READINGS IN MORAL THEOLOGY NO. 1:
MORAL NORMS AND CATHOLIC TRADITION

READINGS IN MORAL THEOLOGY

No. 1:

Moral Norms and Catholic Tradition

Edited by
Charles E. Curran
and
Richard A. McCormick, S.J.

PAULIST PRESS
New York/Ramsey/Toronto

ACKNOWLEDGEMENTS

The articles reprinted in *Readings in Moral Theology No. 1: Moral Norms and Catholic Tradition* first appeared in the following publications and are reprinted by permission: Peter Knauer, "The Hermeneutic Function of the Principle of Double Effect," *Natural Law Forum* 12 (1967); Louis Janssens, "Ontic Evil and Moral Evil," *Louvain Studies* 4 (1972); Joseph Fuchs, S.J., "The Absoluteness of Moral Terms," *Gregorianum* 52 (1971); Bruno Schuller, S.J., "Direct Killing, Indirect Killing," first appeared in German in *Theologie und Philosophie* 47 (1972) under the title "Direkte Tötung—Indirekte Tötung: Franz Scholz "Problems on Norms Raised by Ethical Borderline Situations: Beginnings of a Solution in Thomas Aquinas and Bonaventure" appeared in *Theologische-Practische Quartalschrfit* 123 (1975) as "Durch Ethische Grenzsituationen aufgeworfene Normenprobleme"; Bruno Schüller, S.J., "Various Types of Grounding for Ethical Norms," is reprinted and translated from the original article "Typen der Begründung sittlicher Normen," *Concilium* 120 (1976), pp. 648-654, German Editions Benziger Verlag Einsiedeln, Zurich; Matthias Grunewald Verlag, Mainz, with permission of Seabury Press; Walter Jeffko, "Processive Relationism and Ethical Absolutes," *American Benedictine Review* 26 (1975); Albert R. Di Ianni, S.M., "The Direct/Indirect Distinction in Morals," *Thomist* 41 (1977); John R. Connery, S.J., "Morality of Consequences: A Critical Appraisal," *Theological Studies* 34 (1973): Paul Quay, S.J., "Morality by Calculation of Values," *Theology Digest* 23 (1975); Richard A. McCormick, S.J., "Reflections on the Literature," appeared as "Notes on Moral Theology" in *Theological Studies* 33 (1972), 36 (1975), 38 (1977) and 39 (1978); Charles E. Curran, "Utilitarianism and Contemporary Moral Theology: Situating the Debates," *Louvain Studies*, 6 (1977).

Library of Congress
Catalog Card Number: 79-84237

ISBN: 0-8091-2203-0

Published by Paulist Press
Editorial Office: 1865 Broadway, New York, N.Y. 10023
Business Office: 545 Island Road, Ramsey, N.J. 07446

Printed and bound in the
United States of America

Contents

Foreword

This volume is the first of an ongoing series, with subsequent volumes to appear annually. The purpose of the series is to identify and make available in more usable form influential studies in the field of moral theology. We foresee that some volumes will gather around a theme or trend; at other times we will simply bring together what we believe to be important studies whether or not they cluster around a theme. Since "moral theology" and "Christian ethics" are not denominational terms and properties, it is our intention that the selective process will be as ecumenical as is the discipline in contemporary academic circles.

Having said that, a word is required about this first volume. It concerns itself with moral norms and the Catholic tradition. This would seem at first glance to represent a parochial concern. Actually, that is not the case. The Catholic tradition was but one of the major vehicles for an understanding of moral norms that was shared by other religious groups and other non-religious persons. In its recent official teachings, it has—in contrast to some other groups and individuals—maintained such an understanding, particularly in areas such as birth control, direct abortion, and direct killing of innocent persons (e.g., euthanasia). Disagreement about some of these areas has opened onto the broader discussion of moral norms, their origins and meaning.

During the past decade a lively discussion has taken place on these matters, touching on such key concepts as intrinsic evil, the direct and indirect voluntary, moral absolutes, teleology versus deontology, etc. It is this discussion we report here, conscious of two facts: (1) the discussion is far from finished; (2) many articles (from both moral philosophy and theological ethics) have necessarily had to be omitted because of the limits of space.

Our attempt is to select in a way that will give the reader a sense of the flavor or direction of the discussion. Therefore we have included both sides of the question, though we ourselves (as is obvious from out own contribution) are associated with one side of the development. But that is of no great importance. What is important is that the truth appear. We are convinced that, in difficult moral matters, this is a process, and one necessarily involving questioning, exchanges, disagreements, hypotheses, reversals, etc. That is what this volume, and this series, is all about.

Charles E. Curran
Richard A. McCormick, S.J.

The Hermeneutic Function of the Principle of Double Effect

Peter Knauer, S.J.

The principle of double effect leads a marginal existence in the handbooks of moral theology and appears useful only in making possible a species of hairsplitting. It is, in reality, the fundamental principle of all morality. It responds to the question whether the causing or permitting of an injury is morally evil. I speak of its hermeneutic function because the principle of double effect enables one to grasp—much more effectively than usually happens in traditional ethics—the meaning of the fundamental concepts of traditional morality in their interrelation in the tradition itself.

I
PRESUPPOSITIONS

How does man recognize whether an act is morally good? Traditionally, the morally good has been determined in three distinct ways: Either it is that which "orders man to his last end, that is, God." Or it is that which "corresponds to human nature." Or it is "the simply good."

The first definition is pious but it remains, in the final analysis, abstract. It does not say what concrete acts are ordered to God. In reality an ordering to God is recognized when an act is seen as morally good in itself. This logical order is not convertible.

1

Moreover, it may be asked whether man acts directly in relation to God.

The second definition, requiring "correspondence to human nature," is more concrete. But this formula gives a reasonable meaning only if human nature is defined as "openness to reality in general." Taken rigorously, the correspondence required is not to particular human nature but to the whole of reality.[1] But the formula remains still ambiguous. It does not yet reflect the distinction between physical and moral evil. In fact, a physical evil, such as a sickness or an error or any injury, is not yet in contradiction to nature in a moral sense; such an evil is not a moral evil, even if moral evil is definable only in relation to it.

The most exact is the third definition, according to which the morally good is "the simply good." By "good" is here meant nothing other than the physical goodness of any reality whatsoever, that goodness by which something becomes desirable in any sense, according to the axiom *ens et bonum convertuntur*. What is "simply" good, and therefore morally good, is such a value, if it is willed in such a way that the physical evil possibly associated with it remains objectively beyond the intention of the person willing. Then the good alone, that is, "the simply good," determines the intention.

What is physical evil is known by everyone from experience. Sickness or error or other destruction is never willed for itself but only on account of some other associated good. The question is whether, by reason of this good, the permission or causing of the evil is justified or not. The unjustified permission or causing of evil signifies simply that the evil itself is also intended; then, by intention, the act becomes morally evil.

The principle of double effect, rightly understood, responds to the question whether in a given case the permission or causing of evil is justified or not. In answering this question it reveals itself as a principle which provides the criterion for every moral judgment.

Moral evil, I contend, consists in the last analysis in the permission or causing of a physical evil which is not justified by a commensurate reason. Not every permission or causing of physical evil is a moral evil, but every moral evil depends on the permission or causing of physical evil. This relation, of course, as far as cooperation in the sins of others is concerned, is indirect.

It is essential now to come to a more exact understanding of the proper meaning in ethics of "commensurate reason."

II
AN OLD FORMULATION AND A MODERN ONE

1. The principle of double effect appears to have been first formulated by Thomas Aquinas.[2] He argues for the permissibility of self-defense by force in the following way:

> I reply that it must be said that nothing prevents there being two effects of one act, of which one effect alone would be in the intention and the other would be beyond intention. But moral acts receive their species according to what is intended, not from what is beyond intention, since the latter is accidental as appears from what has been said above.

> Therefore, from the act of someone defending himself a double effect can follow: one is the preservation of his own life, the other is the killing of the attacker. An act of this kind in which the preservation of one's own life is intended does not have the character of the unlawful, since it is natural for everyone to preserve himself in his being as far as he can.

> But some act arising from a good intention can be made unlawful if it is not proportionate to the end. And so, if someone in defending his own life uses greater violence than is necessary, it will be unlawful. But if he moderately repels violence, it will be a lawful defense.[3]

It must first be noted that the concept of "effect" is not used here as a correlative to "cause," but in a more general sense; "aspect" might be a more exact term. It is evident that the good effect here is not different from this object as elsewhere the effect from its cause.

In the interpretation of the text it is also important to pay attention to the third paragraph, where in reality the only one possibility of a moral offense is noted. Thomas does not use the criterion of "correspondence to nature." The approach taken is this: In sinning, man seeks a real good, but his act in its total existential entirety is not proportioned to this good. Then the evil arising thereby, whether it is desired or not, belongs objectively to the act and is objectively what is "intended."

In the text of Thomas the expression "what is intended" provides the most matter for consideration. The concept of intention in ethics evidently means something different from what it means in psychology. In ethics an injury can be "intended" even if the person acting would have preferred its absence or was not thinking much about it. Conversely, as in the killing of an aggressor, an effect can be beyond moral intention, although the person acting was psychologically concentrated on it.

Several other relevant points should be observed in reference to the traditional teaching on "the sources of morality" (*fontes moralitatis*). According to what St. Thomas says elsewhere, moral acts are "determined" by the end of the act, by the *finis operis*.[4] In the present text he says that moral acts are determined by "what is intended." At first glance it seems surprising to say that what must be meant here is not the "end of the person acting" (*finis operantis*) but the "end of the work" (*finis operis*). Yet in order to avoid contradiction with the passages elsewhere, the "end of the act" must mean "what is intended." What results from taking this approach?

By *finis operis* there should not be understood—as unfortunately often happens—only the external effect, the effect that could be photographed. In ethics, *finis operis* means the act which is willed and intended as such. The classic example in the manuals runs as follows: Someone giving alms has as *finis operis* the relief of the needs of a poor man.[5] But almsgiving is not merely a physical act. It becomes a moral act through the intention of the donor. The external action consists in money going from one hand to another. Is this action payment for a purchase or the giving of a present? Is it money lent to the other? Is it the repayment of a debt? Is it a bribe? Whatever in fact the action is depends on what the person transferring the money wills the action objectively to be. That is not a matter of his arbitrary declaration but of his actual intent. All physical evils which are not justified, and which arise in the pursuit of a value, are in the moral sense *eo ipso* morally intended and belong to the *finis operis* itself.

The *finis operantis*, which is regarded as a second "source of morality," is not to be identified merely with the moral intention of the person acting. By *finis operantis*, the external end, there is meant the act towards which the person acting relates his first action. Thus someone may give alms in order to obtain a tax advantage. The *finis operantis* of the first act is related to, and is indeed identical with, the *finis operis* of this second act. If someone performs a single act without relating it to another act, he has only a *finis operis* of his act, and, to speak exactly, there is no *finis operantis*.[6]

In addition to the *finis operis* and the *finis operantis*, another traditional source of morality is the circumstances of an act. Their only function is to determine the act quantitatively. A theft is a theft according to the *finis operis* whether the amount stolen is large or small; but the gravity of the offense depends on the amount. If the theft is connected with breaking and entering, then this fact is not the addition of another circumstance but a change in the *finis operis* itself.[7]

The division of *finis operis* and *finis operantis* into an external physical act and an internal intention cannot be maintained in one and the same act; this is an arbitrary distinction arising on Cartesian foundations. Neither the pure external happening nor the psychological intention is morally understandable alone; only the objective relation, in which both have a part, is understandable. This conclusion means that the moral species of the *finis operis* depends on whether this relation is one of correspondence or one of final contradiction, while the *finis operantis* relates to the *finis operis* of another act.

For the time being I will rest with this formal definition of *finis* in ethics; at a later point I shall return to the topic to give a more exact definition.

2. Today the principle of double effect is most briefly formulated as follows:

One may permit the evil effect of his act only if this is not intended in itself but is indirect and jusified by a commensurate reason.

The modern formula seems to be different in more than one respect from that of St. Thomas. He required the act to correspond to its end (*actus sit proportionatus fini*). The present formula speaks of a "commensurate reason" (*ratio proportionata*). The principle of double effect is, I believe, rightly understood if it is recognized that in fact both requirements mean the same thing.

Thomas also held that the evil might not be effected directly. According to him, the intention must be accidental (*per accidens*); it must be beyond intention (*praeter intentionem*). The usual explanation of this terminology understands the pair of concepts, "direct-indirect," in the sense of direct or indirect physical causality; but this explanation is questionable. *I say that an evil effect is not "directly intended" only if there is a "commensurate ground" for its permission or causation.* There are not two distinct requirements when I speak of the "indirect causing" of evil and of "a commensurate reason" for the act. The principle may be adequately formulated as follows: One may permit the evil effect of his act only if he has a commensurate reason for it.

The objectivity of all ethics depends on the determination of commensurate. A "commensurate reason" is not an arbitrary X, equivalent to "serious reason in the circumstances." The customary deformed understanding of this concept identifies "commensurate" with "serious"; from this deformation, an unhealthy confusion in ethics has resulted. These observations must suffice for now; I shall return later to attempt further clarification.

III
THE SAME PRINCIPLE
IN A VARIETY OF EXPRESSIONS

The key concept in the modern formulation of the principle of double effect is the requirement of a "commensurate reason." This concept can be found in various other chapters of traditional ethics: "Cooperation in the Sin of Another," "Intrinsic Malice and Extrinsic Malice," "Affirmative and Negative Laws of Nature." In scholastic ethics all of these articles were put in different drawers. But in each there is rediscovered the structure of the principle of double effect: the causing or permitting of a physical evil is morally permitted because of a commensurate reason; without a commensurate reason the act is morally evil.

1. "Formal" cooperation in the sin of another is absolutely forbidden in every case. "Material" cooperation is permitted if there is a commensurate reason.[8] If a commensurate reason is lacking, material cooperation in the sin of another becomes formal and therefore forbidden. The absence of a commensurate reason is decisive.

It is evident that the permission or causing of evil on behalf of another becomes moral evil only through the application of the principle of double effect. If I have a commensurate reason for permitting or cooperating with the evil, the evil remains indirect for me. I only participate materially therein, while the formal content of my act is distinct from the evil, so that my act in reality is good. But if my act lacks a commensurate reason, I directly and formally cause or permit evil on behalf of another and become guilty myself. In short, the pair of concepts, "formal"—"material," as they are used in the teaching on cooperation in the sin of another, are fundamentally the same as "direct" and "indirect" in the modern formulation of the principle of double effect.

2. There is a way of acting, which, according to the common teaching, is "intrinsically" evil and therefore universally forbidden. Other ways of acting are only "extrinsically" evil and therefore permitted in the presence of commensurate reasons. But if there is no commensurate reason, then they also are absolutely forbidden in every case. This teaching means, I maintain, that then they are "intrinsically" evil. What is intrinsically an evil act is brought about when no commensurate reason can justify the permission or causing of the extrinsic evil, that is, any given premoral physical evil or injury. This is a thesis which has special significance for contemporary ethics. It says that "morally evil" and "intrinsically evil" are synonymous expressions.

Yet, are there not acts which universally are intrinsically evil so that the question of whether there is a commensurate reason or not is simply superfluous? For example, is not murder under all circumstances forbidden? Such a judgment of universal condemnation is only reached by an implicit application of the principle of double effect. As long as an act is judged according to its external appearance and independently of the character of its reason, it is not understandable as a human act; it is not something that can yet be judged morally. Once it is determined whether or not the reason for an act is commensurate, the moral species of the act may be determined. Murder, for example, consists by definition in causing the death of a man without a commensurate ground. If the same external act, such as causing of the death of a man, has a commensurate ground, then it is from the beginning an act morally different from murder—either self-defense or a lawful act of justice in order to protect the community.

Again, the same conclusion is reached: The terms examined are contained in the principle of double effect. The pair of concepts, "intrinsic—extrinsic," signify the same thing as "direct" and "indirect" in the formulation of the principle.

There are further pairs of concepts which also stand in the same relation to the requirement of a commensurate reason. There are, for example, *per se*—*per accidens* and "in intention"— "beyond intention" in the text cited from St. Thomas. The use of these different concepts for one and the same reality reveals that the scholastics had not reflected thoroughly enough on their meanings.

3. Especially instructive is a comparison of the principle of double effect with the traditional teaching's distinction between affirmative and negative laws of nature.

Negative laws (for example, "You shall not murder," "You shall not lie") oblige, as the manuals say, "always and everywhere." They permit no exceptions but are universally valid.

There are, however, affirmative laws corresponding to the negative laws. For example, corresponding to the instances given above, these are, "You shall revere and protect human life," "You shall speak the truth." In contrast to the negative obligations these affirmative laws only oblige *"semper, sed non pro semper."* A commensurate reason justifies the nonobservance of such laws. If a commensurate reason is lacking, however, no justification is possible. In such a case the affirmative laws becomes absolute, "*semper et pro semper*," exactly like the negative law.

The negative law, in fact, is already contained in the affirmative. The negative law is only the application of the affirmative in cases in which there is no commensurate reason excusing from nonobservance. The pure nonobservance of the affirmative law is already indentical with active infraction of its negative form. A permission of evil which is not justified by a commensurate reason amounts morally to positively causing it. The physical distinction between these cases is very secondary for moral judgment. It is only the more exact specification of the behavior which depends on this ground—for example, when we want to distinguish between homicide and murder.

But the affirmative laws go further than the negative laws in their power of obligation. The sphere where their application is unconditioned is identical with that of the negative laws, which must always be observed if there is a lack of commensurate reason. The "*semper*" of the affirmative laws is to be observed without restriction. But attention is to be given them even when a commensurate reason permits their present nonobservance.

What do I mean by this? I will give a medical decision as an example. There is a therapy against cancer based on present knowledge of the cells, a therapy which produces disturbances in the blood. To cause such disturbance without commensurate reason would be injury to the health of the patient and so an intrinsically evil violation of negative law. But if such therapy holds the promise of improvement in the total health of the patient, the physician permissibly accepts in exchange the unavoidable evils which accompany it. He has a commensurate reason which makes "indirect" his action of causing an evil. His act is a justified nonobservance of the affirmative law which demands that he have care for the healthy state of blood in his patient. This value in his work evidently manifests an affirmative law corresponding to the negative law, but going beyond it.[9] If the physician is dispensed from the direct observance of the affirmative law, it remains valid, and he may not content himself forever with the necessity which forced it not to be observed. He is obliged to seek better solutions. In this obligation the meaning of the affirmative law controls the negative. If a better therapy is developed, what has been permitted can no longer be applied.

This example also shows explicitly what in ethics is unchangeable natural law. In ethics, only the obligation to seek the best possible solutions in their total existential entirety is unchangeable. The best solutions cannot be determined in advance as in a catalogue; they must be developed within the dynamic of the affirmative obligation that there be development. In this development only the prohibition of direct permission or causing of evil is unchangeable.

Negative and affirmative precepts thus constitute still another area ruled by the principle of double effect. To the negative law there corresponds the absolute prohibition of directly causing or permitting evil in any way. To cause or permit evil indirectly is like the nonobservance of an affirmative law where this nonobservance is justified by a commensurate reason. A commensurate reason would evidently be the observance of another, more compelling affirmative law which in existing conditions could not be observed at the same time as the first law. The obligation would remain to seek the possibility of being able to observe both laws. In the principle of double effect there is a commitment to advance in all the interrelated areas of reality.[10]

IV

WHAT IS A COMMENSURATE REASON?

I have indicated that the expression "commensurate reason" determines the meaning of all the other concepts. Through lack of a commensurate reason material cooperation in sin becomes formal; extrinsic malice becomes intrinsic malice; affirmative law takes the shape of an unconditional negative. The principle of double effect means that to cause or permit an evil without commensurate reason is a morally bad act. The evil is no longer accidental in the intention of the person acting, but it becomes constitutive of the moral content of the act, the *finis operis*, or internal object. If a commensurate reason is present, the permission or causing of the evil becomes indirect and is *objectively no longer the object of moral intention.* The commensurate reason occupies the same area as what is directly willed and alone determines the entire moral content of the act. *If the reason of an act is commensurate, it alone determines the finis operis, so that the act is morally good.* The permission or causing of a physical evil is indirect or direct as there is or is not present a commensurate reason. Self-defense is a good example. The external operations are the same as those of a murder, for there is a use of deadly weapons. The moral distinction is recognized only when the unavoidable death of the attacker has a commensurate reason in self-defense. The object of the act is then the commensurate reason which consists in the preservation of one's own life against attack.

But when is the reason for an act a commensurate reason? There is a reason for every act even if it is morally evil. One can only will something on the condition that he is able to see a value in it in some aspect. The freedom of the will is grounded in this fact. Because the will by its nature is directed to the good as such, it can either will a good positively insofar as it is good or reject it insofar as it is only one good and not simply the good. The possibility of both decisions is based on the same judgment according to which the object is really a (but not the) good.[11]

Thus the reason for each act is an actual good. A thief steals only because he hopes for a use from the money. Even the one who acts from pure hate against the moral law seeks an actual value, although in a mistaken way. In his existential decision he wills to determine himself. But does he reach in this way what makes the freedom worth striving for?

For an act to be morally good it is not enough that it always seek a value and so always have a reason. What is required is that this reason be commensurate. What does this mean? "Commensurate" to what?

This question is commonly answered in this way: The good achieved must correspond to the evil accepted in exchange, and indeed the good must outweigh the evil. But this answer is no advance. Such a quantitative comparison is not possible, as it is a matter of qualitatively different values which cannot be compared with one another. When some years ago in Germany the speed limit in city traffic was experimentally abolished, the death toll in traffic accidents rose threefold, and therefore the fifty-kilometer limit was very soon restored; but the death toll was still quite high. Could the loss in human life be compared with the advantages which a speedier traffic system brings? The different values which are measurable by themselves are incommensurable with each other. There is no common measure for them.

A comparison becomes possible if it is established what function one value has for another. A faster traffic causes a loss of more human lives. But if there were no traffic, the preservation of life as a whole surely would not be greater. The preservation of life in great part depends on a sound economy, which, in turn, today depends on the fastest possible traffic. Thus the complete throttling of traffic would not serve the preservation of human life as a whole. By this standard, this end would not be a commensurate reason. At the same time, faster traffic is a greater good the more it is accompanied by safety. This valuation rests on the foundation that the value sought is commensurate when it is achieved in the highest possible measure for the whole.

The example of traffic is instructive in another aspect. Speed limits, regulation of automobiles, and other limits on the freedom of individuals serve in fact to produce faster traffic and greater safety in relation to the whole. The limitations of freedom directly serve to achieve the greatest possible freedom for the whole. The violator of traffic rules contradicts the value as a whole which he wishes to realize for himself. There is a contradiction between his deed and its foundation.

A student may desire to learn the most possible. He can be successful in this pursuit only if he interrupts his work from time to time. If he is so bent on his objective of learning that he injures his own health, perhaps for a short time he may achieve something above average but the result on the whole will be less. In an extreme case he becomes sick from overwork and cannot accomplish anything. Then in the last analysis he contradicts his own purpose. Something similar happens in any immoral act. An objective is sought which has an appropriate price (*tantum—quantum*), but it is sought at any price. In unmeasured desire there is sacrificed what alone would assure the greatest possible achievement of the end.

The government of a developing country has a plan to better

the living standard of its people. This objective may be reached only through an ongoing industrialization which requires an extensive renunciation of immediate accomplishments. If, instead of such a program, the administration forces immediate sharing of goods by use of the police, it may indeed achieve an elevation of the living standard. But this approach quickly leads to a destruction of the economy, and the need becomes greater than before. In seeking an immediate achievement of the objective there has been a neglect of the total conditions of possibility and thereby a contradiction of the objective itself. In this example there is especially clear what could be called the feedback effect or the reciprocal function of two values. On one hand, a rise in the living standard requires industrialization. Industrialization is not a higher value than a better living standard—the possibility of such a comparison has already been denied—but industrialization is of the greatest urgency if a higher living standard is to be achieved. On the other hand, industrialization cannot be achieved if at the same time there is not at least some beginning of a rise in the living standard, because no industry can be developed with hungry workers.

All of these examples may illustrate that unintelligent and therefore immoral acts are in the last analysis self-contradictions and consist in unmeasured desire taking the fruit from the tree before it is ripe. There is an isolation of the objective from its proper conditions. A good is sought while the conditions for the highest possible realization of the good are abandoned. This state of affairs is described by the language of the old moral theology when it singles out an immoral act as an act against nature, *contra naturam*. There is a destruction of reality itself when part of reality is isolated from its inter-relations. If someone pays a price for a good which is not commensurate with the good but, rather, contradicts it and makes the highest possible achievement of the good as a whole impossible, he irresponsibly causes injury. When the expression *contra naturam* is used in ethics, there is not meant physical evil which is against nature only in a premoral, physical sense. What is meant is a physical evil caused or permitted without commensurate reason—that is, in this act there is a long-run contradiction in reality between the value sought and the way of achieving it.

Immediately in the short run there may often be a remarkable achievement. Irrationality first emerges when consideration is given to all the interrelationships and when it is asked if the objective existentially achieved, seen in terms of the whole, best corresponds not only to a particular person but to the totality. What this distinction between individual and totality means may be clarified by the example given above of freedom in traffic. The moral consciousness poses this universalizing question. The distinction between the two approaches is rigorously objective. Whether a reason for an act is commensurate or not is beyond all subjective arbitrariness.[12] The reason for an act is not a commensurate reason if there is a contradiction in the last analysis between the act and the reason.

A similar result is reached if the modern formulation of the principle of double effect is compared with the formulation of St. Thomas. As I noted earlier, Thomas instead of requiring a commensurate reason (*ratio proportionata*) says that the entire act must correspond to its end (*actus sit proportionatus fini*); but end means nothing other than reason for the act. It is simply a matter of a correspondence between the act and its proper reason. Both requirements, that the reason for an act be commensurate (that is, that it be one commensurate to the act itself) or that the act must correspond to its reason, mean the same. An act becomes immoral when it is contradictory to the fullest achievement of its own end in relation to the whole of reality. A short-run "more" of the value is paid by a "lesser" achievement of the same value in the long run.

V

THREE DIFFERENT MEANINGS OF "END"

So far I have used the expression "end" (for which "intention" could be substituted) in an entirely specific sense as identical with reason. It is important to note this in order to avoid an easy misunderstanding. "End" can also have another meaning and simply signify a determinate concrete fact. Thus a band of bank robbers has the end of entering the treasury of a bank. It would be absurd to measure the morality of this act by asking if the band is using the most appropriate means of achieving its end. Such a determination is not meant when I speak of the correspondence required between the act and its proper end. In this requirement what is meant by end is not a concrete fact but what in a particular fact makes it worth acting for, its *ratio boni*. In the sense I use it, in which the end of an act is identical with its reason, it must be said that the value the robber band is seeking is to become rich. At this level the question is posed whether breaking and entering leads in the long run to the greatest realization of riches as a whole or whether it is in contradiction to such realization.

If end is used as identical with reason, it is still not a concept of ethics. As I have already shown, both good and bad acts have a reason in this sense, as reason means a value. The reason of the worst act is never an evil but always a good, that is, something in fact worth striving for. Therefore, a source of morality is not reached when reason or end in this sense is reached.

In a moral sense the end of an act is what is "intended"—the *finis operis* and, eventually more broadly, the *finis operantis*, the ordering of the act to the *finis operis* of a more comprehensive act. These expressions signify the reason of the act insofar as it is in correspondence with the totality of the act or not. In this moral sense, the reason is no longer considered alone but in its relation to the act itself. If the reason of an act is a commensurate reason, it is in a moral sense the end of the act and intended. It is then completely identical with the *finis operis*, so that the eventual concomitant evil, even if it is considered necessarily part of the exchange, falls outside the *finis operis*. The *fini operis* of the act is, then, simply good.

When the reason of an act is not a commensurate reason so that between it and the act in terms of the horizon of the whole reality there is a contradiction, the reason in itself may be as good and as important as possible, yet the *finis operis* of the act is no longer constituted by this reason; the reason is in contradiction to the act, and the *finis operis* is constituted by the evil effect which accompanies it. In the example of bank robbery, the chief evil effect is the harming of other people in the taking of their property. This harm is intended in the moral sense in a bank robbery, although the gangsters have only their own enrichment in view.

In Part VIII I shall return to the threefold meaning of the

concept of end in a discussion of the distinction between mutilation and medically necessary amputation.

VI
THE MORAL GOOD AS THE BÉST POSSIBLE

Every human act brings evil effects with it. The choice of a value always means concretely that there is denial of another value which must be given as a price in exchange. If the chosen value is sought in its entirety in a commensurate way, the evil falls outside what is directly willed. In other cases when the reason of the act is not commensurate, the evils which arise are themselves directly willed even if they are not in the least desired in themselves.

I shall seek to make the matter still clearer through the development of a statement of Aristotelian ethic. I refer to an easily understood alternative to the scholastic procedure. According to Aristotle, morally right behavior is a mean between two extremes which can be recognized as too much or too little. It is observed that in consideration of the good, the mean itself is an extreme.[13] Thus, for example, bravery is a mean between foolhardiness and cowardice. Aristotle declared that bravery appears more closely related to one of the two extremes, foolhardiness. This observation, which is made by Aristotle himself with some surprise, provides an opportunity for asking whether there is not also a name for right behavior which appears to lie closer to cowardice, the other false extreme. There is, in fact, prudence. It belongs inseparably with bravery. It is clear to everyone that bravery without prudence is in reality only cowardice. If foolhardiness consists in too great a risk so that in the end too little is achieved, bravery consists in achieving the most possible of that for which the entire risk is undertaken. Again, there is the criterion of commensurate reason; that is, of a proportionality of the act to its proper objective. Bravery is readiness for any risk which is justified by the end in its existential entirety. Bravery is thus accompanied by prudence, which holds the risk to the smallest degree possible so that the greatest possible gain may be achieved. Cowardice lacks this measure. It wagers the least, but thereby loses too much of the whole.

The formal structure of winning and losing which is implied in this example is founded on the principle of double effect. Evil may be accepted in exchange if, in relation to the whole, the smallest possible evil is exchanged for the highest possible gain. The whole is the determinative point of view for morality; it distinguishes ethics from a technique based on experience in a particular area. When an act neither sacrifices too much nor gains too little, there is conduct which is commensurate to the end sought. Immoral acts consist in preferring the success of the moment to true gain and thereby spoiling the achievement of true gain in the act which is carried out. A coward naturally always says that he is prudent, and a fool often holds himself to be brave. They both refer to their good intentions, but they are both unmasked when consideration is given to the complementary virtue. Where is the bravery in the pretended prudence of a coward? Where is the prudence in the asserted bravery of the fool? In the presence of the complementary virtue there is recognized that the act has a commensurate reason; that is, it is recognized that the act is in proportion to its end. Liberality accompanied by economy is distinguished from extravagance; economy is only avarice unless it is liberal. Progress is not a pure seeking of what is new but a preservation of what is good in the old; there is in fidelity to tradition only a spiritless severity unless it fosters the creation of the new. Zeal and discretion go together; otherwise zeal in reality becomes fanaticism, and instead of discretion there is mediocrity. "Be wise as the serpent and simple as the dove" (Matthew 10.16). Such a demand is not paradoxical but excludes slyness and stupidity together. Christian hope works out its salvation "in fear and trembling" (Philip. 2.12); one without the other is either presumption or despair. There are many other examples. This square is of universal applicability.

Moral good consists in the best possible realization of any particular value envisaged in its entirety. This assertion is fundamentally different from the rigorist thesis which says that among different goods the highest must be always chosen. Here, rather, there is freedom as long as the particular value chosen is not itself subverted.

A particularly good example is the problem of the vocation where the choice has to be made between several morally good possibilities. A false model of this choice is provided if vocation is understood as "a specific call which God himself has implanted in me in advance." The will of God which is knowable objectively consists in being able to decide for oneself among different good possibilities. A so-called vocation should not be understood objectively as an advance determination to one possibility. Vocation consists rather in the possibility of having appropriate motives for the way to be chosen. This is the grace of a calling. It is completely possible that someone be called in this sense to different vocations, so that he himself must make the actual choice. Only in an unusual case where there is an extraordinary need can there be an obligation which is binding in one direction from the beginning; in such a case any other choice would be self-contradictory, because the other possibilities depend for their realization on a condition which must be realized at any cost.

VII
BAD MEANS

The explanation I have given to this point of the principle of double effect is very different from the usual explanation given in the teaching on what is *voluntarium in causa*. This is usually given the following sense: If an evil is the further physical consequence of the good which is willed, or at least does not precede the good which is willed, then the permissibility of the act depends on what is intended by the act. If the evil permitted or caused accompanies the good to be achieved only as a consequence or a concomitant, the act is permitted; otherwise not. But if the evil physically precedes the willed good and so is "the means" to its achievement, then it is directly willed and makes the entire act evil, just as if the evil was intended by the act. In this case, the principle of double effect is replaced by another principle: A good end does not justify bad means.

Such a contrast between these two principles involves a logical error. In the principle that the good end does not justify the bad means it is already assumed that the means are morally bad.[14] The principle is only applicable if the moral judgment has already been formed; in the moral evil of the means something new is not discovered; the evil was already established. In the principle of double effect, in contrast, a moral judgment of this kind is in the process of being determined. The two principles are not parallel in their applicability. That a means is morally bad signifies in our sense that the reason for the application of the means is not commensurate. The pure determination that the means entails physical evil is not enough to qualify it as morally evil. It may well be that the permission or causing of this evil is only indirect because of a commensurate reason. Provided that an end is sought in its existential entirety in a truly commensurate way, the means determined by this end which can contribute to the best possible realization of the end may justify accepting physical evil in exchange. Of course, one must be satisfied that this price is the smallest possible. In this sense the axiom is valid: *Finis determinat media*.

The principle that the good end does not justify the bad means may rightly be understood in either of the two following senses. On the one hand, it may be a matter of a single act whose reason is a good end. The principle asserts that this end, however serious and good in itself, cannot justify the permission or causing of physical evil in the course of its achievement if it is not a commensurate reason in the sense I have indicated. The act must correspond to the value sought not only in the short run but in its existential entirety. On the other hand, the means may itself consist in a proper act which can be recognized without reference to a further objective as having a reason in itself which suffices for the positing of the act. If this reason is not a commensurate one, then the act may not be morally saved, even if it can be related to another act which is an achievement of an end that in itself is good. The means in the last analysis would contradict the act.

In the second sense, St. Thomas says at the conclusion of his analysis of self-defense that it is not permitted to will the death of the aggressor as an act in itself.[15] Self-defense then would be the *finis operantis* and no longer the *finis operis*. The death of the attacker would be willed even if it were not determined to be necessary in fact for self-defense. Such an act would obviously not be permissible.

But clearly there are cases in which the causing or permitting of an evil precedes the achievement of the end without the act thereby becoming morally bad. The evil is justified by a commensurate reason; although the cause is physically direct, it is not direct in a moral sense. The following example is classic. A dangerous fortress may be made harmless only by being stormed by force, but in the outer bastion of the fortress there are innocent hostages who will lose their lives before the proper end of the action, the storming of the fortress, can be achieved. In traditional ethics this action is permissible as long as there is no other way to avoid the evil. The decisive question is not whether the evil, the deaths of the prisoners during the storming, follows the good which is sought or precedes it; the decisive question is in what way the evil is willed. The act is morally bad if the evil is direct or formal, that is, if the act is willed in such a way that there is no commensurate reason for it and therefore is irresponsible. The purely physical series of events is irrelevant to the moral qualification of good or bad. One and the same means can in one aspect be a value or lead to the realization of a value and simultaneously be a physical evil in another aspect. If there is a commensurate reason for the permitting or causing of the evil, the means is effectively willed only in its good aspect. The effect or, more exactly, the aspect which is physically evil remains morally outside of what is intended.

When the categories direct and indirect are confused with purely physical categories, a blind hairsplitting is introduced into ethics. Removal of a cancerous uterus is permitted even though as a consequence the fetus within the uterus loses its life. But to remove only the fetus, because the uterus may still be healed, is said by some theologians to be murder; they think the death of the fetus is used as a means and so is directly willed. In other words, a solution which includes both the death of the fetus and the removal of the entire uterus with consequent sterility is said to be better than that the fetus alone lose its life. Who can understand this?

In the case of an ectopic pregnancy it is almost certain that the woman together with an unborn child will die if the fetus is not removed as early as possible. The "insight" that this is immoral is scarcely demonstrable to any doctor. It is agreed that direct killing is forbidden. But in my opinion, some scholastic moralists have assumed incorrectly that the saving of the mother, which in the normal case is probable if there is immediate removal of the ectopic fetus, is a direct killing. Negative laws (You shall not kill, You shall not speak an untruth, You shall not take the property of another) are understandable only as the prohibition of direct and therefore formal permission or causing of these physical evils (death, error, loss of property, etc.), in cases where by definition there is no commensurate reason. Whether there is a violation of a commandment (that is, whether an act is murder, lying, theft) can be ascertained only if it is established that the reason for the act in its existential entirety is not commensurate. Without a commensurate reason an evil is always willed directly, even if attention is not expressly directed to the evil but it is desired that there be no such evil.

VIII
EXCEPTIONS IN ETHICS

In the recent literature of moral theology there has been evoked from time to time what is called the principle of totality, a principle contrasted with the principle of double effect. The latter is said to relate only to the justification of the "barely permissible," while the principle of totality relates to the "justification of an effect willed for itself by reason of its connection with the whole order of purposes and goods."[16] The principle of totality justifies an act such as the removal of a sick organ in order to save the whole organism.

In my opinion the principle of totality is in reality not distinguishable from the principle of double effect. The latter bears not merely on the passive permission of an evil but relates to the most active kind of permission; concretely the act itself may cause or effect the evil; the evil is not direct unless it is willed without commensurate reason. In fact, it is not true, for example, that a medically necessary amputation is willed in the moral sense as a removal of an organ. What is willed is only the removal of what is an obstacle to health in its entirety. That this obstacle is identical with the hitherto useful member of the body is accidental for moral judgment (*existimatio moralis*),[17] because a commensurate reason justifies the acceptance of the loss. For the eventual preservation of the organs the existence of the person itself must certainly first be assured. There is not a quantitative relation between a part to the whole, but a priority of dependence of one upon the other. If there is a commensurate reason, the removal of an organ is justified, and the operation is not the mutilation of the organism, which is always impermissible.

The example may also serve to clarify the distinction I have already made between the three meanings of "end." In the operation the surgeon does not think of anything except the skillful removal of the limb of the patient. This removal is the concrete thing which is willed by him, and one can say that this act is "the effect willed in itself." But the morality of the act is not determined on this level. Whether the removal of a limb is a health measure or a mutilation of the patient cannot be recognized in the concrete actuality which might be photographed. The reason why the surgeon removes the limb must be looked at. What value does the act seek to serve? It is done because of the health of the patient. But this by itself does not determine the morality of the act. A purely good intention in the psychological sense does not determine the moral goodness of an act. It must be established that this reason is a commensurate one. If, in the given circumstances, the act is the best possible solution of the problem in terms of the horizon given by the whole of reality, it may be said that the act is morally good. In a moral sense, what is then intended is not the taking of the limb, but the health of the patient. That the obstacle to be removed was once a useful limb falls in a moral sense outside of what is intended and is not directly willed. It is another case if the reason for the removal is not commensurate—for example, if it would be possible to achieve the objective of health in a way which would cause less loss. The removal of the limb would then contradict the best possible achievement of the end. In such a case, in a moral sense the removal of the limb in its function as member of the body would be directly willed, even if the surgeon did not direct his attention to this aspect.

In another respect the example is instructive. In the usual thoughtless dichotomy between physical act and intention any act whatsoever might be labeled by any intention whatsoever. But this is in reality not even possible on the psychological, premoral level. Suppose that blood poisoning could be healed by the injection of a new serum so that the objective of health would not require removal of the poisoned limb; it would be logically impossible to prefer the limb's removal for the same reason as before the discovery of the serum. If a physician desired to carry out such an amputation, he would in fact do it for some other reason, e.g., the avoidance of unusually high expenses. But as to this new reason the question would again have to be asked: Is it a commensurate reason or not? In this example it is seen that the permissibility of a medically necessary amputation is not an exception to the prohibition of mutilation, but in a moral sense is an act which is not a removal of the limb but a healing of the sick.

In a similar way a series of other apparent exceptions to the moral law may be clarified. To return to the example of self-defense, the death of an aggressor may be caused if there is no other way to save oneself. Similarly, the lawfulness of the death penalty in traditional morality has been upheld under certain circumstances. In this case Thomas himself thinks that the death of the criminal is directly intended.[18] I do not agree with his formulation. But many moralists have followed him in thinking that the commandment, You shall not kill, is to be understood in a restrictive sense admitting certain exceptions: The guilty may be killed, and an unjust aggressor has already given up his right to life. This analysis is not persuasive. First, one may repel the aggression of an insane man although he is incapable of a moral act and therefore completely incapable of a guilty deed. Conversely, one may not kill an aggressor, however unjust, if in other ways one can save oneself and other possible victims. It is false that a criminal condemned to death has no right to life. How else explain that it is murder if one on his own authority shoots a man on his way to execution?[19] The execution of the judgment of death is not direct killing, and so not murder, because there is no other reasonable possibility of self-defense for the human community. Then the *finis operis* of the execution is only the self-defense of the community. I do not thereby contend that one can be satisfied for all time with this solution. The obligation remains to seek better solutions within the realm of the reasonably possible. That in a certain historical situation the death penalty was rightly judged permissible does not indicate that it remains fundamentally and absolutely permissible.

If someone in extreme necessity takes the property of another because it is necessary for him to preserve his life, he does externally what a thief would do. But a theft is only the taking of the property of another without commensurate reason. A thief wills to enrich himself, but the value of possession assumes a legal order. Through the violation of this order the thief contradicts his own end in its existential entirety. The reason for his act is therefore no longer commensurate. A thief is thus guilty morally of the evil he has caused. It is different as to the poor man in extreme need for whom there is no other possibility of saving his life than the taking of the property of another. In order to be reasonable the legal order which protects property rests on the assumption that everyone has a right to life. The poor man in extreme need does not contradict his end, which is the preservation of his life; and he does not contradict it even in terms of a universal observation (and this point of view is the decisive one). Therefore he does not will directly that the former possessor lose his property and suffer injury. It seems to me false to explain this case by asserting that the possessor had no property right in these circumstances to his property, so that he allegedly has suffered no injury.

A lie consists in telling what is false without commensurate reason and therefore directly or formally causes the error of another; trust is expected and at the same time subverted. If such behavior were permitted, then trust in its existential entirety would be impossible; truth could not be shared. But it is something entirely different if, in order to preserve a secret, a false answer is given to an indiscreet question. Then the case is parallel with self-defense; the error of the other is not directly willed. Morally, the answer has the meaning that I will not give away my secret. That the questioner is deceived is an evil which is rightly accepted in exchange for preservation of the secret. I assume, of course, that the question of the other is illegitimate, so that he has no right to the knowledge of the fact, and I assume that in no other way can the secret be preserved. In many cases a clearly evasive answer or the attempt to use ambiguous language, assuming that one has the presence of mind to think so quickly, is entirely inadequate to protect the secret. In these circumstances a false answer instead of such language is not the same as a lie.

A concrete example will make my meaning clearer: A family in East Berlin before the building of the Wall wishes to flee to West Berlin. While it is gathering some small household effects to take to West Berlin, some neighbor remarks on its activity and asks, "Is it true that you are going to West Berlin?" The detection of such preparation for flight carries with it a serious punishment in prison in East Berlin. How can such a question be answered? If answer is evaded ("What does this matter to you?"), all is betrayed. To avoid an answer without betraying the secret, the only course is to repel with scorn the suspicion of desiring to flee. Such a response in my opinion has as little to do with lying as the death of an aggressor in the case of necessary self-defense has to do with murder. On the contrary, it would be objectively immoral to betray a secret which should rightfully be preserved.

Usually an attempt is made to solve this kind of problem of speech with a theory as to ambiguous language. But it must be clear that any answer to an unjustified question, however the answer is phrased, is ambiguous in its nature in that it may in reality merely refuse to give what the inquirer has asked. To an illegitimate question any possible answer, contrary to the tenor of the words used in the answer, may be nothing but a refusal of the correct answer.

IX
SITUATION ETHICS

Scientific ethics has scarcely coped with the preoccupations of so-called situation ethics. Situation ethics asserts that the moral judgment of an act can be given only in the concrete, particular situation; and that a moral judgment in terms of a general, abstract law, which is valid forever, is impossible. According to this doctrine, ethics ceases to be universally reasonable or capable of being objectified.

The basis for this approach is the following misunderstanding.

It is thought that the principles of traditional ethics entail substantive statements and moral qualifications which are then universally applied to particular cases. In fact, this appearance is given as long as the negative laws (You shall not kill, You shall not speak an untruth) are not formally understood as prohibitions of what is the direct causation or permission of any given physical evil not justified by a commensurate reason. In this approach the distinction between physical and moral evil is obscured. Situation ethics then develops, not unmasking this error, although refusing to accept its consequences.

A moral judgment is naturally possible only when in a concrete act it is established whether the reason for the act is commensurate or not. On that depends whether the cause or permission of the associated physical evil is indirect, or direct and thus morally bad. With this determination the core of truth in situation ethics is taken into account without destroying the foundation for an objective morality. The answer to the question whether the reason for an act is commensurate or not depends on rigorous objective criteria and not on merely subjective or even imaginary good intention.

But another endeavor of saving the core of truth in situation ethics is erroneous. This is the distinction made between the specific and the individual lawfulness of an act. For example, according to this distinction, an act of marital intercourse without love is lawful according to its *finis operis* and so is in its species unobjectionable, although it lacks individual lawfulness which is determined by the *finis operantis*. Here there recurs in more subtle form the false distinction between the mere externals of an act as the *finis operis* and the inner intention as the *finis operantis* which I have already criticized. The *finis operis* of any act is definable only in relation to an individual intention. An act is only morally good if its reason is commensurate; conversely it is only bad if the reason of the act is not commensurate. A marital act completed with external correctness, but not intended as the expression of personal love, is already bad in its *finis operis*. A special individual ethics is superfluous, because all true ethics is individual.

In response to what I published earlier on the principle of double effect, several critics raised the objection that my thesis served the cause of ethical relativism. This objection is unjust. In what I have asserted up to this point, I have attempted to demonstrate that the fundamental insights of traditional ethics show that an act is morally bad if it implies in the last analysis a self-contradiction, and thus becomes unreasonable. This criterion for *malum intrinsecum* amounts to a universal, unconditional, objective and nonrelative rule. An immoral act is the seeking of any value in the short run while in its total existential reality the act destroys the value. The justness of this criterion cannot be denied by anyone who defends an objective ethics. I believe that this criterion is precise and not manipulable in any way, and that in using it I am a clear opponent of situation ethics. But how could my reflections have given the impression of ethical relativism? The chief reason seems to be that my critics did not sufficiently observe that the concept of a commensurate reason must be understood differently than it is commonly and inexactly understood. It is not my meaning that any act at all is permissible as long as there is a "serious reason" for it. Such a conclusion would indeed be the most evil form of ethical relativism. But a commensurate reason in my thesis is not the same as a serious reason.

A second cause for misunderstanding has been that it is assumed that certain acts like murder, unchastity, hatred of God, etc., are morally evil in advance, so that there is nothing more to prove. This is indeed just and true. If it is once established that the act is murder, then it is established that the act is morally evil. I put the question at an essentially earlier point: How can it be recognized that an act is murder? To do this, the physical fact which could be observed in a photograph does not suffice. As Thomas puts it, "Moral acts are defined by what is intended in them," or by what is directly willed in them.[20] I have sought to establish that the concept "direct" correlates with the concept "commensurate reason." If the concept "direct" is understood in the sense of direct causality or direct attention of the person who is acting, then my thesis is understood in a false sense. It would be the worst relativism if it were seriously asserted that the moral qualification of an act depends on whether or not the person acting concentrates his attention on the good intention.

In one sense, however, I plead for a kind of objective relativism in ethics. I think that there are no prefabricated judgments which can be made, but that the judgment of conscience depends on what a particular event is in reality. Whether, for example, particular behavior is hatred of God cannot be known in advance; it requires examination. It may be that the hatred is directed to a false image of God which the person refuses to serve. Similarly, a fool observing the killing of an aggressor could say, "You shall not kill," and be filled with the prideful consciousness that he spoke his verdict on behalf of the unchangeable and absolute moral law. He would still have to be told that the killing was not a direct killing in the sense of the commandment.

X
PROBABILISM

In our discussion of the distinction between affirmative and negative laws of nature we already saw that what is fundamental is the affirmative obligation to realize in the best possible way all the values of creation. At the second level and only as it contradicts its own end is the direct permission or causing of an evil forbidden. The negative laws are applications of the affirmative laws in particular cases. Based on an understanding of this relationship probabilism asserts that one may not prevent an act which is possibly good, for the simple reason that one is not sure whether in fact it is good. As long as one is not sure that an act is morally bad, it is established that it is perhaps morally good and the fulfillment of the affirmative obligation to realize the good may be found in it. Because of the priority of the affirmative obligation to the good, it would be in the last analysis a lack of responsibility if such an act were impeded. The tutiorism which is opposed to probabilism is like the conduct of the servant entrusted with the talent who, for fear of losing it, buried it and so made no profit.

The moral system of probabilism already contains the principle of double effect as I have explained it. The simplest example is the one I have already often cited of a medical decision to be made. The doctor is obliged to determine as far as possible whether the therapy he plans is in fact the best possible; but a decision can be so pressing that he cannot wait long. The patient would be dead before the doctor reached the theoretically best medication in the books.

If he could know in advance what would be the best possible measure, he would be obliged to apply it to the exclusion of all other methods. But in the actual situation because of the time pressure, the doctor is bound to put aside the achievement of ideal knowledge and is permitted to use the solution for the problem which has apparently the least risk and offers a probability of success. Concretely, he then acts in what is the best possible way considering the matter in its entirety. Care for the health of his patient would not be a commensurate reason which would justify him in letting time elapse while he pursued a long investigation. Such behavior would not be responsible. True responsibility is always a function of the best possible choice in terms of the interrelated whole.

A more general statement is necessary in this connection. In most manuals the principle of double effect is explained in such a way that it concerns only the eventual permissibility of permitting or causing a physical evil in the sense that the act is not expressly forbidden. Exceptions which are justified by commensurate reasons are not, in fact, something indifferent (a human act is never indifferent), but are positively good. They are the observance of an affirmative law which requires the seeking of a determinate value in the best possible way. Every act in which any value is sought in a way corresponding to its existential entirety is *eo ipso* morally good.

My interpretation of commensurate reason shows that someone can be so obliged in given circumstances to the causing or permitting of an evil that there is scarcely any other choice for him. This is the case where any other act would involve the violation of a negative law. For example, in the case of catastrophe the rescue of human lives is to be preferred to the salvaging of valuable goods, unless these on the whole will contribute to the saving of a greater number of human lives.

XI
CONTRACEPTION

My interpretation of the principle of double effect may also contribute to the solution of the question, so controverted today, as to whether any form of contraception is permissible. The contribution will consist above all in a correct formulation of the question itself. In this section I will assume the results reached above, especially the definition of the concepts "direct" and "commensurate reason." Whoever reads what follows without reference to these conclusions and therefore with an inexact understanding of these concepts, runs the danger of misunderstanding the meaning of my assertions.

The teaching of the Church has been expressed as follows by Pius XI: any form of contraception in any way is immoral, just as lying, theft, and murder are immoral. It is asked today if this principle is truly general without exceptions. The more severe moralists hold that a modification of the prohibition is excluded because the Church would have to admit that it had erred on a fundamental question. Their opponents believe that this is not a question of infallible teaching and that new arguments which have developed require reconsideration of the doctrine. These opponents would admit that in certain cases contraception is permissible. The two approaches stand in irreconcilable opposition.

The insolubility produced by the problematic seems to me a sign that the question has been put in a false way. The parties to the discussion seem to take for granted a single concept of contraception derived from the encyclical *Casti connubii* of Pius XI: Contraception is said to be present when the conjugal act, which by its nature is directed to the procreation of offspring, is deprived of this natural meaning and power by intention (*de industria*). It is evident that not even the most weighty ground (*nulla profecto ratio ne gravissima quidem*) can effect that such an act against nature, which is evil in itself, be permitted.[21] This apparently clear and precise determination of the concept is not inadequate or false on more exact examination, but is ambiguous.

That a marital act lose its procreative power is a purely physical evil which does not constitute a human act without further content. Thus Piux XI's definition of the concept in reference to immoral contraception notes that this act is done intentionally, *de industria*. In this concept lies the whole ambiguity. Is *de industria* meant as intentional in a psychological or in a moral sense? Let us recall again the example of the medically necessary amputation of a limb. Psychologically the doctor has the removal of the limb in mind. One can say in a psychological sense that he in fact *de industria* removes the limb from the body. But in a moral sense it is his intention to carry out a justified operation. Morally the act is not the removal of the limb but a healing intervention. In a moral sense the act can be justified by a commensurate reason, and the premoral, psychological action is beyond intention; the doctor's moral intention is to remove a once useful member of the body only insofar as it is an obstacle to health. If an act has a commensurate reason the latter prevents evil from being willed directly or *de industria* in the moral sense, so that what psychological attention may be concentrated on is in the moral sense beyond intention, *praeter intentionem*. In other words, if the expression *de industria* used by Pius XI is understood in a moral sense, it is demonstrated according to the logic of its use that it is completely the same as the fundamental moral concepts "direct" or "formal" or "in intention," which we have already shown must be conjugated with the concept of commensurate reason.

Like all the negative laws, the prohibition of contraception means the direct permission or causing of something which must be considered in some respect a physical evil even if it appears worth being sought in some other respect. By direct is meant a causing or permission without a commensurate reason. In a case where there is a commensurate reason for the prevention of pregnancy, the moral content of the act is not the fact of contraception but the nature of the commensurate reason. Naturally in making this determination, an absolute distinction must be observed between "commensurate" and "serious." Pius XI says with complete correctness that, however serious the reason, it cannot make an act right if it is against nature in the moral sense; the same conclusion is reached in terms of my analysis where a commensurate reason is lacking.

In ethics, care must be taken not to identify the physical or psychological order directly with the moral order. A physical evil may be caused or permitted and willed in a psychological sense, and yet the act is not necessarily a moral evil. It is a moral evil if the act has no commensurate reason but in its existential entirety contradicts the value sought. It then becomes in a moral sense contrary to nature. It can be objected that for an act contrary to nature there is never a reason which can be considered commensurate. But a conclusion as to commensurate reason logically precedes the determination that the act is contrary to nature. The objection runs counter to my assertion that the contrariness to the nature of an act is only recognized when its reason is not commensurate—that is, when between the act and its proper reason in terms of the horizon of the entire reality there is a contradiction which shows that the act is in the last analysis counterproductive.

In ethical discussions a distinction must be made between contraception in its moral sense as a prevention of pregnancy not justified by a commensurate reason and the premoral concept of actual prevention of a pregnancy. The second meaning does not yet in a moral sense belong to the *finis operis* of the act. If the concept of contraception in the statement of Pius XI is understood in its moral sense, his judgment is correct and by definition permits no modification. An act which is not founded on a commensurate reason is evil and remains evil because it is a self-contradiction and in the last analysis unreasonable, and it is then to be designated according to the evil physically caused by it—in this case according to the prevention of pregnancy as contraception.

If *de industria* is understood not in a moral, but in a psychological sense, then the judgment of Pius XI is incomprehensible and meaningless as it gives a moral meaning to a fact understood in a premoral sense. This would be roughly like determining the color of an object from its weight. On this level the discussion naturally reaches no conclusion. As long as the distinct meanings of *de industria* are not separated from each other, every statement must remain ambiguous even if it is believed to be clear and even if it is solemnly asserted by ecclesiastical authority.

What I have said up to now on contraception has been of an entirely formal character. I have not asserted what would be a commensurate reason because of which the prevention of a pregnancy willed in a psychological sense would remain beyond moral intention. But, fundamentally, to give such a reason would be to yield to another false framing of the question which has been seriously harmful to the discussion. A catalog of commensurate reasons is expected in terms of which the act for all time could be regarded as permissible, and it is assumed that there would be no need to consider further such permissible behavior. These expectations are deceptive. A list of reasons which might be composed, whether they are commensurate or not, cannot be definitively established in advance. What is at issue is a concept which depends on a relation.

The permissibility of an act, moreover, does not mean that it is permissible for all time. If a doctor uses a medicine with concomitant evil result, he remains obliged to use it as long as there is no better means, but he is also obliged to seek better solutions. Our case is similar. If what is in fact contraceptive conduct in the premoral sense is justified by a commensurate reason so that it is not an act of contraception in the moral sense, this does not mean that this reason will remain commensurate forever. There is a fundamental obligation to seek a solution for the problem which in the achieving of the values sought accepts in exchange the respectively least evil possible within the entire range of possibilities.

Many moralists content themselves in their argument with a pure proof of physical evil. They confuse the physical and the moral sense of contrariness to nature. This is as though the killing of an aggressor in a case of necessity were identified with killing in a moral sense. It is, to be sure, true that contrariness to nature in a moral sense has a relation to a physical evil which can be defined in a physical sense as contrary to nature; but moral evil comes about only through permission or causing of physical evil without commensurate reason. But this physical evil is not as such a moral evil. The same moralists found the permission of periodic continence on the logically insufficient claim that periodic continence is not an active attack on procreation although in fact a choice of times for intercourse is a pure activity. In fact if periodic continence were practiced without commensurate reason it would not be other than impermissible contraception. This is plain from the text of Pius XII.[22]

The criterion of commensurate reason means that the value whose achievement is realizable only by contraceptive measures in a premoral sense may not in the last analysis be contradicted by these measures by preventing in the long run the highest possible realization of this very value with the smallest possible evil. To prove that a particular act is contraceptive in the moral sense it must be shown that the act in the last analysis does not serve the end of preservation and deepening marital love, but in the long run subverts it.

If it is argued in accordance with scholastic ethics that the foundation of the prohibition of contraception is that the marital act is directed by its nature to the procreation of offspring, this argument is correct only if it is understood in a moral sense. The objective of the procreation of offspring is to be sought in a way commensurate to the objective and not actually subversive of it. It is conceivable that a marital act may lead to irresponsible procreation. Such an act would be a sin both against the expected child and against the children in existence whose appropriate education might not be further provided for. In this moral sense the act would be one hostile to children, an act which could be recognized as a misuse of marriage although physiologically everything appeared to be in order. It would appear that this act was in reality deprived of its natural direction to the procreation of offspring, because there would be no correspondence between the act and its end in the final analysis for the moral judgment which must be made in^r terms of the whole reality.

In this article directed to principles it is not possible for me to enter into further detail. But the following consequences seem valid. If someone may not reasonably be responsible for another pregnancy, the use of periodic continence, where it is not impossible because of external circumstances, seems in the usual case to best correspond to the social and human character of the marital encounter. With adequate motivation it may serve to increase mutual love.[23] Where periodic continence is objectively impossible, the question is posed whether other ways may be used. These means are to be judged as to whether or not they contradict the highest possible realization of the desired value on the whole. If, for example, a man without conscience compelled his wife against her will to have marital intercourse, the wife would have an evident right to use the necessary means to prevent a pregnancy for which she cannot take the responsibility. As a wife she would not have to use force against her husband. Her conduct would have nothing in common with forbidden contraception in a moral sense. It would be a scandalous mistake if I should be accused because of this position of having abandoned the "hard but healthy Catholic teaching."

XII
CONCLUSION

The principle of double effect brings into usage a criterion which is implied in every decision of conscience. That an act is good means that a commensurate reason is recognized as present. Conversely, in an immoral act a lack of a commensurate reason is recognized—that is, in terms of the whole reality the act in its existential character directly contradicts the very value which is intended to be sought. A short-term, particular realization of a value is sought at the price of a greater loss for the same value as a whole. This fact is not always clear in advance because a looking back towards the horizon of reality is necessary. The task of scientific moral theology is to prove in behavior which is condemned as immoral that it contradicts the very value which is expressly sought.[24] It must be cautioned that the reason for an act can prove to be commensurate only if the whole horizon is considered and not some particular aspect. Conscience has to do with the whole.

Notes

1. The concept of nature in ethics does not mean a discoverable and unchangeable particular nature—for example, the nature of man in contrast to that of horses; but according to its origin in Greek philosophy, the concept is a counterconcept to positive human determination (thus *physis* is opposition to *thesis*). It is a human determination that traffic should not move on the left but on the right. This arbitrary determination stems from a necessity arising from "nature" that for the safety of participants in traffic some fixed order be determined. Cf. for the concept of the law of nature the very perceptive article of P. Antoine, *Conscience et loi naturelle*, 317 Etudes 162-83 (1963).

2. Cf. J.T. Mangan "An Historical Analysis of the Principle of

Double Effect," *Theological Studies* 10 (1949) pp. 41-61. There is no substantial foundation for criticism of Mangan's conclusions by J. Ghoos, "L'Acte à double effet—Etude de théologie positive," *Ephemerides Theologicae Lovanienses* 27 (1951), pp. 30-52, esp. pp. 31f.

3. Thomas Aquinas, *Summa Theologiae*, II-II, q. 64, a. 7 in corpore: "Respondeo dicendum quod nihil prohibet unius actus esse duos effectus, quorum alter solum sit in intentione, alius vero sit praeter intentionem. Morales autem actus recipiunt speciem secundum id quod intenditur, non autem ab eo quod est praeter intentionem, cum sit per accidens, ut ex supra dictis patet. Ex actu igitur alicuius seipsum defendentis duplex effectus sequi potest: unus quidem conservatio propriae vitae; alius autem occisio invadentis. Actus igitur huiusmodi ex hoc quod intenditur conservatio propriae vitae, non habet rationem illiciti: cum hoc sit cuilibet naturale quod se conservet in esse quantum potest. Potest tamen aliquis actus ex bona intentione proveniens illicitus reddi si non sit proportionatus fini. Et ideo si aliquis ad defendendum propriam vitam utatur maiori violentia quam oporteat, erit illicitum. Si vero moderate violentiam repellat, erit licita defensio."

4. Id. at I-IIe, q. 1, a. 3; q. 18, a. 2-7. The *finis operis* is identical with the moral object of an act.

5. E.g., M. Zalba, *Theologiae Moralis Compendium* I (Madrid, 1958), n. 10: "Finis . . . dividitur in: a) OPERIS (intrinsecum), ad quem res vel actio objective ex natura sua ordinatur (obiectum morale actionis) in morali hominum existimatione; . . . Sic eleemosyna ordinatur ex se ad subveniendum pauperi." See also A. Vermeersch, *Theologiae Moralis Principia–Responsa–Consilia* I (Rome, 1926), n. 115: "*Finis est id propter quod aliquid fit*. Rationem autem agendi habere, proprium est entis rationalis, Quare finis *dicitur primus in intentione*; nihil magis voluntarium est, ac proin nihil magis morale. *Finis operis seu internus, intrinsecus* dicitur, ad quem opus per se, seu natura sua in *morali existimatione* tendit, ut v.g. internus finis eleemosynae est levamen indigentiae." The *moralis existimatio* commonly spoken of by moralists in their definition of *finis operis* does not mean a kind of vague judgment according to common sense, but a moral judgment of the act—a judgment which includes a reference to the intention and thereby an implicit application of the principle of double effect as it has been above interpreted.

6. Cf. A. van Rijen, "Daden met meerdere gevolgen en de leer over de bronnen der zedelijkheid," in *Jaarboek 1960 van het Werkgenootschap van Kath. Theol. in Nederland* (Hilversum, 1961) pp. 48-82, esp. p. 70; similarly, F. D'Hoogh "Over de afzonderlijke zedelijke handeling," *Collectanea Mechliniensia* 50 (1965), pp. 356-53; 476-96 (especially p. 486) which refers to my first article cited in the asterisked footnote.

7. Cf. Thomas, *op. cit. supra* note 3, at I-II, q. 18, a. 10; q. 88, a. 5.

8. Here it must be observed that the pair of concepts, "formal"—"material," in the teaching on cooperation with evil is used in a different

sense than in the distinction made between "formal" and "material" sin. In a material sin the person acting is in good faith as to the objective permissibility of what he does. For example, he gives his friend candy when in reality it is poison. In formal sin there is complete consciousness of the actual character of transgression in the act, and therefore the person acting is guilty. In the sense in which the terms are used in reference to cooperation, there can be complete consciousness of what one is doing and nonetheless the act may be material cooperation and not formal cooperation.

9. If the principle of double effect appears purely formal in its nature and requires for the morality of an act only the presence of a commensurate reason which then makes indirect the evil accepted in exchange, yet the principle contains a content determined by ontology. Any reason whatsoever may be the reason for an act, and yet one may not conclude that any reason is in fact commensurate to the act. Conversely, the question what is evil may also be answered from ontology: it is the lack of completeness which could be present.

10. Cf. L. Janssens "Daden met meerdere gevolgen," *Collectanea Mechliniensia* 32 (1947), pp. 621-33, esp. p. 632.

11. The postulation of a necessary *judicium ultimo-practicum*, as it is commonly assumed by the scholastics, would contradict freedom and in the last analysis make its rational explanation impossible. It is a false assumption that the fundamental form of free choice is the possibility of decision between several goods, among which one chooses that good which reason, working reciprocally with the will, declares to be the greatest. This explanation contains a logical circle which is disguised with difficulty. In reality there is a *libertas specificationis* not only when one compares several objects with one another, but also when one accepts or rejects a single good in itself. The first form, that is, *libertas specificationis inter plura*, is then only a conclusory application of the second *libertas specificationis quoad idem*. A No is naturally more than the pure preservation of an act of the will on the basis of a so-called *libertas exercitii* which under no circumstances can be designated as the fundamental form of the freedom of the will. I make this observation only because I know of no other satisfactory explanation of the freedom of the will in scholasticism.

12. R. A. McCormick, "Notes on Moral Theology," *Theological Studies* 26 (1965) pp. 603-608, has raised as an objection to my French article mentioned at the beginning of the notes that my explanation of the principle of double effect transgresses the boundaries of an objective ethics. Unfortunately in his account of my work he first confuses "commensurate reason" with any reason ("The formality under which the act is willed is determined by the proportionate reason for acting," p. 604) and then confuses it with a "reason proportionate to the original goal" (p. 604); and he appears to conclude, contrary to my express statement, that any direct quantitative comparison of one value with another value may create

a commensurate reason (p. 606). Above all McCormick objects that I failed to distinguish in my article between "inner" and "outer" "commensurate reasons." In reality I had set out this distinction on pages 360-61 as the distinction between *finis operis* and *finis operantis*. I return to it in Part VII of the present paper. His chief objection is that "this reasoning would destroy the concept of that which is intrinsically evil *ex obiecto*" (p. 605). What I have said in Part III.2 above is a response to this objection. What was lacking in my French article was a failure to make explicit the identity of the morally evil and the intrinsically evil, that is, the evil *ex obiecto*. On this account I am grateful to McCormick for his criticism.

13. Aristotle, *Nicomachean Ethics*, 2.6.15-17.

14. Cf. F. D'Hoogh, *op. cit. supra* note 6, at 487.

15. " . . . illicitum est, quod homo intendat occidere hominem, ut seipsum defendat. . . ."

16. L. Liebhart, "Sterilisierende Drogen," *Theologisch-Praktische Quartalschrift* 111 (1963), p. 192.

17. See *supra* note 5.

18. Thomas, *op. cit. supra* note 3, at II-II, q. 64, a. 3 and 7.

19. See the observations of L. Bender, "Ius in vita," *Angelicum* 30 (1953), pp. 50-62.

20. See *supra* note 3.

21. Pius XI, *Casti connubii*, in *Acta Apostolicae Sedis* (hereafter AAS) (1930) 22:559: "At nulla profecto ratio, ne gravissima quidem, efficere potest, ut, quod intrinsece est contra naturam, id cum natura congruens et honestum fiat. Cum autem actus coniugii suapte natura proli generandae sit destinatus, qui, in eo exercendo, naturali hac eum vi atque virtute de industria destituunt, contra naturam agunt et turpe quid atque intrinsece inhonestum operantur."

22. Cf. Pius XII, "Allocution to the Catholic Society of Italian Midwives," October 29, 1951, AAS (1951) 43:846: " . . . sottrarsi sempre e deliberatamente, senza un grave motivo, al suo primario dovere, sarebbe un peccare contro il senso stesso della vita coniugale. Da quella prestazione positiva obbligatoria possono esimere, anche per lungo tempo, anzi per l'intera durata del matrimonio, seri motivi, come quelli che si hanno non di rado nella cosiddetta "indicazione" medica, eugenica, economica e sociale. Da ciò consegue che l'osservanza dei tempi infecondi può essere *lecita* sotto l'aspetto morale; e nelle condizioni menzionate è realmente tale. Se però non vi sono, secondo un giudizio ragionevole ed equo, simili gravi ragioni personali o derivanti dalle circostanze esteriori, la volontà di evitare abitualmente la fecondità della loro unione, pur continuando a soddisfare pienamente la loro sensualità, non può derivare che da un falso apprezzamento della vita e da motivi estranei alle rette norme etiche.

The expression "serious motive" is somewhat inexact. The real meaning is that of a commensurate reason as in the passage of Pius XII in the "Allocution to the International Society of Hematologists," Sept. 12, 1958, *AAS* (1958) 50:736.

23. Cf. C. Rendu, "La régulation des naissances dans le cadre familial et chrétien," *Nouvelle revue théologique* 87 (1965), pp. 606-31.

24. The Editor, whom I thank for the translation of my article, has asked me to answer this question: Does the principle work also in the sexual area? Take the hypothetical case often used of a woman who is asked to commit adultery in order that her children may be rescued from a concentration camp. If her objective is the saving of the children, is her act contradictory to this objective? Or if a woman for whom prostitution is the only way to keep from starving, is she not like the man in extreme necessity who steals? Why is her act any more adultery than his act is theft?

I would reply first that the difficulty is by no means special to the sexual area. We have the same problem in every kind of extortion or blackmail. For example, someone may be threatened with death if he refuses to take part in the falsification of a document.

The question must be answered in relation to the whole context. Does life or freedom have any value if in the end one is forced to give up all human rights and in principle be exposed to every extortion? This would be in contradiction to the very values of life and freedom. For extortion always works after the pattern of the salami, one slice of which is taken after the other: it is a menace not only for a part but also for the whole.

As for the woman who believes that prostitution is the only way to keep from starving, she is in reality also the victim of extortion. By acceding to an unjust extortion one can never really save anything in the long run.

Ontic Evil
and Moral Evil

Louis Janssens

In the first and by far the longest section of his treatise *De Actibus Humanis*, St. Thomas presents a very painstaking examination of the structure of human action (*Ia IIae.qq.* 6-17). Next, he limits his teaching on the moral evaluation of human action to three questions (qq. 18-20). The sequence and the interrelationship of those two parts is immediately obvious when it is seen that the way in which the morality of the human action is interpreted definitely rests on one's approach to the structure of the action. This is apparent in the history of the discussion about human action. In the medieval tradition, two distinct currents of thought about the structure and the morality of the human action can be found. The first, which influenced the following centuries by the prestige of Petrus Lombardus, accents the importance of the object (*finis operis*) within the framework of the action, and it assumes the position that the object can be morally evaluated by itself (*in se*) without reference to the agent. The second, which had already been advocated by Anselm of Canterbury and had been elaborated by Abaelardus and his followers, was adopted by St. Thomas who thoroughly systematized it. It ties the definition of the structure and the morality of the human action to the agent.[1]

We start from the Thomistic view because it is, in our opinion, a solid basis for the examination of the fundamental problem we will broach in this study. But let us understand St. Thomas correctly, because it is a fact that he is often interpreted in the light of concepts and presuppositions of the views he actually disputes.[2]

From this misinterpretation has originated many difficulties and inconsistencies we find in our textbooks of morality, e.g., the lack of consistency in the moral evaluation of the acts with several effects. The principles which govern this evaluation were formulated in the sixteenth century[3] and are not conformable to the thought of St. Thomas.

I

STRUCTURE AND MORALITY OF THE
HUMAN ACTION ACCORDING TO ST. THOMAS

Thomas approaches the topic of the structure of the human action in the light of his view of the acting subject, the inner act of the will. This appears already in the introduction to his *De Actibus Humanis*, in which he gives us the division of his exposition. First he will deal with the **voluntarium**. He calls this an essential condition (*conditio*) of any explanation of strictly human actions because the will, as **appetitus rationalis**, is specifically characteristic of the human being and consequently, only the acts which emanate from the will (*actus voluntarii*) are properly speaking *human* acts. Next he will go into the study of the acts themselves. In the first place, he will consider the inner act of the will (*actus ab ipsa voluntate eliciti*). Then he will turn his attention to the external actions which are also acts of the will itself (*ipsius voluntatis*) although they depend on other faculties for their realization.[4] The agent, consequently, is so essentially related to the structure of the activity that his activity can only be called *human* to the extent that it originates within a thinking and willing subject who is therefore capable of a free act of the will. "Only those acts of which man is thoroughly in control are properly called human acts. But man is thoroughly in control of his actions by the power of his reason and his will. Therefore only the acts which emanate from the free will, enlightened by the faculty of deliberation (reason), are called human in the proper sense."[5]

Why is it essentially important (*conditio*) to start from the acting subject in order to arrive at an analysis of the structure of the activity? Thomas replies with most convincing reasoning. "It is self-evident that all the actions which emanate from a certain faculty are shaped by this faculty according to the particular nature of its own object (*secundum rationem sui objecti*)."[6] Subsequently, St. Thomas adds, the formal object of the will is that which is good or more precisely that which is apprehended as good (*bonum apprehensum*).[7] Insofar as the action is elicited by the will itself, it is directed toward the attainment of a good. This principle can be applied to each human act, even a sinful act, since in any sinful act, man still intends to reach for something which is apprehended as something good, at least for some particular tendencies, although it is not in accord with the true good of the whole person (*contra naturam rationalem secundum rei veritatem*).[8] That we, in each action, seek and endeavor to realize that which is good—the proper object of the will—means that we aim at this good as the *end* of our action. In this sense St. Thomas writes: "The object of the will is the end and the good. Consequently, it is necessary that *all* human actions be done for an end (*propter finem*).[9] Or still more precisely, the good we strive for through an action functions in the act of the will and therefore in us, who are the acting subject, as an end (*bonum habet rationem finis*).[10] It is clear now that the end is the primordial element of the structure of an action, because it is the proper object of the act of the will. But it is equally clear that the subject or the inner act of the will is involved in the definition of the end. St. Thomas considers this thought over and again. "*Voluntas* **proprie** *est ipsius finis*."[11] "*Finis* **proprie** *est objectum interioris actus voluntatis*."[12] Every end of an action, therefore, is to be taken as an end of the subject, of the inner act of the will, viz., a **finis operantis**. Further on it will be shown that Thomas does not give this principle the sense of a subjectivistic interpretation of human activity. He will emphasize that a definite good, as object and end of an inner act of the will, cannot be pursued by the subject by any kind of action. Nevertheless, he will not abandon the position that the subject or the inner act of the will must be considered as the starting point; on the contrary, he will always stress that the end of the inner act of the will (or the *finis operantis*) determines the concrete structure of the action which fits this end (*finis dat speciem actui humano*).

Our textbooks distinguish between **finis operis** and **finis**

operantis. The intention of the authors is evident; it is an attempt to secure a moral evaluation of the action by itself (*in se*), as related to the object or the built-in end of the action, without any reference to the acting subject. Now it is to be noticed that Thomas never uses this distinction in his *De Actibus Humanis*, although he knows it. He mentions it in his commentary on Petrus Lombardus.[13] But he accentuates immediately that the *finis operis* is always converted into a *finis operantis*: *finis operis semper reducitur in finem operantis*. His reason for this teaching is clear: he draws it from the very definition of end. To the mind of Thomas there is no end without the inner act of the will of the subject and vice-versa. The end is in the strictest sense of the word the peculiar object of the inner act of the will.[14] In other words, the good, which is the appropriate object of the will, can only be termed an end insofar as it is aimed at by the subject in and through his action; it is always a **finis operantis**. According to Thomas, this can be said about both the **finis operis** and the **finis operantis**, as it appears from the definitions he offers in his commentary on Petrus Lombardus: "The *finis operis* is that to which the action is directed by the *acting subject* (*ab agente*); for this reason it is called the cause of the action (*ratio operis*). The *finis operantis* is the goal at which the agent in the end (*principaliter*) aims." Thomas illustrates his definitions with an example. A bricklayer "programs" the operations performed on the construction materials in such a manner that the work becomes a house. The realized house is the *finis operis*; but the profit he derives from this construction, e.g., his wages, is the *finis operantis*. The *finis operis* is a *finis operantis*. The bricklayer must, of course, really want the construction of the house (*finis operis*) in order to satisfy his yearning for wages (*finis operantis*). It is true that one end is not operating on the same level as the other—the *finis operis* is the immediate end of the bricklayer (*finis medius*), the *finis operis* is his main end (*principaliter*).

Consequently, each end is by its very definition the proper object of an inner act of the will, a *finis operantis*. The subject is the center. This view of Thomas is of far-reaching importance because the determining situation of the subject in the activity makes it possible to consider our actions not as a succession of separate and disjointed actions but as the integrated moments of a life history in which unity and wholeness can be realized by virtue of the ends of the agent. In this sense Thomas does not speak of *finis operis* or *finis operantis* in his *De Actibus Humanis*, but he stresses the varied rank and the interplay of the ends the subject strives to achieve: *finis medius, proximus, remotus, ultimus*, etc.[15]

We have seen that Thomas' view centers on the agent and that *ipso facto* the end of the agent is the fundamental element of the structure of the human act. To have a clear idea of this structure, we must take a closer look at the question: "How does the will of the agent aim at the end itself?" Thomas answers that the will aims at the end in two ways (*voluntas in ipsum finem dupliciter fertur*), either in an absolute way when it wills the end in itself and by itself (*absolute secundum se*), or when it wills the end as the reason that it wills the means to the end (*in ratione volendi ea quae sunt ad finem*).[16]

Voluntas

When the will strives for the end itself in an absolute way, St. Thomas uses the term **voluntas**[17] or **simplex actus voluntatis**.[18] Some are of the opinion that a mere *velleitas* was meant by *simplex actus voluntatis*. This interpretation runs counter to the terms Thomas uses in the context: *absolute secundum se*. Evidently Thomas wants to accentuate that the good, as the proper object of the will, can be striven for in itself and for its own sake as an end (*voluntas proprie est ipsius finis*),[19] even if it is not connected with an action. The example Thomas keeps repeating is that we can want health as an absolute end for its own sake, even when we do nothing to stay healthy or to regain our health.[20] It will appear below that this view is of the utmost importance when we handle the problem of morality.

Intentio and Electio

In the second case, the end is also wanted for its own sake, but at the same time it is striven for as the reason of the election of *the means* that make it possible to realize the end: *voluntas fertur in finem ut est ratio volendi ea quae sunt ad finem*.[21] It is therefore not a matter of a *simplex actus voluntatis* but of an *actus compositus*, made up of the end and the means. For the proper understanding of this view it must be remembered that the end of the subject determines the means. Or, in other words, the sense of means can be attributed only to something from the point of view of the end: *ex fine enim oportet accipere rationes eorum quae sunt ad finem*.[22]

Traditional terminology had compiled many terms that were more or less technically suited to describe the diverse elements of the human act. Thomas reduces them to the terms *intentio* and *electio*,[23] of which he left us a precise definition. "The *intentio* is the striving toward the *end* to the extent that it is within the range of the *means*." "The *electio* is the concentration of the will on the *means* to the extent that they bear upon the attainment of the *end*."[24] The material sense of both concepts is the same since they contain the idea of the whole act, end and means. But they are formally quite distinct. The *intentio* is directly aimed at the absolute element of the structure of the action, that is, the end itself which is the reason that the means are willed and consequently is the principle of the act (*finis* as *principium actionis humanae*), the formal element which specifies the act.[25] On the other hand, the *electio* signifies the relative element of the act, viz., the means (by its own definition means indicates a relation to the end) which is only useful until the end has been attained (*finis as terminus actionis humanae*).[26] As we have already said, an end can be striven for in itself and for its own sake. A means *as such* cannot be willed unless the end is willed simultaneously, because it is by nature relative to the end and because the exigencies of the goal specify that which will lead to its realization (*ex fine enim oportet accipere rationes eorum quae sunt ad finem*). For this reason, Thomas writes: "Whenever someone wants a means, he wants the end in the *same* act (*eodum actu*), but the reverse of this phrase is not always true."[27]

The expression *eodem actu* clearly suggests that the will of the end and the choice of the means constitute only one act of the will: "It is evident that the same act of the will is embedded in the striving for the end as the reason for the choice of the means as well as in the striving for the means."[28] Thomas illustrates this proposition as follows: "When I say that I want a remedy (means) to recover from an illness (end), I indicate only one act of the will, since the end is the reason that I want the means. Subsequently, one and the same act of the will combines the object (the use of the remedy) and the reason for this object (the end, viz., the recovery from the illness).[29]

But this one act of the will is a composite act. Thomas uses the terms *intentio* and *electio* to show the structural elements of this complex whole. Because of both elements the act of the will is a single dynamic event of which the end is the formal and primary element (*finis* as *principium*) which so extensively directs and determines the motion of the will toward the means that the act comes to a stop when the end has been attained (*finis* as *terminus*).

Actus Exterior

Since the end is *terminus*, viz., that which must be realized by the act, the dynamic event cannot be confined to the inner act of the will. The action must be *done* in order to effect the end. To act is to be actively in touch with reality (with things, with ourselves, with our fellow men, with a social group, with God). The inner act of the will falls short of this active contact. Our will must rely on the medium of other faculties and our bodiliness as agencies which enable it to effect a real contact with reality. For this reason our action is not only an inner act of the will (*interior actus voluntatis*) but also an exterior event (*actus exterior*).

This brings us again to the question about the unity of the human act. Are the interior act of the will and the exterior event two acts or one? Thomas himself poses this question and writes an entire article in response.[30] He elucidates his answer in a comparison. A reality which is composed of *forma* and *materia*, e.g., the soul and the body of the human being, is only one being (*unum simpliciter*) although it has different parts (*multa secundum quid*). In this way the human act is only one act but at the same time a composite unity of which, on the one hand, the interior act of the will is the formal element and, on the other hand, the exterior act is the material element. In other words, the end which is the proper object of the inner act of the will[31] is the formal element; the exterior act, as means to this end, is the material element of the very same human act: "*Finis autem comparatur ad id quod ordinatur ad finem, sicut forma ad materiam.*"[32] And as the *forma* determines the specific being of a reality, so the end of the interior act of the will specifies the concrete totality of the human act (*finis dat speciem actui humano*).[33]

Now it is clear that Thomas begins with the subject when describing the structure of human action. The end of the interior act of the will is the determining and decisive factor. 1) It can be willed absolutely and for its own sake even without any reference to an action in a *simplex actus voluntatis*. 2) It is also the decisive and determining factor of the action: only from the vantage point of the end can it be seen what are the means properly so called and furthermore, that the means are related to the end in such a manner that the action ceases when the end has been attained.[34]

Having taken the subject or the interior act of the will as the basis of his description of the structure of the human act, Thomas also uses the same basis for the moral evaluation of the will and the act. He states in his treatises *De Lege Aeterna* (*Ia IIae, q.* 93) and *De Lege Naturali* (*Ia IIae*, q. 94) that reason is the measure of morality to the extent that it is a participation in the eternal law (*secundum rationem esse*). In *De Actibus Humanis* he summarizes this view in one article whose main thrust is: "*Quod ratio humana sit regula* voluntatis humanae, *ex qua ejus bonitas mensuratur, habet ex lege aeterna, quae est ratio divina.*"[35] It appears from this idea that the moral goodness of the human act depends on its accordance with reason. This is true both for the *simplex actus voluntatis* in which the end is aimed at in itself and for its own sake and for the *actus compositus* in which the will is directed towards the end in and through the means.

The Morality of the Voluntas

We said that it is Thomas' view that the good which is the proper object of the will is also its end. It is a moral good (*vere bonum*) when it corresponds to reason: *ipse appetitus* **finis debiti** *praesupponit rectam apprehensionem de fine, quae est per rationem.*[36] If it is not within the realm of reason, it is still a good (*apparens bonum*), as far as it is consonant with a particular appetite, in spite of the fact that it is morally vitiated (*contra naturam rationalem secundum rei veritatem*).[37] Whether or not the subject is taking the moral good as the end of his action depends on his inner disposition. In this context Thomas accentuates the meaning of the virtues. The moral virtues (below we will speak about the special place of *prudentia*) are acquired dispositions (habits) which direct us toward the moral good as the end, even when we do not act. Having acquired the virtue of justice, we would, by virtue of an inner *habitus*, love and will the social relations and conditions that fit the dignity of man, even when we do not act or when we find it impossible to overcome certain abuses in our own actions. A virtuous person is directed toward the moral good because he loves and wills it as an end by virtue of an inner disposition. *absolute et secundum se*.

Even in his *De Actibus Humanis* which *per se* concerns human acts, Thomas cannot keep from already mentioning the virtues. He does this particularly in reference to texts of Aristotle.[38] He quotes especially this text of the philosopher: "*Virtus est quae bonum facit habentem et opus ejus bonum reddit.*"

Above all, virtue makes the subject who possesses it a good subject. It is the source of the morally good *simplex actus voluntatis* which enables us to set our will on the moral good in an absolute sense and for its own sake. So the first moral qualification does not concern the particular acts but the subject himself who by virtue of his virtuous dispositions is turned towards the moral good as his end.[39]

But virtue also makes good acts out of the acts of man. Here Thomas quotes the sentence of Aristotle: "*Similes habitus similes actus reddunt.*"[40] In his own doctrine on the virtues he stresses the point that the virtues endow us with a connaturality or an affinity with the moral good and that they help us to discern the concrete actions which can embody the love of the moral good. He who is just, for instance, is tuned to just actions by the virtue of justice.[41]

The Morality of the Human Action

We said that according to Thomas the inner act of the will (end) and the exterior act (means) are one and the same concrete act.[42] No wonder that Thomas concludes that they must also be treated as one from the moral viewpoint: "*Actus interior et exterior sunt diversi secundum genus naturae. Sed tamen, ex eis sic diversis constituitur unum in genere moris.*"[43] For this reason he reacts sharply against those who are of the opinion that the material event of an act can be evaluated morally without consideration of the subject, of the inner act of the will or of the end. As he sees it, an exterior action considered as nothing but the material event (*secundum speciem* **naturae**) is an abstraction to which a moral evaluation cannot be applied. This object-event becomes a concrete *human* act only insofar as it is directed towards an end within the inner act of the will. Only this concrete totality has a moral meaning. It is the end of the inner act of the will which specifies the malice or the goodness of the act: "*Finis secundum quod est prior in intentione,* **secundum hoc pertinet ad voluntatem**. *Et hoc modo dat speciem actui humano sive morali.*"[44] Thomas himself illustrates this as follows. The act of killing a human being (*hoc ipsum quod est occidere hominem*) as the matter-event (*actus secundum speciem naturae*) can be done for several reasons, e.g., the exercise of justice (undoubtedly Thomas is thinking here of the execution of the death penalty—which according to his theories can be justified on certain conditions) or of the gratification of vengeful feelings. Both cases have the same material act in common (*idem actus secundum speciem naturae*) but if we examine them from a moral point of view we will discover very diverse actions (*diversi actus secundum speciem moris*), since in the first case we will find a virtuous act while we will find a vitiated act in the second. It is then possible that acts which have the same features insofar as they are object-events (*actus qui sunt iidem secundum speciem naturae*) fall into very distinct types of morality (*esse diversos secundum speciem moris*) determined by the kind of end of the *will* towards which the matter-event has been directed (*ordinetur ad diversos fines* **voluntatis**).[45] The end which the subject intends to work out by his inner act of the will specifies the morality of the act.[46]

Thus, in order to determine the morality of a human act. Thomas chooses as his starting point the acting subject, the end which is the proper object of the inner act of the will and which impresses the qualities of good or evil on the action: *finis enim dat speciem in moralibus*.[47]

At first sight it may seem that Thomas contradicts himself.[48] For one thing, he says that the *species moris* —the goodness or the malice of the act—is determined by the end, the object of the inner act of the will. For another, he writes that the *species moris* of the exterior act depends on the fact whether or not its object is in keeping with reason (*secundum rationem* or *praeter rationem*).[49] Does he thereby not suggest that the morality of the exterior action can be evaluated by itself and as an element which is disconnected from the subject or the end of the inner act of the will? We must not forget that Thomas immediately proceeds to answer this question as follows: "Nevertheless, the inner act of the will is the *formal* element of the exterior action, because the will itself acts through the medium of the body and because the exterior actions concern morality only insofar as they emanate from the will (*nisi in quantum sunt voluntarii*). From this follows that the *species moris* is formally dependent on the end (of the inner act of the will) and materially dependent on the object of the exterior action."[50] He adds this terse statement: *actus interior voluntatis comparatur ad exteriorem sicut formale ad materiale*.[51]

Let us always keep in mind the primacy of the end, the formal element. This element must be the starting point of the search for insight into the morality of the action. Now Thomas leads us into the alternative: the end itself can be good or bad.

1. First there are the actions with a morally bad end which is not the *finis debitus* sanctioned by reason.[52] The bad end vitiates the entire action because the end is the formal element of the entire event of the action. In Thomistic terms we can say: the bad intention vitiates the entire action. Indeed, as we have said above, in the view of Thomas the intention is to will the end as a *reason* that the action is willed.[53] When the end is bad, the whole action is the fruit of a **mala voluntas** and because the action is only human as far as it emanates from the will (*voluntarius*) it is entirely bad. It is

in this sense that Thomas says that giving alms is a bad action if vanity motivates the giver, at least if the love of vain praise is a real intention, that is, the cause and the reason (*ratio et causa*) of the action: "*Voluntas non potest dici bona, si sit* **intentio mala** *causa volendi. Qui enim vult dare eleemosynam propter inanem gloriam consequendam, vult id quo de se est bonum*[54] *sub ratione mali; et ideo, prout est volitum ab ipso, est malum. Unde* **voluntas** *ejus est* **mala**."[55] Thomas is very well aware of the fact that a donation may help the person in need who receives it, that the *finis operis* of the action (to provide relief) is morally good if *it is intended by the acting subject as an end* (in this sense he says "*quod de se est bonum*"), but in the càse under examination, the *mala voluntas* or the bad *intentio* of the agent is the reason (*causa*) of the entire event, and because there is the most intimate connection between the agent and the morality of the act, we have here an action which is truly bad since the formal element is bad in itself. The situation is still worse when the subject aims at several bad ends with his action. To illustrate this case. Thomas copied an example of Aristotle. Someone who steals to get the money he intends to use to lead someone into adultery is, strictly speaking, more of an adulterer than a thief.[56] He is both, of course; he is primarily an adulterer because the main end of his inner act of the will is to commit adultery (*finis principalis*), but he is also a thief because he *wills* the unjust acquisition of money as an immediate end (*finis medius*) which *enables* him to realize his main goal. The end of the agent—the object of the inner act of the will—consequently, is so determining and cogent that it *communicates its moral malice to the entire action*.

2. Now suppose that the good at which the agent aims as the end of his inner act of the will is a good which is sanctioned by reason (*ipse appetitus finis debiti praesupponit rectam apprehensionem de fine, quae est per rationem*).[57] In this case the entire action is necessarily good if it is not a mere *velleitas* but rather the very will to bring about an end, or in other words, if it concerns a real **intentio finis** which involves the effective will to realize an end for its own sake and also as reason and cause of the action (*ratio et causa volendi*). This thesis does not favor subjectivism. On the contrary, it takes without any reservations the objective aspect of

the exterior event into consideration and assigns it its rightful place in the light of the agent or of the inner act of the will. Thomas explains this in two convergent ways.

(a) He uses in most cases his views on the distinction and the intrinsic cohesion between the formal and the material elements.[58] In one and the same human act the formal element is the object of the inner act of the will, viz., the end, while the object event of the exterior action is the material element. That is true about the structure of the human act. It is also true about its morality. The *moral goodness* of the act of the will is the formal element of the exterior act: **bonitas** *actus voluntatis est forma exterioris actus*.[59] For this reason the end formally specifies the goodness or the malice (*species moris*) of the human act while the material element of the goodness or the badness of this same act receives its material specification from the object of the exterior action.[60] Not any kind of exterior action, however, can become the material element of a morally good end. Thomas emphasizes this: "The end is to the means (exterior action) as *forma* is to the *materia*. According to the way things are, the *materia* cannot receive the *forma*, unless it is properly disposed to it (*nisi sit debito modo disposita ad ipsam*). Consequently nothing can realize its end unless it has been properly directed and ordered toward this goal (*nisi sit debito modo ordinatum ad ipsum*)."[61] So writes Thomas when he deals with the matter of our ultimate end and demonstrates that this can be reached only if the will is correctly directed according to its proper relation to that end (*rectitudo voluntatis est per debitum ordinem ad finem ultimum*). But he evidently intends to give us a principle which is true of the actualization of any morally good end. But how do we ascertain that an exterior action is **materia apta** and in a fitting way is adequate as a medium of the realization of a morally good end? When is the exterior action fittingly directed toward a good end? This cannot be known by viewing the exterior action only as a material event (*secundum speciem naturae*);[62] rather, the object of the exterior action must be left within the whole framework of the act before it can be evaluated according to the measure of morality, viz., the reason (*objectum est ei (= rationi) conveniens vel non conveniens*).[63] As far as it is a material event, sexual intercourse can conceive life both in the act of adultery and in the marital act (*habent unum effectum secundum speciem*), but when sexual intercourse is taken as the material element *of the whole of the action* of which the end is the formal element, the marriage act and adultery are entirely divergent on the level of the *species moris* (*secundum quod comparantur ad rationem, differunt specie*).[64]

(b) Thomas endeavors to explain this in another way by the use of the notions "means" (exterior action) and "end" (inner act of the will). He points out that on account of its very definition, the means is related to the end and therefore, must be adequately proprotionate (*debita proportio*) to this end.[65] To be a real human act he says, the act must emanate from the will (*voluntarius*). This does entail that the acting subject has a rational knowledge of the end (*non solum apprehenditur res quae est finis, sed etiam cognoscitur ratio finis*) and the means. In other words, he must grasp that the means is by its own definition relative and proportionate to the end (*cognoscitur proportio ejus quod ordinatur in finem ipsum*). Only then can the subject in the mental process of deliberation create the distance which brings about the freedom to act or not to act (*deliberans de fine et de his quae sunt ad finem protest moveri in finem vel non moveri*).[65] The exterior act can only be means insofar as it is in proportion to the end (*proportio actus ad finem*), i.e., insofar as it is suited to effect the end.[66] Insofar as it is a means, the exterior act is not willed for its own sake, but for its going out towards the end (*ex ordinatione ad finem*): the will wills the means only to the extent that it wills the end, so that it wills the end in the means (*unde hoc ipsum quod in eis vult est finis*).[67] Consequently the end is the reason (*ratio*) and the cause (*causa*) of the will to will the means.[68] So it is the beginning and the principle of the act (*finis ut principium*).[69] The means is relative to the end. Its characteristic is to serve the purpose of effecting the end. For this reason the action ceases when the end has been effected (*finis as terminus*)[70]: *id quod est ad finem se habet ad finem ut medium ad terminum*.[71]

Consequently, the exterior action is a means and as a means, it is relative to, going out towards, and in proportion to the end which is to be effected. This fits the structure of the human act. It also fits the morality of the human act. The end is morally good when it is in keeping with the *exigencies of the reason* (*conveniens rationi*). The means of the exterior acts participate in this moral goodness when they not only serve the purpose of effecting the end but moreover, when they are in the correct proportion to the end according to reason. This balanced proportion is an intrinsic element of the exterior action (*debita proportio ad finem et relatio in ipsum inhaeret actioni*); from this results the fact that the exterior action participates in the moral goodness of the end which is the cause of the moral goodness (*secundum habitudinem ad [finem] causam bonitatis*).[72] Thomas describes very clearly this *debita proportio* in a summary of his own view:

> Sin really consists of an action which is not in proportion to an end to which it is directed. It must be noted that the correct proportion to the end is measured with a rule. . . . The reason is the immediate rule of the actions which emanate from the will. The eternal law is the highest rule. Consequently, the human act is good when it is directed toward the end in keeping with the order determined by the reason and the eternal law; it is sinful when it deviates from this rule.[73]

Just as in the structure of the action, the end is the reason and the cause of the choice of the means, so is the goodness of the end in the morally good action only the total reason and cause of the exterior action if it leads the subject into doing an exterior action of which the object is properly proportioned *according to reason* to the required end (*debita proportio*). Someone steals, for example, in order to give the stolen goods to a needy person. Judging by the material element of this action, we see that it serves the purposes of the end: *de facto*, the needy person gets relief. But when we judge this action in the light of morality—*secundum ordinem rationis*—we say that there is no *debita proportio* of the action (means) to the end. On the contrary, there is a contradiction between the material and formal elements of the act. The end which is willed by the subject is an affirmation of the right to own property: the thief wants the needy person to own the things he gives him. But, by his exterior action, he disregards the ownership of the victim of the theft.

Now let us put the same material element into a case of

a morally good deed. Suppose, for instance, that there is no other means to save a needy man from death by starvation except by giving him things that are taken from another. In this case there is no contradiction between means and end since, under these circumstances, the right to ownership must give way to the right of use. Therefore, this case is not a case of theft.[74] To give an act the character of moral goodness, it is therefore not enough that the end of the subject is morally good: the act is good only when the exterior action (material element, means) is proportioned to the end (formal element) *according to reason*, when there is no contradiction of the means and the end in the whole of the act on the level of reason (*secundum rei veritatem*). Only then is the undivided and composite action morally good, because the means share in the moral goodness of the end within the totality of the act. In other words, by virtue of the *debita proportio* the formal element of the act, the end, communicates its moral goodness to the material element of the act, viz., the exterior action or the means: *secundum habitudinem ad finem, causam bonitatis*.

It is clear that Thomas does not fall into subjectivism because he always uses the subject or the end of the inner act of the will as his starting point. It is always his view that both constituent parts of the act, end and means or material and formal element, must be judged morally in the light of the objective measure of morality. The intention must aim at an end which is morally good according to reason: *ipse appetitus* **finis debiti** *praesupponit rectam apprehensionem finis, quae est per rationem*.[75] The exterior action too (material element, means) must also be *materia debito modo disposita* to be open to the form of the good end. In other words, the means can only share in the moral goodness of the end if it is correctly proportioned (*debita proportio*) to that end according to our understanding of objective truth and if there is no contradiction between end and means.

We said that the moral virtues direct us toward morally good *ends*. *Prudentia* holds a special place among them. The means (*ea quae sunt ad finem*) are its object. Its function is to safeguard the *debita proportio* of the means to morally good ends.[76]

Let us go more into detail about Thomas' view of *debita proportio* by examining a concrete illustration of his special ethics.[77] We choose this example because it refers to an action whose means obviously imply an ontic evil. This will put us on the way to the main point of our problem: Thomas asks: "Is it permissible to kill someone in self-defense?"

First, he establishes the fact that one and the same act can have two effects, of which one has been intended (*in intentione*) as the intended end (*id quod intenditur*) and the other has not been intended as end (*praeter intentionem*).

Then he mentions the principle which governs the moral qualification of the activity: the acts share in the moral species (their being good or bad) of the intended end, while that which has no bearing on the intention of the end (*praeter intentionem*) only happens **per accidens** and therefore has no moral meaning. Thomas already explained this tersely at the beginning of his treatise **De fine ultimo**[78] and also in his examination of scandal,[79] where he always takes the fundamental principle "**Finis enim dat speciem in moralibus**" as *his starting point*. Thomas now applies this principle when he examines an act of self-defense.

This act can have two effects: self-conservation and the death of the assailant. When the end of the act of my will is only the safeguarding of my own life (*id quod intenditur*), my act is morally right on that level. St. Thomas says that this end is morally good because it is consistent with an urge of human nature: It is natural for each being to protect its existence as much as possible. "*Actus ergo hujusmodi* ex hoc *quod* intenditur *conservatio propriae vitae non habet rationem illiciti, cum hoc sit cuilibet naturale quod se conservet in esse quantum potest.*"[80]

But it is not sufficient that an end of an acting subject is morally justifiable. One is not free to do what he pleases to effect a good end. This would be subjectivism. In order to prevent subjectivism, Thomas introduces the matter of the exigencies of the *debita proportio*. The exterior action—material element or means—must be correctly proportioned to the end within the totality of the act: "*Potest tamen aliquis actus* ex bona intentione *proveniens illicitus reddi* si non sit proportionatus fini."[81]

What does Thomas think this *debita proportio* is in the case of self-defense?

In the case of self-defense violence (means) is used against the assailant. This use of violence naturally causes ontic evil: it is harmful and hurtful to the assailant to the extent that it scares him, wounds him or perhaps even kills him. That is why it must be restrained as much as possible. In other words the use of violence must be kept within the limits of the measures which are the *means* to the conservation of one's own life (*end*). Or, in Thomas' words: it is right to use violence to protect one's self against violence if the defensive violence stays within the limits indicated by the right to safeguard one's own life (*vim vi repellere licet cum moderamine inculpatae tutelae*),[82] for the end of the agent is the reason and the cause of the exterior action which is the means to the end. If it should be necessary to use a kind of violence which causes the death of the assailant, this defensive violence is justifiable as a necessary means. It is still an ontic evil but it is morally justifiable.

When excessive violence is used (*si aliquis ad defendendam propriam vitam utatur majori violentia quam oporteat*),[83] the excess exceeeds the bounds prescribed by the end of self-defense. The excess is not a means anymore. The end does not sanction it as a reason or a cause. Consequently, the excessive use of violence is not disconnected from *praeter intentionem*, but it is implied in the intention as something which is willed for its own sake. When an assailant can be kept under control by meanacing him with a weapon, killing him is not morally justifiable.

The only goal of self-defense must be the safeguarding of one's own life. Thomas distinguishes very clearly between the case in which the death of the assailant has actually been intended as the end (*quis intendit occidere hominem ut seipsum a morte liberet*)[84] and the case in which the death has not been actually intended although the assailant has been effectively killed. In this case the death of the assailant stays within the confines of the use of violence as a *means* to the safeguarding of one's own life, which is the *exclusive end* of the act of self-defense (*quamvis non intendat interficere, sed seipsum defendere*).[85] Thomas says that this is a case of killing an assailant **per accidens** and **praeter intentionem**. What does he mean by that? He makes it clear in another context where he is dealing with the moral problem of scandal.

Scandal (*scandalum activum*) comes about by improper acts or words which can give the impression to others that they are sinful. There are two types of active scandal. In the first case, there is the intention to lead someone into sin by improper acts or words,[86] when he is seduced into sin by inciting, encouraging or showing him how to sin.[87] In the second case, one performs an action (for instance, he commits a public sin) that by its very nature leads others into temptation.[88] Is his sin also a special sin of scandal (*speciale peccatum*)? Scandal can be given **per accidens**, viz., when the agent does not intend it (**praeter intentionem agentis**), e.g., when someone freely resolves to sin by word or deed but does not want (*non intendit*) to be an occasion of sin to someone else. In this case giving scandal is not a special sin because that which happens *per accidens* does not make it a special sin (*quia quod est per accidens, non constituit speciem*). But scandal is scandal **per se** when the purpose of the bad words or bad deeds is to turn someone else into a sinner. This particular purpose brings about a special sin (*ex intentione specialis finis sortitur rationem specialis peccati*). It is always for the same reason: *finis enim dat speciem in moralibus*.[89] Consequently, any sin could be the material element of the special sin of scandal, but this special sin has the special malice of scandal only by virtue of the *formal element*, when the subject has seduction in mind as an end (*ex intentione finis*).[90]

Now we understand why it is the thesis of Thomas that in the act of self-defense the death of the assailant must be something that comes about **per accidens** and **praeter intentionem**. When one specifically *intends* to kill the assailant, self-conservation loses its status of sole intention. Another specifically intended goal then enters the act (*ex intentione specialis finis*) and thus the action **per se** gets *the meaning of murder* because **finis dat speciem in moralibus**. If, on the other hand, the safety of one's own life is the sole end (*id quod intenditur*) of the agent, the sense of the action is self-defense and nothing but self-defense. If it happens that the assailant gets killed as a result of a violent act of self-defense, his death happens only **praeter intentionem** and **per accidens**. Consequently, the end of one's inner act of the will should never be the death of another person because this would make his act **per se** an act of murder.

Now Thomas raises an objection. It does not seem necessary that somebody whose life is threatened does everything possible to spare the life of his assailant because we must love our own life more than the life of others. Why should not the death of the assailant be the purpose and the end of the act of self-defense (*id quod intenditur*)? In his answer Thomas takes up another principle: only the public authorities or their delegates have the right to intend the death of someone (*intendens hominem occidere*) for the safeguarding of the common good (*refert hoc ad publicum bonum*). In this case the killing is an intermediate end (*finis medius*) which serves a higher goal, viz., the safeguarding of the common good (*finis principalis*).[91] This act does not negate the right to life. What matters here above all is the protection of the right to life and to security of those who respect and serve the common good, since this right and this security are essential elements of the common good, which must be defended against those who endanger it even when it means killing them. The *debita proportio* is unquestionable.

But even in this case the act becomes immoral, says Thomas, if he who is responsible for the common good acts with a bad intention e.g., to take revenge (*privata libidine*).[92] **Finis enim dat speciem in moralibus!**

This example evidently concerns exterior actions in which ontic evil is involved. Thomas formulates some rules of the evaluation of their morality. 1. What has been generally said about human acts is also true here. If the exterior action (material element) is a means to a bad end, the act is bad. The bad end of the subject is the formal element that vitiates the act. 2. To bring about ontic evil can be justifiable if the act which brings it about remains within the bounds of the measure of *means* to the good end. I have the right to use violence within an act of self-defense to keep myself alive: and if need be, killing my assailant does not exceed the bounds of that which I must use as *means* to my end. 3. According to Thomas, it is permissible to will in itself an act which causes ontic evil, provided that certain conditions are present and if this act itself serves a higher end, e.g., the right of the public authorities to kill someone who by grievous offenses endangers the common good. These points show, in any case, that there is a *difference* between ontic evil and moral evil, while there is also a connection between them. This leads us finally to the heart of our problem.

II
ONTIC EVIL IN OUR ACTS

Of old, a distinction between *malum physicum* and *malum morale* was made. Nowadays, we prefer the term "ontic evil" to the term "physical evil," because the contemporary meaning of "physical" corresponds more to the meaning of "material." It is true, of course, that there is evil in the material world. We say that an earthquake which destroys human lives and entire regions is an evil. A devastating flood is evil: generally speaking, all natural disasters are evil. There are evils which disrupt the corporal life of man, e.g., death (which radically defeats our will to live), pain, sickness. It is true that pain is like a signal which is good because it warns us that something is wrong with our health. But it is also true that it is a signal which is sent forth by something that displeases us and that in itself is ontic evil. Wear and tear of the body, fatigue, etc., are evils. There is spiritual and mental evil. Every human being suffers the handicaps and the shortcomings of his own individual psyche—not to mention psychoses and neuroses—which make life difficult for him. And are we not always crippled by our ignorance, which makes us aware of a frustration of our urge to know? Because we are human beings we want to govern our actions: only *human* acts that emanate from the will suit us. But from the beginning of his *De Actibus Humanis*, Thomas encounters the problem of invincible ignorance and error, which can keep our acts from being human acts in the real sense.[93] We call ontic evil any lack of a perfection at which we aim, any lack of fulfillment which frustrates our natural urges and makes us suffer. It is essentially the natural consequence of our limitation. Our limitation itself is not an evil—to be created to be limited—but, because we are thinking, willing, feeling and acting beings, we can be painfully hampered by the limits of our possibilities in a plurality of realities that are both aids and handicaps (ambiguity).

How does this situation concern our actions? By action, we do not mean here the inner act of the will, but the concrete act made up of the material and the formal element (means and end). We feel that we may take the position on this level that each concrete act implicates ontic evil because we are *temporal* and *spatial*, live together *with others* in the same *material world*, are involved and act in a *common sinful* situation.

Our Temporality

Our actions follow each other in the course of the different moments of time. It is true that we can do some things by force of habit while we deliberately keep ourselves busy with another thing. But from the moment our actions demand our full attention and endeavor, we can do them only successively, i.e., where ambiguity enters our freedom of choice (*liberum arbitrium*). Our ability to resolve which action we want to effect at a certain moment is an expression of our autonomy, of our self-determination. Henri Bergson very correctly stated that our freedom is "*la détermination du moi par le moi*." In this sense the fact that we have the *ability* to decide and to determine what we do, is the positive aspect of our freedom. But there is also a negative side. When we choose a certain action, we must at the same time, at least for the time being, postpone all other possible acts. This is the meaning of Bergson's words: "*Tout choix est un sacrifice*"; or as the traditional terminology puts it, each **commissio** (act) includes an **omissio**. Usually this does not strike us as bad because we can postpone until another time what we cannot do now: all is not lost that is delayed. But the situation can be one which makes us painfully aware of our temporary limitation. The fact of an unavoidable *omissio* may even become a moral problem. The matter of the moral problems involved in the question of the *omissio* and the conflict of duties and values came up often in our textbooks.

However, the point of the question is not the conflict of the duties or the values—all duties and values by their own definition have some connection with the fulfillment of the human person and consequently, are not conflicting. The conflict is directly related to our temporality. A husband, for example, can be very busy with his professional duties; he must also spend enough time in the company of his wife; as a father he must be interested in the education of his children; as a religious man he feels the need to spend time reading and meditating on religious topics; he has also to keep up his social life and he has a need of friendship, recreation, etc. All these realities are very valuable. But to do all this he needs time, more time than he has. He has the feeling he is lacking something when he becomes aware of his inability to realize all these different values as much as he pleases. So there is ontic evil. This ontic evil is *distinct* from moral evil—we speak here about limits and restrictions which force themselves upon man. But at the same time there is a *connection* between moral and ontic evil: it occurs every day that people who are busy in several ways experience the problem of the conflict of duty and of *omissio* to the degree of the sensitivity of their own conscience. This problem comes from the temporality of our existence and our activity.

Our Spatiality

By this way we mean that our *corporal being* and the reality of the *world* in which our activity is embedded are material and subject to physical laws that escape our freedom. Here, too, we are facing a fundamental ambiguity.

Our corporal being has a share in our subjectivity; it forms part of the subject we are. It enables us to communiciate by way of social relations. It gives us the capacity for acting as a subject on the things of this world. But at the same time our body remains a part of the world, and because it is material, it is necessarily subject to the laws which govern matter. Our power to act on things is limited and graded by our corporeal capacities (which can always become more refined, stronger and wider with the help of technical aids). Our actions are unavoidably limited by the fact that we are subject to tiredness, need to sleep, sickness, physiological wear and tear etc. Our body is a means to action. But it is also a handicap which impedes our action. This hindrance may hurt us as an ontic evil.

But the ambiguity is not only present in our own corporal being; it becomes more intense when our activity deals with the *material* things of this world. These things are governed by laws which we have not created and which we cannot change by our free will. But the very fact that these things have their own nature and are governed by fixed laws makes them aids and means to our fulfillment. We can count on them: e.g., if by their own nature bricks did not retain their solidity, our free will could not use them as proper construction materials. Because we can count on things and because their laws are fixed, we can change with our work the world of nature into a cultural environment (objective culture) wherein we can live and continually improve the standards which correspond to the dignity of man's existence (subjective culture). This presupposes that we first become familiar with the things and their laws. Referring to Hegel, Marx wrote that necessity is only blind as long as it remains unknown. For instance, as long as man was ignorant of the laws of electricity, he could only fear it as the blind and destructive force of thunderstorms. Because scientific knowledge helped him formulate the necessary laws of electricity, man can use electricity as a source of light, power and heat. Generally speaking, we can say that the more we learn about the material reality, the better we can harness it as an aid to action.

But this knowledge remains limited. The material world, moreover, is pluriform and is subject to many and very diverse laws. We can make an efficient use of some of them as a means to certain ends of our existence because we have tapped their power in a scientific and technological way. But other forces and processes handicap our actions. To a certain extent things act with degrees of hindrance and usefulness for man and place him in a situation of ambiguity.

As temporality involves man in the problem of the *omissio* and the conflict of duties or values, so our spatiality involves him in the problem of acts with several effects. Scientific and technological progress have meant for man an enormous increase in the output of goods which has accompanied the rise of "Big Technology," yet we cannot manage this big-scale industry enough to prevent the pollution of the environment which threatens to engulf us. We have succeeded in organizing very high-scale traffic by air, land and sea which binds up the world in a web of communication routes at a rate of speed the world has never known, but the detrimental side-effects are the enormous number of traffic accidents and the psychological stress and strain caused by the noise level and the hectic pace of life.

We control our material reality only imperfectly and partially. Detrimental consequences flow from the use of things in the constant accompaniments of every day, e.g., a walk gives me rest and fresh air but it also wears out my shoes.

We do not usually pay attention to the ambiguity of our daily actions caused by our spatiality. But once ontic evil increases considerably we start seeing very clearly that the problem of activities with many effects becomes a very important moral question. Who would still dare to deny that the problems of the pollution of the environment and the soaring statistics of traffic mishaps involve no need for moral thinking? It would be very hard to lose sight of the moral problems that crop up constantly in the field of medicine. They become more and more complicated since medicine introduces more and more *things of the material world* to work on the processes of our physical life, after having made them into products of science and technology; thus, the ambiguity of both our physical being and the material things manifests itself. The technological means (material things) used in the field of surgery serve the health and life of man, but a loss of integrity of the body may be the consequence of their incursion into the processes of life. More and more effective medicines are continuously available to man, but are there any medicines which are not detrimental at the same time?

Our Togetherness

Our human existence is also *being with*, *by and for each other*; our life is togetherness. Ambiguity also runs through this dimension of man's life. Our being is open to the totality of the reality. Within this intentionality our openness to each other or our social being evidently plays an important role. Child psychology has sufficiently proven that only through the achievement of openness to others and integration into a human "togetherness" can the child become a human, responsible and self-asserting subject—

only *with* and *by* those who are already human will man become human. Having become a responsible and self-asserting subject, man can by virtue of his essential openness unfold and achieve himself only by engaging himself in and for others in the forms of social relations which suit man. Our self-fulfillment can only be realized in our being *for* each other.

This sounds quite positive. Neverthless, there is a fundamental ambiguity in our social life. Consider this example. Probably the most important aspect of the social dimension of life is that we must be able to share the cultural achievements, fruits of the collaboration. When we share the same *spiritual* values, we are not disturbing one another. On the contrary, an educated person does not become less educated when he transfers his knowledge to his students. When many share the same spiritual value, one's share is not made smaller by the sharing with others. What is said about the unifying power of spiritual values is so true. Think of the spiritual affinity and the ties of people who are interested in the same branch of science, share the same religious conviction, have a common love and appreciation of esthetic values. This too sounds very positive. But we find also a relationship to material things in social life. Social ties, too, grow out of a common sharing of interest in the material environment. If we did not have this sharing of interest, living-together would not become a working-together which produces these material goods. But, community life also means that all of us take something of the products of the corporate enterprise. Whatever is consumed or used by one member of the community is not available to another at the same time. In other words, although we profit from living for, by, and with others there remains a seamy side to the way society is related to the allocation of the resources made available to man. As to the need of regulating the use and the consumption of goods according to moral laws which guarantee the dignity of man, there is no doubt. The moral controls put on this aspect of social life will vary according to the nature of the use of these goods and of the goods themselves. For example, we use only a section of the highways for a certain time. Others use other sections before, after and near us. But when the traffic becomes very heavy because of the many dozens of vehicles which use the highway, a system of traffic laws becomes absolutely necessary.

The controls will affect other fields still more. There are things which must always be available to our basic needs. They must be owned by us. Even Marx defended the right to own the useful goods and the consumer goods because it fits the dignity of man (personal property). Thus, without social controls man is constantly in the way of other men in a world where material goods must be shared. Without social controls, this state of confusion would make a decent social life impossible. Ethical controls must be imposed on individual freedom for the sake of the safety and the freedom of all who live in the human community.

Our Sinful Condition

The outstanding fact about these problems is that we cause ontic evil when we act immorally. And so we move to the question of the fundamental source of ontic evil—our sinful condition. There is no need to emphasize the obvious fact that a very great amount of ontic evil is caused or is tolerated by the immoral behavior of individuals or groups, e.g., the inhumanity of man to man, the evils of racial discrimination, the starvation of two thirds of the population of the world, the destruction of life and property during wars, etc. All these forms of evil cannot be whitewashed by the claim that temporality, spatiality, the shortage of economical goods, etc., are sources of ontic evil. It is a sad fact that much ontic evil is the fruit of moral evil. If individuals and groups, in their mutual intercourse, always acted according to their inner inclinations (which Aristotle already said give moral goodness to the acting subject and his deeds), the level of ontic evil present in this world would drop considerably.[94]

III
DISTINCTION AND CONNECTION
BETWEEN ONTIC AND MORAL EVIL

We have tried to show why ontic evil is *always* present in our concrete activity. If this approach is true, it cannot be concluded that it is inevitably morally evil to cause ontic evil or to allow it to remain in this world by our actions. If this were the case, there would not be any way to act morally. We must act. "*Nous sommes embarqués*," said Blondel. Our humanity is imperfect, it is a being-potentiality and at the same time it is a dynamic tendency pressing forward the fulfillment of this potentiality (to expound this we should make a study of our inclinations, but we take it for granted). As *open* reality we can realize our potentialities only as we realize our relationships with things, men, social groups to which we belong and God. The realization of all these relationships, within the measure of morality, of course, presupposes our effective engagement, our activity as an active intercourse with reality. To be man means to tend dynamically toward self-realization. Now self-realization can only be the fruit of our actions. We must act. Consequently, it cannot be said that all activity is essentially tied up with moral evil, although ontic evil is always present in the activity. Ontic evil and moral evil, hence, are not the same.

Yet, there is a connection between ontic evil and moral evil. As we have said, ontic evil is a lack of perfection which impedes the fulfillment of a human subject (this subject could be ourselves or other individuals or a group of individuals). In any case, it is harmful and damaging to human beings. And since morality is chiefly concerned with the human relationships and the well-being of human beings, it cannot remain unconcerned about the ontic evil which in all its forms handicaps and harms the development of individuals and communities. If we accept this view, we must ask ourselves: When and to what extent are we justified in causing or allowing ontic evil?

We have accentuated that, according to Thomas, a human act is morally good when the exterior act (material element, means) has a **debita proportio** within the measure of reason to the morally good end (formal element). It seems to us that a further examination of Thomas' understanding of this **debita proportio** will help us find the answer to that question.

The authors who try to answer the question in the light of the principles of the acts with more effects also appeal to the notion of **debita proportio**. One of the principles they start from is that the directly intended good effect must have a **debita proportio** to the indirectly willed bad effect: the value realized in the direct effect must at least counter-balance the bad, indirect effect. Mangan claims that this principle is a Thomistic one.[95] He refers to Thomas' article on self-defense: "*Illicitum est quod homo intendat occidere hominem ut seipsum defendat.*" Mangan asserts that **intendere** implies both end and means. Both of them are *directly* intended and so they must be morally good. Mangan is right when he maintains that according to Thomas **intendere** applies to the end and the means. But his affirmation will no longer serve when he juxtaposes end and means as though both of them were equally **direct** objects of the intention. According to Thomas, the end is intended *absolute secundum se*, and it is the reason and the cause of the willing of the means. In other words, the end is the formal element and the means or the external action is the material element. Well, as material element the means or the external action has to be a **materia bene disposita** or in due proportion to the end. Consequently, in Thomas' view due proportion is an *intrinsic* requisite in the one but composed action; it is a due proportion between means and end, between the material and the formal element of the action, while the principles of the acts with more effects require a due proportion between the direct and indirect effect.

According to another principle (the most important) of the moral evaluation of acts with several effects, the act must be good in itself or at least indifferent; in other words, the use of bad means to attain a good end is never permissible. This principle supposes that the external action (means) can be morally evaluated in itself without any consideration of the end or the effects. Our analysis of the structure and the morality of a human action has led us to our firm claims that this position is one of the currents of thought contested by Thomas. According to Thomas a moral evaluation is only possible about a concrete action, considered as a whole, composed of end and means. And two questions must be answered. First, is the end of the agent morally good? Secondly, is the external action a material element able to be actuated by the end as formal element or is it a *true* means? On account of its very definition, means involves being-related-to-the-end. Hence, it is not subject to a judgment that considers it as an absolutely unrelated thing. The judgment must judge the **debita proportio** of the means by virtue of which the totality of the act participates in the moral goodness of the end.

We should never overlook the **debita proportio** of the means to the end in a composite action. In order to explain it, we will examine successively different aspects (without distinguishing, it is not possible to describe), but even now we must say that it is necessary to grasp the interrelationship of all those aspects in order to define all the requirements of a *debita proportio*.

1. If ontic evil is **per se** intended, the end itself (object of the inner act of the will) is morally bad and, being the formal element (reason and cause of the exterior action), vitiates the entire action.

We have already stated that any dimension of ontic evil is a lack of perfection, a deficiency which frustrates our inclinations. We label it *evil* when it affects a human subject insofar as it appears to the consciousness as a lack and a want, and to the extent that it is detrimental and harmful to the development of individuals or communities. It follows from this definition that we should never **per se** will ontic evil. In the final instance, the entire set of moral laws and principles exists for the real well-being and the true development of man and society. Therefore, it is obvious that we would fall into immorality if we should strive for ontic evil itself and *for its own sake*, because ontic evil necessarily impedes and precludes the development of man and society. In other words, ontic evil should never be the end of the inner act of the will if by end is meant that which definitively and in the full sense of the word puts an end to the activity of the subject *(finis* as *terminus)*. In this sense, Thomas said that a private individual is never justified, not even in the case of self-defense, in willing the death of a human subject as an end, because this would make his act **per se** an act of murder.[96] However, Thomas says, *under certain conditions*, it can be right to intend an ontic evil as end of the inner act of the will, if that end is not willed as a final end, but only as *finis medius et proximus* to a higher end. Referring to this principle, Thomas teaches that the public authorities who are bound by their office to be responsible for the public good, have the right to *will* the death of a criminal as the immediate end *(finis* *medius*), if it is a necessary means to the higher good of the community (**intendens** *hominem occidere . . .* **refert hoc** *ad publicum bonum*).[97] We can now establish the principle that we never have the right to will ontic evil as the *ultimate end of our intention*, because the formal element of our action, viz., the end, the object of the inner act of the will, would be morally evil, and the malice of the end determines and characterizes the grade of morality of the entire action.[98]

Unless we remember this fundamental principle, it is not likely that we will understand Thomas' explanation of the sin of scandal. When someone sees that I am doing something which is sinful or which looks sinful to him,[99] my action "scandalizes" him (occasion of sin). What he sees me do can cause trouble for him; it can lead him into wanting to do the same thing. This set of circumstances is detrimental to him and is, therefore, an ontic evil. So my action causes ontic evil. But does that make it a special sin of scandal (*speciale peccatum scandali*)? According to Thomas, if we will only the sinful act we commit and if we do not intend to lead others into temptation (*non intendit alteri dare occasionem ruinae, sed solum suae satisfacere voluntati*) we do not commit the sin of scandal. Because the ontic evil which has been effected has not been willed **per se** (as end). It stays outside the end of the inner act of the will (*praeter intentionem agentis*). But when we actually intend to lead others into sin (*intendit alium trahere ad peccatum*), we want the ontic evil *for its own sake* and so the end is immoral. Because the end is immoral (*ex intentione* **specialis** *finis*) we are guilty of the special sin of scandal (*finis enim dat speciem in moralibus*).[100] Each sinful action can be the *material element* of a special sin of scandal, because its ontic evil is its potentiality of scandal. But the moral evil of the special sin of scandal only comes to the fore when the inner act of the will involves the intention to lead others to sin, because this end is the formal element which specifies the totality of the action.[101]

Leaving this example out of our study, we can formulate as a general principle that any action, insofar as it involves *ontic evil*, becomes the material element of an immoral act, if this is ontic evil is *per se* the end of the intention since this makes the end of the acting subject into an immoral end which, as a formal element, contaminates the totality of the action with its malice.

2. When the single and composite act is viewed from the point of view of reason (*secundum rationem*), it must be found without an intrinsic contradiction between *the means* (exterior act as material element) and the morally good *end* of the inner act of the will (formal element).

The first condition for a good act is the goodness of the end of the agent (*debitus finis secundum rationem*). However essential this condition may be, it is not yet sufficient. Thomas taught us that the moral end as formal element only deserves to be labelled as the reason and the cause of the exterior action if this action is a means which, in conformity with reason (*secundum rationem*), has a *debita proportio* to the end, which only in these conditions puts the stamp of its moral goodness on the totality of the act.[102] I mean that no intrinsic contradiction between the means and the end may be found in the total act when the act is placed in the light of reason. Put into terms of the philosophy of values, this means that the means must be consistent with the value of the end. Or, according to a more abstract formulation, the principle which has been affirmed in the end must not be negated by the means.

By stealing something from my fellow man, I cause damage to him, and I do something he dislikes because it causes an ontic evil for him. If I take something away from him to keep it for myself and to enrich myself, my action is an act of immoral theft, because this act involves an intrinsic contradiction between the means and the end: my end is the affirmation of the right to ownership (for me), while the means I use is the negation of the same right to ownership (for the victim of the theft). Now suppose that I take something away from him because I need it to save myself from utter misery. This time there is no intrinsic contradiction. I only signify that the right to use has priority over the right to ownership. Viewed from the angle of morality, this act is not an act of theft. What ground underlies this different moral evaluation? Reason is fundamentally ordered to truth (*appetitus veri*). Given that I am sure that I have evidence of something or that it seems to me that I have it (because I can be mistaken in good faith), I cannot but register this evidence cognitively even when it concerns a truth which displeases me or which interferes with my own profit or pleasure. Reason is disinterested. Thomas calls it a *facultas liberalis*. It submits itself necessarily and gratuitously to the truth which it embraces as evidence or as something which has all the appearances of evidence. It affixes to the truth the strictest connotation of necessity, absoluteness and universality so that it rejects any suggestion of a negation of itself. When it is obvious to me that I, the subject of the whole action, use a means which is the negation of the value (or the principle) I am affirming in my idea of the end, I am forced to be aware of this contradiction. This contradiction is the source of my feelings of guilt: the awareness of the inner disunity of the subject which has turned its free will against its rational understanding when it aimed at an end it could not rationally sanction or when it used a means by which it negated the value it affirmed by the end. My self is a united self, a subject which is undivided, and I preserve this unity only when I apply my will to use the means and to realize the end to my reason. My reason is *necessarily* ordered to the truth. It is like a pivot on which everything hinges. My power to will is *free*. Hence, there is only one way to preserve myself as a united subject: I must order all the aspects of the act of my will to the disinterested understanding of my reason. That is the fundamental axiom of morality.

Knauer pointed out very well that the axiom of the *debita proportio* or of the unwarrantableness of the inner contradiction between means and end is the central norm of each human act;[103] and he applied that fundamental norm to a problem of conjugal morality.[104] According to *Gaudium et spes* the marriage act must be ordered to the conjugal love and to the human transmission of life, viz., to responsible parenthood. This must be the end of marital intercourse; each conjugal act must include a *debita proportio* to this end. Consequently, if the marriage partners engage in sexual intercourse during the fertile period and thereby most likely will conceive new life, the marital act may not be morally justifiable when they foresee that they will not have the means to provide the proper education for the child. The rhythm method, too, can be immoral if it is used to prevent the measure of responsible parenthood. But the use of contraceptives can be morally justified if these means do not obstruct the partners in the expression of conjugal love and if they keep birth control within the limits of responsible parenthood. Marital intercourse can be called neither moral nor immoral when it is the object of a judgment which considers it without due regard for its end. A moral evaluation is only possible if it is a study of the totality of the conjugal act, viz., when one considers whether or not the conjugal act (means) negates the requirements of love and responsible parenthood (end).

The question to which we refer here is known as the problem of the relation of the *debita proportio* and ontic evil. If the presence of ontic evil as such would always endanger the *debita proportio* of our action, it would be impossible to act morally, because it is impossible to prevent ontic evil. The danger lies in the fact that *moral* evil is mentioned too soon. This happens every time a moral judgment of an exterior act does not include a judgment of the end and of the agent. This is taking ontic evil for moral evil. For example, it is said that "to say something which is not true" is "to lie," and the generally accepted meaning of "to lie" suggests moral disapprobation. This judgment is not sufficiently discriminating to be true. It passes over the distinction between **falsiloquium** (ontic evil) and **mendacium**. Each *falsiloquium* is undoubtedly an ontic evil, and it clashes with the ideal of absolute truthfulness (an ideal which from a moral point of view is of the utmost importance as will be shown below). But is each *falsiloquium* (ontic evil) at the same time a *mendacium* (moral evil)? To answer this question, we must consider what reason tells us about the meaning of human speech.

We can deal with language as an objective reality, as a system of phonemes which has its own structure (structuralistic approach). But when a subject utters language, the utterance becomes a very human means of communication: one individual says something about something to *another person*. We are social beings and in our social behavior language plays a fundamental role. The question is then if each *falsiloquium* contradicts the objective meaning of our human relations.

No doubt we would use speech in the most commendable way if we always used it to utter only the truth. If we feel that a person does not care very much for the truth, we lose our faith in him. Faith in others is a necessary condition of good social relations. The rule about "never be untruthful" is valid in most cases: *valet ut in pluribus*. It suggests an ideal, and it certainly means that if it were always permissible to utter *falsiloquia* this would be the end of all faith in our fellow men which is a condition for truly human relations. Reason dictates that we use our speech to *reveal* truth, if truth is the means to the furtherance of truly human social relations and of the faith in others which leads to this kind of relation (end). But the same end will also often dictate that we *keep silent* about certain truths, e.g., the duty of keeping something a secret. If certain secrets, e.g., professional secrets, are not kept under certain circumstances (which are indicated by the standards of a truly human social life), faith in others which is so indispensable to truly social relations is also eliminated. To be silent is the best way to hide a secret. But it may happen that somebody wants us to reveal a secret and that silence may be interpreted as a revelation of the secret. When someone has no right to know our secret, we must defend our right of secrecy by the necessary means, even by a *falsiloquium* if it is the only means and although it includes an ontic evil. We could also speak about our relation to people who at least for the time being could not take a certain truth. . . .

But it is sufficient to mention the example of secrecy to explain our intention. The ontic evil of a *falsiloquium* is not willed here *per se* as the ultimate end of our intention (we regret on the contrary that it is inevitable, because there are people who want to know something they have no right to know or who would not be able to take the truth should they know). Our end is morally good: we want to hide a truth insofar as this is necessary to make good human relations possible. We implicate ontic evil in our speech only insofar as we want to use an effective means. No contradiction exists between means and end. The meaning of the entire act is secrecy and consequently, we intend only to preserve the trustfulness of all who expect that their secrets be kept. This should not be called a lie, because every lie enters the ontic evil of a *falsiloquium* as an end or as a means to an immoral end, or its implication in an action causes this action to absolutely contradict a good end.[105]

It will be said that this opinion does not agree with the view of Thomas, although we take Thomas' idea of the structure and the morality of the activity as our starting point. This is an objection well taken.

But first of all, when Thomas begins his study of the lie, he grounds it immediately and explicitly on his view of the structure and morality of a human act:

A moral act is specified by two elements, viz., the object and the end, because the end is the *object* of the *will* which is the first principle (*primum movens*) of the moral act. But the faculty too which is put into motion by the will has *its own object*. This object is the immediate object of the voluntary act (**proximum objectum**, consequently ordered to the end as **objectum voluntatis**) and is related in the act of the will [in the singular!] to the end as a material element to a formal element (*se habet in actu voluntatis ad finem sicut materiale ad formale*).[106]

How strikingly and succinctly Thomas sums up the fundamental givens of his *De Actibus Humanis* in very few sentences! These givens serve as basis of his definition of the lie. The material element of the lie is "to utter a falsehood" (*falsum enuntiatur*). This is not yet a lie. One can be mistaken in good faith. A mistake is not a lie: *falsum materialiter, sed non formaliter, quia falsitas est praeter intentionem dicentis*.[107] To be a lie, this material element must be embraced by the *formal* element, viz., the end of the inner act of the will, the *intention* to utter something that is not true (*intentio voluntatis inordinatae . . . ut falsum enuntietur*).[108] Then and only then the act clashes formally and directly with the virtue of veracity: "*Sic ergo patet quod mendacium directe et formaliter, opponitur virtuti veritatis.*" This contradiction appears from Thomas' definition of the **virtus veritatis** or veracity:

Potest dici veritas **qua aliquis verum dicit,** *secundum quod per eam aliquis dicitur verax. Et talis veritas sive veracitas necesse est quod sit virtus, quia* **hoc ipsum quod est dicere verum** *est bonus actus, virtus autem est quae bonum facit habentem et opus bonum reddit.*[109]

Thomas' argument is very logical. He argues that telling the truth—the object of the virtue of veracity—is a good act (*dicere verum est bonus actus*). Hence, when one has the *intention* (the object of the inner act of the will, end) of uttering a falsehood (*voluntas falsum enuntiandi*),[110] he commits a sin against the virtue of veracity. Thomas calls this sin a lie.

However, Thomas adds restrictive clauses to his definitions. Talking about veracity, he admits that it is not good to utter any truth anytime: it is bad, he says, to talk without reason about one's own virtues, even if they are real (*etiam de vero*) or to talk about one's sins if nobody profits by this conversation.[111] Moreover, one of the reasons why Thomas advocates veracity is that "people must be sure that they can trust each other." Now it is obvious that trustworthiness can be preserved by keeping secrets or by revealing the truth.[112] Evidently Thomas encounters the same difficulties when he reflects about his definition of the lie. He understands very well that just keeping silence is not always a good means to hide a truth if the revelation of the truth has bad consequences or is immoral. We shall not speak about the ways Thomas, just like Augustine, juggles words to absolve certain biblical saints from mendacity.[113] It is not permissible to tell a lie in order to save somebody from a danger, but it is permissible to practice a bit of prudent dissimulation (*aliqua dissimulatione*) or to veil the truth with many figures of speech.[114] One gets the impression of veracity. Or let us consider the question of the secret of the confessional. Thomas says that the confessor even has the right to declare under oath that he does not know anything. Thomas claims this right for the confessor for the following reason: *qua* human being he does not know anything because he knows it only the way God knows it since he represents God. "Et ideo absque laesione conscientiae potest jurare se nescire, quod scit tantum ut Deus."[115] It is a pity that Thomas does not speak anywhere about professional secrets. Would he perhaps have said that those who must keep professional secrets have the moral right to declare that they do not know anything because they *qua* private individuals, do not know anything and because they *qua* professionals, must defend the professional secret in the name of the rights of society?

Let us accentuate that these arguments of Thomas are brilliantly consistent with his views on the structure and the morality of the human act. But we dare think that he has not sufficiently analyzed the meaning of speech and consequently loses sight of the "speech behavior of man in society." In every form of speech something is said about something (*enuntiatio, locutio*) by somebody to somebody (*communicatio*).Thomas knows this. He writes that on Pentecost Day the Apostles received the grace of the Holy Spirit to pass it on to others. This is signified very well by the figure of the fiery tongues, he says, because *the tongue is instrumental in the communication with others by way of speech (lingua per locutionem est communicativa ad alterum).*[116] Now, in his definition of the lie, Thomas mentions only the *locutio*, the fact that something is said about something—so the material element of the lie is the utterance of a falsehood (*falsum enuntiare*) and the formal element is the intention to utter a falsehood (*voluntas falsum enuntiandi*). Evidently, Thomas is right when he says that a sin of lying is committed when the *end*, the object of the inner act of the will, is to speak a falsehood. To will *per se* an ontic evil as the end of the intention is sinful. But the question is whether the utterance of a falsehood—ontic evil—in a *voluntary* falsehood is always willed necessarily as *end*. If speech is viewed only as *enuntiatio*, the way Thomas views it in his definition of the lie, it must follow that "to say something about something" is the formal element of a *human* act. But this leads to a view which is at variance with reality. Is it not a fact that in many *voluntary falsiloquia* the *end* of the object is certainly not to say something which is false *only* because it is false (*intentio voluntatis inordinatae . . . ut falsum enuntietur*). In other words, in these cases there is a **voluntas falsum enuntiandi** but this *voluntas* cannot be identified as **intentio** *finis*, the way Thomas does. Thomas' distinction between a material and a formal element of the lie is excellent. The weakness of his view is in the fact that he applies this distinction to an incomplete analysis of human speech. In his definition of the lie he considers only the *enuntiatio*, "to say something about something," and it slips his mind that he mentions elsewhere that speech is a social phenomenon—*somebody* talks to *somebody* about something (*lingua per locutionem est communicativa ad alterum*). This is the totality of the phenomenon in which we must look for the formal and the material element. Thomas applies this distinction only to a partial aspect of the phenomenon we call human speech. Therein seems to be his weakness.

Obviously, language is a social phenomenon—it reveals our

social being and it is at the same time a fundamental instrument of the realization of a truly human community. Think, for example, about the ways speech is indispensable to the common endeavors to realize a human culture and to give to all the opportunity to share in the cultural resources. This is actually the *end* we should aim towards as speaking subjects: the realization and the promotion of a truly human community life (social relations). It is evident that, in order to achieve this end, we need the *locutio*, the utterance about something, as a means (material element) to turn this end into reality (*finis* as *terminus*). But what must we say? It is obvious that generally speaking our speech must truthfully *reveal* a reality. If it were not this, it could not be a *positive* contribution to truly human relationships, could it? But it will also happen that speech will *conceal* a truth, also for the good of social relations. This is its *negative* function, viz., to safeguard the conditions of a truly human community life against those who do not stay within the bounds of their rights (e.g., by attempting to know a secret they have no right to know) or in relationships with those who cannot yet take a truth. If keeping silent is not sufficient, a *falsiloquium* may be the only *effective* means to the end. The implication of an inevitable ontic evil in this act does not keep this act from having the sense of a rightful secrecy which benefits truly human relations.

We can establish as a principle that it is impossible to pronounce a moral judgment on an exterior action which contains ontic evil—e.g., to kill somebody, to utter a falsehood—if this action is viewed only as a factual and actual event (*secundum speciem naturae*) and without paying attention to the end of the inner act of the will. We can further establish that, in order to be able to make a moral evaluation, we must consider: 1) if the end of the agent, the object of the inner act of the will, is morally good; 2) if the exterior action has a *debita proportio* to this end or if, on the contrary, it contains the negation of the value or the principle which is affirmed in the end.

From all of this, it follows that it would not be morally justifiable to keep all forms of ontic evil out of our actions in such a way that we would make it impossible to realize morally good ends. This would be presumptuous; it would be a failure to see our human condition as it really is. It would be an illusion which paralyzes our moral life. Traffic accidents, for example, evidence a considerable amount of ontic evil—material damage, the mutilation of thousands of people, the death of many. This sad situation imposes very serious duties on public authorities—the construction of good highways, the enforcement of coercive measures against those who break traffic laws, adequate traffic laws, driver education, etc. But if the authorities should want to prevent this ontic evil, they would have to prohibit the use of the entire road system, and by doing this, they would paralyze economic and social life. The sad fact of traffic accidents also imposes serious moral obligations on those who use the road system—obedience of traffic laws, the practice of caution and courtesy. But if they too should be of the opinion that this ontic evil should be completely eradicated, they would have to give up all use of the road system, and in doing this, they would have to stop practicing essential rights and duties that are inherent in life. Another illustration: It is beautiful that people are giving all they have to the tasks of their chosen vocation or profession. But it happens often that very committed people are annoyed by the fact that they must set aside time to sleep, to rest, to relax, etc. But if they do not set aside time for leisure, they will become ill, weak, and too tense. In other words, they will lose their inner balance and their mental zest. And they will cause many other ontic evils which keep them in the long or the short run from accomplishing their work at all.

We can conclude that we must accept the inevitable fact that we will run into ontic evil when we act. We cannot do away with ontic evil without depriving our actions of their effectiveness and without sooner or later endangering the realization of our morally good ends. Within these restrictions, the implication of ontic evil in our actions does not mean that no attention should be given to the *debita proportio* of the means to the end.

3. We have the moral obligation to reduce as much as possible the ontic evil which comes about when we act.

This thesis is implied in the fact that ontic evil should never be the ultimate goal of our intention (point 1) and that we must preserve the proper proportion of the means to the end (point 2). We have already said that ontic evil always enters our consciousness as an impediment and a frustration of the ends of man and society. Since the very object of morality is to promote the truly human growth of the individual and the social communities, it is bad to will ontic evil which obstructs this growth. And this happens from the moment we bring about or tolerate more ontic evil than is necessary to make our actions into effective actions. If our actions contain more ontic evil than they must have to be the proper means, they are not ordered properly to the goals of man and society. Consequently, they are immoral.

At face value, this thesis sounds quite negative. But it has a very positive sense, and it is pregnant with stirring contents. Indeed, it throws light on the dynamic character and the need for the historical evolution of morality. The progress of science and technology makes it more and more possible to lower the level of the nocivity (ontic evil) of things and increasingly raises the level of their usefulness. To the extent that we have more cultural resources at our disposal, we can reduce more forms of ontic evil and actualize the positive chances for a truly human development of each individul and of humanity. If it is immoral to let ontic evil exist when it is possible to cause it to diminish, it is our pressing duty to actualize those possibilities for the well-being of each and every individual. That which can be used to further the development of individuals and society thereby becomes a moral dictate. Consequently, morality is dynamic. What Ricoeur calls *"le souhaitable humain"* becomes the object of a moral obligation from the moment it becomes possible to realize it.

At the moment it becomes economically possible to bring about a steady and very substantial output of products and a more equitable distribution of the consumer goods which would give to each and everyone the opportunity to live at a truly human level of prosperity, this possibility becomes a source of moral obligation; further, it is immoral to tolerate the ontic evil of hunger and misery. To the extent that medicine discovers increasing possibilities to prevent or to cure the ontic evil of sickness, it becomes a moral obligation to organize a system of social medicine which is motivated by *"le souci de mettre à la portée de tous les ressources d'une médecine de qualité."*[117] When it becomes possible in a country or all over the world to lessen the ontic evil of the lack of education, it becomes a moral obligation to provide the means of education to each and everyone. . . .

We could say more about these topics, but these examples will suffice to explain that wherever ontic evil can be lessoned it must be lessened. This obligation reveals the dynamic character of morality. There are two reasons for this obligation. The first one follows from the definition of morality: moral activity fundamentally concerns the truly human development of man and society and the struggle against ontic evil which impedes this development. The second reason follows from the meaning of our activity in the world: by our activity we must turn the world of nature into a world of culture. In other words, our activity is ordered to the realization of the objective culture for the promotion of the subjective culture of each and everyone. In this respect, ontic evil is anything which impedes the progress of objective culture and the increase of the share of each and everyone in the resources of objective culture. If we do not care to eliminate ontic evil to the best of our ability, we neglect our duty to ensure a truly human life in a truly human world for each and every human being.

4. In the actualization of a good end and the deliberation about the means to this end, the genuinely important question is what place this end has in the totality of human existence.

We have said that Thomas defines the ends of our actions as the proper object of the inner act of our will. Something becomes an end insofar as the subject aims at it. It should not amaze us, therefore, that Thomas carefully avoids the use of the expression "*finis operis*" in his *De Actibus Humanis*. To him, the exterior action is a means insofar as it is ordered by its object to the realization of the end of the subject. To act, consequently, means that a *subject* actualizes his intentions in and by an active contact with reality. If we begin this way from the acting and willing subject, it is possible to look at our actions as something more than a succession of isolated, diversified and scattered acts. As moral subject man can understand that he, as a dynamic being, must actuate, in a way which *in truth* fits his being-a-person, his spiritual consciousness and his openness to the totality of reality (things, fellow men, communities, God). Thus, his existence becomes a meaningful event, a history of acts that are unified and integrated into this event by his *ends*. Thomas has this destiny in mind, when he places the subject at the center of the activity and when he concerns himself with the hierarchy and the reciprocal connection of the ends which the subject endeavors to realize in and by his acts. For this reason he starts his study of morality with a treatise on the total and ultimate end to which man must order all his acts. And for the same reason he examines—always in the light of this total end—how in daily life, on account of the hierarchy and interrelationship of ends (*finis proximus, medius, remotus,* etc.), human acts, in spite of their diversity and frequency, are not necessarily isolated and contradictory, but can and must be integrated into the meaningful totality of a human and decent life by way of their good ends.

This integration demands not only that the particular ends we aim at in our concrete acts be morally good, but also that we take their relativity into consideration. It demands that we aim at them in such a way that we do not lose sight of the place and the rank they have in the whole of a meaningful human existence. In other words, it demands that we do not lose sight of the intensity (the urgent character) and the hierarchy of values in our behavior. "Personal and social growth would be endangered if the true scale of values were lost."[118]

The full significance of this moral axiom can be best shown by a look at the problem which is nowadays called "world politics." We have already said that "*le souhaitable humain*" or the "desirable level of humanity" should be provided to each and every human being from the moment and to the extent that this becomes possible. *Populorum Progressio* gives us a clear perception of the stepping stones to the ideal (or utopia) which is called "increased level of humanity." They are:

> to move up from the level of misery to the level of the ownership of the basic necessities of life, to end the social wrongs, to raise the level of education, to engage in the pursuit of culture. They are also a growing appreciation of the dignity of the fellow man, an attitude of the spirit of poverty, the united efforts toward the common good, the will and the yearning to create peace. Even more significant is man's appreciation of the highest values and of God who is the source and the ultimate end of the highest aspirations of man. Of the highest significance are: faith, a gift of God to which man's good will responds and the unity in the love of Christ who calls all of us to be His children and to share in the life of the living God, the Father of mankind.[119]

Is this many-sided growth an object of real concern to us? For many years already the affluent countries have advocated economic expansion — a higher level of production of consumer goods which would lead to more job opportunities and to a higher consumption potential. But more and more this intent to expand the economy has become the butt of criticism. The question has been asked whether there is not a kind of idolatry of the improvement of economic conditions. It seems that many are only concerned with material wealth, riches, comfort, prestige and power based on the notion that what one *has* rather than what man *is* is the measure of his greatness. Is this not materialism? Is it not the tyranny of a one-dimensional life?

More and more, voices clamor for a mentality which is not shot through with a yearning which is slanted too much toward *prosperity*. They call for a quest for the true *well-being* of individuals and communities. Mansholt is advocating a thorough change and broadening of objectives. He is strongly in favor of a strong lowering of the *per capita* consumption of economic products, compensated by a considerable rise of interest for other objectives: social provisions, especially for forgotten groups; intellectual and educational provisions for the leisurely unfolding of reason or feeling, etc.[120] Theologians, too, react against the one track mentality of a theology of the activist type which regards man exclusively as a worker who changes the world and makes it fit to live in. Theology turns again its full attention to religious cult, prayer, meditation, contemplation, mysticism, suffering, joy, etc., which are realities that are on the outside of the useful and the profitable, but are of enormous significance in the practice of the faith.[121] At the same time the specialists of the problems of the development of the underdeveloped countries remind us of the old problems of asceticism and mortification of the natural inclinations, not only at the level of the individual life, but on the scale of the affluent countries which should lower the ceiling of consumption in order to have more goods available for projects that are directed to the "improvement of the human condition" in underdeveloped countries.[122]

The problems of the hierarchy of objectives and of the relationship of the objectives to the totality of a meaningful human existence, at the individual and social level, are becoming pressing problems at this time, when the dimension of the future moves more and more to the focal center of attention. The study of the future becomes a science (*futurology*). More and more means to plan the future are at our disposal, so that terms like prognosis, prospective, etc. come more frequently into use. All this has mainly to do with the future of man himself and of the entire range and scope of man's life in society. Undeniably, the sense in which we opt for our priorities and the exact nature of those priorities is of utmost importance. It has become a problem of *debita proportio* on a world-wide scale of the ends we set for ourselves and the means we are ready and willing to order toward these ends.

IV
Conclusion

We have undertaken this study to explain the meaning and the significance of the *concrete material norms* of morality. This category of norms prohibits *ontic evil*. They show us that we should not kill, maim someone, utter falsehoods, harm others (e.g., by taking something which rightfully belongs to someone else, by failing to return something that has been entrusted to us: *deposita sunt reddenda*, etc.), fail to act to eliminate ignorance, sickness, hunger, etc. They are reducible to: you shall *neither* bring about (cause by your *actions*) *nor* tolerate (allow to grow by your *omissions*, by failing to act) ontic evil.

It clearly follows from the foregoing that the fundamental basis of these norms is an ideal. We must work toward a society wherein there is less and less need to kill, wherein all are so respectful of rights that there is no need for self-defense and the use of defensive violence, and wherein, at the level of international relations, conflicts can be prevented or, in any event, resolved without wars. In a truly human society there must be solicitude about moral education, so that everybody becomes able to cope with the truth he should hear and be discreet enough to keep from prying into the secrets of others, so that for the sake of the smooth course of truly human relations, ontic evil can be lessened more and more. Briefly, concrete material norms invite us to bring about the ideal relations which lessen more and more effectively all forms of ontic evil which by their definition hamper the development of human beings and communities.

I am of the opinion that it is quite necessary to accentuate these points, since, in this era, we are more and more equipped to "create" the future of man and of society by planning and prospecting. Nowadays the word "utopia" has a positive ring. These days very much is said and written about utopia. There is still a long way to go to a consensus of opinion about it. But in spite of the differences of opinion, it always appears from discussions that a positive and a negative meaning is assigned to the term utopia: the perfect and the absolute conditions of a dream which has not yet found its place in the present era and which is the wish and the hope of mankind to secure a place for a perfect world in the future. The utopian speculation is in the field of the polarity of the present and the future. It originates in a contrast conception: beyond the ills and the defects of the present times which disgust us, we see the opposite image of the truly human and attractive way of life which lies over the boundaries of the things which are now. This insight into a better world originates in the dynamic qualities of our human nature which is essentially tending toward the future. In other words, the utopian speculation is inherent in the history of man; what the past generations have already accomplished and have made into events of history does not satisfy us and cannot satisfy us because we are dynamic beings. This should not lead us into underestimating the positive results of the traditional and past endeavors, as often happens in the name of utopia when there is a criticism of the existing structures that goes too far afield.

The utopia is also an expression of the faith that history has a future; and it is an expression of the idea that we must feel responsible for the ideal of the betterment of the world when we act. The *concrete material norms* of morality hold the ideal of the utopia before us and continually suggest a future which is more suitable for man. These norms are a constant protest against the different forms of ontic evil, and as we have said already, they pronounce us guilty of immorality when we bring about or tolerate more ontic evil than is necessary to realize the moral objectives of our human existence. The negation of anything which hampers the development of man and society appears strongly from their negative terms: *no* killing, *no falsiloquium*, *no* tolerance of ontic evil, etc. Consequently they are the negation of the negation (= all forms and shapes of ontic evil). By way of this negative dialectic they point to the *formal norms* which turn attention to that which ought to be done positively, since they show which moral dispositions must inspire the agent and which moral ends the agent must realize by his contact with reality.

Insofar as they express *the ideal*, the concrete material norms concern the "desirable degree of humanity" (*le souhaitable humain*). Insofar as they are *norms*, they imply only the obligation to realize that which is possible for man. We have already demonstrated that it would not be right to try to do away with all the forms of ontic evil because it would become impossible to actuate moral objectives. We must make allowance for our human limitations. That is why Thomas already said that the concrete material norms (*precepta magis propria*) are not applicable in all cases: *valent ut in pluribus*.[123] He illustrates this with an example that comes from Plato. Generally speaking it will be true that we must return something that has been entrusted to us if the owner claims it (*ut in pluribus verum est*): but when we know that he demands that we return a weapon because he plans to use it to commit murder, the restitution of the weapon would clash with the universal and constantly valid norm of morality; viz., that we must act reasonably (*apud omnes enim etiam hoc rectum est et verum, ut secundum rationem agatur*). Thomas even lists several exceptions to the rule "you shall not kill" which concerns the fundamental value of human life (licit self-defense, death penalty, deaths caused in a justified war). We could add some restrictions of our own to his. The concrete norms are *relative*: they only forbid that we cause or tolerate ontic evil which exceeds the boundaries of the measure of means to the actualization of good ends.

But we have shown that these boundaries are made smaller by cultural progress. More and more ways are at our disposal to lessen the ontic evil in this world and to keep us from bringing about or tolerating ontic evil. This fact casts light on the *historicity* of the concrete material norms. Historicity does not mean a negation of the past. On the contrary, long ago before our time, mankind had already made history and had discovered concrete material norms to preserve the riches of culture. The fundamental concrete norms which guard the essential values—life, human integrity, truthfulness in social relations—will always be valid. But historicity means also that we, dynamic beings with inexhaustible possibilities, never cease to plan and to construct new ways of truly human life. Consequently, in the measure that a possibility becomes an actuality of the desirable level of humanity, concepts of norms must be adjusted to the new state of affairs of humanity. We have already said that all forms of ontic evil hamper the development of men and society and that morality which is at the service of this development, consequently, demands that we should not bring about or tolerate ontic evil which can be kept out of this world. We also said that we should eliminate this ontic evil whenever possible. Morality tries to affirm this moral obligation and mission throughout history by new concrete material forms.

When Karl Marx wrote his *Communist Manifesto* in Brussels in the year 1848, children were put to work in Belgium at the average age of twelve. Only the children of rich families had the opportunity to study. At that time, too, the idea of giving all children a chance to procure a good education was an attractive idea; but it was also an "impossible dream" because the *primum vivere* was the most compelling urgency. Now, at least in the affluent countries, it is possible to postpone making a living until the eighteenth year. Consequently, it has become possible to give to each child a time of youthfulness, and at the same time it has become financially possible to expand the educational system and to differentiate it in such a way that the ontic evil of lack of education can be reduced and that each child has an opportunity to choose an education which suits his talents. This possibility becomes *ipso facto* a moral obligation; that is why morality establishes norms of the democratization of the system of education. We could mention other examples: it is more and more possible to prevent and to cure illnesses, to eliminate hunger and misery, etc. Morality establishes new norms for all those new situations, because it demands that ontic evil be eliminated whenever and wherever possible. This negation of the negation is the core of the utopian speculation and implies the exigencies of the human activity which in a dynamic morality is governed by norms which shine forth from an ideal.

Notes

1. A good analysis of the existence and the orientation of those two currents of thought can be found in F. J. Van den Berge, *De morele kwalifikatie van het menselijk handelen. Klassieke en scholastieke achter-*

gronden van een modern probleem. Doctoral thesis, Faculty of Theology. (Privately printed. Louvain, 1972).

2. See W. van der Marck, "De autonome menselijke samenleving als sakrament van de Godsgemeenschap," in *Tijdschrift voor theologie* IV, (1964). pp. 151-176.

3. J. Ghoos, *"L'acte à double effet: Etude de théologie positive,"* in *ETL* XXVII (1951), pp. 30-53.

4. *Ia IIae, q.* 6. introduction.

5. *Ia IIae, q. 1, art.* 1.

6. *Ia IIae, q.* 1, *art.* 1.

7. *Ia IIae, q.* 1, *art* 1 and *q.* 8, *art.* 1.

8. *Ia IIae, q.* 6, *art.* 4 *ad* 3 and *q. art.* 6 *ad* 3.

9. *Ia IIae, q.* 1, *art* 1.

10. *Ia IIae, q.* 1, *art,* 4 *sed contra* and *in corp.*

11. *Ia IIae, q.* 8, *art.* 2.

12. *Ia IIae, q.* 18, *art.* 6.

13. *In II Sent., dist. 1, q. 2, art. 1.*

14. *Ia IIae, q. 18, art.* 6.

15. *Cfr. b.v. Ia IIae, q.* 1, *art.* 3 *ad* 3; *q.* 12, *art.* 2 and 3; *q.* 13, *art.* 3 *ad* 2; *q.* 14, *art.* 2.

16. *Ia IIae, q. 8, art.* 3.

17. *Ia IIae, q. 12, art. 1 ad 4.*

18. *Ia IIae, q. 8, art.* 2 *in corp* and *ad 1.*

19. *Ia IIae. q. 8, art.* 2.

20. *Ia IIae. q. 8, art. 3; q. 12, art, 1 ad 4.*

21. *Ia IIae. q. 8 art. 3 ad 1.*

22. *Ia IIae, q. 1,* introduction.

23. This has been demonstrated very well by W. van der Marck, *art. cit.* It seems to me that he does not sufficiently stress the significance Thomas attaches to the **voluntas or simplex actus voluntatis,** as order of the inner act of the will to the end by itself and for itself (*absolute et secundum se*) even outside the context of an action. To me, this element seems to be an essential one, because it accentuates even more that Thomas' starting point is the subject, the end of the inner act of the will, and because this point is of great importance in any study which concerns Thomas' doctrine on the virtues and the moral evaluation of an act.

24. *Ia IIae, q. 12, art. 4 ad 3; cfr.* also *q. 12, art. 1 ad 4.*

25. *Ia IIae, q. 1, art.* 3.

26. *Ia IIae, q. 1, art.* 3.

27. *Ia IIae. q. 8, art. 3 ad 2* and *ad 3; q. 12, art.* 4.

28. *Ia IIae, q. 8, art.* 3.

29. *Ia IIae, q. 12, art.* 4.

30. *Ia IIae, q. 17, art.* 4.

31. *Ia IIae. q. 8, art.* 2.

32. *Ia IIae, q. 1, art.* 4.

33. *Ia IIae, q. 1, art. 3 ad 2.*

34. Thomas often compares the way the act is composed of a formal

and a material element (end and means) with the way the agent himself is a composition of soul and body. This goes, of course, with his axiom: *agere sequitur esse*. This analogy has an important function in his description of the structure and the morality of human activity. For this reason we will look at it more closely.

Thomas disputes a *monistic* view of man. Man is not only material. He is more than matter; he is also spiritual. Consequently, there is a certain duality in his single being. Thomas puts this into a philosophical term. He says that the soul is *forma subsistens* (*Ia, q. 76, art. 1 ad 5*). The analogical sense which is applicable to the human act is obvious: the proper object of the inner act of the will is the end, which can be intended in itself and absolutely, even outside the context of an action. The end is the *forma* of the totality of the act in the way of a *forma subsistens* and therefore as the proper object of the will or the *simplex actus voluntatis*.

Although Thomas teaches that there is duality in the human being, he is strongly opposed to a *dualistic* view of man. Man is one single subject, one single being, a unified composite. In order to signify this unity of the unified composite Thomas says in philosophical terms that the soul *qua forma subsistens* is at the same time *forma substantialis* of the oneness of the human being: "The soul communicates its own *esse* in which it subsists to the corporal matter, so that both elements make up one single being in such a way that the *esse* of the unified composite is the *esse* of the soul. This is not the case for the *formae* which are not *subsistentes*" (*ibid.*: see also *Ia, q. 76, art. 5; art. 6 ad 3; art. 7 ad 3*). On account of the communication of its own *esse* to a part of the material world, the soul makes this material part into human corporality of a single human subject. In this way, the body remains a material part of the material world but it participates at the same time in the subjectivity and belongs to the single human subject. As the formal element, the soul gives to the compound whole the *specification* of *humanity*: the *forma* specifies a reality. Again the analogy of the human being and the human act is clear. Thomas repeats again and again that our actions are a unified composite: the formal element is the end of the inner act of the will (*actus interior voluntatis*), the material element is the exterior action (*actus exterior*). And as the soul is the *forma* of the human subject which specifies the human being, so the end is the formal and specifying element of the structure and the morality of the action; the end of the agent or of the inner act of the will makes the exterior action into a means (*Ia IIae, q. 1*, introduction: *ex fine enim oportet accipere rationes eorum quae sunt ad finem*) and at the moral level it determines the *species moris* (the moral goodness or the malice) of the entire action (*IIa IIae, q. 43, art. 3: finis enim dat speciem in moralibus*).

35. *Ia IIae, q. 19, art. 4.*
36. *Ia IIae, q. 19, art. 3 ad 2.*
37. *Ia IIae, q. 6, art. 4 ad 3; q. 8, art. 1; q. 18, art. 4 ad 1.*
38. *Cfr. b.v. Ia IIae, q. 18, art. 5 sed contra; q. 19, art. 1 sed contra; q. 20, art. 3. 2a obiectio and ad 2; q. 21, art. 2 sed contra..*
39. Abaelardus already contributed this thought in *Dial, inter phil.,*

iud. et Christ. (*PL*, t. 178, col. 1652B): "*Quaedam etenim bona aut mala ex seipsis proprie et quasi substantialiter dicunter, utpote virtites vel vitia; quaedam vero per accidens et per aliud, veluti operum nostrorum actiones, cum in se sunt indifferentes, ex intentione tamen ex qua procedunt, bonae dicuntur vel malae. Unde et saepe cum idem a diversis agitur vel ab eodem in diversis temporibus, pro diversitate tamen intentionum, idem opus bonum dicitur atque malum.*" Moral goodness is, in the strict sense of the word, a qualification of the virtues, the good dispositions which make the subject into a good subject and which are the sources of the orderly relation of the inner act of the will and the moral good which is the end that communicates its moral specification to the exterior action. Without any doubt Thomas thinks along these lines.

40. *Ia IIae, q. 18, art. 5 sed contra.*
41. *Ia IIae, q. 19, art. 1 sed contra.*
42. *Ia IIae, q. 17, art. 4.*
43. *Ia IIae, q. 20, art. 3 ad 1.*
44. *Ia IIae, q. 1, art. 3 ad 2.*
45. *Ia IIae, q. 1, art. 3 ad 3.*
46. *Ia IIae, q. 1, art. 3; q. 18, art. 6.*
47. *Ia IIae, q. 43, art. 3.* Cfr. also *Ia, q. 48, art, 1 ad 2*: "*Bonum et malum non sunt differentiae constitutivae nisi in moralibus, quae recipiunt speciem ex fine, qui est obiectum voluntatis a quo moralia dependent; et quia bonum habet rationem finis, ideo bonum et malum sunt differentiae specificae in moralibus.*"
48. *Ia IIae, q. 18, art. 2, 4, 5, 6 and 7; q. 19, art, 7 and 8; q. 20, art. 1, 2, and 3.*
49. *Ia IIae, q. 18, art. 5 and 6.*
50. *Ia IIae, q. 18, art. 6.*
51. *Ia IIae, q. 18, art. 6 ad 2.*
52. *Ia IIae, q. 19, art. 3 ad 2.*
53. *Ia IIae, q. 12, art. 4 ad 3.*
54. Here Thomas uses the terminology of the line of thought he disputes: *id quod de se est bonum.* But this intention is obvious. Almsgiving is usually the *materia* which can be specifically made into a moral action by a good end of the subject (to help the needy). But no moral judgment can be made about the material event as such (*secundum speciem naturae*) and as an element which has been abstracted from the end which is the formal element. The example given here by Thomas, shows that the material event "alms-giving" belongs to a bad action, if a bad end is the reason and the cause of the exterior act (*actus exterior*). According to Thomas' terminology in his commentary on Petrus Lombardus, the *finis operis* of alms-giving is the alleviation of misery. But "*finis operis semper reducitur in finem operantis.*" In other words, a goal, on account of its very definition, is the object of the inner act of the will of the subject. Consequently, it relates to morality only if it is willed by the subject (*ab agente*) as the *ratio operis* (see note 13). The actions "*recipiunt speciem ex fine, qui est objectum voluntatis a quo moralia dependent*" (see note 47).

Alms-giving, consequently, is *per se* good on the condition that the *subject* makes it into the end of his inner act of the will. Only then can the *finis operis* be properly called "end" because *finis* is by definition *objectum* **voluntatis**. This is so in the case of the action Thomas describes here.

55. *Ia IIae, q. 19, art. 7 ad 2.*

56. *Ia IIae, q. 18, art. 6.*

57. *Ia IIae, q. 19, art. 3 ad 2.*

58. *Ia IIae, q. 1, art. 3; q. 4, art. 4; q. 17, art. 4; q. 18, art. 6 in corp.* and *ad 2; q. 19, art. 10; q. 20, art. 1 ad 3.*

59. *Ia IIae, q. 20, art. 1 ad 3.*

60. *Ia IIae, q. 18, art. 6.*

61. *Ia IIae, q. 4, art. 4.*

62. *Ia IIae, q. 1, art. 3 ad 3.*

63. *Ia IIae, q. 18, art. 5.*

64. *Ia IIae, q. 18, art. 5 ad 3.*

65. *Ia IIae, q. 6, art. 2.*

66. *Ia IIae, q. 6, art. 2.*

67. *Ia IIae, q. 8, art. 2.*

68. *Finis als ratio: Ia IIae, q. 8, art. 3; q. 9, art. 3; q. 12, art. 4; q. 13, art. 5; q. 19, art. 10. Finis ut causa: Ia IIae, q. 19, art. 7 ad 1* and *2; q. 20, art. 1 ad 3.*

69. *Ia IIae, q. 1, art. 3.*

70. *Ia IIae, q. 1, art. 3.*

71. *Ia IIae, q. 12, art. 4 sed contra.*

72. *Ia IIae, q. 18, art. 4 in corp.* and *ad 2.*

73. *Ia IIae, q. 21, art. 1. Cfr. q. 18, art. 4 ad 2; q. 19, art. 8.*

74. *Ia IIae, q. 18, art. 7, obiectio and in corp. Cfr. IIa IIae. q. 110, art. 3 ad 4: "Non licet furari ad hoc quod homo eleemosynam faciat, nisi forte in casu necessitatis in quo omnia sunt communia."*

75. *Ia IIae, q. 19, art. 3 ad 2.*

76. *Ia IIae, q. 19, art. 3 ad 2; q. 20, art. 3 ad 2. Cfr. Ia IIae, q. 65, art. 1: "Ad rectam electionem non solum sufficit* **Inclinatio In debitum finem** *quod est* **directe per habitum virtutis morallis,** *sed etiam quod aliquis* **recte eligat ea quae sunt ad finem** *quod fit* **per prudentiam** *quae est consiliativa et indicativa et praeceptiva eorum quae sunt ad finem. Similiter etiam prudentia non potest haberi nisi habeantur virtutes morales, cum* **prudentia** *sit* **recta ratio agibilium** *quae sicut ex principiis procedit* **ex finibus agibilium** *ad quos aliquis recte se habet per* **virtutes morales."***

77. *IIa IIae, q. 64, art. 7.*

78. *Ia IIae, q. 1, art. 3.*

79. *IIa IIae, q. 43, art. 3.*

80. *IIa IIae, q. 64, art. 7 in corp. Cfr. Ia IIae, q. 94, art. 2.*

81. *IIa IIae, q. 64, art. 7 in corp.*

82. *Ibid., in corp.*

83. *Ibid., in corp.*

84. *Ibid., ad 1.*

85. *Ibid., ad 3.*

86. *IIa IIae, q. 43, art. 1 ad 4.*
87. *Ibid., in corp.*
88. *Ibid., ad 4.*
89. *IIa IIae, q. 43, art. 3 in corp.*
90. *Ibid., ad 1:* "*Omne peccatum potest* **materialiter** *se habere ad scandalum activum, sed* **formalem** *rationem specialis peccati potest habere* **ex intentione finis**."
91. *IIa IIae, q. 64, art. 7 in corp.*
92. *Ibid., cfr. Ia IIae, q. 1, art. 3 ad 3.*
93. *Ia IIae, q. 6, art. 8.*
94. We said that mental defects and spiritual deficiencies, such as ignorance and error, can be listed as ontic evil. We can leave them out of the study of the ontic evil of our *human* acts, since acts are not *human* when ignorance, error, mental disturbances, etc. are the *cause* of the behavior. Thomas would say that they keep an act from being *actus voluntarius*—an act which emanates from the will—and a human act. It is possible that certain defects—ignorance, error, etc.—are *voluntarii*, but this brings us back to the question of sin as a source of ontic evil. See *Ia IIae, q. 6, art. 8; q. 19, art. 5 and 6.*
95. J. Mangan, "An Historical Analysis of the Principle of Double Effect," in *Theological Studies* X (1949); pp. 41-61.
96. *IIa IIae, q. 64, art. 7 in corp. and ad 1.*
97. *IIa IIae, q. 64, art. 7 in corp.*
98. See notes 45, 46, 51, 55, 59, 72, 73, 76, 79.
99. *IIa IIae, q. 43, art. 1 ad 1.*
100. *IIa IIae, q. 43, art. 3 in corp.*
101. *Ibid., ad 1.*
102. See note 98.
103. A. Knauer, "La détermination du bien et du mal moral par le principe du double effet," in *NRT* LXXXVII (1965), pp. 356-376.
104. A. Knauer, "Überlegungen zur moraltheologischen Prinzipienlehre der Enzyklika Humanae Vitae." in *Theologie und Philosophie* XLV (1970), pp. 60-74.
105. Is this not always so in the case of a voluntary *falsiloquium*? It is true that each *falsiloquium* always runs counter to the faculty of cognition which by its own nature and consequently necessarily and directly is ordered to the truth. This is precisely the definition of ontic evil: each ontic evil runs counter to the aim of one of our *inclinations*. That is why we experience it as an imperfection. The problem of moral evil concerns *the activity*. The gratuitous cognitive act comes in here as a measure which examines: (1) whether the intended goal is really good, and (2) whether there is really no intrinsic contradiction between the means and the end.
106. *IIa IIae, q. 110, art. 1.*
107. *Ibid., ad 1.*
108. *Ibid., in corp. and ad 1.*
109. *IIa IIae, q. 109, art. 1.*
110. *IIa IIae, q. 110, art. 1 in corp.*

111. *IIa IIae, 1. 109, art. 1 ad 2.*
112. *IIa IIae, q. 109, art. 3 ad 1.*
113. *IIa IIae, q. 110, art. 3 ad 3 and ad 4.*
114. *Ibid., ad 3 and 4.*
115. *In IV Sent., dist. 21. q. 3, art. 1 ad 3.*
116. *IIIa, q. 72, art. 2 ad 1.*

117. Letter from the Vatican to the chairman of the 38th "Semaine Sociale de France," in *Santé et Société: Les découvertes biologiques et la médecine sociale au service de l'homme,* Paris, 1951.

118. Paul VI, *Populorum Progressio*, March 26, 1967, n. 18.

119. *Ibid., n. 21.*

120. M. Mansholt, "Brief van N. Malsatti" (February 9, 1972) in *Sélection hebdomadaire du journal 'Le Monde'* from April 6 to 12, 1972, pp. 6-7.

121. Cf. H. Schaeffer, " 'Politieke theologie' in een tijd van 're-ligieuze renaissance,' " in *Tijdschrift voor Theologie* XII (1972), pp. 226-242.

122. J. Zinbergen, *Een leefbare aarde.* Amsterdam-Brussels, 1970.

123. *Ia IIae, q. 94, art. 4.*

The Absoluteness
of Moral Terms

Joseph Fuchs, S.J.

Christ's mission was not to establish a new moral order, new moral laws. Nor was it His primary intent to teach a moral doctrine corresponding to creation. The significance of His coming was rather to redeem sinful mankind, to transform him interiorly by grace, to make him one who believes and loves. Loving faith must and will bear fruit; it must express and verify itself in morally correct conduct, i.e., by doing what is right, thus giving witness to the truth by "doing the truth"—*testimonium veritati*. Under the dynamic of faith and love, the Christian is concerned not only with living in faith and love, but also with carrying them out by a way of life proper to "man as Christian." Indeed, faith, love, and salvation do not depend upon the rectitude of the norms of living that are basic to one's life practice. Yet faith and love are not genuine, if there is no effort to manifest through one's life practice the "right" mode of life, i.e., corresponding to the reality of human-christian existence. Thus, under the dynamic of faith and love, the problem of the absoluteness of moral norms arises in this present age of "uncertainty" and "revolution." Have we perhaps overstressed the absoluteness of our system of moral norms, and precisely for this reason failed to achieve the "right" life practice as an expression of our faith and love? Or are we perhaps to the point of renouncing the absoluteness of an inherited system of moral norms, and so running the risk of faith and love no longer manifesting themselves in the "right" day-to-day manner?

No small number of convinced Christians are allergic to "absolute" norms; not indeed to the possibility of "right," "objective" and therefore "absolutely" binding judgment in concrete instances, and consequently of moral imperatives, but to "universally binding" and in *this* sense absolute norms of moral action. They make their judgment on experiential grounds, so that what was yesterday an absolute, i.e., presented as always and without exception right, must today yield to other insights. They fear that the so-called absolutes, or universally valid norms characteristic of a static world-view, cannot be absolute for men of a dynamic world-view. They hold that the cultural fact of the discovery of moral norms in the past cannot be taken as a final conclusion, rather, that man must ever address himself anew to this fact, to examine the conclusions reached, to deepen and enlarge and adduce new experiences and evaluations. Their great concern is that abstract and therefore timeless and in *this* sense "absolute" norms do not perhaps take due account of the times; i.e. are not sufficiently realistic and responsive to the concrete mode of reality represented by (redeemed) creation; and that consequently they can obscure rather than illuminate the "objective" and in *this* sense "absolute" task of the present day. That this concern for relevant behavior on the part of the believing and loving Christian and for absolute fidelity to the order of (redeemed) creation in its concrete manifestations is genuinely "Catholic" is unquestionable.

Other convinced Catholics incline toward a view just as typically "Catholic." They fear that with the "dissolution" of so-called absolute ordinances and norms, in the sense of "universally valid" and "timeless" truths, truth itself would be lost. They think that if "absoluteness," understood as "immutability" and "universal validity," yields to the principle of change and historical conditioning, faithfulness to reality, i.e., to (redeemed) creation, will no longer determine concrete action, as the expression of faith and love, but will be replaced by a relativistic subjectivism. They presume that deviation from absoluteness (i.e., timelessness and immutability) might imply also a swerving from absoluteness understood as objectivity oriented to the reality of the (redeemed) created order.

Basically, both tendencies share the same interest: the believing-loving Christian must concern himself with recognizing the *absolutely* valid, or that which always corresponds *objectively* to the concrete human (Christian) reality in a moral matter. For this is the Will of God based on creation and redemption—so that what is objectively right partake somehow in the absoluteness of God. The problem is whether and in what degree the absolute in the sense of the objective as applied to universal or universally valid norms is conceivable or in any sense guaranteed. When we address ourselves to this question, we do so in the conviction that global solutions of the problem are not solutions; nuanced consideration is required. Neither the opinion that love should be the sole moral absolute, nor the conception of natural moral law as an all-embracing set of invariable norms is satisfactory, although there is some truth in both these points of view. It will not escape the informed reader that the problematic thus presented is of importance not only for (Catholic) circles within the Church—particularly in the present climate of "uncertainty"—but also for dialogue with those non-Catholic Christians who are experiencing and dealing with the same problematic on a broad scale, and with all men concerned with genuine morality. For God will judge Christians, Jews and pagans alike according to their works (cf. Rom. 2, 9-11) the righteousness of which they can know fundamentally in their "hearts" (cf. Rom. 2, 15). Accordingly, the following considerations are limited to the shaping of life within the world, i.e., innerworldly, to actions relating man and his world.[1]

I
ABSOLUTE: UNIVERSALLY VALID OR OBJECTIVE?

"Absoluteness" in moral imperatives is directly opposed, obviously, to all arbitrary judgment and to all relativism, and thereby positively affirms the objectivity, grounded in human reality itself. The real problem, we repeat, lies in determining to what degree the absolute, in the sense of the non-arbitrary but objective, is comprehensible and guaranteed in the case of universally valid norms. We are accustomed to having moral ordinances placed before us in the guise of norms purporting to be universally valid: in *Revelation* (Holy Scripture), in the teaching of the *Church*, in the formulated tenets of the *natural moral law, conscience* finds itself confronted with moral imperatives in the form of moral norms. In what follows we shall consider what (degree) of the absolute character of norms is implied in the individual instances respectively.

Norms in Holy Scripture

Moral imperatives in Holy Scripture are of the greatest interest, for God's word has absolute value, since He is The Absolute. And since He speaks, therefore, via human concepts and so in terms of universals, Christianity with good reason has been inclined to understand the moral precepts found in Holy Scripture as "universal," ever valid and unchangeable norms, and in this sense, as "absolute." On the other hand, God's speaking in human mode signifies that the moral imperatives appearing in Holy Scripture should not be interpreted as direct divine "dictates." Thus we are inevitably faced not only with the question as to which moral imperatives are actually to be found in Holy Scripture, but also with the question by which hermeneutic rules they are to be understood and evaluated.[2] There is no doubt that here moral theology will have to go to school to contemporary exegesis, to avoid lapsing into unauthorized good-will reading.

Holy Scripture was never meant to be a handbook on morality: consequently it may not be so used. Inasmuch as it speaks of God's ways with mankind, it must speak also of man's behavior—his religio-moral behavior—toward God. Indeed, since Scripture is concerned with the conversion and salvation of the sinner, and therefore with his personal transformation, statements regarding the religio-moral situation of man are central to the Bible. Nevertheless, it is not the particular moral imperatives which have this central position, but the fundamental imperative of fidelity and obedience to God, of the following of Christ, of life according to faith and baptism or, as with John, according to faith and love. But *these* moral-religious imperatives are transcendental, that is, they refer to the personal human being as a whole and not to specific moral conduct. And even though Holy Scripture speaks also of particular attitudes and values—goodness, mildness, mercy, justice, modesty—these are still not "operative" norms of behavior, since it has yet to be determined which actions are to be regarded as just, modest and kind. Certainly, Scripture knows "operative" norms of conduct as well—a few at least. The question is precisely with reference to these, insofar as the absoluteness of moral norms is the point at issue.

We shall limit ourselves to the New Testament. References there to concrete moral behavior, norms of activity, are relatively few; but these few are important. The critical question is: In what sense are they absolute—in the sense of objective—in the sense of objective, non-arbitrarily grounded imperatives, or more than that, universal norms admitting of no exception? The answer to this question is not altogether easy.

The Christian centuries have tried earnestly to understand the demands of the Sermon on the Mount (Mt. 5-7). No Christian doubts their absolute validity, absolute to be understood in the sense of objective. The question is: absolute validity, as what—as universal norms, or as models for the behavior of the believing and loving citizens of God's kingdom who will be ready for such modes of conduct, perhaps, under determined conditions not individually specified by the Lord? The latter interpretation seems probable from the context and manner of expression. In recent years there has been renewed and heated discussion of the Lord's word about the *indissolubility of marriage* (Mt. 19, 3-10). Regarding the scope of this word, it is asked: Is it a question of a moral imperative or of something more? Is the moral imperative to be understood as a norm to be followed as universal practice or as an ideal? The discussion makes at least this much clear: The acceptance of an absolute in the sense of an objectively valid moral affirmation in Scripture does not necessarily involve recognizing it as an absolute in the sense of a universal norm.

It should be noted first of all that while Paul ascribes to the Lord definite sayings regarding moral behavior (indissolubility of marriage: 1 Cor. 7,10f.) and attributes others to his own personal understanding in the Holy Spirit (virginity: 1 Cor. 7,12.25), he *presupposes* that most of the behavioral norms of which he speaks are valid. This is particularly to be inferred from the many ordinances in which he accepts the moral wisdom of the "good" men of his time, both Jew and Gentile; one thinks, among other things, of the tables of domestic rules and the catalogue of vices. On the one hand, this means that Paul does not present himself as a teacher of moral living, still less as a teacher of specifically Christian norms of conduct; what he does have to transmit is something quite different from a moral code. On the other hand, his having assumed a given morality can lead us to consider whether such a morality, at least in many of its regulations, is not historically and culturally conditioned. It could scarcely be supposed that the Stoic, Judaic and Diaspora-Judaic ethos which Paul represents was in all respects a timeless ethos. If it is self-evident to us today that the Pauline directives concerning woman's position in marriage, society and the Church (1 Cor. 11,2-16; 14,34-36; Eph. 5,22-24; Col. 3,18; 1 Tim. 2,11-15) are to be regarded as conditioned by his times, reflecting Jewish tradition and the position of woman in the culture in which Paul and his contemporaries lived, we must indeed ask ourselves with what criterion we decide that those directives which Paul seeks to validate, even theologically, are historically conditioned and thus not absolute (i.e. universal), that they hold as absolute in the objective sense rather for the age whose ideas on the position of women they reflect. Consequently, such directives cannot be normative for a period in which the social position of women is essentially different. Holy Scripture itself gives us no criteria for such a judgment, but it comes from our knowledge of the difference in the social position of women in various ages together with our own insight into moral imperatives which arises out of the various social situations. This same power of discernment will permit us perhaps to make a judgment—at least in principle—as to which suits the nature of women in society better, and hence the moral ideal, the social position of women in Paul's cultural milieu or that of women in our cultural milieu—along with corresponding moral demands.

By analogy with the instance of woman's position in marriage, society and the Church, a further question inevitably arises, whether the possibility of similar considerations regarding other behavioral norms to be found in the Pauline corpus are to be absolutely excluded—on the theoretical level at least, especially since the criteria for such reflections are not provided us by Holy Scripture itself. For the affirmation that certain explicitly mentioned modes of conduct ban one from the kingdom of God, from companionship with Christ and from the life given by the Spirit remains true if these modes were to be judged negatively, in accordance with the moral evaluation proper to the age and accepted by Paul. Paul therefore did not teach such evaluation as thesis, but admitted it as hypothesis in his doctrinal statement on the Christian mystery of salvation. Thus, it remains to be established whether in Paul's cultural milieu, because of the actual conviction of the morally high-ranking segment of society, every "honorable" Christian had to share exactly this conviction, or whether this conviction was the only objectively justified one and was not based on definite options.

(In Paul we have actually a model for "Christian" discovery of moral norms. With him such discovery derives neither from Christ alone nor from the Old Testament alone. It occurs within an existing culture and as a consequence of its established moral values. It draws from Jewish tradition and from Greek popular philosophy, just as it carries along the culture in which Christianity took root. This does not exclude the fact that Paul himself also reflects upon the values he found already present, as, for example, the social position of women, and that, in particular cases, he himself independently—in the Holy Spirit—recommends practices like virginity or that he appeals to the word of the Lord).

The foregoing considerations obviously do not permit us to conclude that the norms of behavior found in the New Testament are no longer valid today. Only, we must reflect whether the criterion of their possible absolute (i.e., universal) validity is Holy Scripture itself, whether it can be and is intended to be.[3] The moral behavioral norms in Scripture are directed to actual persons of a definite era and culture. Hence their character of absoluteness would not signify primarily universality, but objectivity; and the latter can denote either the objectively right evaluation in a particular culturally conditioned human situation or necessary conformity to the moral views of the morally elite in a given society.

Norms of the Ecclesial Community

Neither from Christ nor from Paul or John has the Church inherited a system of moral norms. On the other hand, the ecclesial community—how could it be otherwise?—always maintained definite moral norms and passed them on to later generations. But in this connection it may by no means be said that there was ever in the Church a definitive or in all respects universal code of precepts. Nevertheless, the Church community had "their" morality which, even if it did not derive purely from Revelation, was regarded as being connected with or compatible with Christian belief. This morality—as being the morality of the Christian community—was "Christian" morality. Insofar as it had been handed down, it was a more or less codified morality, which just for this reason was lived in the *one* Church in *different* cultures and epochs. Naturally, this brief exposition is a simplification. But it enables us to understand how the Church, unlike Paul, begins not only to set forth dogmatically particular moral concepts—indissolubility of marriage (word of the Lord) and virginity (Paul's opinion, in the Holy Spirit)—but *in principle* the whole compass of the morality practiced by the Christian community which Paul had not taught but rather "presupposed," as also did the Church *after* Paul with regard to many questions. While Paul, earlier, expressed himself "in obliquo" and hypothetically on moral questions, the Church slowly began to do this "in recto" and dogmatically. The Church teaches in rebus fidei *et morum* and indeed, as she repeatedly declared during Vatican Council II, also in regard to moral questions on which she had no explicit revelation. Now the question: If the Church addresses herself thematically and dogmatically to moral questions, have we then pronouncements that are true universals? Is the claim of absoluteness for the norms transmitted by the Church a claim of universal norms? Does the Church give us thereby a system of universal morally valid norms which God has not given us in Holy Scripture?

In general, then, unlike Paul, the Church "teaches" norms of moral conduct. Why, really? The answer often given runs: Because the Church has to teach the way to salvation and true morality is the way to salvation. This answer might be considered valid if taken *cum grano salis*. For ultimately there is the question whether marriage, for example, is to be understood and lived according to Congolese or Western European style; surely not an unimportant cultural and ethical question, but not in itself deter-

minative of salvation. Still the matter admits of a different interpretation. The manner in which faith and love—which do determine
salvation!—are expressed in daily life, by premarital abstinence or
premarital intercourse, for example, is not a matter of totally free
choice. And since man must strive to incarnate his faith and love in
the "true" way of human beings, the Church assists him by her
"teaching." Clearly, this answer also does not entirely satisfy. In
any case, it remains true that the materiality of culturally and
ethically right mastery of the concrete reality of life—education,
economy, technology, sexuality, etc.—are not directly concerned
with salvation, or union with God; only faith and love, *together
with the effort* to incarnate this materiality in the "true" way in the
reality of life are thus concerned. That the material mode of this
Incarnation can represent only a secundarium, already makes it
reasonable that within certain limits moral pluralism might well be
possible. If, for example, faith and love have to be espressed in the
maintenance of the "right" social position of woman, then the
concrete expression in the Pauline conception and in the twentieth
century Western European conceptions must (!) be regarded as
necessarily differing from each other. Yet the Christian community
is obliged to see to it, that moral behavior as an expression of faith
and love does not come down to fulfilling one's own wishes, as also
it must not fail to manifest the unconditional character of faith and
love by unconditionality in stating moral precepts. However, it
could follow from what has been said that this quality of absoluteness does not represent primarily the universality of a norm, but an
anti-thesis to arbitrary judgment; or, positively stated, orientation toward concrete human (total) reality, and in this sense, "objectivity," "truth." This objectivity-truth is achieved, on the one
hand, through right understanding of the revealed word of God,
insofar as it contains morally significant affirmations; on the other
hand, through the right moral understanding of man's concrete
reality, in which connection, obviously, the light of revelation and
the moral understanding of man are not to be viewed as two
completely unrelated possibilities.

With respect to norms of moral behavior, the light of the
Gospel does not manifest itself in formally expressed statements
alone. Rather there is also the possibility suggested by Vatican II in

the Constitution on the Church in the Modern World, when reference is made to the necessity of judging contingent realities in the world of men in light of the Gospel.[4] Edward Schillebeeckx alludes to this statement;[5] nevertheless, he is of the opinion that the Christian, on the basis of his faith, can more easily assert negatively the incompatibility of a given social situation with his faith than discover positively how the situation might be changed. Karl Rahner has spoken, in the sense of Vatican II of a moral faith-instinct.[6] Maurizio Flick and Zoltán Alszeghy have pursued in greater detail the question of the significance of the Gospel—which itself gives no directives—for moral judgment of contingent human realities.[7] They maintain that it is possible, especially for a believer, to draw "an objective *picture* of revealed reality" on the basis of the content of revelation. Inasmuch as the development of dogma has not rarely been indebted to such an "objective picture," a great deal might be gained also for the proper mastering of concrete human reality via such an "objective picture." However, they are also of the opinion that actual problems, those, for example, pertaining to development and progress, can find direct solutions neither in the Gospel and faith, nor in theology, but only in a Christian ideology, which, of course, must be approached in terms of the eventual possibility of a critique by the Gospel and theology (and their "objective picture of revealed reality"). Only on this condition can a "political theology" venture an attempt to make the Gospel and faith effective for the reality of the world.[8] The "imperatives,"[9] known or determined corresponding to a "political theology," do not follow directly from faith and the Gospel, therefore, but only from an ethical interpretation ("political ethics"). And this ethics is "human" ethics; theological only to the extent that it has been projected by the believer as an imperative of a Christian theology which, in turn, depends in any case on an "objective picture of revealed reality."[10] It need scarcely be said that the imperatives of a Christian theology so projected are not absolutes in the sense of universalia. They represent the attempt to be as objectively relevant as possible to given realities through man's reflection in light of the Gospel, as described above; they are not to be artitrary precepts, therefore, but the most objective possible, and in this reduced sense, absolutes.

The assistance of the Holy Spirit has been promised to the endeavors of the Church. Inasmuch as the Church, to a far greater extent than Holy Scripture, has begun to address herself directly and dogmatically to moral questions, she becomes, in a much higher degree than the Scripture, concretely important because of the assistance of the Spirit of Christ. Some concepts of moral theology create the impression that the Holy Spirit slowly began to impart via the Church what He had not conveyed through Scripture—a vast collection of moral behavioral norms proclaimed for the whole world and for all time; absoluta, in the sense of universally valid norms. However, under this aspect, the Church is seen often in an all too spiritualized way; how very much the Spirit is merely "incarnated" in the Church is overlooked; in other words, how very human the Church is and remains despite the assistance of the Spirit. She arrives at norms of moral conduct only by way of a long process of learning to understand and to evaluate. And this comprehension and evaluation are accomplished not only by the hierarchy of the ecclesial community who, it may be, ultimately provide a decisive orientation, but by the Church as a whole, within the community of believers— where, not rarely, a special role falls to the theologians. It is far from true that a moral question is submitted to the pastors of the Church, so that in solitary reflection they can reach an authoritative decision. Before there is question of "decision" the "teaching" Church is in all instances a "learning" Church. The Spirit assists the *whole process* of teaching and leading in the Church; i.e., comprehending, discovering, evaluating, mutual listening, deciding.[11] He guarantees that error, which in human comprehension-discovery-evaluation-listening-deciding, can never be absolutely excluded, will not become in the end an essential component of the Church. Will not, perhaps, the same ecclesial community or a particular cultural group within it—pluralistic, therefore— occasionally begin to experience and evaluate in a new and different way, regarding specific points? In this connection it is noteworthy that in the two thousand years of the Church seemingly no definitive doctrinal decision on moral questions has been made, at least insofar as these would be related to natural law, without being at the same time revealed. On the other hand, this is not to say that the non-definitive authoritative orientations of the Church are meaningless, as if one might ignore them, oblivious to the fact that they also come under the assistance of the Spirit of Christ abiding with the Church. Hence a certain "presumption" of truth must be granted them. Yet one may not see in such instances any conclusive legislation or doctrinal laying down of an ethical norm, the validity of which would be guaranteed by the Holy Spirit. Declarations by the Church *in rebus morum* can be understood in all cases as an attempt to formulate "absolute," i.e. non-arbitrary, but objective imperatives, properly conformed to a concrete human reality and expressed in terms of a *presumptively* valid ecclesial orientation. If, on the contrary, such pronouncements had the assurance of infallibility, they could be set forth as universally valid norms, guaranteed to hold true always, everywhere and without exception. But even in such a case there would have to be a reservation; for it can be imagined and probably demonstrated if need be, that a strict behavioral norm stated as a universal, contains *unexpressed* conditions and qualifications which as such limit its universality.

The Church arrives at moral pronouncements—in the sphere of natural law morality, at least—via man's reflection on himself. But man is not a static being, whose nature is incapable of development. Furthermore, man is not by nature a Christian and a member of the Church. Thus, new questions will come up again, because of new experiences, insights and evaluations, therefore, in a new light and a changed culture. Even Christian man is obliged to question in retrospect, to go back to the past in order to find out what was once believed in the Church—even authoritatively, perhaps—about the right way to embody faith and love concretely. And more than this, without losing contact with the Christian wisdom of the past, he must always be thinking out once again various questions that affect his life, one time this way, one time that way.[12] It cannot be that the Christian and ecclesial past (from which year to which year?) enjoyed the prerogative of finding the (non-revealed) "truth" about moral behavior, while future Christians would have only the task of recording, confirming, applying the "truth" of the past—conclusive, absolute and universal in the strict sense—without advertence to really new problems never before reflected upon or resolved. Furthermore, it happens not infrequently, that old problems presenting themselves in a new guise are, at bottom, new problems. Also, it is scarcely conceivable that all Church traditions or decisions concerning moral behavioral norms would be in the full sense timeless and unconditioned, i.e., absolute, in the sense that they would be completely explicit and not in some respect conditioned either by fixed ideas or value judgments or by man's limited understanding of himself.[13] For example the opposition of the Church in the past to religious freedom is understandable if religious freedom and indifferentism are equated conceptually. Moreover, it is today an historical fact that the sexual morality handed down in the Church came under the influence of certain non-Christian (Jewish and pagan) evaluations in the first Christian centuries and is conditioned by them. The Church is not a "spiritualized" reality, thinking, speaking and existing in a vacuum, unrelated to any actual culture, and under such conditions devising norms of moral conduct that are in the purest sense "universal." But if norms of conduct can include culturally and historically conditioned elements, only then is there a possibility that they can be expressed in a manner that will respond to concrete human reality; i.e., be objective, and in this sense, absolute. ("Can" means that even in the moral judgment of a real situation, the Church could err.)

The Natural Moral Law

If Holy Scripture and the Church do not provide a system of universal moral norms, one expects this at least from the moral law of nature (natural moral law, natural moral order, order of creation, natural law). A well-defined concept of natural law underlies this expectation. Natural law is understood to be the summary of precepts which are based on the given and unvarying nature of man as such and which can be deduced from it. In his critical study, "The Natural Law Yesterday and Today,"[14] E. Chiavacci terms this concept "preceptive." According to this view, "immutable" nature points out to the man who "reads" and "understands" her what right behavior can and must be once and for all in the different areas of reality. A concept of this sort ends in a codifiable summation of the numerous precepts of natural law, which, because rooted in an unchangeable nature, are unvarying and universal. Thus it is maintained that all these precepts (norms) are to be applied in actual life situations appropriately, to be sure, but unequivocally.

This notion of a static-universal system of norms is valid to the extent that it believes man is and always will be man (tautology!) and that he must always conduct himself rightly—that is, as man. But this quite accurate perception does not entail as a necessary consequence a static-universal system of moral norms. The state of being man does not, *in the first place*, exclude that the human state may differ in different epochs and cultures, just as it is actualized in different individuals and life situations without placing man's nature in question. Against this assertion of the unchangeableness of human nature stands Aquinas' affirmation of its mutability.[15] The two positions are not in conflict if man along with his component structures and his ways even of being human, together with their structures, are differentiated rather than divided. Only there must be no attempt to distinguish what precisely is changeable from what is unchangeable. For even that which essentially constitutes man, that which therefore belongs to his nature unalterably, as also his permanent structures, is basically mutable. Mutability belongs to man's immutable essence; irrevocably, man is man (tautology!). To be sure, a priori, some essential elements of man's nature can be identified: body-soul unity, personality, accountability, interpersonality; while one cannot say with equal a priori validity, respecting other components of existential man, whether they belong necessarily and unchangeably to human nature. But even these a priori and inalienable elements of man's nature subsist in it in variable modes, a fact which can be correspondingly significant for moral behavior.

The question of mutability-immutability, secondly, is connected with the historicity of man.[16] History is possible only in virtue of the mutability of that which remains ever the same. Now man is an historical being; not only in terms of the successive variations of past, present and future, but above all in the sense that man himself designs and brings to realization the plot-lines of his given existence and its progress on into the future. He has to actualize what is sketched out for himself as possibility. In the process of his self-realization, he continually modifies his existence. In his spiritual and bodily aspects and his external relationships (environmental change), he becomes to an ever increasing degree a different person. Morality would have him live rightly the actual man, i.e., the man (humanity) of each actual moment, the present with the past enfolded within it and the projective future: that is, starting from each present reality he should "humanize" himself and his world. Whatever leads to our unfolding, in the fullest and best sense of the word, is good.[17]

Mutability and historicity, thirdly, are connected with the fact that man is person and nature in one. Person and nature can be placed counter to each other, so that nature expresses the intrapersonal given of man and his world, while person represents the I, possessing and shaping itself in terms of the given nature. However, one's personhood also is *given* and in *this* sense it is nature, indeed the determining element of one's humanness, and in this sense of human nature. The nature of man consists above all in his being a person (i.e., possessing ratio). Nature is not understood as human, unless it is thought of as a *personal* nature. Thus, it is not enough to say nature (for example, sexuality) "belongs to" the human person.[18] For then it would be possible to understand nature (sexuality) as non-personal;[19] hence one could speak of the meaning of sexuality, rather than of the meaning of *human* sexuality and make the consideration of this meaning (i.e., sexuality) a moral problem for the person reflecting upon his sexuality. The term "law of nature" is not merely open to misunderstanding; it frequently is responsible for it. It would be possible and perhaps more meaningful to speak of "person" as moral norm instead of "nature."[20] But then there would be danger that "personhood" would be viewed too onesidedly; that is, with practically no consideration of nature, provided person and nature are to be thus differentiated. In any case, nature, considered infrapersonally, cannot be the norm of moral behavior. Rather man is essentially person and has to understand himself therefore as person—"in a human nature"—and achieve self-realization according to this self-understanding. Self-realization entails that he himself must discover the available possibilities for his action and his development and determine on the basis of his present understanding of himself which of these possibilities are "right," "reasonable," "human" (in the full and positive sense of these words), and so contributive to "human progress." In this way he arrives simultaneously at the moral judgment of a concrete situation and the affirmation of moral norms.

In reality, this is tantamount to the traditonal statement that the lex naturalis is a lex interna (or indita), not a lex externa (or scripta). The preceptive understanding of natural law as a summary of precepts conformable to nature is not quite in keeping with this traditional concept; for, thus, a lex interna becomes furtively a lex externa resembling general positive or postively formulated laws. The lex interna signified the possibility and duty of man (humanity) to discern, as he himself evaluates himself, what in concrete "human" action is capable of being—inasmuch as man is essentially person-reason—and what can be affirmed propositionally in the problem area of "behavioral norms." Here we are obviously dealing with moral perceptions of an absolute nature. But it is equally obvious that absolute means at least primarily correspondence of behavior to personal human reality; objectivity, therefore, and not, or at least not primarily, universal validity.

Conscience

As explained according to traditional manuals, the function of conscience was the application of the moral law, or its norms, to the concrete case, a formulation founded on a "preceptive" understanding of the moral law, oriented to the specificity of positive law. The traditional statement has, naturally, some validity; in forming the dictates of conscience, we never begin at pure zero. We always bring to our actions existing orientations and norms. Yet conscience—as judgment of concrete action—is not only and not on the deepest level, the application of general norms. Knowledge of the essential function of conscience casts light also on the essence and meaning of behavioral norms.[21]

The function of conscience is to help man, as agent, make his action authentic (i.e., self-realizing). Hence conscience ought to assist action toward objectivity, toward truth, in conformity with the concrete human reality. It is necessary *above all* that action be conformable to the evaluating judgment (of conscience) with respect to the given concrete moment and its options. For this judgment itself belongs at the moment of action to the concrete human reality; it is, so to speak, its final form, so that the agent is enabled to realize himself only by fidelity to this judgment (mediating truth to him, yet erring occasionally). Clearly, *for this very reason*, the agent must strive for objectivity in forming this judgment regarding the concrete reality; i.e., that ratio which makes the judgment may be *recta ratio*. (The terms ratio-recta ratio derive from scholastic tradition. Here they signify, rather than specifically discursive thinking, an evaluative observing-understanding-judging, which can also occur "intuitively.") Now the behavioral norms of the moral law should also be recta ratio; only insofar as they are recta ratio, are they behavioral norms and can they, as such, objectively have a meaning for the function of conscience as recta ratio in action. The difference between judgment of conscience and norm of action consists basically in the fact that man with his evaluating ratio forms a moral judgment of his conduct *either* at the moment of action and in reference to it *or* in advance and not with reference to the actuality of the particular event as such. In terms of the concrete situation, then, it is clear that the norm of action cannot represent an exhaustive judgment of the actual reality, and that the actor must judge in light of his conscience to what degree a norm of conduct corresponds morally to a given situation.

Insofar as only the ratio (recta ratio) of conscience judges the reality ultimately and comprehensively in terms of the concrete element in it that is to be actualized, it exercises merely an auxiliary function, as compared to the ratio (recta ratio) of behavioral norms. As a consequence, the *decisive* aspect of such norms, is that they are *recta* ratio, thus their objectivity; to the extent that they are objective, they are absolute. Of course, they can be behavioral *norms* only insofar as they are discernible *in advance*; therefore they are necessarily abstract and in some way generalized. On this point further consideration is called for.

II
THE ABSOLUTENESS OF HUMAN BEHAVIORAL NORMS

The title of this section requires clarification. Our previous reflection on behavioral norms in Holy Scripture, Church teaching and natural law, should have made it evident that the affirmations in Scripture and in the teaching of the Church on absolute norms of behavior are not as definitive as might be supposed, particularly if the absoluteness denoted is to be primarily synonymous with universality. In addition to this, Christian behavioral norms, in their material content, are not *distinctively* Christian norms, that would hold only for Christians, but "human" norms, i.e. corresponding to the (authentic) humanness of man, which we have traditionally called norms of the natural moral law, or moral law of nature.[22] These observations suggest the need for further reflection on the absoluteness of moral norms of behavior considered as *human* (related to natural law), hence, insofar as they can be discerned by man himself as recta ratio.

The Human as Recta Ratio

We shall continue to employ the traditional term recta ratio. The human is in it, that which is humanly right. Whatever is not recta ratio is necessarily non-human, not worthy of man, antithetic to a steadily advancing "humanization." Recta ratio does not mean innate discernment or moral truth, "inscribed" somehow, somewhere. Hence it does not denote a norm of conduct "inscribed in our nature," at least not in the sense that one "could read off" a moral regulation from a natural reality. The "nature" upon which the moral law is inscribed is preeminently and formally nature as ratio, but only, of course, as recta ratio. From this viewpoint, the preferred expression would probably be that of Paul in Romans: the moral law is "engraved on the heart" (Rom. 2,15).[23] Apart from this, realities of the natural order, ratio excepted, can neither provide a basis for, nor affirm, any "moral" laws. Considered positively, then, the task of homo-ratio in "discovering" or "projecting" behavioral norms consists in understanding man himself, his own total reality, together with his world, in order to assess the significance of the alternatives for action available to him and so arrive at a moral affirmation. There will be some a priori and hence self-evident affirmations: for example, that man has to act responsibly and in an inter-personal and social context. Others will presuppose experience; for instance, conduct as related to the life of another or sexual behavior. In this regard some things will be immediately evident, e.g., that there should be respect for life (it may not be destroyed at will), that sexuality has to be viewed in relation to a particular culture, etc. Still other affirmations call for long and perhaps varied experience, until man understands the value of different possibilities for the realization of genuine humanness. How mankind and the Christian centuries as well have striven in the most diverse ways to come to an evaluative understanding of sexuality and marriage and their actualization!

Criteria of Evaluation

Do criteria for the evaluating ratio exist? A prime criterion is obviously correspondence of behavior, hence also of the behavioral norms to be discovered to the "meaning," in general, of being man and to the significance of particular givens; i.e., sexuality and marriage as *human* givens.[24] It is probable that penetration of meaning occurs far less frequently on a priori or metaphysical ground than has often been supposed. It implies varied experience on the part of man (humanity) and a long apprenticeship in unprejudiced weighing of these manifold experiences. And it is not only the "meaning" itself of experienced realities that constitutes a criterion for the evaluating ratio, but also practical knowledge of the outcomes and consequences which determined modes of conduct can have— and this under all kinds of presuppositions,[25] for example, in the economic sphere, in social life or in the area of sexuality and marriage. Of itself experience yields no norms of conduct; assessment of its outcome is required to enable us to perceive in which direction to seek or not to seek—genuine human self-realization. A basic criterion for true penetration of human reality, as well as for a just appraisal of experience, is to be found in the interpersonality of the human person.[26] The conduct of individual persons in the different areas of life has to be scrutinized in terms of its interpersonal significance and implications. No one is a self-enclosed individual; each one lives as a person in relation to persons. Humanness essentially involves inter-human relations. Technological and economic progress, for instance, cannot be assessed in the concrete as "human values," unless interpersonal and social aspects are fundamentally involved in the judgment.

To arrive at a behavioral norm regarding, for example, pre-marital intercourse or birth control, a whole *complex* of factors obviously has to be considered. (It should not be necessary to add that this takes place in an *explicit* manner only in scientific reflection.) What must be determined is the significance of the action as value or non-value for the individual, for interpersonal relations and for human society, in connection, of course, with the total reality of man and his society and in view of his whole culture. Furthermore, the *priority* and *urgency* of the different values implied must be weighed.[27] By this procedure, man as assessor (the evaluating human society) arrives at a judgment, tentatively or with some measure of certitude, as to which mode of behavior might further man's self-realization and self-development. As soon as this judgment has been made, it is recognized as a moral norm by the ever-present conviction reflected in it, that this human action is bound absolutely to recta ratio. Simultaneously asserted is the fact that the many values to be considered according to their priority and urgency, or non-values, do not, strictly speaking, belong as yet to the moral sphere; that is, they are not as yet moral precepts, but are, in this connection, pre-moral. Only the all-embracing view and total appraisal which, as such, determine the mode of action that is good for men, lead to a *moral* statement. This implies that one or other aspect of an action cannot of itself and without regard for the remaining factors determine the morality of an action.

Relativism?

Facts—social, cultural, technological, economic, etc.—change. Man's experiences, i.e., those of human societies, likewise change, on the basis of changing data. Evaluations also, the mind's grasp of human realities, and self-understanding can be altered. One thinks, for example, of the efforts toward an expanded conception of marriage and sex in the milieu of the Catholic Church in the recent past. And in the process, man (that is, human society), oriented toward development and progress, also changes himself. All these manifold possible—and actual—alterations have to be brought into the moral judgment of human conduct. Such "new" aspects could call for action, which, independent of such aspects would be out of the question; or they might exclude a course of action which would be commanded under other circumstances. If the minimum family income set decades ago is linked to certain social and economic factors, if the institution of private property in our present economic, social and political situation must be viewed as differing in its concrete signification from previous decades or the Middle Ages, if conceptual grasp and interpersonal and social experience in the realm of family and marriage necessarily co-determine behavior in this area, then on principle corresponding "changes" regarding the "right" human behavior in *other* spheres of life cannot be ruled out. Under this aspect, behavior norms have, at least theoretically, a provisory character.

Changes in the data, differences in concepts and experiences—or even interpretations—occur not only in successive cultures, if not, in cases of actual pluralism,[28] within the same culture. This is readily understandable if heterogeneous economic, social or political situations admit, respectively, of different modes of behavior. But what if varying experiences and concepts and varying self-images of men in different societies or groups lead to different options and so to a diversity of statements on behavior norms in relation to similar bodies of facts? One might point out, perhaps, that in many cases a given self-concept and a given viewpoint and form of a reality, e.g., marriage in, let us say, a certain African tribe, may not "in themselves" correspond in all respects to recta ratio. Then, of course, the question arises, whether another form of marriage, presupposing another culture, may legitimately be imposed upon men belonging to an endemic culture—by missionaries, for instance[29]—provided the indigenous culture itself has not changed by a rather gradual process, and provided it admits of a "human" form of marriage. But might it not be assumed also that on the basis of dissimilar experiences, a *heterogeneous* self-concept and *varying* options and evaluations on the part of man (humanity) "projecting" himself into his future in human fashion—secundum rectam rationem—are entirely possible, and that these options and evaluations within the chosen system postulate varied forms of behavior? Who would expect human individuals, groups or societies to arrive at self-understanding and values exempt from all one-sidedness or merely from incompleteness? There recta ratio which is to guide our conduct has to allow for such conditionality, essentially connected with humanness; without it man de facto does not exist. Moreover, must it not be supposed that the behavioral norms encountered in a particular civilization or cultural area were formulated partly in consideration of just this civilization and culture, hence for them alone? And this despite the fact that definitive or generally valid norms of conduct were actually intended, simply because one does not advert to the possibility of other civilizations and cultures.

Is this relativism? Some time ago, when H. J. Wallraff called Christian social doctrine a "structure of indeterminate propositions"[30] and in connection with the institution of private property accepted only a few general statements on social ethics, the realization of which depended heavily upon economic, social and political factors, he found himself vulnerable to the charge of relativism. The title of his work was "Vom Naturrecht zum Relativismus: an Beispiel des Eigentums."[31] Exception was taken to the subsequent statement: "Principles for a normative science would have to be drawn from the social reality."[32] Here the decisive truth was overlooked, that if behavioral norms are to be operative, the entire pertinent reality (including the social factor) has to be taken into account and enter into the judgment. The a priori, hence universal, non-historical social ethics that stands opposed to this, that provides norms in advance for every social reality, sacrifices the indispensable objectivity and therefore validity of duly concrete solutions to an a priori universalism. The critical question, then, is not one of relativism but of objectivity, or the "truth" of the action which must be in conformity with the whole concrete reality of man (of society). Now Wallraff had

spoken earlier of indeterminate propositions that must be concretized through *political decisions* (thus involving some compromise), but still in relation to the given social reality. Our own
previous consideration, however, had to do with *moral behavior
norms* which men (humanity) "discover" as being appropriate to
their actual civilization, experience, etc. We asked: Is this relativism? And now the correlative question: Is it not rather the
necessary connection with concrete human reality to which human
behavior must be adapted if it is to be "objective" and "true" and
so "right," secundum rectam rationem? The demand to be this is
absolute! Rightly does Chiavacci point out[33] that the objectivity
of morality is not necessarily based on an unchangeable being (in
other words, on a "preceptive" understanding of natural law), but
on the indispensable correspondence of act to being.

III
The "Applicability" of Moral Norms

If the absoluteness of moral norms is constituted primarily by
their objective effectiveness vis-à-vis the given reality and thus not
preeminently by their universality or their universal validity, the
question inevitably arises concerning the applicability of moral
norms to reality in the concrete.

The So-Called Exceptions to the Norm

A very small step in the direction of universal validity in
applying moral norms brings home the realization that possibly
they cannot be stated, as we once believed they had to be, so as to
apply, to all epochs or in all cultures, or social groups or in all
conceivable individual cases. And so we have the problem of the
exception to the moral norm, a matter discussed chiefly in Anglo-
Saxon circles in past years. The title of an Irish article is symp-
tomatic: "Toward a Theory of Exceptions."[34] The author, N. D.
O'Donoghue, starts with the possibility and the fact of exceptions
to behavioral norms, understood, actually, in the same way as by

Fletcher and Robinson, for instance, when they concede absoluteness in the sense of admitting no exceptions to only *one* norm—
that of love.[35] An ethical system, according to O'Donoghue, is
possible only because, despite change and diversity, man and his
structures abide, yet since the same man and his structures also
exhibit changes and differences, exceptions must occur, in such a
way, however, that they remain exceptions. The conclusion is
then: Moral norms necessarily admit of exceptions. Princeton
University's renowned theologian, Paul Ramsey, the "most influential and most prominent advocate of a 'Principles Ethics' "
among his Protestant colleagues, holds the contrary opinion. His
title is significant: "The Case of the Curious Exception."[36] Ramsey
reasons as follows. If there is an exception, it must be based
objectively on the actual situation, so that when the same situation
is repeated, the same exception must hold. This means, however,
that the norm to be applied in general is not meant for the case at
hand, or that it must give way to a "better" norm. The "exceptional case" obliges us, therefore, to a "refining" of the previous
norm, since it did not take into account certain elements of the
particular situation or perhaps considered them only implicitly.
Accordingly, Ramsey's solution is: Fundamentally, there are no
exceptions—provided the formulation of the norm becomes ever
more refined and precise. This solution is the correct one. Frequently our statements of norms are inexact, inasmuch as they do
not—perhaps cannot—take into consideration all the possibilities
of the human reality. When, as he must, Ramsey finally confronts
the question whether *all* norms can be "refined," the question will
really be asking, at least logically, whether all the already "refined" norms are to be refined still further. In this connection one
thinks of the changeableness and historicity of man (of humanity),
of his culture, his value systems, etc. Ramsey appears to incline
rather to a static concept of man. Thus the "refining" entails not
only the ever improved and more precise comprehension and
articulation, but also a "re-formulation" for modes of reality which
hitherto could not be taken into consideration

Dennis E. Hurley, Archbishop of Durban,[37] has published
another attempt to advocate the simultaneous validity of the norm
and the justification of the exception. In his view, where a case of

conflict occurs, duties and rights stand in opposition to each other. An overriding right can cancel the obligations of certain absolute norms of morality and so make permissible some (not all) "intrinsece mala" (killing, stealing, lying, etc.). Charles Curran[38] appeals to a "theory of compromise," in terms of which—particularly in virtue of man's situation in consequence of original sin—what really ought not happen, may and must happen on occasion. The often invoked theory of the lesser evil (or the greater good), like the two attempts just mentioned, also seeks to maintain simultaneously the validity of the norms and the vindication of the exceptions.[39] Yet would Ramsey not rightfully reply, that the justification of the exception in view of the overriding right, of the necessary compromises and of the lesser evil, must be objectively based on (human) reality itself; i.e., the norm sustaining the exception is not stated with sufficient precision, and, given this formulation, does not at all represent the true norm governing the concrete reality? The justification of the apparent exception lies in the fact that the supposed norm simply does not possess the range of validity it appears to have, judging by its inexact formulation. This does not militate against the validity of the (true) norm; rather it permits the objectively-based, so-called exception to call attention more pointedly to the objective range and true validity of the norm.[40]

Further consideration leads to a like result. Hurley maintains that killing, stealing, lying, etc. are intrinsically evil; yet they might be warranted in view of important opposing obligations. According to press reports, a French bishop is supposed to have said in a presentation at a Conference of French bishops on *Humanae vitae* that, according to *Humanae vitae* the use of contraceptives is an *evil*, like killing; but killing in a morally justified war of defense and the use of contraceptives in certain cases of conflict would not be morally culpable (in no sense wicked). Have we not overlooked the distinction—crucial in this case—between *evil* and *wickedness*; that is, between evil in the *pre*moral (physical, ontic) sense and evil in the *moral* sense (wickedness). Objectively, there is no conflict of moral precepts, only a conflict of value judgments (bona "physica") in the *pre*moral sense.[41] Only the right—"secundum rectam rationem"—solution of this conflict makes the "absence of conflict" evident in the *moral* situation. Killing is a realization of an evil, but it is not always a moral evil. In this regard, there is also no moral norm applying to *killing*, but only such as designates *unjust* killing as immoral. If someone (with *Humanae vitae*) regards the use of contraceptives as a *malum*, but considers certain exceptions morally justifiable, he must understand that the *malum* of contraceptive use affirmed by him in this form lies in the *pre* moral sphere ("it is evil") while only the objective *unjustified* realization of the evil belongs in the area of the moral ("it is wicked"). In general: Whoever sets up negative norms, but regards exceptions as justified, by reason of overriding right, or warranted compromise, or for the sake of the lesser evil (or the greater good), shows by this that the malum repudiated by the norm is *not* (yet) to be understood as *moral* evil. Hence its realization to avoid another malum (or for the sake of a relatively higher bonum) can be justified *morally* on the ground mentioned previously. If, on the contrary, it is preferred to give this norm moral validity, its formulation in universal terms has to be restricted, and the "exception" is no longer an exception. The norm is *objective* only within the limits of the restriction.

Moral and Premoral Evil

The basic distinction between moral and premoral evil[42] should be carried still further in the interest of clarifying the significance of moral norms for concrete behavior. Morality, in the true (not transferred or analogous) sense is expressible only by a human action, by an action which originates in the deliberate and free decision of a human person. An action of this kind can be performed only with the intention of the agent. One may not say, therefore, that killing as a realization of a human evil may be morally good or morally bad; for killing as such, since it implies nothing about the intention of the agent, cannot, purely as such, constitute a human act. On the other hand, "killing because of avarice" and "killing in self-defense" do imply something regarding the intention of the agent; the former cannot be morally good, the latter may be.

Here we take up the question: When is human action, or when

is man in his action (morally) good? Must not the answer be: When he *intends and effects* a human good (value)—in the premoral sense, for example, life, health, joy, culture, etc. (for only this is recta ratio); but not when he *has in view and effects* a human *non-good*, an evil (non-value)—in the premoral sense, for example, death, wounding, wrong, etc. What if he intends and effects good, but this necessarily involves effecting evil also? We answer: If the realization of the evil through the intended realization of good is justified as a proportionally related cause,[43] then in this case only good was intended. Man has almost always judged in this manner. A surgical operation is a health measure, its purpose is to cure, but it is at the same time the cause of an evil, namely, wounding. This, however, appears to be justified in view of the desired cure and is capable of being incorporated in the *one human* act—a curative measure. The surgical operation is *morally* right, because the person acting desires and effects only a good—in the *pre*moral sense—namely, restoration of health. If the surgeon were to do more than was required in performing this operation, that "more" would not be justified by the treatment indicated; that is, it would be taken up *as an evil*—in the *pre*moral sense—into the surgeon's intention; it would be *morally* bad. The conclusion in definitive terms is: 1) An action cannot be judged morally in its materiality (killing, wounding, going to the moon), without reference to the intention of the agent; without this, we are not dealing with a human action, and only with respect to a human action may one say in a true sense whether it is morally good or bad.[44] 2) The evil (in a premoral sense) effected by a human agent must not be intended as such, and must be justified in terms of the totality of the action by appropriate reasons.

These considerations are not without significance for the question of the application of norms to the concrete case. We have already seen this in connection with the so-called exceptions to the norm. The problem presents itself also in the form of the traditional doctrine of the three sources of practical morality (tres fontes moralitatis). According to this doctrine, morality in a comprehensive sense, as applied to a concrete action is determined not only by the morality of the act as such, but also by the morality of the circumstances and purpose of the action, with the reservation, however, that neither the purpose nor special circumstances can rescind the negative morality of an action. This point has the value only of a "rule of thumb" (although it has also the theoretical force that something *morally* bad cannot become morally good in view of a good purpose). In theoretically precise reflection, one must, of course, establish some additional points. For 1) a moral judgment of an action may not be made in anticipation of the agent's intention, since it would not be the judgment of a "human" act. 2) A moral judgment is legitimately formed only under a *simultaneous* consideration of the three elements (action, circumstance, purpose), premoral in themselves; for the actualization of the three elements (taking money from another, who is very poor, to be able to give pleasure to a friend) is not a combination of three human actions that are morally judged on an individual basis, but a single human action. A surgical operation is not made up of several human actions (wounding, healing, for the purpose of restoring health), but it is only one healing action, the moral quality of which is based on a synchronous view of the three—premoral— elements in conformity with an evaluating recta ratio. The same thing could be said about the transplant of an organ from a living human organism, about underground coal-mining with its threat to health, about the moon-landing and the incalculable dangers involved, etc. But now the critical question: What value do our norms have with respect to the morality of the action as such, prior, that is, to the consideration of the circumstances and intention? We answer: They cannot be moral norms, unless circumstances and intention are taken into account. They can be considered as moral norms only because we tacitly assume to judge the action in the light of possible circumstances and intention. But since, *theoretically*, this is impossible, and since *in practice* these elements of an action are necessarily incomplete, we cannot rule out the possibility that in the practical application an objectively based instance of conflict—the exceptional case—can show that the norm does not have, objectively, the range of validity previously supposed. The absoluteness of a norm depends more upon the objectivity of its relationship to reality than upon its universality.

   "The end does not justify the means," that is, the morally bad means. This tenet is, of course, correct. When and to the extent that it has been established that an action is morally bad, it may not be performed as a means toward attaining a good end. On the other hand if there is question only of evil in the *pre*moral sense, such as death, wounding, dishonor, etc., the intention and the realization of a good can possibly justify the doing of an evil, e.g., the evil of a surgical operation in the interest of health, or a transplant. Needless to say: 1) the performing of the evil is not judged independently of the intention as *morally* bad; 2) in the *one* human action (health care, transplant) the performing of the evil is not an isolated (human) action, but only an element of the one action. Therefore, a morally bad (human-) action, is not being used as means to a good end. This point was often overlooked in the traditional statement of the principle of an act with a double effect. Thus, in cases in which, during the course of the action, the bad effect preceded the good, temporally or physically, opinion was always inclined toward prohibition, on the grounds that otherwise the good effect would be achieved *through* the realization of the bad effect (as means). Actually, many good Christians cannot understand why, in a situation where life is endangered, as, for instance, ectopic pregnancy or uterine diseases, the removal of the fetus was prohibited, while the removal of an organ from the mother, whose serious illness was anticipated because of the pregnancy, *together with* the fetus was permitted; although in both cases, there was liability involved with respect to the life of the fetus—a (premoral) value.[45] The theory failed to take into account that the evil involved is such, not on moral but on *pre*moral grounds (like wounding, loss of honor, death, etc.) and that consequently its actualization occurs, not as a separate human act with its own morality and not, in this context, as an immoral means to a good end, but as a component of one action which is specified through the intention of the agent. Once more: moral norms are not likely to be fully expressed so long as intentions and circumstances are not taken into consideration, at least implicitly. They are objective, therefore, only when this qualification can be presupposed.

"Ethical" Norms and "Abstract" Norms

Under this title Edward Schillebeeckx has treated the problem of the applicability of norms to real cases in the third volume of his collected works[46] and in 1968 in *Concilium*.[47] He points out that some Catholic theologians—G. de Brie, Karl Rahner, Josef Fuchs are named—in view of the all-too-simple solutions of the problematic of situation ethics, have attempted to compensate by having the moral requirement of the situation from abstract norms drawn from the concept "man" as well as from strictly situation-conditioned elements. Against this solution Schillebeeckx cites the epistemological difficulty that *two* norms are posited by it. In reality, however, there would be solely the concrete reality of the particular individual's ethical norm. The *abstract* norm would not be an *ethical* norm at all, that is, a demand of reality. Rather, it would only repeat the ethical norm in the abstract and inadequately and would have moral significance only in virtue of its existential connection with the concrete reality. This significance would lie in the fact that it is "the inadequate indeed, but still real referent to the single operative concrete ethical norm";[48] i.e., in the direction indicated by it, the ethical norm is to be sought, without its being itself capable of providing this ethical norm satisfactorily. Apart from the question of terminology, the authors cited above legitimately suppose, precisely as Schillebeeckx, only a single ethical norm (as required by the actual case) and admissibly understood the relationship of the "abstract" to the concrete reality as "ethical" norm epistemologically in precisely the same way as he; they have said this explicitly.

But the question of interest to us here, is rather that of the significance of the abstract norm for the concrete reality as ethical norm. Schillebeeckx probably does not mean to say merely that an abstract norm cannot form the basis of an exhaustive judgment of a concrete reality. He would doubtless also wish to say that only in the confrontation with an actual situation will the moral value and the moral exigency, toward which the abstract norm merely pointed in a partial manner, be fully revealed and understood. Or he has in mind that the abstract norm can only be arrived at via the concrete reality through abstraction and conceptualization. But this would imply that the concrete reality to which it is to be applied later on, is *conceivable* of a different *kind* than the concrete reality that represented the point of departure. Thus, it can no longer serve as the ethical norm; i.e. as meeting the concrete requirements of the new reality. If he indeed meant to say this, he perceived the problem treated above and sought to solve it in his own way: the norm for concrete action is constituted by the *one* moral judgment of the whole complex (the action in abstracto, circumstances, intention) and not by the moral judgment of an action in abstracto *and* the added judgment of circumstances and intention.

"Intrinsece Malum"?

The question of the applicability of moral norms may arise in still another form known from tradition. If the absoluteness of the moral norm signifies objectivity more than universal validity, can moral norms be universal at all, in the sense of being applicable always, everywhere and without exception, so that the action encompassed by them could never be objectively justified? Traditionally we are accustomed to speak of an "intrinsece malum."

Viewed theoretically, there seems to be no possibility of norms of this kind for human action in the inner-wordly realm. The reason is that an action cannot be judged morally at all, considered purely in itself, but only together with all the "circumstances" and the "intention." Consequently, a behavioral norm, universally valid in the full sense, would presuppose that those who arrive at it could know or foresee adequately *all the possible combinations* of the action concerned with circumstances and intentions, with (pre-moral) values and non-values (bona and mala "physica").[49] A priori, such knowledge is not attainable. An a priori affirmation would not come to be a moral judgment by way of the premoral. Add to this that the conception opposed to this does not take into consideration the significance for an objective understanding of morality attached to, first, practical experience and induction, second, civilization and cultural differences, third, man's historicity and "creative" perceptions.

Despite all this, we often make statements connoting "universal validity." But "Thou shalt not *kill*" is obviously too broadly stated; it would be better to say, "Thou shalt not *commit murder*"; that is, "Thou shalt not kill unjustly." This last formulation is universal and exact. Nevertheless, a high price has been paid for this advantage over the formulation "Thou shalt not kill." For while "killing" expresses an unequivocal fact, "murder" does not, since it leaves undetermined when killing is lawful and when it is not. Accordingly the inference is self-evident: A precise description of an action as a statement of fact would, theoretically, scarcely admit of a universal moral judgment in the strict sense. An operative universal moral norm contains a *formal element* not yet defined materially, "lawful," "in an authorized manner." Hence the attempt on the part of moral theology to discover which values, realizable in this world can justify "killing" and which cannot. If it is believed that, in moral theology, the line between "lawful" and "unlawful" has to be precisely drawn, we have once again a definitive statement of fact and, within its limits, a universal moral judgment. But here we must pause for further reflection. How could one make a judgment that would take in *all* the human possibilities—even granting that one had succeeded in understanding rightly and judging rightly those possibilities that were foreseen? Today, actually, such reflection begins thus: Might there not be at the present time and in the future a society in which—as distinguished from earlier societies—by reason of its social and cultural structures, capital punishment would not be an appropriate and therefore warranted means of administering justice? Further, is there meanwhile no life situation that might justify suicide, as for example, the only means of preserving a state secret, a possibility which presumably is open to consideration, inasmuch as it was excluded indeed in the norm as stated in the past, without however having been reflected upon at any time. "Killing" vs. "murder" was mentioned as only one example that might shed more light on the problem of the applicability of behavior norms stated as universals.

Theoretically, no other answer seems possible: Probably there can be no universal norms of *behavior* in the strict sense of "intrinsece malum." *Practically*, however, norms properly formulated as universals have their worth, and indeed on several counts. 1) Such norms, insofar as they are based on true perception, indicate a value or a non-value in the premoral sense. But negative values are to be avoided; in particular, as evil they may never serve as intentions for human action, and only for adequate reasons may they be actualized concurrently with relatively higher or more urgent values. 2) There can be norms stated as universals, including, that is, a precise delineation of the action, to which we cannot conceive of any kind of exception; e.g., cruel treatment of a child which is of no benefit to the child.[50] Despite misgivings on the level of theory, we get along very well with norms of this kind. 3) Norms can be stated as universals (in the case of a specific culture or society, particularly), corresponding to human and social situations that have been actually experienced. In these instances, Aquinas' opinion concerning so-called secondary principles of the natural law, including, therefore, "operative" behavioral norms, holds true by analogy: They can be applied in *ordinary cases* ("valent ut in pluribus").[52] And this for the reason that they are stated so as to suit conditions wont to occur in practice (and only for such); they suffice for ordinary use in practical living. 4) The extent of the inapplicability of a norm to a concrete case (for which it was actually not intended), the degree to which specific norms of our society are stated with precise relevance to present-day conditions in our society, or to those of yesterday's society (from which our present one derives) and so are not relevant to ours; or are generalized and so apply to other societies and cultures as well— such difficulties can neither be presumed as free of doubt, nor may they be completely ignored. Where the first suspicion of one or other of the conditions mentioned above exists, a point of reference is at hand for a thorough examination, to determine the factor upon which the delimiting process should be objectively based.

The absence of a distinction—made only later on—between *theoretical* and *practical* possibility characterized not only the moral-theological discussion of the past on "intrinsece malum" and the universality of behavioral norms, but also, by way of consequence, the official ecclesiastical use of these expressions. Apart from this, the terms would have a better meaning if they could be aligned with the term "absolute" in the sense we have given it above. Every action that is *objectively*—secundum rectam rationem—not justified in the concrete human situation (according to Schillebeeckx, the sole norm and only adequate norm of conduct) is "intrinsece malum" and therefore absolutely to be avoided.[52]

IV
NORMS AS AUTHENTIC ORIENTATION

To summarize: Moral theology is concerned primarily with objectivity—its true absolutum—which consists in the recta ratio of a human-Christian actualization of the concrete reality. Recta ratio can be satisfactorily present only in a conscience situation. But human society requires and "discovers"—"creates"—norms stated as universals; the same is true of scientific moral theology. Nevertheless, universality in norms has certain limits, at least theoretically, because of the objectivity required of a true absolutum. What are the practical implications?

Formal Principles and Material Norms of Action

Undoubtedly there are universal ethical statements in the strict sense. Nevertheless they always remain *formal* in a certain sense, at least insofar as they are not *material* norms of action, i.e. norms which indicate whether actions exactly described materially are ethically permissible or not. That our actions must be authentic self-realization, or what is the same, that we have to do the good and not the evil, is nothing other than the formal formulation of man's ethical self-understanding. This formal and hence absolutely universal formulation can be applied to *different spheres of life* without losing its formal character: the imperative to be just, chaste, and merciful thus materially states nothing about the materially determined actions which can express justice, chastity, and mercy. Likewise the formal formulation of the ethical self-understanding can express itself in *transcendental norms*, which thus do not describe the material content of actions, for example, that the Christian man has to realize himself as Christian, that he should live faith and love, baptism and the following of Christ in every action. They are universal. *Categorical evaluations* on the other hand may be influenced to a certain degree by determined experiences, by factual options in a given society, and by a specific self-understanding. Above all this applies to the *hierarchy* of values, for example, in the area of marriage and family. This applies in the same way and even more to *"operative"* norms of action, which were treated above. In this case to defend as a theoretical possibility the complete universality of ethical statements—perhaps on the basis of an *a priori* metaphysical understanding of determined actions—is to succumb to the utopia of rationalism.

Moral-Theological Reflection

Ethical, or moral-theological, reflection is always associated with moral experience. This however, can never be a solipsistic experience. Its substance is always related to the moral consciousness of the community.[53] But this moral consciousness is shaped by manifold experiences and diverse influences. In the Christian community led by the Spirit, the human-Christian self-concept is always the matrix and potential corrective of the moral understanding, even when the Christian message as such transmits behavioral norms that are scarcely "operative," definitive and universal. On the other hand, it cannot be denied that in the course of the centuries, Old Testament-Jewish concepts and the ethical opinions of non-Christian ideologies of various kinds exercised their influence. It is likewise undeniable that in the Christian communities of those centuries "errare humanum est" and that error in the moral sphere cannot therefore be excluded *a limine*.

If today in Christian as well as non-Christian sectors, the universality of norms is being questioned on theoretical and on practical levels as well, with very manifest consequences, the fact still remains that *men of today* also and the Christian community of today are susceptible to *error*. There is equal a priori probability, however, that, in their reflections, they can achieve *true* insight. In this connection, where might the basis be found that would validate the right or necessity of questioning or "rethinking," for without penetrating and common reflection in relation to this basis, will not a community run the risk of deviating from "its own" *clear-sighted* moral sense, which has developed within it and in virtue of its own particular reality? Theoretically speaking, three possibilities that could warrant doubt or re-thinking come to mind. *First*, it can be shown that in the Christian past, faulty evaluations were made and false norms set. If such could be and were identified hitherto, similar identifications could *in principle* be made also today. Those erroneous evaluations and norms could have been objectively "false" for men of earlier times as well, although today we could probably show why the errors were scarcely avoidable or even not avoidable at all because of the state of knowledge—or awareness—at that time. *Second*, inasmuch as we ourselves formulate moral norms, such norms may well be imprecise or the most likely eventuality, stated in too generalized a manner, either because there was only an implicit awareness of limits, or because limits were not adverted to at all. This helps to explain why, *third*, particular inherited moral statements can be related very accurately to a social situation, a culturally conditioned evaluation, a partially developed self-concept, and the like, rather than to a designated era of the past, whereas for us today those situations and evaluations are "past." In cases where we can prove this and where it is clear that a moral statement has its basis in precisely those givens that have since changed their bases, a moral reformulation is not only conceivable; it is called for.

The Individual and His Conscience

Undoubtedly, the question of the absoluteness of moral norms has considerable significance for the individual and the forming of his situation-conscience, in light of which (not, then,—directly—in light of the norms!) he acts. For since we never begin at zero to form our situation-conscience, but always include norms in our starting point, the question of absoluteness, i.e., universality, regarding the norms of the individual and his concrete behavior, becomes important. To repeat, we are not solipsists either in forming a situation-conscience or in developing a moral sensibility or in appropriating moral norms. Rather, despite the uniqueness of the individual, there is a human orientation to moral questions only in terms of a group, a community, a society, conceived of as a whole. In his moral convictions and in forming his situation-conscience, the individual cannot simply detach himself from his roots in the moral convictions of the community; nor may he forget that he will find the (i.e. "his") right solution of many an individual moral problem only by relating to the moral perceptions and the self-concept of his community. Specific problems usually occur in an integrated context and cannot easily find their distinctively appropriate solutions in another context. In the *ecclesial* community, it is to be noted further, moral traditions can also be co-determined, in that a Christian member's self-concept and ideal of morality, springing from faith (even though the inferences may be partially undeveloped), can contribute to the ratifying of a moral evaluation. On the other hand, doubts and reversed judgments occuring justifiably in a community can also, naturally, influence the mental attitude and the formation of conscience taken by the individual according to his capacity and responsibility, when he decides to participate in the reflective evaluations of his community and follow the judgment of his adviser. Doubtless, much depends on a responsible discernment of spirits, perceptible through[54] and dependent upon a moral faith-instinct (K. Rahner), which, however, must not be equated with mere susceptibility to what has been traditionally handed down.

There is, of course, the theoretical possibility that the "curious exception" (Ramsey) may present itself, not only as a public phenomenon in the life of the community, but also independently in a justified individual case. For the actuality of this possibility, one should not only deal with the uniqueness of the individual and of the particular case—this would be very superficial—but with the basis which in itself is objective and demonstrable—perhaps along the lines of one of the possibilities mentioned in the previous section, "Moral-Theological Reflection." Nevertheless the individual case, granting the demonstrability of the objective basis, probably will be presented as a rule within the community in a similar and analogous manner and be carried through to a competent (not necessarily authoritative) judgment.

The "Pedagogical" Value of Norms

The moral task of the Christian is not to fulfill "norms" but to "humanize" (Christianize) each of man's concrete realities, understood as a divine call. Norms of moral behavior should "help" to bring this about rightly, "objectively." The true significance of these norms consists in this "pedagogical" service—not in a universal validity that could compromise objectivity. Accordingly, the function of the norms is then "only" pedagogical.[55] They are guides to right actualization, that is, they are not intended, being abstract, to be the concrete solution, nor can they even, at least theoretically, designate with precision their own range of validity.[56] Yet, practically speaking, they are indispensably important, because no one who is incorporated in a community is without norms. The "pedagogical" service of norms reaches its highest intensity in cases where the individual (as a member of his community) is not entirely capable of finding his way.[57] To be sure, precisely in such instances norms are liable to be understood and lived as law or taboo because they do not clearly manifest their proper limits.

Once again: the moral task proper to man is not to fulfill norms, so that in the final analysis life's reality would serve merely as material, so to speak, for actualizing moral values; that is, of obeying norms. Inversely, the concrete reality of life itself—that is its actualization—is the real task; hence the mandate to take up a given reality and to form it, "creatively" and in a spirit of self commitment, into something "worthy of man" (and therefore of his Creator and Redeemer).[58] The understanding of concrete reality itself could by itself enable the evaluating individual (Christian) to judge which "designs" of his shaping action are really "human" (Christian). By forming this judgment he would simultaneously and, at least, implicitly recognize the norms, which he has probably carried over; just as the full meaning of the norms "carried over" reveals itself totally only in a comprehending evaluation of the concrete human reality. Nevertheless, in the foreseeable future man will carry over, presumably, less numerous, less detailed and fewer behavioral norms known in advance to fulfill the work of performing responsibly the many tasks involved in shaping man's world. Rather, there will be, probably, fundamental principles, a deepened insight into human and Christian values and a heightened sense of responsibility.[59]

If moral behavioral norms have their "relative" significance for the human and Christian realization of man's world, a reflection on their absoluteness belongs to the task of a theoretical consideration of questions regarding Christian morality. Only theoretically neat attempts at solution, not apologetical efforts, can assist praxis effectively. Indeed, not only should these attempts at solution include a designation of limits, but also the indication of the limits of the designated limits. In other words, abstract discussion is not enough. There should be further reflection on how the theological analysis and its outcomes affect the daily life, not only of the "experts" but also of the "ordinary Christian." This latter provision is of very great importance, because moral judgments — concerning really contingent realities—do not require metaphysical proof, only a so-called moral certitude; *with this we may be and should be content.*

Notes

1. Blasphemy is not infrequently referred to as an "intrinsically" bad act. It should be noted, however, that blasphemy, if it is really such, means *expressly* a contradiction addressed to God, i.e. the real essence of immorality, therefore—different from any other innerworldly acts. An analogy would be an act directed against the salvation of one's nearest and dearest.

2. Cf. J. Blank, "New Testament Morality and Modern Moral Theology," *Concilium* 5, 3, pp. 6-12. Cf. also A. Grabner-Haider, "Zur Geschichtlichkeit der Moral (Biblische Bemerkungen), *Catholica* 22 (1968), pp. 262-270; W. Kerber, Hermeneutik in der Moraltheologie, *Theol.u. Phil.* 44 (1969) pp. 42-66, esp. pp. 52-60.

3. So also H. Rotter, "Zum Erkenntnisprobleme in der Moraltheologie," in J. B. Lotz (ed.), *Neue Erkenntnisprobleme in Philosophie und Theologie*, Freiburg, 1968, pp. 226-248, on pp. 238ff.

4. *Gaudium et spes*, n. 46.

5. E. Schillebeeckx, "The Magisterium and the World of Politics," *Concilium* 6, 4, pp. 12-21, esp. p. 16.

6. K. Rahner, "Zum Problem der genetischen Manipulation," in *Schriften zur Theologie* VIII, pp. 303ff.

7. M. Flick-Z. Alszeghy, *Metodologia per una teologia dello sviluppo*, Brescia, 1970, pp. 47-68, 91-99.

8. *Loc, cit,; cf. Diskussion zur "politischen Theologie,"* ed. by H. Peukert, Mainz and Munich, 1969.

9. K. Rahner distinguishes between norms and imperatives, *The Dynamic Element in the Church*, London, 1964, pp. 13-41.

10. In his article " 'Politische Theologie' in der Diskussion," *St. d.*

Zt. 184 (1969) 289-308, J. B. Metz rightly saw that political theology can lead to action only by way of political ethics (pp. 293-296). Yet it is not made clear why "political ethics" precisely as an "ethics of change" (in distinction from an "ethics of order") is assigned specially to political *theology* as a "specifically Christian hermeneutics."

11. Cf. R. A. McCormick, "The Teaching Role of the Magisterium and of Theologians," in *Proceedings of the Catholic Theological Society of America* 24 (1969), summarized by the author in *Theol. Studies* 30 (1969), pp. 647f. On the action of the Spirit in the Church, cf. also K. Demmer, "Kirchliches Lehraüt und Naturrecht," *Theol. u. Gl.* 59 (1969) pp. 191-213; B. Schüller, "Bemerkungen zur authentischen Verkündigung des kirchlichen Lehramtes," *Theol. u. Phil.* 42 (1967), pp. 534-551.

12. Cf. for the conditioned, not a-historical, character of the moral pronouncements of the Church, Alf. Auer, "Die Erfahrung der Geschichtlichkeit und die Krise der Moral," *Theol. Qu* 149 (1969), pp. 4-22; C. E. Curran, "Natural Law and the Teaching Authority of the Church," in *Christian Morality Today*, Notre Dame, Indiana, 1966, pp. 79-91; "Absolute Norms and Medical Ethics," in *Absolutes in Moral Theology?* Washington, D.C., 1968, pp. 108-153; esp. 127ff; L. Sartori, "La legge naturale e il magistero cristiano," in L. Rossi (ed.), *La Legge Naturale*, Bologna, 1970, pp. 219-244. According to Curran, changes in the moral teaching of the Church are to be understood as development, not as contradictions of the past: "Natural Law . . . ," p. 87.

13. Cf. E. Chiavacci, "La legge naturale ieri e oggi," in F. Festorazzi *et al.*, *Nuove prospettive di morale coniugale*, Brescia, 1969, pp. 61-91 on p. 75.

14. See the foregoing note.

15. Chiavacci, *loc. cit.*, pp. 65 ff., is of the opinion that Thomas, although he cites many "auctoritates" for other formulations also, basically does not consider detailed norms as natural law; and that this conception derives from other sources. Cf. also D. Mongillo, "L'elemento primario della legge naturale in s. Tommaso," in *La legge naturale* (see note 12), pp. 101-123; D. Capone, "Ritorno a s. Tommaso per una visione personalistica in teologia morale," Riv. di teol. mor. 1 (1969), pp. 85ff.

On the whole problem of change with regard to moral questions, cf. J. Grundel, *Wandelbares und Unwandelbares in der Moraltheologie*, Düsseldorf, 1967, esp. pp. 46-73.

16. Cf. Alf. Auer, (see note 12); I. Lobo, "Geschichtlichkeit und Erneuerung der Moral," *Concilium* 3 (1967), pp. 363-375; A. Grabner-Haider (see note 2); M. Sheehan, "History: The Context of Morality," in W. Dunphy (ed.), *The New Morality, Continuity and Discontinuity*, New York, 1967, pp. 37-54.

17. Cf. Alf. Auer, *loc. cit* (see note 12), p. 12: "Gut ist immer nur, was der Wachstumsbewegung der menschlichen Person und der menschlichen Gemeinschaft dienlich ist. Aber das lässt sich eben nicht

nur aus der Vergangenbeit bestimmen; es bedarf auch der Hinwendung zur Zukunft." J. Fuchs, "On the Theology of Human Progress," in *Human Values and Christian Morality*, Dublin, 1970, pp. 178-203, esp. pp. 185-190. From the moral psychologist's point of view cf. I. Lepp, *La morale nouvelle*, Ital. ed.: *La morale nuova*, Milano, 1967, p. 78.

18. This terminology occurs in the encyclical *Humanae vitae* n. 10.

19. Cf. C. E. Curran, "Absolute Norms . . . " (see note 12), pp. 118f.

20. B. Quelquejeu's phrasing tends in this direction, "Brèves notes à propos de 'Nature et Morale' ": Supplement de *La vie spirituelle*, n. 81 (1967), pp. 278-281; also L. Janssens, *Personne et Société*, Gembloux, 1939, pp. 199-243; *Personalisme en Democratisering*, Brussels, 1957, pp. 93f; H. Mertens, "De persona humana ut norma moralitatis," *Coll. Mechl.* 44 (1969), pp. 526-531.

21. This is not the place for an analysis of the phenomenon of conscience; only *one* aspect—a fundamental one-conscience as judgment, is being considered.

22. Cf. J. Fuchs, "Gibt es eine spezifisch christliche Moral?" *St. d. Zt.* 185 (1970), pp. 99-112; "Human, Humanist and Christian Morality," in *Human Values and Christian Morality*, Dublin, 1970, pp. 112-147; B. Schüller, "Zur theologischen Diskussion über die lex naturalis," *Theol. u. Phil.* 41 (1966), pp. 481-503; "Inwieweit kann die Moraltheologie das Naturrecht entbehren," *Leb. Zeugnis*, Mar. 1965, pp. 41-65; Alf. Auer, "Nach dem Erscheinen der Enzyklika 'Humanae vitae.' Zehn Thesen über die Findung sittlicher Weisungen," *Theol. Qu.* 149 (1969), pp. 75-85, esp. pp. 75-78; F. Böckle, "Was ist das Proprium einer christlichen Ethik?" *Z. f. ev. Ethik* 11 (1967), pp. 148-159; K. Demmer, "Kirchliches Lehramt und Naturrecht" (see note 11), p. 200; R. A. McCormick, "Human Significance and Christian Significance," in G. H. Outka-P. Ramsey (ed.), *Norm and Context in Christian Ethics*, New York, 1968, pp. 233-261; J. McMahon, "What does Christianity Add to Atheistic Humanism?" *Cross Currents* 18 (Spring, 1968), pp. 129-150; J. M. Gustafson, *Christ and the Moral Life*, New York, 1968, esp. Chap VII.

23. J. Fuchs, *Human Values . . . loc. cit.* (see foregoing note), pp. 140-147. In the encyclical *Humanae vitae*, n. 12 states: "leges in ipsa viri et mulieris *natura* inscriptae."

24. R. A. McCormick insists, probably against J. G. Milhaven (see following note), upon far-reaching effects and consequences of actions whose significance is known without experience: "Human Significance . . . ," *loc. cit.* (see note 22), esp. pp. 25f.

25. So, especially J. G. Milhaven, "Toward an Epistemology of Ethics," in *Norm and Context* (see note 22), pp. 219-231; published also in *Theol. Studies* 27 (1966), pp. 228-241.

26. W. Van Der Marck, *Toward a Christian Ethic. Renewal in Moral Theology*, Shannon (Ireland), 1969, advances the thesis (perhaps somewhat onesidedly) that the moral value of actions consists exclusively in their significance for the creation of positive interpersonal relations. With

this can be compared the thesis of J. Fletcher and J. A. T. Robinson regarding love as the sole absolutum; also J. M. Gustafson, "Love Monism, How Does Love Reign?" in J. C. Bennett el al., *Storm over Ethics*, United Church Press, 1967, pp. 26-37.

27. Cf. B. Schüller, "Zur Problematik allgemein verbindlicher ethischer Grundsätze," *Theol. u. Phil.* 45 (1970), pp. 1-23 esp. pp. 3f.

28. On the problem of a morality in a pluralistic society, cf. R. Hoffmann, "Das sittliche Minimum in der pluralen Gesellschaft," *Theol. Qu.* 149 (1969), pp. 23-38; also A. Hertz, "Sitte, Sittlichkeit und Moral in der pluralistischen Gesellschaft," *Neue Ordn.* 18 (1964), pp. 187-196; W. Schöllgen, *Moral–fragwürdig? Uber gesellschaftlichen Pluralismus und Moral*, Hückeswagen, 1967.

29. On the problem "norms of morality and the Christianization of the nations" cf. E. Hillman, "The Development of Christian Marriage Structures," *Concilium* 5, 6, pp. 25-38; "Polygamy Reconsidered," *Concilium* 3, 4, pp. 80-89.

30. H. J. Wallraff, "Die katholische Soziallehre—ein Gefüge von offenen Sätzen," in *Eigentumspolitik, Arbeit und Mitbestimmung*, Cologne, 1968, pp. 9-34.

31. H. Schwandorf, "Zum Standort der katholischen Soziallehre heute," *Gesellschaftspolitische Kommentare* 1970, no. 11, pp. 130-132; continued in no. 12, pp. 144-146.

32. *Loc. cit.*, p. 132.

33. *Loc cit.*, (see note 13), p. 81.

34. N. D. O'Donoghue, "Towards a Theory of Exceptions," *The Irish Theol. Qu.* 35 (1951), pp. 217-232.

35. J. M. Gústafson, "Context Versus Principles: A Misplaced Debate in Christian Ethics," in *New Theology No. 3*, ed. by M. E. Marty and D. G. Peerman, London 1966, on p. 86.

36. P. Ramsey, "The Case of the Curious Exception," in *Norm and Context* (see note 22), pp. 67-135. Cf. also the excellent contribution by D. Evans, "Love, Situation and Rules," *ibid.*, pp. 367-414.

37. D. Hurley, "A New Moral Principle: When Right and Duty Clash," *The Furrow* 17 (1966), pp. 619-622.

38. C. E. Curran "Dialogue with Joseph Fletcher," in *A New Look at Christian Morality*, Notre Dame, Ind., 1968.

39. Thus, e.g., the commentary on *Humanae vitae* presented at the meeting of French Bishops, n. 16: *Docum. Cath.* 65 (1968), pp. 2055-2066.

40. To the cited attempts at solution one might compare N. J. Rigali's critique "The Unity of the Moral Order," *Chicago Studies* 8 (1969), pp. 125-143.

41. Cf. J. De Broglie, "Conflit de devoirs et contraception," *Doctor communis* 22 (1969), pp. 154-175.

42. For this distinction, cf. W. Van der Marck, *Toward a Christian Ethic* . . . (see note 26); P. Knauer, "The Hermeneutic Function of the Principle of Double Effect," *Natural Law Forum*, Vol. 12 (1967), pp.

132-162; B. Schüller, "Zur Problematik . . . " (see note 27).

43. Cf. P. Knauer, *loc. cit.*; the decisive question treated by Knauer is: What is a "proportionate" reason? C. J. Van der Poel, "The Principle of Double Effect," in *Absolutes in Moral Theology?* (see note 12), pp. 186-210. V.d.P. obviously depends on W. van der Marck, *Toward* . . . (see note 26), pp. 65-74, and *Love and Fertility*, London, 1965, pp. 35-63. Cf. also C. E. Curran, in "Absolute Norms in Med. Eth." (see note 12), pp. 112-114.

44. Reference is made to this especially by W. van der Marck, C. van der Poel and P. Knauer (see foregoing note).

45. Cf., e.g., P. Knauer, *loc. cit.*, p. 149: "In other words, a solution which includes both the death of the fetus and the removal of the uterus with consequent sterility is said to be better than that the fetus alone lose its life. Who can understand this?" Similarly, C. E. Curran, "Absolute Norms . . .," *loc. cit.*, p. 112; W. van der Marck, *Love* . . ., *loc. cit.* pp. 49-52.

46. E. Schillebeeckx, *God and Man*, New York, Sheed and Ward, 1969.

47. E. Schillebeeckx, "The Magisterium . . . " (see note 5), pp. 15f.

48. *Loc. cit.*, p. 16.

49. P. Knauer, has a similar statement in "The Hermeneutic Function . . . " (see note 42), p. 138: "What is intrinsically an evil act is brought about when no commensurate reason can justify the permission or causing of the extrinsic evil, that is, any given premoral physical evil or injury." Cf. B. Schüller, "Zur Problematik . . . " (see note 27), p. 4 and 7.

50. Cf. J. A. T. Robinson, *Christian Moral Today*, London, 1964, p. 16.

51. Thomas Aquinas, *Summa Theol.* Ia-IIae 94, 4.

52. So also J. Coventry, "Christian Conscience," *The Heythrop Journal* 7 (1966), pp. 152f; also C.E. Curran, "Absolute Norms in Moral Theology?" *Norm and Context* (see note 22), p. 169.

53. Rightly does J. M. Gustafson insist strongly on this in "Moral Discernment in Christian Life," in *Norm and Context* (see note 22), pp. 17-36.

54. Cf. Gustafson's significant title: "Moral Discernment in Christian Life" (see foregoing note).

55. By analogy with the Pauline conception of law as a "pedagogue" leading to Christ, R. Marlé in his work, "Casuistique et morales modernes de situation," in E. Castelli (ed.). *Tecnica e casuistica*, Rome, 1964, pp. 111-120, speaks of a pedagogical function of moral law with respect to the concrete situation.

56. With Thomas Aquinas, J. de Finance, *Ethica generalis*, 2d ed., Rome, 1963, p. 186, points out that even an aggregation of norms—being abstract—can never produce a concretum.

57. In opposition to many psychoanalysts, I. Lepp, from the standpoint of a moral psychologist, also maintains that the "closed morality"

with its norms and also the "superego" are extremely important for the individual as well as for society, so long as there has not yet occurred a breakthrough to an "open morality" as he calls it: *loc. cit.* (see note 17). pp. 91ff. In his article "Maßstäbe sittlichen Verhaltens. Zur Frage der Normenfindung in der Moraltheologie," *Die Neue Ordnung* 23 (1969), pp. 161-174, on p. 164. A. K. Ruff speaks of norms as having an irreplaceable "exoneration function."

58. Cf. the dynamic contribution of P. Antoine, "Situation présente de la morale," *Le Supplément, no.* 92, 23 (1970), pp. 8-27; also A. Jonsen, "Responsibility . . . " (see note 12); J. M. Gustafson-J. Laney (eds.), "On Being Responsible," *Issues in Personal Ethics,* Harper Forum Books; J. Rief, "Moralverkündigung angesichts der Krise der Moral," *Theol. pr. Qu. 117* (1969), pp. 124-138.

59. For this reason as extreme opponents to this theme, P. Ramsey was obliged to write *"The Case of the Curious Exception,"* in *Norms and Context* (see note 22) and J. Fletcher "What's in a Rule. A Situationist's View," in *Norm and Context* (see note 22), pp. 325-349.

Direct Killing/
Indirect Killing

Bruno Schüller, S.J.

The treatment of the fifth commandment in any textbook of Catholic moral theology would show that the significance attached to the distinction between direct and indirect killing is very fundamental. Direct suicide, for example, would never be justified. Indirect suicide, however, could be morally justified in certain circumstances: for a proportionate good. Exactly the same would apply in the case of killing another man who is innocent. Only if it could be considered as indirect killing could it be allowed or even commanded for a proportionate good. If the killing were direct, it would have to be considered illicit in all circumstances.

One always hesitates a bit before casting doubt upon a distinction which has been accepted unanimously in a long tradition, and which is likewise so practically important. That is to say, there is hardly any reason for doubting that one could make a purely descriptive distinction between direct and indirect killing. But there is reason for doubting that traditional moral theology has been correct in attributing to this distinction the overwhelming significance that it has for establishing ethical norms. It is easy to recall that earlier moral theology distinguished just as sharply and carefully between direct and indirect sterilization. Someone who since then has judged for himself that the traditional moral assessment of methods of contraception could not be maintained no longer considers it necessary to fall back on the earlier distinction. He can, if he so desires, make the distinction, but he makes it purely descriptively. Since he now judges direct sterilization according to the same principle as the indirect method, allowing even direct sterilization for the sake of a proportionate good, he will understandably consider the distinction between the "direct" and the "indirect" to be morally irrelevant. This could come as a surprise, for all at once one can do without that tool which one previously considered indispensable. And from this surprise emerges the following question: How did it happen that in the traditional way of building norms so great a moral importance has been attached to this distinction?

Once one has reached this question, one becomes aware that moral theology has had to use this distinction between direct and indirect acts only in setting norms for a certain few types of acts. Among these are leading another into sin (*scandalum activium*) and cooperation in the moral failure of another (*cooperatio cum peccato alterius*), and also acts such as suicide, killing a man who is innocent, and contraceptive interventions.[1] The question raised before can then be expanded: What do the aforementioned actions have in common? Can a common means of establishing norms be discerned from these common traits? Does this means of establishing norms make it understandable on its own why moral theology has found it necessary to distinguish between direct and indirect acts in a morally meaningful way?

I

"DIRECT" AND "INDIRECT" AS DISTINGUISHING
CHARACTERISTICS
OF INTRINSICALLY EVIL ACTIVITY

Traditional moral theology classifies all the acts mentioned above as intrinsically evil acts, as acts that are morally evil by their very nature. Clearly it does this for different reasons. It is fairly obvious why leading another into sin and cooperating in the sin of another should be considered evil by their very nature. Inasmuch as one leads another into sin or cooperates in his morally evil act, one affirms moral evil, one promotes another's doing it, or one performs it along with another. To affirm evil in this way and to bring it into existence can be nothing else but morally evil. This is immediately apparent. The intrinsic immorality results here simply from the morally evil quality of the intended result of the activity (sin).

Moral theology proceeds differently in establishing that suicide and the use of contraceptives are morally evil by their very nature. The respective consequences, namely the individual's death or the unfruitfulness of the marriage act, are not in themselves morally bad but are rather a non-moral evil. So far it is not readily apparent from the (intended) result of the acts why suicide and the use of contraceptives by their very nature should be considered morally evil. Actually, in these cases moral theology does not establish norms on the basis of the consequences of the acts, but from a special modality of the acts. Suicide is not allowed because it would occur without the required authorization (*ex defectu juris in agente*). The intrinsic immorality in contraceptive birth-control follows from the fact that these means would make the marriage act unfruitful in a way contrary to nature. The process for establishing each of these norms has been different. Keeping that in mind, it can be said that the normative sentence "no one may lead another into sin or participate in the sin of another" is to be considered as analytic, while the sentence "suicide and the use of contraceptives are always forbidden" is the expression of a synthetic judgment. Why is one required to distinguish between direct and indirect in the case of both the analytic prohibitions and the synthetic prohibition?

II

DIRECT AND INDIRECT LEADING ANOTHER INTO SIN

The sense of the normative sentence "one may not lead another into sin" is understood only if one knows exactly what is meant by the word "lead." Moral theology presents an exact account of the meaning of "leading another into sin." This account should not be simply repeated. Rather, we should make an attempt to reconstruct the problem and the considerations by which moral theology was eventually able to give the explanation of this concept as exactly as in fact it does. It is universally agreed that a man is responsible for all foreseen (negative) consequences of a free act.

Working from this understanding of human responsibility, one could try to define "leading another into sin" as follows:

> To lead another into sin means to make a free decision from which one foresees that it will have as a consequence the sin of another man.

In light of such a definition, the prohibition would run as follows:

> You shall not make a decision from which you know that it will have as a consequence the moral transgression of another.

One can see at first glance that if measured by this norm many acts would have to be considered illicit which one would usually consider licit or even morally obligatory. For example, a civil legislator can foresee, on the basis of common experience, that every penal law will lead an indefinite number of people to use the knowledge they have obtained to blackmail people who have committed criminal acts which have not yet come to the knowledge of law enforcement agencies. Thus, according to the principle that one may not make a decision which he knows will result in morally objectionable acts of others, the legislator would not be allowed to pass any penal law. This is obviously absurd. On the other hand, one cannot exclude the negative consequences of an act from the responsibility of the one who performs the act. It would seem that one could not do anything if the negative consequence consisted in a sin, even if the sin is another's. Sin is an absolute non-value, another's sin no less than one's own. Therefore, it must be avoided unconditionally. It is unthinkable that one could justify condoning what is morally evil. But what does the phrase "to avoid sin unconditionally" mean? To wish unconditionally that sin not exist? But such a desire does seem to imply that one is resolved to avoid anything that could in any way help sin to come into existence. But then one would have returned to the prohibition that one knows is not acceptable: i.e., one may not make a free decision, from which one can foresee that it would result in the sin of another.

It is well known that for many years a solution to this dilemma has been sought in trying to distinguish in the free attitude of the moral agent toward moral evil a positive desire, intention, or working for the evil on one hand and an allowance, a toleration, an accepting something as a by-product on the other. The absolute non-value of sin demands only that one not positively desire or intend it in any circumstances or at any price; granting this, it is thoroughly consonant with the absolute non-value of sin that one permit it, if one has a proportionately grave reason.

This way of solving the dilemma remains a bit obscure in spite of its general trustworthiness. Be that as it may, one thing seems to stick fast: the distinction between an intending will and a merely permitting will becomes necessary when one is faced with the free attitude of the moral subject toward moral evil. The absolute non-value of sin—one might eventually conclude (without logical contradiction?)—would entail an absolute avoidance, which as absolute would be incompatible with any willing or intention of sin. But such avoidance of sin would lead to consequences which one could for good reasons consider to be absurd. And the Christian (the theist) has an absolutely cogent reason for so thinking. For such an avoidance of sin is incompatible with the will of the Creator to create a being that is moral and capable of sin. To avoid such a conclusion, one must introduce a tolerating or permitting will, of which we could say: Under certain conditions this attitude of permission is morally justifiable, allowed, or even commanded, even in the face of the absolute non-value of sin.[2]

It should be clear, then, that leading another into sin, as this is understood by moral theology, must be considered morally evil by its very nature. For it takes this term to mean an act which has the sin of another as its foreseen *and* intended consequence.[3] It calls an act so characterized a *direct* (formal) leading another into sin. If an act results in another's sin, but this is merely allowed, according to everything that has been said, this act can under certain conditions be allowed or can even be obligatory. It is called an *indirect* leading another into sin.

III
THE FREE ATTITUDE TOWARD A NON-MORAL EVIL

From the preceding considerations it can be conjectured that a permissive will and an indirect act are required as ethically meaningful categories only for moral evil. As soon as one establishes the proper moral attitude toward non-moral evils such as error, pain, sickness and death, the decisive reason which led to the distinction between intended and allowed, direct and indirect, namely the absoluteness of the disvalue, disappears. If we judge that a disvalue ought to be avoided, removed, or prevented, it seems that a non-absolute, a relative disvalue is such that it is to be avoided only conditionally.

The condition under which a relative disvalue should be avoided is this: if it does not concur competitively with another relative value but one that is to be preferred to it, or with an absolute value. An illness is to be avoided, but not at any price, e.g., not if it means that one would spend all his money for medicines and cures and would therefore reduce his family to most dire straits. One may not inflict pain on another, except in cases in which it is only through inflicting pain that one can gain a certain desired result, e.g., a therapeutic or even a pedagogical result.

In short, insofar as it is necessary for the realization of a preferable value, one is allowed to cause a relative disvalue, and at times one *should* cause it. But in such a case, isn't the causing like an indirect act, so that the disvalue that has been caused would be considered an indirect result, merely allowed and accepted as a side-effect of an act? Even if one wanted to accept that, he would still have to use such linquistic convolutions as would strike most men as downright unusual, if not nonsensical. One would have to say, for example, that a man who would give a spanking to his obstinate child with a purely pedagogical purpose would have not to desire and not to intend that the spanking also cause pain; he would accept this effect of the spanking only as a side-effect. One would be constrained to assert that the health police who force quarantine on someone who has caught typhus intend only to prevent an outbreak of typhus; the police merely allow or regretfully tolerate the isolation of the sick man which they forced on him. In ordinary speech, one would rather say in such cases that the causing of evil would serve a good end, would be a necessary means to this end. But one says of the use of a means that it proceeds from an intending will; that it is direct activity. So, too, the axiom: whoever desires an end desires also the means necessary to reach his end. It is not easy to see why one should abandon this way of speaking. On the contrary, this way of speaking expresses clearly the differing attitude one should have toward moral evil and non-moral evil. For the sake of a correspondingly important good, one may merely permit a moral evil or cause it indirectly. But he may intentionally desire and directly cause the non-moral evil.[4]

Apparently, this is also the interpretation of Catholic moral theology. It considers some acts which result in non-moral evil as morally allowable, without demanding as a condition that the effect or result not be intended. Some examples might help: one may expose the hidden faults of another, may even damage his reputation or honor, in order to ward off a proportionately grave harm from one's own person or from a third party.[5] One may break his word in violation of an oath if this is the only way one has of keeping a "proportionately grave" evil from his person.[6] Not to keep a promise is by any standards an evil for him to whom the promise was made. But "the duty of promised silence ceases if this is justified by the threat of greater personal harms . . . if an innocent person would be condemned . . . if the common good would be damaged."[7] The breaking of a promised secret has the character of a non-moral evil for the one interested in having the secret kept. In none of the cases mentioned do moral theologians see themselves obliged to declare that the negative consequences of the acts may not be intended and that they are ethically acceptable only as permitted. One can consider this as a sort of confirmation for the acceptance of the idea that not a relative disvalue but only the absolute disvalue of sin forces the moral theologians to establish the category of "indirect act."

IV
COOPERATION IN THE MORAL FAILURE OF ANOTHER

Exactly the same problems we encountered in the case of leading another into sin confront us when we consider the classic topic of cooperation in the moral failure of another. That direct (formal) cooperation cannot be allowed follows, as it were, from the definition of direct cooperation: it consists in one's approving the morally objectionable deed of another and thereby sharing in its performance. But what of the case where someone disapproves of the immoral act of another but nonetheless helps in its performance? One could say that the person concerned does not properly disapprove of the evil deed; otherwise he would resist cooperation in the deed at any price. How Catholic moral theology answers this is already well known: it is morally justifiable under certain conditions to accept the sin of another as a negative byproduct of an act.

It can be doubted that one has to fall back upon the category of the non-intended or indirect consequence of an act in order to justify material cooperation. Whether one lends material cooperation or refuses it has no effect on the sin of another but only on the evil consequences of this sin. A case may be useful to illustrate this. The cashier of a bank, threatened by a robber with a drawn pistol, is faced with these alternatives: either let himself be shot, or remove the stacks of bills from the safe and hand them over to the robber. Does his decision have any effect on the sin of the robber? Could he say to himself that a murder is a morally worse crime than a robbery, that therefore he must prevent the murder and allow the robbery, and therefore hand over the money? Actually, in normal circumstances he would have to hand over the money, not because in so doing he lessens the moral guilt of the robber, but because the loss of money which the bank suffers is a lesser non-moral evil than the loss of a human life. The measure of the moral guilt of the robber is determined by his determination to commit even murder if necessary. It is not possible for the decision of the cashier to lessen the degree of this moral guilt, but only the amount of non-moral evil which the robber is determined to commit. Therefore, the cashier in these circumstances may will the loss of the money for the bank for the sake of saving his own life. One need not view the harm to the bank as a negative result of the cashier's choice which he may accept only as a side-effect of his action. No, one may intend a relative disvalue as the consequence of his act, if only it occurs in the service of a proportionately important end.

But however one understands the negative consequences of material cooperation, whether as a moral or as a non-moral evil, it suffices as a response to the question raised at the beginning to establish that traditional moral theology saw itself obliged to fall back upon the category of the indirect effect of an act because it understood that the negative effect of such cooperation consists formally in the sin of another man. The first part of the question posed above has thus been basically resolved. The analytical prohibitions—one may not lead another into nor cooperate in the sin of another—have forced us to make the distinction between the direct and the indirect consequence of an act because the result of the prohibition seems to consist in the absolute disvalue of sin.

V

The Indirect Consequence of an Act in Cases Where Norms Are Established Deontologically

As was already established at the beginning, the intrinsic immorality of leading another into sin and of cooperating in the sin of another derives from the consequences intended in these acts. So far the method of establishing norms has been teleological. It is different in the case of suicide, of killing another person who is innocent, and of using methods of contraception. The consequence of these acts is a non-moral evil, a relative disvalue. Therefore, from the consequence of the act it cannot be immediately shown why these acts are intrinsically evil, why they must be forbidden in all circumstances. That is to say, Catholic moral theology does not use purely teleological means to establish norms for these acts in every case. It ascribes to these acts the further characteristics either of being an arrogation of a right (killing, suicide) or of being contrary to nature (contraception), characteristics which are not immediately derivable from the consequence of the act itself. One may long for his own death, if he does so for an unobjectionable motive. Likewise, one would be allowed to wish that the marriage act remain in fact unfruitful for a proportionate reason. But one may not promote either of these results by his own actions. Exactly this fact, that one may not intend as a result of his act what can be legitimately longed for and desired,

makes it obvious that we are not establishing norms here teleologically. With C. D. Broad, we want to name this unique way of
establishing norms "deontological."[8]

This leads to synthetic prohibitions such as: You may never
kill yourself no matter what results this might have in an individual
instance. Therefore, you may not do this even if you know that you
could thereby save another man from certain death.

In the foregoing there was no question of proving whether this
deontological method of establishing norms is conclusive. However, it is my opinion that it is not conclusive, as I have attempted
to point out in earlier essays.[9] The question here is merely this:
Why does moral theology see itself obliged to distinguish in a
morally relevant way between direct and indirect effects precisely
where there is question of acts for which moral theology uses
deontological norms?

To analyze this question, we will use the deontological prohibition against killing: You shall not kill either yourself or another
innocent man. Once again, the practical importance of this norm
depends on what should be understood by the word "kill" in this
context. One can suggest that by "kill" is understood the knowing
and willful causing of the death of oneself or of another. But this
response merely transfers the problem to the word "cause." From
a teleological standpoint, one would say that this word reaches just
as far as a man's responsibility for his own life and for the life of
another. One could give this definition: To cause the death of a man
is to reach a free decision which one knows will result in his own
death or in the death of another. Furthermore, for killing understood in this way, one could use norms that are mostly deontological on the grounds that man as a creature has no right to make such
a decision. On first glance, this would seem plausible. Anyone who
can decide whether a man lives or perishes seems in fact to be able
to act as Lord of life and death. One would usually look upon this as
an appropriation of divine prerogatives. The prohibition of killing
would then be worded as follows: You may never make a decision
which you know will result in your own death or in the death of
another. However, the consequences of such a prohibition of
killing will appear to most as unacceptable and contradictory.

To prove this it is sufficient to give a couple of typical examples of self-killing and of killing another. Some man, tired of his life, slits his wrists. Another man gives the last place in a lifeboat to someone else. A third man takes over the care of plague victims, realizing that he can soon infect himself and die of it. These cases all give examples of self-killing, according to the accepted definition of the word *"kill"* that is, a decision from which the subject knows that it will have as a consequence his own death. Or some other examples. A doctor performs a craniotomy in order to save the life of a mother. Another doctor refrains from performing the craniotomy, knowing that his decision means the death of the mother. A third doctor performs a hysterectomy on a pregnant woman, which is warranted on medical grounds (carcinoma). In these three cases there would be an example of the killing of an innocent man according to accepted definition of the word "kill." If one wanted to apply the principle here that no one may kill himself or another man who is innocent, then all the actions described in the examples would have to be judged as morally forbidden. But this appears to be thorough nonsense. Especially unacceptable is the notion that it makes no difference whether a doctor prescribes a craniotomy in order to save the life of a mother or refrains from the craniotomy knowing that it will result in the death of the mother, because in either case he makes himself guilty of the forbidden killing of a man.

How can one avoid these unacceptable or contradictory consequences and still retain deontological norms? In any case, we must define more precisely that killing which is generally considered to be unjust; we may not understand by this term every free decision which results in death. That can be done first of all by excluding the free decision for an *omission* with the foreseen result of death from illegal killing. In this way the classic distinction between killing and letting die took form. It is only killing that is considered to be generally unjustifiable, not letting die. Certainly a person must be morally responsible for the decision which he makes to let another die, but basically this decision admits of a moral justification. If it takes place for a proportionate reason (*propter rationem proportionate gravem*), it is permissible or even obligatory. Hence we have the attitude, rather generally shared, that the doctor could not be obliged to prolong the life of an unhealthy sick person at any price and by all available means.

These discussions are familiar and seem to be self-evident. Precisely for this reason it is necessary to be aware of two things: (1) to do and to allow may have the same result: the death of a person; nonetheless—judged morally—they are very different. The ethical weight is shifted from either the free decision on one hand or from the value of a human life on the other to a middle position: to the different ways a man has to achieve definite results. There is something strange about this: that is, one would think that the only crucial matter is whether the life of a man is saved or lost. It makes no ethically relevant difference whether that happens through doing something or through "allowing" something to happen. (2) Since "allowing to die" is excluded from the category of unjustified killing, one creates the possibility of using teleological norms for it. Death, as a non-moral evil, is now seen in its relationship to another concurring evil. This is proved by the fact that if death is seen as the lesser evil, then it is morally permissible, if not obligatory, to omit everything which could delay or prevent death. It is important to establish this. The deontological prohibition of killing becomes more plausible precisely because "allowing to die" is removed from the prohibited category and is submitted to a teleological norm.

It could still be asked whether it is morally permissible to intend the death of a man as the consequence of a freely willed omission. The etymological affinity of the words "omit" and "permit" could lead to the assumption that a death which results from an omission is a morally responsible act only as a permitted death, as a not-intended death. But this assumption does not prove right. Only if the death of a man were an absolute evil in the sense of moral evil is it necessary to appeal to the notion of permission (*voluntarium indirectum*) to establish its moral licitness.

Catholic moral theology has excluded not only "permitting to die" from those killings controlled by deontological norms. Beyond that, even among the *acts* which result in death it has undertaken an exceptionally subtle distinction. It may happen that some act has an immediate second effect besides the death of a man, e.g. the healing of another man from a threatening disease. There is a question here of something like a double action, if we allow an act to be specified by its consequences: an act which has the character of a therapeutic operation and also the character of a killing. As a therapeutic operation, the norms for the act would be established teleologically in the view of moral theology, and in the majority of cases it would be morally permissible or even obligatory. As an act of killing, however, it must be considered morally evil, it seems, *ex defectu juris in agente*. Here a question occurs: May one resolve to perform such an act, which one could look upon as morally permissible and forbidden at the same time? Moral theology concludes that one may perform such an act, but under the condition that one intends only the therapeutic effect and merely permits the death. Thus such a killing—called "indirect"—would not fall under the prohibition that admits of no exception, but would be morally justifiable for a proportionate reason.

Again, it is apparent that it is the free attitude toward the moral evil that leads to the distinction between the direct and the indirect act. If moral theology were to consider the killing of an innocent person not as an act that is intrinsically evil, if it would see in this act the negation of a value which, though fundamental, is still a non-moral evil and would attempt to establish norms from this starting point, then it would not have to carry through this distinction. We have a striking proof of this in the different ways and means that moral theologians use to explain killing in self-defense. They all consider such a killing to be morally justified. But—and this is noteworthy—some consider it morally justifiable because in their opinion such killing is *indirect*; others consider even a direct killing in the situation of self-defense to be allowed. How is this explained? By a different wording of the deontological prohibition of killing. Some propose the idea that the individual as a private person may not at any time kill anyone, not even an unjust aggressor.[10] Consequently, for them, killing in self-defense can be morally justified only if it can be understood as indirect killing. The others restrict the deontological prohibition to the killing of an innocent man,[11] but the unjust aggressor is *ex definitione not innocent*.[12] Thus killing him does not fall under the deontological prohibition. Hence there is no need to explain the killing of an unjust aggressor as an indirect killing.

Finally, the usual understanding of the teaching of the act with a double effect is a proof for the fact that it is the attitude toward moral evil that made the category of indirect effect necessary. In this teaching, the negative consequence of the act is seen either as a moral evil in itself, or at least as intended.[13] This can be seen most clearly from the ever present demand that both the good and the bad effects must proceed with equal immediacy from the act. If the good result proceeds from the bad, then the act would be forbidden, since a good end does not justify a bad means. Bad means can mean only a morally bad act. Since as often as a non-moral evil may be intended as the effect of an act, it is ethically irrelevant whether the good effect appears at the same time or only later, if only it is proportionate to the evil. For example, in the case of vaccination, the positive effect of immunization follows only from a negative act, an artificially induced infection. No moral theologian will object that vaccination must not be allowed because the good end does not justify the bad means. From this it can be taken as established that one has to fall back on the category of indirect effect only where the effect of an act in itself (as with the sin of another) or at least the intending of the consequence of an act (death of an innocent) is to be considered as morally evil.

The distinction between direct and indirect relates to the prohibition of killing in a way similar to the distinction between acting and allowing. If indirect killing is exempted from the deontological prohibition, this prohibition's sphere of application is reduced a few degrees, and so it becomes more plausible. Indirect killing comes to be covered by teleological norms, that is to say, it is justified by a proportionate good. And so it is that a deontological establishment of norms becomes acceptable to the extent that it lets itself be restricted in favor of a teleological establishment of norms.

It should be mentioned only very briefly that moral theology judges contraceptive measures in exactly the same way. The marriage act can be unfruitful because one has decided for himself to omit something that would make it fruitful, e.g. a medical treatment. The moral norms in the case of this decision for an omission are established teleologically. The same is true of an act that is indirectly contraceptive. It is only for the direct use of contraceptive measures that norms are established deontologically, i.e., considered to be "contrary to nature." Presented schematically, it appears:

Decision	Omission		Teleological
to	Act	Indirectly	Teleological
		Directly	Deontological

One short glance at this outline is enough for one to recognize that if it be demonstrated that the deontological method of establishing norms for killing and for birth control cannot be maintained and should therefore be replaced with the teleological method of establishing norms, then it would be useless to continue to distinguish as before among omission, indirect act, and direct act. For whether it is a question of omission or action, in both cases the principles of teleological norms would have to be used. If one judges that contraception cannot be proscribed because of its supposed "contrary-to-natureness," one is abandoning for this instance deontological norms. This is the reason why one is able to get along very well without that tool which the teaching on the act with a double effect places in one's hand.

Even if one regards the deontological method of establishing norms for killing and birth control as erroneous, one cannot help but admire the ingenuity which led to the development of the teaching on the act with a double effect, an ingenuity surely in the service of an excellent purpose, as indeed any theologian must admit. The teaching on the act with a double effect restricts the scope of the deontological norm in favor of a teleological norm, as far as this is at all possible. But even this cannot prevent the deontological method of establishing norms from betraying its highly questionable character in certain situations. In their book, *Respect for Persons*, R. S. Downie and Elizabeth Telfer call attention to this questionable character:

> If the deontologist is correct, it is theoretically possible that the performance of a duty could on a given occasion make the world a worse place than it would have been if the duty had not been performed. It might be argued that the very fact that a

duty has been performed must mean that some good consequences will be brought about. But even if we grant that the
mere fact of duty-performance is itself good, it still may be the
case that the total state of the world after the duty-
performance is worse than it would have been if the duty had
not been performed. And if this is a consequence of the deontologist's interpretation of moral rules his interpretation must
be rejected as a bad case of rule-worship.[14]

A moral theologian could prove through actual examples the
things that Downie and Telfer mention as theoretical possibilities.
B. Häring takes the case of a doctor who had to operate on a
woman in the fourth month of pregnancy for an adnexal tumor.[15]
Because of complications, the doctor found himself faced finally
with the following alternatives: either the removal of the uterus
together with the fetus, or the removal of the fetus while saving the
uterus. He decided in favor of the second alternative. In this way
the woman, who had not as yet had any children, was still able to
conceive and give birth. Later the doctor, as he himself reports,
was told by a moral theologian that although the doctor had acted
in good faith, objectively speaking, he had acted wrongly. He
"would have been allowed to remove the bleeding uterus with the
pregnancy, but not to interrupt the pregnancy and thereby save the
uterus. The first would be an abortion for the sake of saving the
mother, which is not allowed; but the other would be a permissible
prima intentio, as in the case of cancer of a pregnant uterus. So
the consideration that he would be saving the woman's fertility
and thereby would possibly be saving the marriage in certain
circumstances, would play no decisive role." Häring himself considers that the moral theologian in this case illustrates what Catholic casuistry ought not to be: "The application of principles of
moral theology may not be confused with the manipulation of a
slide rule. The act is much rather to be viewed in its entirety."
With this comment Häring shows moral common sense, but he
shows also that he has not grasped the problematic revealed by
the report of the doctor—the problematic of deontological
norms.
As far as a non-medical person can understand the operation

performed by the doctor, this must actually be considered as a direct killing to save the life of the mother. He who is concerned, confused, or terrified by this cannot extricate himself from the affair by asserting that in this case the ethical principles which he himself espouses have to be used not as principles but merely as rules of thumb. There are only two possibilities left open to him: either to stand squarely by the consequences of his principles, or to become critical of them and to question whether there is not something wrong with them. In saying this, anyone who considers any direct killing of an innocent to be intrinsically evil says also that any such killing would have to be avoided in individual cases, no matter what the consequences. The permanent inability of a woman to bear children and the childlessness of a marriage are not the worst (non-moral) evils which can come from one's refusal on the grounds of his duty to directly kill another. To use deontological norms for killing *eo ipso* means that there can be situations in which adherence to one's duty results in a greater measure of non-moral evil than acting against one's duty.

One may not incorrectly overvalue this last assertion. It characterizes deontological norms, but does not disprove them. A deontologist can answer pointedly that the moral value of acting according to one's duty should be valued unconditionally higher in every case than any non-moral evil which can result from acting according to one's duty. No theologian can contradict him in this, as long as he recognizes the unconditionality of moral value. One can refute deontological norms only if one can show that the reasons brought forward to validate them are not sound, for example, if one could establish that the so-called "opposition to nature" of using contraceptives cannot be ethically normative. Even the norm (grounded purely teleologically), "One may not lead another into sin," must obviously be considered with the condition "whatever the consequences may be." These consequences could be terrible; for this norm also affirms that "one may not try to get another to act against his *erroneous* conscience." But this norm is analytically evident; its justification comes only from the meaning of the words used in it.

The conclusion of the preceding analyses can be summarized as follows:

    1. If one establishes norms exclusively on teleological

grounds, then the distinction between a direct and indirect act is ethically meaningful if, and only if, the consequence of the act is in itself morally evil. This holds true certainly in the case of leading another into sin.

2. If one establishes norms partly on teleological grounds, partly on deontological, one can still use the distinction in the case of acts for which norms are established deontologically. By so doing, one has the great advantage of being able to avoid many seemingly unsupportable consequences of this way of establishing norms.

Notes

1. O. Lottin, *Morale Fondamentale* (Tournai 1954) 286ff. names as the major cases of this: "scandal direct et scandale indirect, et cooperation au mal . . . homicide direct et homicide indirect . . . la luxure volontaire en soi et dans sa cause."

2. Cf. J. de Vries, "Theodizee," in W. Brugger (ed.), *Philosophisches Wörterbuch* (Freiburg[13] 1967) 381: God can "not positively will" the morally evil. . . . But it is indeed possible that God allows evil, i.e., does not prevent it, even though he foresees it and has the power to prevent it." J. B. Schuster, in W. Brugger, *op cit.* 49, "Why does holy God, who can never will, cause, or sanction evil, allow evil; or why does he not prevent the beings which he created from misusing their freedom unto evil? This permission, which includes no positive sanctioning and responsibility for evil, is motivated by compensating values." The terminology used is not always the same. Cf. J. Hellin, *Theodicea* (Matriti[2] 1957) 337: "Mala autem moralia Deus non vult per se nec per accidens; nam ob suam sanctitatem non vult peccata directe, nec vult ea indirecte (!) ut media ad fines bonos obtinendos." F. Diekamp, *Kath. Dogmatik*, Bd. 1 (Münster 11 1949) 216: "Reason validates the notion that there is no good that outweighs the greatness of moral evil . . . Therefore God cannot will sin, he can merely allow it." Cf. also J. M. Dalmau, "De Deo Uno et Trino" in *Sacrae Theologiae Summa*, Vol. II (Matriti 1955) 177.

3. The question need not be explored here in what sense the moral failure of another can be called the result of my act. On this cf. A. Vermeersch, *Theologia Moralis*, T. 1 (Romae 1947) 108.

4. J. de Vries, *op cit*: "God can not only allow physical evil, but he can positively cause it as a means to reach a higher goal." W. Brugger, *Theologia Naturalis* (Pullach 1959) 412, distinguishes as follows: to intend something as a goal (in se et propter se); to intend something as a means to a goal (in se, non propter se); to allow something, neither to intend it as a

goal nor as a means, but also not to prevent it, although one be in a position to do so. He continues: an evil as such, whether a moral evil or a non-moral evil, one could never intend as a goal in itself, but only as a means or, not intending, simply allow it. It would be morally justified to intend a non-moral evil and to allow a moral evil, when this happens for the sake of a "bonum praevalens." In my opinion, one should also understand in this connection under the term "means" that non-moral evil that is necessarily entailed in an intended goal, even if it is only a side-effect of that goal. The decisive factor might be that the intended goal can be reached only if one pays a price for it. Whether the price must be paid before reaching the goal or after makes no morally significant difference.

5. Mausback-Ermecke, *Kath. Moraltheologie*, Bd. 3 (Münster[10] 1961) 582.

6. O. Schilling, *Handbuch der Moraltheologie*, Bd. 3 (Stuttgart 1957) 70.

7. O. Schilling, *op. cit.* 61.

8. *Five Types of Ethical Theory* (London[9] 1967) 206: "Deontological theories hold that there are ethical propositions of the form: 'Such and such a kind of action would always be right (or wrong) in such and such circumstances, no matter what its consequences might be.' "

9. Cf. B. Schüller, "Zur Problematik allgemein verbindlicher ethischer Grundsätze," in ThPh 45 (1970) 1-23: and "Typen ethischer Argumentation in der katholischen Moraltheologie," in ThPh 45 (1970) 526-550.

10. So, it seems, Thomas, S. Th. II—II q 64 a 7 c: "occidere hominem non licet, nisi publica auctoritate propter bonum commune . . . illicitum est quod homo intendat occidere hominem, ut seipsum defendat, nisi ei qui habet publicam auctoritatem." Very significantly, H. Merkelback, *Theologia Moralis*, Bd. 2 (Brugis[11] 1962) 357: "Directa (occisio) non est iusta, nisi ex auctoritate publica, erga malefactores, et erga hostes nocentes in bello iusto, non autem erga innocentes, nec mere privatis (!); licita tamen esse potest occisio indirecta etiam mere privatis, iustae defensionis vel conservationis causa."

11. So, among others, M. Zalba, *Theologia Moralis*, Bd. 2 (Matriti 1953) 275: "occisio vel mutilatio innocentis (!) directa est semper grave peccatum."

12. The expression "not innocent" is in this context merely a synonym for "unjust," concerning which moral theology is known to be of the view that an attack justifies self-defense if it is unjust only objectively, though it may be subjectively innocent. This view is especially vulnerable and somewhat disquieting if one uses the following saying as an argument: right need not soften unright. But that is not particularly germane here.

13. A. Vermeersch, *Theologia Moralis*, Bd. 1 (Romae[4] 1947) 105, clarifies the negative result of an act: "Effectus malus, i.e., talem hoc loco vocamus qui nec intendi nec eligi honeste posset." According to this, one must accept that "malus" here means simply "morally evil." But the

consequence of an act judged by deontological norms is not evil in itself, but only as the intended consequence of an act. From this it follows that not only evil such as death and sterility count as "effectus mali," but even the pollutio which should hardly be qualified as evil. It counts as "effectus malus" because it is contrary to nature and therefore it is morally evil to intend it as a consequence of one's actions.

14. R. S. Downie and Elizabeth Telfer, *Respect for Persons* (London 2 1970) 34; so also G. E. Moore, Ethics (London[1] 1912, Oxford Paperback 2 1966) 93.

15. B. Häring, *Das Gesetz Christi*, Bd. 3 (Freiburg[8] 1967) 126.

16. On the same, cf. B. Schüller, "Zur Rede von der radikalen sittlichen Forderung," in ThPh 46 (1971) 321-341, esp. 327ff. As to the moral relevance of the distinction between killing and letting die, cf. my essay "Various Types of Grounding for Ethical Norms" later in this volume.

Problems on Norms Raised by Ethical Borderline Situations: Beginnings of a Solution in Thomas Aquinas and Bonaventure

Franz Scholz

Ethics can be defined as "normative anthropology." That means that moral theology in its search for concrete (secondary) norms must consider the verified results of the human sciences. Humans are historical beings, and moral theology must therefore listen to the questions and problems of contemporary people and at the same time preserve continuity with Church tradition. What beginnings of a solution to current contemporary problems of norms do we find in Thomas Aquinas and Bonaventure, two important teachers of Christendom who died just over 700 years ago?

I
QUESTIONS CURRENT TODAY

1. In the debate over the revision of Par. 218 of the West German Penal Code the churches properly emphasized the non-disposability and the value of every human life. Yet the ethicist can question whether this is an absolute inviolability in the sense that there can never under any circumstance be moral justification for interfering directly in unborn life. This is not to question the validity of the norm as such, but whether it is valid without

exception.[1] In the discussion of the German penal law reform no one, including the Church, wished to include the case involving grave medical indications in the list of punishable misdemeanors, but ethically the position of the Catholic Church in this borderline case was unclear. Even earlier some uncertainty could be seen; if in such cases those concerned (mothers, physicians, etc.) were in good—even though erroneous—faith, they were not to be imprudently disturbed.

Of the four bills aimed at the reform of Par. 218, the one closest to the traditional Catholic understanding[2] also excepted direct interference based on medical indications from penal law. The question then arose whether this legally permitted interference does not nevertheless remain just as objectionable morally as one based on ethical, eugenic, or social indications. In the discussion of this question the unambiguous official pronouncements of the Church of an earlier day proved to have little staying power.[3] Instead, a careful reorientation appeared during the course of the discussion. The position taken jointly by the German Evangelical and Catholic Churches in 1970 reads: " . . . from the moral viewpoint an offense against the principle of the inviolability of developing life is acceptable only in the case of a collision with higher or at least equal legal goods and of a resultant conflict of conscience and duty."[4] Thus what had previously been the official Catholic position became once again a *quaestio disputata*.[5]

The Bishop of Augsburg, J. Stimpfle, spoke out clearly on the matter: "Whoever commits an abortion, unless to save the life of the mother, sins seriously and lays on his conscience the death of a human life."[6] To put it theologically, the previous proclaimed norm remains valid and remains law, but at least in the case mentioned an exception is deemed possible. Then the rule no longer stands as exceptionless. A principle, from a logical perspective, is made a "rule of thumb" for usual cases. In fact, we are standing in the midst of a realignment of borders, in which we are experiencing a kind of change of norms. Is this process legitimate? How does it agree with the traditional concept of the "intrinsically evil act," a category which included the direct killing of the innocent?[7]

2. A second example of the admission of exceptions to norms previously declared valid without exception is the prohibition of any direct interference in organs and bodily functions not covered by the so-called "principle of totality." The donation of organs for life-saving transplantation, along with all other interventions not serving the donating organism itself, seemed sinful presumptions against God. Dominican theologian Bender, for example, taught in 1954 that any removal of tissue for transplantation was always forbidden.[8] In 1961 G. Ermecke still held that every intervention not covered by the principle of totality, i.e. by being of service to the donor himself, is an "improper, impossible attempt at disposing of one's own property." Partial self-mutilation is not permissible and cannot be justified by any motive.[9] A short time later the Franciscan Simeoni declared that disposing of organs for this purpose is certainly permitted.[10] The Dutch theologian Pethegen[11] taught the same. B. Häring also tended in this direction already in 1961: "One may therefore not obstruct the way of medicine by an axiomatic No to organ-transplantation."[12]

Here too we see the tendency to transcend an exception-lessly valid ban. Many sensed correctly that someone offering one of his two healthy kidneys to another person otherwise doomed to death could call upon the words of the Lord: "A greater love has no one than that he lay down his life for his friends" (Jn. 15:13). They did not agree with moral theology that this is a question of a sinful offense against the entire body, but rather held that this "price" could be "paid" in the name of Christ for the neighbor. That led to the abrogation of the consistent validity of the hitherto advocated principle that direct intervention can be justified *only* by the principle of totality.

3. A further example illuminates the situation. The principle that no one may take his own life directly or permit it to be taken was held for centuries. Now, however, there is also a crisis over this principle. B. Häring, for example, asks: "Is it permitted for spies to commit suicide?" He declares: The fifth commandment forbids only autocratic and arbitrary assaults on life, not every direct killing. If, in the spy's opinion, in his special situation it is morally certain that he can fulfill his charge to serve his country

and the cause of freedom only by, in conformity with a received command, taking his own life, that is, in Häring's opinion, not suicide. The point can be argued. The spy is not acting autocratically, but in fact fulfilling a command. The brutality of modern dictators who extort every fact by torture must be considered. If it is not an absolutely necessary sacrifice in the service of an indisputably good thing, then it is indeed a matter of autocracy and thus of suicide, which can never be justified.[13]

In the above cases we see a tendency to deviate from the claim to exceptionless validity. The examples can be multiplied. Those mentioned serve only as matter for that type of prohibition which in traditional thought *never* admits of exceptions. We now ask: Is the claim of consistent validity for these prohibitions— *Never* kill an innocent person directly! *Never* give false witness! *Never* practice contraception!—really well-founded or can one justifiably question their consistent validity and admit of exceptions? We here face a very real current question of principle and wish to investigate what beginnings toward a solution are to be found in Thomas Aquinas and Bonaventure.[14]

II
WHAT DOES THOMAS AQUINAS SAY ON THIS THEME?

1. *The natural moral law is a creation of human reason*, something produced by reason itself.[15] This reason is actively at work in the genesis of the natural moral law. It is not only passively determined by the lower natural structures, drives, and similar things, but even more it is itself actively engaged in "constituting." For Thomas in any case the moral natural law is a product, something which human *ratio* in the light of the *ordo rationis*—not arbitrarily—grasps and actively constitutes, not simply receives passively. Inferior "levels," which humans share with other animals, cannot be declared "natural" in reference to their biological legitimacy and finality without a reflective judgment of reason. That is decisive: conformity to physical law is still not in itself a *moral* precept. It becomes morally binding law only through a considered judgment of the reason. Reason is

creaturely; it apprehends only from a perspective, determined by time and situation; it penetrates ever more deeply.

2. *Reason is therefore the principle of the properly human act and omission.* If human conduct corresponds to the order of reason, it is morally good; if not, it is morally evil. To categorize an act ethically one must confront it with the challenge of reason.[16] This is the first yardstick of all moral conduct. "Whatever is contrary to reason is against human nature."[17] Human acts and omissions are considered good and evil on the basis of a comparison with reason.[18] To act according to reason is the first principle, which must be realized always and without exception in the various decisions of life,[19] just as the innumerable concrete individual precepts must be reduced to this basic principle. All individual acts must therefore be measured by the criterion of reason; they must thus also be able to be made intelligible to reason. Reason must therefore inquire behind the theories presented for elucidation—in this case about the existence of intrinsically evil acts in the sphere of relative values. In the establishing of concrete natural morality it is not legitimate to invoke revelation as though it could replace rational insight. Reason also demands a critical differentiation of precepts which lay claim to "naturalness" and thus to consistent validity as well. Thomas strongly advocated this differentiation, later neglected by the Neo-Scholastics.

3. *There are consistently valid natural laws and those required only "in general."* Reason thus constitutes the moral natural law. For the sake of clarity, the double sense in which Thomas speaks of "natural law" should be explained first.

(a) In the *most narrow* and *proper* sense it comprises, formally considered, the immediately intelligible principles of the practical reason and all resultant insights which obtrude *necessarily*, i.e. without special reflection.[20] In this Thomas is following William of Auxerre, who first defined natural law in the strict sense as that which natural reason commands without any, or at least without considerable, deliberation.[21] So, for example, the statement "one must act according to reason"[22] is immediately recognized as a universal, consistently valid principle. Corresponding to that which is naturally recognized by the intellect, there is that which is naturally sought by the appetites, and "only that *which thus pertains to the nature of reason and will*" is for Thomas in a narrow and proper sense "given by nature" or "according to nature."[23] In reference to such immediately intelligible first principles (Good must be done, evil is to be avoided! One must act in accord with reason! Justice should prevail!) the natural moral law possessed *exceptionless* binding force.[24] So considered, it has the stability which Thomas ascribes to the original intention of the lawgiver.[25] Anyone who thinks differently is a relativist.

(b) But in a wider, improper and even problematic sense Thomas occasionally describes conclusions arising in concrete applications as natural law, although these imperatives (e.g. You should not directly kill the innocent!) can claim neither uniformity nor consistent validity. These *deductions* become more inaccurate as more details are included.[26]

In the *Commentary on the Sentences*,[27] Thomas accordingly distinguishes two kinds of laws. One includes those which are immediately evident to reason, that is, those which themselves comprise the original intent of the lawgiver. Such abstract precepts of the "principle" type are always conclusive and are valid without exception; they belong to the natural moral law in the strict sense.[28] *Alongside* these, however, there is another type of precepts. These likewise demand consideration "in themselves" (*secundum id quod sunt*), but in a collision with other values their limitations may be revealed. Thomas compares them with laws of nature that govern frequently but not without exception and which themselves depend on immutable, higher laws.

This second kind of laws—the derived, concrete precepts—holds therefore only conditionally: as long as in such a collision the original intent of the lawgiver does not justify, or even demand, the causation of physical evil in the service of a higher value.[29] Thomas presents the following example: Justice customarily demands the return of a deposited pledge. This uncontested claim however retreats when faced by the opposing interest of society if someone who has gone crazy demands his sword back. Reason, which is obligated to immutable rights, always likewise demands a realization appropriate to the changing situation, a realization whose concrete form can be ascertained only in the light of careful consideration by the intellect. Original justice demands such flexibility. For precisely for the sake of protecting original justice the deposited weapon in the above case may *not* be returned. Thomas appeals to Aristotle: "That which always is, is the ground and source of that which is often and seldom. . . . Therefore the latter is referred to the former."[30] That means that the same unchanging original justice, precisely in order to prevail in the vicissitudes of life, demands forms of concrete actualization which accommodate themselves to it, whether it be the return of the pledge or the refusal.

Here we find the same underlying idea as in the *Summa Theologica*. Only the most abstract, formal, immediately obtruding insights are consistently valid. The derivatives have still only the quality of a rule of thumb, which can no longer take into account all situations. Clarity would be served if the natural moral law as a consistently valid principle were also terminologically delimited to the immediately evident original principles and the inferences made without reflection. It ought to remain clear to what extent we are dealing with consistently valid precepts, natural law in the narrowest sense, and where the simple rule of thumb begins.

The degree of derivation must therefore be noted. With Thomas we hold unconditionally that the highest principles— such as "Good should be actualized!" "The will of God must always be fulfilled!" "Reason (illuminated by faith) should prevail!"—are valid without qualification and accordingly without exception. Equally obligatory are the applications of these original principles to the unchanging human challenges, such as "Practice self-control!" "Treat your neighbor as one who has dignity of himself and may never be degraded to a means for your purposes!" "Be helpful, truthful, loyal and brave, etc.!" In contrast to moral positivism, Thomas emphasizes the immutability and consistent validity of the above *basic tendencies* of human acts and omissions. Seen from a Christian perspective, discipline, an orientation to a Thou with the demands included therein, belongs to the very essence of the human.

The question becomes complicated and also controversial at

the point at which the derivative (here in the third degree) moves into the immense field of concrete realizations. Just as the norms of tendency and disposition (first and second derivatives) are consistently valid, so the contents of the *concrete* imperatives, especially the prohibitions, are conditional and limited. We ask whether it is really possible to say: "The direct killing of an innocent person is never permitted!" "Even if the world comes to an end, there is no reason for speaking an untruth!" "Every direct interference in organs, members and functions not covered by the principle of totality is an outrage against God's supreme authority!" Or are there special situations in which the claim of such concrete applied norms to consistent validity is no longer tenable?

As the claim to consistent validity is broadened, then, the *inflexible invariability* of the concrete actualization necessarily enters into the area of applications, which according to Thomas are flexible and claim validity only for usual cases. The following will attempt to show that Thomas and Bonaventure treat even the precepts of the second table (fifth, sixth and seventh commandments) as applications which admit, even though seldom, of exceptions.

4. *Even the precepts of the decalogue are dispensable.*

(a) *The problem.*

Peter Lombard had already asked "Are the precepts of the decalogue dispensable?" in connection with the exceptions that are reported in the Old Testament[31]: Abraham's readiness to sacrifice his son Isaac at God's directive,[32] God's command to the Israelites to borrow gold and silver vessels from their neighbors and to take them along in the exodus,[33] and the demand that the prophet Hosea contract a marriage with a harlot.[34] The difficulty consists in that God, one assumes, has in enjoining exceptions himself brushed aside the exceptionlessly valid natural law which he himself had given. The essential properties of the natural moral law worked out in the Middle Ages, especially by Thomas[35]—immutability, unity, and consistent validity—would thus be put in question by God himself. That seems a challenge. We wish to see how Aquinas copes with it. The question provoking and moving us is simply: Can God dispense from the moral natural law as it is clearly defined in the second table of the decalogue?[36]

(b) *The presupposition of any possibility of exception or dispensation: tension between the letter and the sense.*

Thomas on the above question[37] first investigates the presuppositions of *any* possibility of dispensation at all. Dispensation is in principle impossible if a precept reproduces the original intent of the lawgiver (thus, that one must act reasonably, that justice must prevail, that the common weal is to be preserved). There can never be any dispensing from such basic demands of original justice which contain the unmediated original intent of the lawgiver. Dispensations and exceptions are therefore in these cases impossible in principle. For God can never contradict himself. He remains faithful to himself (2 Tim. 2:13). If, however, the intent of the lawgiver (God) is directed always at the universal common weal, the common good is guaranteed by original justice. Such laws articulating the original intent of the lawgiver thus by definition tolerate no dispensation.

A possibility for exceptions in the way of exemptions opens up, then, only if—corresponding exactly to the teaching on epikeia—a conflict exists between the formulated *letter* of the law and the intended *sense* of the precept (the intent of the lawgiver). Thus Thomas considers the case in which the letter of a precept (*verbum legis*) does not catch the divine intent (*intentio legislatoris*). The discovery that such tensions between the original meaning and the written formulation of a positive precept are possible is no surprise. Upon this Thomas builds his doctrine of economy, *epikeia* (the claim of the conscience against legal formulations).[38] What is astounding for today's reader is that Thomas applies the reflections which are completely plausible in reference to positive-human laws to the precepts of the second table as well in order to establish a possibility of dispensation even from the precepts of the decalogue, usually looked upon as firm. The *corpus articuli*, of course, is silent on this intended conclusion. In the *Sed contra*, as well as at the end of the corpus, he writes as though the tension presented above did not exist for the second table, with the result that the basic presupposition for dispensation disappears. He explains, "The precepts of the decalogue contain the original intents of God and are therefore completely indispensable!" This global assertion found adherents and is also customarily considered the authentic Thomist teaching.[39] Yet it is not Aquinas' final word. The response to the third objection opens for the first time a perspective far exceeding the previous line of thought, a perspective in which the distinction between letter and meaning of laws developed earlier yields a positive result.

(c) *The tension between letter and meaning also prevails in the second table.*

The fifth commandment is the uncontested classic example. The letter of this commandment does forbid, it is objected, the destruction of human life. In war, however, and in carrying out the death sentence, human beings "dispense" from this prohibition. How, in this case, can the assertion in the *caput articuli* that the decalogue is consistently valid be maintained in reference to the fifth commandment? In putting together his argument Thomas goes into the matter more closely. The fifth commandment—he makes the distinction—does not simply forbid the destruction of human life. It was never intended to be consistently valid. God's intent is directed only at prohibiting the *morally improper* destruction of life[40] which alone opposes original justice. "The commandment thus contains the actually intended demand of original justice."[41] The usual wording is thus not pointed enough; it does not hit God's intent precisely enough. It makes claims which are not covered by God's intent. The precept "Thou shalt not kill" clearly admits a tension between its formulation and the really intended meaning—with all the inferences for possible exceptions.

The *letter* of the fifth commandment obviously forbids the physical destruction of human life in general because average cases (*ut in pluribus*) dominate the formulating thought process. Here, however, the precise meaning of the commandment, which applies only to *unjust* killing, or murder, is stretched too far. God's actual precept is not directed against every destruction of human life, as the letter would purport, but only against killing against God and humanity—that is, against murder. Therefore the wording of the fifth commandment is only *conditionally* valid, specifically only for cases in which the destruction of human life is contrary to the original intent of God ("Thou shalt not kill unjustly, i.e. thou shalt not murder!"). Only in this sense, not expressed in the wording, is the precept consistently valid.

The *letter* thus logically has only the quality of a rule of thumb for average cases, and not of a consistently valid principle. Because the rule of thumb by its nature suffers from fuzziness, exceptions in those situations not embraced by it are possible from the beginning. In distinguishing objectively between "to kill" and "to murder" (letter and meaning) Thomas's distinction between the factual concept (to kill) and anti-value-laden concept (to murder) aids in clarification. The misunderstanding results from the equation of fact and anti-value-laden concepts (to kill = to murder). The solution of the problem is therefore begun by distinguishing the two concepts. Only the *meaning* of the law, the formally understood prohibition which forbids murder (the intent of the lawgiver) is indispensable, because it infringes on original justice. The injustice which the fifth commandment is to prevent thus does not adhere to the physical deed as such but to the "circumstance" of injustice which supervenes and is thus separable from the physical deed. From the merely empirical knowledge of a "destruction of human life" alone, it cannot be determined whether it was a killing corresponding to divine intent—from a medieval perspective—or an outrageous murder which was committed. The very same *physical* act actually admits of more than one *moral* evaluation; it is thus, seen abstractly, value-neutral, indifferent; it can conflict with original justice (in average cases, according to Thomas), but it can also, if seldom, correspond to it. In the first case it is to be assessed as murder, in the second as permitted killing.

Thomas thus also admits a tension between the letter and meaning on the second table; by suggesting the difference between factual concept and anti-value-laden concept he reveals from the perspective of the meaning of the law the possibility of exceptions with reference to the *letter* of the law. A dispensation from the *meaning* of the law is obviously never possible. The letter however does not hit the meaning in all cases. It has only a rule of thumb character (*ut in pluribus*). Thomas—as we have seen—unfortunately did not take up this fundamental distinction in the *corpus* of the article. Therefore the global and imprecise formula, "The precepts of the decalogue . . . are indispensable," could easily cause problems. Indeed the *corpus* should already have presented the fundamental restriction which the third response supplies: insofar as the verbal formulation coincides with the authentic intent of the lawgiver . . . otherwise not. In later times the imprecise, static formulation of the *corpus articuli* was more adhered to than were the provocative assertions to the third objection. Our investigation here is concerned with helping this dynamic beginning to new life.

Thomas, at closer view, moves near the thesis of Bonaventure, still to be presented; Bonaventure had from the beginning advocated a more flexible standpoint in reference to exceptions from natural law. Thomas had thus ultimately, contrary to the inexactness of his presentation in the *corpus*, conceded that the fifth commandment does not forbid every killing indiscriminately, as he would have had to conclude from the *corpus*, but only that which "has the character of the improper" (*rationem indebiti*). To put it the other way around: "Thus (i.e. if the condition of the not improper is fulfilled) it contains the essence of original justice."

(d) *The "exceptions" (dispensations) in reference to the sixth and seventh commandments are also explained according to the model of the fifth commandment.*

Taking along the vessels in the exodus from Egypt was not theft[42] but a permitted act, because God as supreme ruler had transferred the former property of the Egyptians to the Israelites.[43] Although "stealing" and "taking along" others' possessions are physically the same thing, just as physically to murder and to kill are the same, they are distinguished in a moral respect by the circumstance of being either proper or improper. God forbids only the improper killing, taking, etc., but not the "proper." Thomas explains Genesis 22 in a corresponding way. Abraham had an intent to kill which was pleasing to God; he did not entertain a plan to murder.[44] The killing of an innocent person as a physical act is thus not forbidden without exception. On "divine authority" it can be permitted.

Nor did Hosea err by his sexual intercourse with a "harlot."[45] God as the sovereign ruler of the institution of marriage had assigned this woman to him as partner. "She is become his by divine command." Here too, the model is valid. Sexual relations in a socially disordered liaison can, on God's sign, be allowed. Thus in a higher perspective there is a permitted killing which is not murder, a permitted taking of others' possessions which is not accounted theft, and a permitted sexual relationship in a socially unrecognized relationship which presents no sexual transgression. Thomas saw in these unique exceptions. Here it is sufficient to begin by noting that such "re-evaluations" are metaphysically possible so that God, who ordained them, does not place himself in contradiction to himself.

What Thomas says in the introduction to the *caput articuli* is only now fully set into relief. As for the fifth commandment, there are also according to Thomas for the sixth and seventh commandments tensions between the formulated letter and the real meaning of the precepts, tensions which open up surprising, even bewildering, possibilities for exceptions. The familiar distinction between factual and anti-value-laden concepts (to kill—to murder) is in a more comprehensive horizon also relevant for other commandments.

Thomas concedes considerable marginal blurring in the case of not only the fifth, but also the sixth and seventh commandments. Through such exceptions God gave supplemental instruction to humans, to whom these distinctions—we must conclude—were as yet unknown. In God's comprehensive perspective exceptions are possible which at that point had scarcely entered into society's field of experience. It can be asked whether such exceptions[46] cannot commonly enter into human perspective today as well. Thomas concludes his explanation (ad 3): "Thus the precepts of the decalogue are immutable (only) in reference to original justice coming to expression in them." Thomas thus limits consistent validity to the meaning, not to the letter, of the precepts. In this way, however, he highlights the unquestionable permanent core much more clearly. In light of these limits "surprises" which would have been amazing in the past have become possible. Unequivocally and indisputably this permanent core transcends time and space;[47] equally broad, according to

Thomas, is the diversity of judgments on whether individual physical actions actually are theft, murder or adultery or not. The
moral evaluation as to whether a physical killing is also to be
judged a murder, whether carrying off another's possessions is
also theft, or whether a socially unaccepted sexual relationship is
a sexual offense can change through new, morally cogent
circumstances—"in some cases . . . as in marriage, by divine
authority alone . . . sometimes (mandated) by human authority."
This mutability in the moral evaluation of physically identical
procedures rests, according to Thomas, on a phenomenon which
was later designated "change of matter." Before we return to this
"change," it should still be noted that Thomas is recommending
that a forbidden concubitus outside socially recognized marriage
should no longer be designated as fornication or adultery. These
"changed" acts should no longer be covered by the anti-value-
laden concept.[48] Thomas by his retreat to the factual concept[49]
indicates that the physical acts appear value-neutral and do not
necessarily have the character of the morally inferior in the sense
of an *actio intrinsece mala*. In other words, God can never command a murder, a theft or a sexual offense—nor, we can add, a
lie. But whether a physical, freely performed act really is murder,
etc. and not merely a permitted killing, etc. cannot be *asserted a
priori*.[50]

(e) *The re-evaluation is possible because of the "change of
matter."* We turn now to the extremely important occurrence
which later was suitably designated "change of matter": conduct
which according to the letter of the law did indeed appear deviant
is so altered that it conforms with God's intents. This is not a
matter of throwing off the "yoke of the commandments," but of
corresponding to God's holy will. The solution[51] presented by
Thomas is explosive; it is full of a revolutionary dynamic which
was almost completely defused in Neo-Scholasticism.[52] Thomas
does actually stand uncompromisingly for the inviolable base
against which any attempt to argue for exceptions shatters. But
this unyielding granite foundation finds its adequate expression
not in the articulated letter but only in the original will of the
lawgiver which stands behind it, though it cannot be formulated
precisely.[53] From this basis of original justice, the intent of the

lawgiver, even God cannot dispense without self-contradiction.

How is it then possible that an act which looks like murder is in fact not murder and no longer contradicts the original intent of the lawgiver? Thomas rejects Ockham's solution of appealing to the *potestas Dei*. He respects the limits drawn by God's self-affirmation; God cannot act against the fundamental meaning of God-given precepts. "He cannot disown his own self" (2 Tim. 2:13). God can neither will nor command a murder, nor a theft, nor a lie, nor a disordered sexual activity.[54] From this base Aquinas undertakes the solution which entered moral history under the catch-word "change of matter" (*mutatio materiae*). How does Thomas present the circumstances which we too will designate briefly as "change of matter"? We must go back to his analyses of the fifth commandment, which are *structural* models. Killing is forbidden only by the usual blurred formulation, but not the meaning, of the precept. The "matter," i.e. the subject, of the prohibition is of course not all destruction of human life, but only unjustified killing, or murder, although this limitation is not expressed in the customary wording of the fifth commandment. A just killing—in Thomas' view perhaps the carrying out of the death sentence, capital punishment—is no longer matter which is subject of the prohibition. The physical occurrence of "killing" then no longer falls under the prohibition. The "matter" has so altered that it avoids the prohibition.[55] There is indeed a deliberate killing but no murder. Humans (the judge, the representative of civil executive power) have by virtue of the change of matter ordered the killing. Thomas, through the above differentiation between formulation and meaning of the law, between letter and spirit (*epikeia*), between "generally" valid rules of thumb and principles valid without exception, between factual and value-laden concepts, systematically prepared for the comprehension of the "change of matter." What he developed in reference to the fifth commandment he has applied to the explanation of the exceptions within the compass of the sixth and seventh commandments.[56]

In God's comprehensive perspective[57] an intent to kill an innocent Isaac directly is not sinful in every case but only when authorization is lacking. The same is true for the sexual relations of Hosea and for the carrying off of the gold and silver vessels by the Israelites. Considered abstractly, such physical actions must be seen as value-neutral. By the additional "circumstance" of authorization they become morally permissible. Only in contrary cases, lacking authorization, are they *morally* evil. They are always and consistently deviant only in the inadequate perspective of the *cursus communis* (that is, in the ordinary course of events). If an authorization is involved—could it not lie in the broadest interpretation of *causa proportionate gravis excusans*, valid before God?—the matter (subject) changes (in reference to the *cursus communis*, and only to this) in a moral respect. An act which in the first horizon is considered theft becomes a permitted taking when seen in the perspective of the *meaning* of the precepts: murder becomes killing, sexual transgression becomes a relation no longer in conflict with God's intent. The same physical facts of a case (like killing) can according to the circumstances (whether authorized or not) be morally permitted or forbidden. The *moral* quality thus changes without a *physical* change. That purports a "change of matter." At bottom Thomas applies here the *via facti* against the possibility of "intrinsically evil acts" laid out especially in Neo-Scholasticism. He does not draw out this beginning, however; he admits in the same place intrinsically evil acts (*actiones intrinsece malae*) whose apparent insoluble monolithic unity he here dissolves by searching more deeply into an indifferent physical object and a merely additional ethically significant circumstance (authorization).[58]

This authorization (*auctoritate divina et partim humana*) must not be thought of as an *arbitrary* decision in Ockham's sense; rather it shows the illumination of the immutable original divine intent in a rare concrete situation which humanity has still not generally considered thoroughly. The authorization therefore, according to Thomas, never encroaches on the original meaning of the precepts; it corrects only the setting of conditioned false boundaries by inadequate verbal formulations.[59]

(f) *Dispensations, exceptions and deliberations on change of matter would not be necessary if we possessed formulations of norms which included all situations.* But comprehensive formulations of that kind surpass our possibilities. Humans can always only generalize from many single experiences of concrete cases, but not anticipate all possible human situations and bear them in mind in formulating norms. Such generalizations are time-conditioned. They may not be upgraded into timeless essence-concepts. Therefore, instructed by new experiences (situations), we must strive for more pointed articulations. What Thomas said in another context is valid here: "As long as there is a still higher principle (here: the divine original intent) the matter in question can still be submitted to it. As long as the ultimate norm (*finalis sententia*) has not entered the field of vision, the judgment remains in suspension."[60] That would mean that in an ultimate horizon extending beyond the horizon of the *cursus communis* (that is, in the ordinary course of events) the claim of precepts to consistent validity must remain in suspension. In other words: There can again and again be completely new "situations" in the face of which the system of norms elaborated in the past fails.[61]

(g) *The outcome of the reflections*. The inquiry and search for God's real intent does not cease. There are here no absolute concrete applicatory norms removed from the historical dynamic. The abstract highest and higher norms, such as "The human good is to be done," and "Justice must prevail," remain, of course, consistently valid. As soon as the precept, however, also includes the *concrete* kind and manner—even if only in generalized form—in which these unchallenged consistently valid but abstract norms should be concretely realized, the area for possible surprises begins.[62] Even venerable maxims (like parts of the second table) show their weakness in that they can no longer demand obedience as consistent principles but only in usual cases. Actually it is surprising that Aquinas holds the application of *epikeia* possible even to the verbally formulated moral natural law (insofar as it is concerned with concrete applications). Here Neo-Scholasticism has not followed him inasmuch as it has not explained the "change of matter" effected by "authorization" in Thomas as *epikeia*.

The change of matter explained in connection with *epikeia* also draws our attention to another distinction already alluded to, that between the *morally evil* and the merely *temporal evil*. God commands physical acts which are apparently evil (the killing of

Isaac, the "robbing" of the Egyptians). Causing this physical evil is thus no sin if there is authorization (*cause proportionate gravis?*). In other words Thomas is able to distinguish precisely between physical evil and moral evil. The famous axiom "The end does not justify the means" can accordingly only purport, "A good end never justifies morally evil means." In the variation "A good end can justify physically evil means," the axiom would stand in agreement with the above start of Aquinas, who can distinguish sharply between moral evil and temporal evil.[63] In the last version there is a possibility of apparent exceptions inasmuch as the standard verbal norm cannot render the meaning of the norm objectively and exhaustively. It lacks in reality the breadth of validity which it appears to have only because of an inexact formulation. Nothing is taken from the significance of the true norm—the original meaning of the law, the intent of the lawgiver. The opposite is true: the objectively grounded so-called exception shows the true breadth of validity of the norm more exactly than the former customary verbal norms.[64]

III

How Has Bonaventure Solved the Question of "Exceptions" from the Natural Moral Law?

The Seraphic Doctor turns to our theme in his *Commentary on the First Book of Sentences of Peter Lombard.*[65] He asks, "Can God enjoin evil?" In the response he first of all distinguishes—as Thomas also suggested—between *contingent* temporal (physical and social) evils and absolute, religio-moral evils. The first, relative because temporal, he calls *mala in se*, a formulation here translated as "of itself temporal evil." This evil contrasts with the absolute religio-moral evil that operates much more deeply because it immediately disturbs, or destroys, the basic relationship with God (*malum secundum se*—the in itself evil). The of itself (temporal) evil,[66] according to Bonaventure— and let us notice that from the beginning—does not stand in necessary and exceptionless contradiction to God, the final goal. From this beginning God can therefore order the performance of temporal evil (*mala in se*) without any necessary divine contradiction.[67] But God could never order the religio-moral evil (*malum secundum se*) forbidden by the first table. Bonaventure appeals here to Bernard of Clairvaux,[68] who had also adjudged the possibilities of exceptions in reference to the first and second tables as entirely different. Bonaventure's beginning is clear. God can indeed command the performance of temporal, physical and social evil on the higher ground of divine wisdom,[69] but God can *never* will religio-moral evil. Thus the first and second commandments are valid without exceptions. Dispensations from the basic life-bond with God are nonsensical and unthinkable.

Bonaventure differs, however, on the performance of temporal evil. It too is "of itself" improper and troubling, but not, however, without exceptions and in all cases. And here it is relevant to our subject. The performance of such evil does not always and without exception disturb the basic relationship to God; for the actualization of higher values, lesser temporal evil may apparently be brought about. The precepts of the second table are valid therefore only in "usual cases."[70] Logically, they have the more modest character of a rule of thumb rather than that of consistently valid principles. From this basis the problem of exceptions in salvation history can be more easily approached.[71] Obviously Bonaventure concedes that the conscious causing of such evil in *usual* cases also disturbs the relationship with God, but this effect is *not always necessarily* induced. Exceptions are in principle possible. Thus not every killing is to be judged as murder, not every seizure of another's property is to be judged as theft, and so on. So value-neutral factual concepts like "killing," "taking others' things," etc. emerge as independent of the anti-value quality ("murdering," "stealing") customarily associated with them. Killing and taking property of course usually disturb the relationship to God, but not without exception. Thus situations in which God—for reasons of divine wisdom—commands that temporal evil be done are conceivable.

Temporal evils, the *mala in se*, lie for Bonaventure on another plane than the *mala secumdum se* which infringe on the basic relation to God and thus endanger the ultimate goal. Moral evil disturbs the meaning of life; it offends against the immutable original intent of the lawgiver. In the perspective of Bonaventure's thought, then, the basic difference is between the abundant temporal contingent evils (second table) and the absolute religio-moral evils (between *relative* and *absolute* anti-values). The "exceptions" appear in him as a kind of authorization to actualize temporal contingent evil in the service of higher meaning values. Although for Bonaventure too only God possesses the power of judgment to command such "exceptions," the basic distinction between the absolute evil and relative evils is nevertheless clearly presented. This differentiation receives practical significance if it is established[72] that in certain spheres humans themselves are in the position to recognize when a reasonable judgment of matters orders an "exception."

Thomas, from another beginning (*epikeia*), came very close to Bonaventure in result. In reference to the fifth, sixth and seventh commandments Aquinas conceded the possibility of *epikeia* and in this way relativized the stability of the second table. Bonaventure had already included their relativity in his beginning.[73]

Duns Scotus (d. 1308 in Munich) followed the Seraphic Doctor on this tract.[74] For him too the second table contains neither the highest practical principles nor compelling inferences from such. The actualization of temporal anti-values forbidden by the second table does not necessarily lead to a contradiction of the divine essence.

IV
SYNOPSIS AND OPEN QUESTIONS

Thomas and Bonaventure have approached the question of the possibility of exceptions from the natural moral law from different points, yet in result they come very close. The solution for our examples presented at the beginning are obvious. Such developments are possible. Looking back we reaffirm especially in reference to Thomas:

1. The original meaning of the law, the intent of the lawgiver, is and remains the critical yardstick for the breadth of validity of the verbal formulation. Where both are not fully covered, as in our earlier examples, exceptions from the verbal formula are possible but only in the spirit of the authentic intended meaning. Original justice is here—as in the teaching of *epikeia*—the critical measure of literal justice. Human reason is here capable of producing clarity.

2. In a broader horizon accessible to God—at times also to humans—a "change of matter" is possible, so that deeds physically the same change their quality by the entrance of a morally significant circumstance. In Thomas' view physically identical acts in the sphere of the fifth, sixth, or seventh commandments can be judged complete opposites morally. Here obviously there must be a sharp differentiation between factual and value-laden concepts.

3. Change is possible through "authorization," which results partly from God, partly from humans. Authorization results, however, according to the context in which Thomas presents his concept, not arbitrarily but in virtue of original justice as opposed to mere literal justice.

4. As concerns the timeless, consistent and enduring meaning of the precepts, no exceptions are conceivable. Talk of exception and dispensation has meaning only in the perspective of justice according to the letter.

5. This concept suggests further questions to us. How far can the "change of matter" or the entrance of morally cogent circumstances ("authorization" by appropriate weighty reason) be established by humans? Is it not possible that humans of growing maturity enter so far into the divine perspective, i.e. the meaning of the law, that an appropriate serious reason could be recognized as authorized by God? Do our customary formulations of norms, especially those given out as principles (e.g., Never kill an innocent person directly! Never use a lie!), have the precision demanded by Thomas? Do we draw the systematic consequences which result from the prevailing tension between the letter and meaning of the precepts of the second table? Have we precisely outlined and thoroughly reflected on all the implied conditions

and restrictions under which the usual norms must attempt to lay claim to validity?

How is an *actio intrinsece mala absolute* in the sphere of the second table possible, proceeding from the attempt developed here?

6. It follows in consequence of the beginnings presented here that even unborn life possesses no absolute inviolability. Can one then not perceive in strong medical indications an authorization in the Thomistic sense which justifies interfering in innocent human life in this border case? Should something corresponding not be true of donation of organs, contraception, and prevarication? Thomas and Bonaventure have offered beginnings to an affirmative answer.

Notes

1. This seemed already decided. Pius XII in his address to the midwives of Italy on Oct. 29, 1951, declared: "Saving the life of the mother (is) a very noble goal, but the direct killing of the child as a means to this goal is not allowed."

2. The bill sponsored by Representatives Heck and comrades (Records of the House of Parliament 7/561 of 15 May 1973).

3. The official understanding can be seen in the following writers: A. Lehmkuhl: "To directly kill an innocent person is always a most serious offense" (*Theol. mor.*, Freiburg, 1914, no. 1000); D. Pruemmer: "Craniotomy and other surgical interventions which directly bring about the death of the fetus are wholly forbidden" (*Man. Theol. mor.*, Freiburg[7], 1933, no. 134; Noldin-Schmitt: "Abortus is then also forbidden if the mother is in certain danger of death and there is no other means to save the mother" (*Summa Theol. mor.*, Munich[18], 1933, no. 343, 4); M. Zalba: "A directly caused abortus is always strictly prohibited" (*Theol. mor. Summa*, Matriti, 1951, no. 212, 2); B. Häring: "The Church maintains inexorably the principle that it is under no circumstances permitted to attack directly the life of an innocent child in the womb" (*Das Gesetz Christi* III, Freiburg, 1961, 261f.). In practice however he is of a more lenient opinion (cf. III, 226); G. Ermecke speaks of the "absoluteness of the moral prohibition in this area" (*Kath. Moraltheol.* III, Münster, 1961, 272.

4. J. Doepfner and H. Dietzfelbinger, *Das Gesetz des Staates und die sittliche Ordnung* (Guetersloh, 1970), 30.

5. Criticism of the official ecclesiastical standpoint, which encouraged rigorism in borderline cases, was never entirely silenced. M. Jocham (d. 1893) and F. X. Linsenmann (d. 1898) had already raised it in the nineteenth century.

6. Declaration of 27 April 1974. Cf. *Kirchenzeitung* fuer die Dioezese Augsburg, "Ein schwarzer Tag," 4/5 May 1974.

7. In regard to such acts one spoke of a malitia "intrinseca conditionata." Cf. Ermecke, I, 240.

8. Cf. "Organorum humanorum transplantatio, "*Angelicum* 31 (1954), 160.

9. Ermecke, III, 253.

10. "De mutilatione quadam, "*MF* 55 (1955), 59-87.

11. "De Moraliteit der Biologische Overplantinsen," *CollGand* 4 (1954), 351-365; cf. also J. F. Groner, "Die Organverpflanzung beim Menschen in moralischer Sicht," in R. Hauser and F. Scholz, *Der Mensch unter Gottes Anruf und Ordnung* (Düsseldorf, 1958), 194-200.

12. Just how natural Catholics consider these interventions, earlier condemned as outrageous, can be seen in two reports in *Weltbild* (a "magazine for critical readers," which is published by order of the German bishops by the ecclesiastical center for the pastoral care of men in Augsburg), which applauded the donation of a kidney as a work of Christian love of neighbor (cf. no. 28/29 of 26 June 1974, 44-47).

13. B. Häring responds, *Remscheid* (1966), 61-63.

14. By "beginnings" (Ansaetzen) are meant possible intellectual starting positions, even if these were not developed—or not logically enough developed—by the authors themselves, or were simultaneously blocked by other structures.

15. S. the. 1,2 q 90 al ad 2 aliquid per huiusmodi actum (= per rationem) constitutum; 1, 2 q 94 al c aliquid per rationem constitutum; cf. also 1, 2 q 90 al c . . . quod lex quaedam regula est et mensura actuum . . . regula autem et mensura humanorum actuum est ratio, quae est principium primum actuum humanorum. . . .

16. S. th. 1, 2 q 19 a3 et a8.

17. De malo q 14 a2 ad 8; cf. S. th. 1, 2 q 71 a2 c.

18. S. th. 1, 2 q 18 a5 c.

19. In III. Sent, dist 37 q 1 a3.

20. S. th. 1, 2 q 100 a3 c; q 94 a2 c.

21. Summa aurea in 4 1b. Sent. (Paris, 1500); quoted in O. Lottin, *Psychologie et morale aux XIIe et XIIIe siècles* (Louvain, 1948), 1, 2/76, n. 1.

22. S. th. 1, 2 q 94 a4 c; In III, Sent, dist 37 q 1 a3 resp.

23. Arntz, "Die Entwicklung des naturrechtlichen Denkens innerhalb des Thomismus," in F. Boeckle, ed., *Das Naturrecht im Disput* (Duesseldorf, 1966), 97.

24. In III. Sent, dist 37 a3.

25. S. th. 1, 2 q 100 a8 c.

26. S. th. 1, 2 q 94 a4 c . . . conclusio propria . . . quidem . . . ut in pluribus verum est . . . sed . . . in paucioribus potest deficere. . . .

27. In III. Sent, dist 37 a3 et a4 ad 2.

28. Considered precisely, we are dealing with logically compelling, unanimous assertions in which the idea of human good is interpreted *a priori*: Be just! Practice self-control! Love your neighbor! etc.

29. Killing in self-defense is, e.g., a physical-temporal evil, but it can be justified, indeed even obligatory.

30. In III. Sent, dist 37 a3.

31. III. Sent, dist 37.

32. Gen. 22:1-18; God's command seems to go against the fifth commandmment.

33. Ex. 12:35f.; the command seems to contradict the seventh commandment.

34. Hos. 1:2; the demand, in medieval opinion, was pointed against the sixth commandment.

35. S. th. 1, 2 q 94 a4 et a5.

36. We are consciously limiting ourselves here to the commandments of the second table, to the so-called world-ethic.

37. Utrum praecepta decalogi sint dispensabilia? S. th. 1, 2 q 100 a8.

38. S. th. 2, 2 q 120 a1.

39. This is the usual understanding of Aquinas; e.g., R. Erni, *Die theol. Summe* II (Lucerne, 1949), 197; W. Stockums, *Die Unveraenderlichkeit des natuerlichen Sittengesetzes in der scholastischen Ethik* (Freiburg, 1911), 84; Pruemmer, I, no. 154.

40. Occisio hominis . . . secundum quod habet rationem indebiti.

41. Ipsam rationem justitiae.

42. "Theft" here is the anti-value-laden concept corresponding to "murder."

43. Corresponding to permitted killing.

44. What is amazing in the case of Isaac is that God as sovereign has displaced the criteria of distinction between killing and murder previously valid in moral consciousness, so that what appeared to the contemporaneous moral consciousness as murder is declared to be a permitted, indeed commanded, killing of an innocent.

45. Cf. S. th. 2, 2 q 154 a2 ad 2.

46. Which lie in the horizon of traditional formulation of norms.

47. As the original intent of the lawgiver, natural law in the strict sense.

48. Like "murder," "theft," "illicit sexual relations."

49. To kill, to take, to have illegitimate sexual relations.

50. Cajetan, the famous interpreter of Thomas, hits the mark precisely when he emphasizes that God can never permit or command a murder, a theft, a lie, or a deviant sexual relationship (cf. his Commentary on S. th. 1, 2 q 100 a8). The formulation of Caramuel (d. 1682) is similar: "God can bring it about that all those acts which are forbidden on

the second table do not morally oppose the divine goodness," after which he very clearly showed the distinction between physical evil and moral evil (*Basis Theol. regularis*, II concl. 1 et 7, no. 136, 141).

51. S. th. 1, 2 q 100 18 ad 3.

52. Thomas himself favored such a "defusing" inasmuch as the *sed contra* and the *corpus articuli* offer smooth, global, non-differentiating formulations according to which the *articulation* of the second table appears simply as the expression of the consistently valid original justice. In this case, of course, a basis for any "exception" would be avoided from the outset.

53. The latter is for its part bound to original justice.

54. Dispensations, as we saw, are always possible only in reference to the inadequate articulation, never in the perspective of the original intent of the lawgiver.

55. Stockums, 78f.

56. Cf. S. th. 1, 2 q 100 a8 ad 3; 2, 2 a 154 a2 ad 2.

57. Praecepta quantum ad rationem justitiae.

58. Cf. In III. Sent, dist 38 a1 resp.

59. These ideas are not sufficiently emphasized by Stockums, *op. cit.* He overlooks the fact that Thomas intends to unknot the problem after the model of dispensation (I, 2 q 96 a6; q 97 a4) or *epikeia* (2, 2 q 120 a1).

60. S. th. 1, 2 q 74 a7 c.

61. Cf. the examples at the beginning of the article.

62. Moral positivism denies the consistent validity of the principles which are here presupposed as self-evident. We are concerned whether in the realization of consistently valid first principles, certain concrete physical acts are forbidden without exception.

63. This beginning is not carried through to its logical end by Thomas.

64. Cf. J. Fuchs, "Der Absolutheitscharakter sittlicher Handlungsnormen," in *Testimonium Veritati*, ed. H. Wolter (Frankfurt a. Main, 1971), 228-233.

65. In I. Sent. dist 47 a1 q4.

66. What is meant is evidently the conscious *performance* of bodily, spiritual, social harm.

67. Cf. the indicated factual concept in Thomas.

68. In his "Ueber Dispens und Gebet," chap. 3, no. 6.

69. Cf. "authorization" in Thomas.

70. In the ordinary course of things, *ut in pluribus*, in Thomas.

71. Killing an innocent (Abraham-Isaac), sexual intercourse with a non-spouse (Hosea), and carrying off another's property (Ex. 11:12) do indeed in this perspective present an evil, but only a physical, temporal evil, which need not be prevented at any price.

72. Cf. Thomas, S. th. 1, 2 q 100 a8.

73. Bonaventure, just like Thomas, did not carry to its logical end the beginning developed here in reference to the eighth commandment (In III. Sent. dist 38 a1 q2, III 843). "The character of the intrinsically evil adheres more to the false statement (mendacium) than to theft or killing."

74. In III. Sent, dist 37 q unica, no. 1-7.

Various Types of Grounding for Ethical Norms

Bruno Schüller, S.J.

In the last decade a variety of Catholic moral theologians have sought to sketch the outlines of a normative ethics. Their efforts can only be understood if we keep in mind the problems which they were trying to resolve by these efforts. The problems are readily identifiable by the catchwords used: the "use of artificial contraceptives," the "indissolubility of marriage" and the "killing of an innocent human being" (medically indicated abortion). Insofar as the actions identified by these phrases are concerned, Catholic tradition asserts that they are to be condemned ethically in each and every case.

To many this moral judgment no longer seems plausible. What is their objection to it? Well, insofar as contraception is concerned, tradition says that it is impermissible no matter what its consequences may be. In contrast to this it is said of the fulfillment of a promise that consequences must be taken into consideration. A doctor is obliged to carry out an operation that cannot be postponed, even if he is thereby forced to forego a promised visit to a friend. To form a judgment on this sort of ground would seem to indicate that the ethical character of an action is decided by its consequences. Thus when people express criticism of such norms as the traditional prohibition on contraception, the reason seems to be that they do not see how a pattern of behavior or way of acting can be condemned ethically unless the consequences of the action are taken into account.

In line with the two rival basic types of normative ethics described by C. D. Broad, the two viewpoints noted above are

184

called a *deontological* ethics and a *teleological* ethics respectively. Broad stipulates the following basic definition of the two types. Ethical theories of a deontological type maintain that there are ethical postulates of the following sort: "Such and such ways of acting are always ethically right or wrong under such and such circumstances, no matter what their consequences may be." Ethical theories of a teleological type, on the other hand, maintain that a particular way of acting is ethically right or wrong, depending always on whether it produces certain consequences which are good or bad in themselves. Broad is of the opinion that *purely* deontological and *purely* teleological theories are ideal-types, borderline-limit cases. Most theories espoused in fact are usually mixed theories, sometimes predominantly deontological and sometimes predominantly teleological.[1]

If one sticks with Broad's classification, then one finds oneself compelled to arrange and catalogue a plethora of normative theories according to the varying mix of deontological and teleological elements in them. This allows for greater differentiation, but at the expense of any quick or easy overview. That may be one of the reasons why today we often encounter a somewhat different subdivision of normative theories. People say that the label "teleological" should be applied to those theories which maintain that *all* actions are to be ethically judged *solely and exclusively* on the basis of their consequences. Deontological theories, then, are defined in contrast to this definition of teleological theories. A theory is "deontological" if it maintains that *not all* actions are ethically specified solely and exclusively on the basis of their consequences. This fashionable approach provides a neat and complete disjunction. One can then take any imaginable theory and arrange it neatly under one of the two types. One result, of course, is that the deontological type of ethical theory now embraces a wide variety of differing theories.

In view of the problem pressing on him right now, it seems advisable for the Catholic moral theologian to follow Broad's division, at least to begin with. He can then ask himself: Are deontological norms asserted validly? Are there certain ways of acting which must be judged to be ethically right or wrong, independent of their consequences? From the relevant literature it is evident that a theologian tends to express his doubts about this in a way that is characteristic for him. Christian ethics seeks to be an ethics of love. It seems scarcely comprehensible that the chief commandment of love could harmonize with any deontological norm. How, for example, could love require us to leave an innocent human being to the cruelty of his enemy rather than to protect him from that enemy with a "lie"? One can readily get the impression that a legalistic misconception of ethical norms underlies deontological norms, that it is almost as if human beings existed for the sake of ethical norms rather than vice versa.

Lest we overestimate the practical magnitude of the problem, we should remember that deontological norms constitute only a relatively small segment of all the ethical norms and rules for behavior handed down by tradition. The principal areas involved are the prohibitions against false statements, suicide, and the killing of an innocent human being; the indissolubility of marriage; and the impermissibility of any sexual behavior which is regarded as going against nature, as is the case with the use of artificial contraceptives.

It is hardly surprising that even moral theologians of earlier generations sensed the problematic nature of deontological norms. This is evident, first and foremost, in the fact that they expounded such norms in the most restrictive terms possible. The clearest and simplest example is the fact that they interpreted the concept of false statement so narrowly that double-meaning assertions do not come under that heading. They thus retain the possibility of passing ethical judgment on double-meaning assertions on the basis of their consequences. Even though such assertions may lead the listener into error, they may be ethically justified if they are the only way to protect another person from serious harm. The aim of this restrictive interpretation seems to be to minimize the instances in which the fulfillment of deontological norms results in disproportionate harm to an individual or society.

In all likelihood restrictive interpretation of the same sort applies to the traditional distinction between direct and indirect killing.

Many theologicans of more recent times are of the opinion that the indissolubility of marriage should not be regarded as a commandment to be fulfilled, as tradition does, but rather as a commandment which sets a goal. They appeal to the Sermon on the Mount to justify this position. If the indissolubility of marriage is interpreted as a goal, as this view suggests, then obviously it could no longer be reckoned among the deontological norms.

To sum up, then, for centuries there has been a clear tendency in Catholic moral theology to restrict the jurisdiction of deontological norms as much as possible in favor of teleological considerations. Insofar as the former have continued in force up to now, Catholic tradition has appealed to two types of argument to support its deontological norms. The first argument starts from natural ends, which are attributed to human speech, the human body and its organs, and in particular the sexual act. In these natural ends tradition sees the providential wisdom of the Creator at work: *Deus (natura) nihil facit inane*. Thus, for example, God gave speech to humans so that they might live together in community through truthful talk. Untruthful talk frustrates this divinely appointed goal and is therefore impermissible. This conviction is at bottom teleological in its presentation. It ends up in deontological norms only because its proponents appeal to the supreme wisdom of God in order to show that a natural end is unassailable. The speech of human beings must be truthful even though this may bring serious harm to another.

In this way certain particular non-ethical values are elevated to the rank of absolute preferability, to the detriment of other potentially competing values. In this way the integrity of certain biological laws can be a value to be preferred absolutely. This approach is thoroughly a-teleological in its consequences. For example, tradition maintains that the use of artificial contraceptives *as such* is impermissible; on the other hand it judges that the Knaus-Ogino (rhythm) method is ethically permissible.

I will only mention the following here by way of criticism. Insofar as we human beings judge certain natural ends to be true and applicable, we are also justified in seeing the wisdom of the Creator at work in them. However, the extent to which these natural ends are to be respected in an individual case depends on whether they are to be judged to take preference over other potentially competing values. The making of this judgment, if one chooses, is the natural end of the capacity for judgment given to human beings by God.

A second type of argument is used to justify deontological norms. In this case it is asserted that human beings are not permitted to justify certain ways of acting at all because such justification is the prerogative of God alone. The most well-known example here is the age-old argument for the prohibition of suicide. God alone, it is said, is the master over life and death. A human being usurps God's right, then, if he brings his own life to an end.

Formally speaking, we can say that there is a *petitio principii* involved here. From a theological standpoint the precise question is whether God does or does not exercise his mastery over the life of a human being in such a way that, through the ethical demands of given situations, he thereby empowers the human being to put an end to his own life. For a long time now there have been theologians who have recognized the faultiness of the aforementioned argument. They have looked for other bases of argument, and to a significant degree these arguments have had a thoroughly teleological character. Such, for example, is the effort to find an analogy between the absolute prohibition against suicide and the indissolubility of marriage on the one hand and a law enacted to forestall a general danger on the other hand (*lex lata ad praecavendum periculum generale*).

Thus when we examine the normative ethics of Catholic tradition more closely and compare it to the framework provided by C. D. Broad, we find that it is overwhelmingly teleological. It seems to narrow down as much as possible the already small space allowed to deontological norms. Where it does arrive at norms that operate deontologically by appealing to divinely appointed natural ends, it basically argues on teleological grounds even though it may make a mistake in the process. The efforts to transform even the second type of argument into a teleological line of argument are particularly instructive. Not only do they clearly indicate how dear the teleological approach is to Catholic moral theologians; they also call attention to the *possibility* that traditional ethical norms, which at first glance bear all the hallmarks of being deontological and having no grounding in consequences, may be shown to be justified on teleological grounds upon closer and more careful re-examination.

If one attempts a systematic reconstruction of the teleological type of ethics elaborated by Catholic tradition, one runs up against a difficulty. In the handbooks of fundamental moral theology one will look in vain for a tract that deals directly with what is called "normative ethics" today. Tradition occupies itself with the question as to what constitutes the standard of ethical behavior: right reason or human nature. But no matter which way that question is resolved, in special ethics all argue the same way. Tradition is concerned with clarifying what is meant by "natural moral law" or "natural law." In so doing, however, it tackles questions which only indirectly concern a normative ethics: e.g., the objectivity of ethical value-judgments, the relationship of axiology and ontology, the distinction between *phýsei dikaion* and *thései dikaion*, and the relationship between an ethics of reason and an ethics of faith.

This absence of an explicit presentation of a teleological line of argument is best explained by Wittgenstein: "The aspects of things that are most important to us are concealed under their simplicity and their everyday nature. (One cannot notice the thing because it is always right in front of our eyes.)"[2]

Insofar as theologians look on deontological norms as alien within the context of an ethics of love, we can assume that they will present their teleological theory in the form of an ethics of love. They take it for granted that the ethical goodness of a human being is summed up in the fulfillment of the twofold commandment of love. This love is, first of all, an inner disposition of benevolence and respect. Only as an inner disposition can this love live rooted in the free self-determination of the human being serving as his or her very own love and therefore as love in the ethical sense. It is a love that human beings owe to God and their neighbor: to God because of his absolute goodness, to their neighbors because of their dignity as persons. Because tradition grounds love, as something owed and obligatory, on the goodness of the one to whom it applies, it gives priority to the concept of goodness over the concept of obligation. In this many see the hallmark of a teleological way of thinking.

Love as an inner disposition is translated into deeds of love under two conditions. (1) The other person must be dependent on such acts of love for his welfare. (The healthy person does not need a doctor.) (2) One must be in a position to accomplish such acts. (Those who are extremely poor can hardly alleviate the poverty of another.)

On the whole, both conditions are always fulfilled among human beings, but the first is always more all-encompassing than the second. Human beings are not in a position to do everything for each other that would be required if everyone wanted to be called good in every sense of the word. The good things which constitute the welfare of a human being can come into conflict with each other, so that the only thing possible is to choose the more important ones. The paradigm here is the injured person who must allow his arm to be amputated in order to save his life.

The interests of one person can conflict with the interests of another person. One person may be able to ward off serious harm to his own goods and chattels only by harming the goods and chattels of another. Thus each person is confronted with limited possibilities for acting. Each must ask himself: For whom and for what am I to be primarily responsible? What each person is bound to do in the way of active love is determined by a correct choice of priorities among competing values. The rightness of such a choice is decided by the proper principles of priority governing the values at issue. These principles can be called "rules of priority." Awareness of these principles enables people to determine what is required in the way of acts of love in a given case.

Catholic moral theology has brought these rules of priority together in a tract that is usually entitled *De ordine caritatis*. Nevertheless this does not make clear the extent to which these rules of priority represent the nodal principle for the elaboration of special moral theology as a whole. This work remains to be done. Romans 13:8f. provides the biblical reference point for this work. Insofar as the task undertaken by G. Gillman in his *Le Primat de la Charité* is concerned, it should be viewed in terms of the more recent approach which distinguishes between a teleological type of grounding and a deontological type of grounding.

The person who acts out of the disposition of love acts in an *ethically good* way. Of course it may happen that he misjudges the situation and causes greater harm, though he was trying to alleviate some harm. By the same token, a person may do good for another person even though he was prompted only by selfish motives. In that case he acts in an *ethically bad* way. Viewed in these terms, it would seem that the ethical character of a certain way of acting is decided only by the inner disposition of the agent, not by the consequences of the action.

Here a distinction is necessary. Suppose a person feels obliged out of love to help someone and hence chooses to help, but by mistake causes harm. By mistake he does exactly the opposite of what love demands *in deeds*. To that extent his way of acting is *ethically wrong* even though it is at the same time *ethically good* because it springs from the best intentions or inner dispositions. By the same token, a person may do something that is *ethically right*, that contributes to the welfare of another human being, and still be doing something *ethically bad* because he is motivated solely by self-seeking designs.

The distinction between ethically good and ethically right behavior, between ethically bad and ethically wrong behavior, holds true even from the standpoint of a deontological ethics. Kant similarly makes a distinction between an action done out of duty (*Handeln aus Pflicht*) and an action in accordance with duty (*pflichtmässiges Handeln*). Normative theories are principally concerned with the question as to how a certain way of acting becomes an *ethically right* way of acting.

Since the individual is an ethical subject of action, there is a danger that the teleological determination of ethically right action may be mistakenly construed in individualistic terms alone. One may erroneously assume that each individual is *directly* responsible for the welfare of *all* and hence must decide which of the actions open to him will best serve the interests of all. In reality, of course, the ethical duty of the individual must be viewed in connection with the ethical duty of society. Thus a normative ethics must confront not one but two basic questions. First, there is the question of the individual: What should *I* do for whom? Then there is the question of the many, the group: What should which of *us* do for whom?

In principle at least, some sort of division of duties is always undertaken in normative ethics, so that the welfare of *all* is to flow from the actions of *all*. Coordinating the activities of all in the interests of all usually takes the form of institutions. The corresponding determination and specification of what is ethically right in this area usually goes under the name of "institutional duties" (as opposed to "natural duties"). They constitute a considerable portion of the ethical rules for conduct that are generally recognized. Many of them seem so obvious to us that it takes a real effort for us to realize that they are of an institutional nature. Take, for example, the presumptive duties to keep one's word and to honor contracts. Their teleological basis of validity is supplied by the institution to which they appertain.

Like natural duties, institutional duties are usually classified according to ethically relevant characteristics, and they are marked off from one another as dintinct virtues (= types of ethical value = ethical principles). The specific obligation to stand by one's word is called "fidelity." The duty to fulfill contracts constitutes a sector within the broader field known as "justice." People accordingly talk about duties of fidelity and duties of justice, so that fidelity and justice are envisioned as grounds for some obligation.

When we come to moral theology, certain duties of love also show up in this classification of ethically right behavior. A person may help someone in need even though he or she is not obligated to do this by some promise or contractual agreement. In such a case the person acts in an ethically right way, but he or she is not fulfilling a duty of fidelity or justice. What kind of duty is the person fulfilling? Authors customarily characterize such behavior as an act of mercy or an act of love.

Thus in Christian ethics the word "love" serves a twofold purpose. It signifies the quintessence of ethical demands in general, and also a special segment of ethically mandated behavior. This may lead someone to misunderstand the import and thrust of a teleological ethics. If one takes the word "love" in the second sense just noted, that is, as a special type of ethically right behavior, then one is bound to think it absurd to regard that kind of love as the universal basis for determining all ethically right behavior.

One would assert that other demands, such as the demands of fidelity and justice, must be recognized alongside the duties of love.

It is obvious that love, as the universal basis for all ethically mandated behavior, can only be the love which is recorded in the New Testament as the chief commandment. This love is characterized by the fact that it is concerned with the whole and complete welfare of human beings. Insofar as fidelity and justice clearly serve human beings in their own proper way, they must be viewed as special instances of that love.

Within moral theology it is not unusual to find that a normative ethics of a teleological cast is spelled out as an ethics of love. Anglo-American writers on ethics, of course, usually do not talk about "love." They talk about "benevolence" (wishing people well) and "beneficence" (doing good). For them the main problem is whether the principle of benevolence suffices for determining what is ethically right, or whether at least one more equally basic principle is needed: i.e., the principle of justice. As is evident from their debate with Kant, most of them reject the view that an action can be ethically right or wrong no matter what its consequences may be. That may be a further reason why they, unlike Broad, define deontological theories as the direct opposite, the direct contradiction of, teleological theories. They can then formulate their basic question as follows: Is the ethical character of every action teleological, that is, determined solely by the principle of benevolence (= solely by its consequences)? If still another principle is determining, if the ethical character is not determined solely by the consequences, then the right normative ethics should be called "deontological." This formulation of the issues is certainly not new for the Catholic moral theologian, but it must be clearly distinguished from what are called "deontological" norms in Broad's sense.

A large number of Anglo-American philosophers are of the opinion that besides the principle of benevolence there is need for a distinct principle of justice. Here the theologian would say that those who maintain this are not interpreting the principle of benevolence in exactly the same way as the commandment of love is usually understood by theologians. In fact W. K. Frankena has this to say: "It has been said that justice is included in the commandment of love insofar as the latter, in its second part, requires that we love our neighbors as ourselves: that is, love them to the same extent we love ourselves. If we interpret the commandment of love in that way, then in fact it becomes a twofold principle. First of all, it requires us to exercise benevolence. Secondly, it requires us to exercise this benevolence in equal measure."[3]

If we recall that in the New Testament the commandment to love one's neighbor (in the version of Leviticus 19:18) and the golden rule (Mt. 7:12) apparently are viewed as equivalent, then there seems to be no doubt that the commandment of love not only demands beneficence but also gauges it by the standard which Frankena describes as justice. What should we say then: that the commandment to love one's neighbor contains two commands in itself, or that it derives from two principles? The question is hardly of any practical importance. One brief comment may suffice here. At first glance it may well seem strange that morality, which is undoubtedly a unified way of life in itself, could derive from two principles which do not refer back to one another nor to some third principle outside them both. Be that as it may, when a theologian asserts that he is advocating a normative ethics of a teleological type, then in all likelihood he means an ethics which is rooted in the chief commandment of love.

In conclusion I should like to touch briefly on two problems which may be discussed quite apart from the choice between deontological and teleological ethics, but which present themselves with particular clarity when and if one proposes a teleological ethics. If a person judges the ethical rightness of an action on the basis of its consequences, he or she may be inclined to succumb to calculations and petty accounting. In certain situations that comes off as moral philistinism.

Consider this question, for instance: When is wasteful extravagance not only not a vice but actually a virtue? When must we reckon and calculate carefully, and when must we drop that? The problem is brought out vividly in Mark 14. A woman broke "an alabaster jar of perfume made from expensive aromatic nard" and began to pour the perfume on Jesus' head. Some of those present reacted indignantly: "What is the point of this extravagant waste of perfume? It could have been sold for over three hundred silver pieces and the money given to the poor." Some people, reminded of this passage, might well suggest that the evangelists often give figures that are too high and that the value of the perfume could not have been so high. But it still seems that the action of the woman is an instance of wasteful extravagance.

In 1 Corinthians 7 Paul advises slaves to remain slaves even though they might obtain their freedom. Why? To bear witness to the fact that in the last analysis the only thing that counts is their freedom in Christ. That, too, is extravagant waste—in this case, of something worth much more than three hundred silver pieces. But here again the point seems to be that this wastefulness gives one's profession of faith its overwhelmingly persuasive force.

A person may protest against some serious injustices, knowing that he will not accomplish anything by that. He protests nevertheless, fully realizing that he will have to pay for his action with his life. That is useless and pointless, but for that reason *alone* one cannot say that it is meaningless.

Another person may give up certain advantages even though his action may not improve the lot of others. He gives up things simply because he does not want to have a better time of it than other people do. His action is motivated by pure feelings of solidarity.

Joseph II of Austria (1741–1790) seems to have followed an ethics which left no room for the virtue of wasteful extravagance. With an uncommon feeling for social justice, he abolished serfdom, made every effort to improve the lot of the peasantry, and tried to inculcate work habits in the nobility, promoting education and scholarly science. At the same time, however, he clearly exemplified what is called moral philistinism. He abrogated the right of contemplative religious orders to exist. In the interest of frugality he forbade people to leave lighted candles on the graves of their loved ones. And for some strange reason he regarded all poets as "poultry" and criticized Mozart for using too many notes in his operas.

Actions such as the anointing of Jesus in Bethany are called "symbolic actions." As such they are directly grounded on the same ethical standard which governs human speech in general.

They should be truthful. The question which they give rise to in people's minds concerns their costliness. A purposeless protest, for example, can also be *too* costly. Here one recalls G. Gundlach's stand on a defensive atomic war: "Even in the possible case where the only result (of a defensive atomic war) would be a manifestation of the majesty of God and his order, which we owe him as human beings, one can imagine a case where there would be a right and a duty to defend such supreme values. Even if this should bring about the destruction of the world, that would be no argument against our line of argument."[4] In terms of rationally purposeful criteria, what Gundlach calls "defense" is no longer "defense" at all; it is simply self-destructive protest. In my opinion, however, this assertion alone does not suffice to refute Gundlach's thesis. Even though an action is purposeless or even anti-purposive, we cannot immediately conclude from that basis that it is meaningless also as a symbolic action. Instead it would seem that in the case of a symbolic action we may not pay such a high price as Gundlach seems prepared to pay. In any case these few observations on the costliness of symbolic actions are simply meant to call the reader's attention to the whole problem-complex involved here.[5]

The second problem concerns the ethical relevance of the distinction between doing something and allowing something to happen. It would seem that a proponent of teleological ethics would have to deny any ethical weight to this distinction. For him, it would seem, only the consequences of man's free decisions can count for something. Whether they are the consequences of a free decision to do something or a free decision to let something happen would be only a difference in the technique used to produce the consequences. Whether one kills someone or lets him die makes no difference. Only the result matters: a human being loses his life. The person who lets a human being die would seem to dispose of a human life just as much as a person who actually kills a human being.

Insofar as we can say anything about the *de facto* ethical awareness of Christians, it does seem that there are plenty of cases in which we really do judge the matter in the above terms. *Gaudium et Spes*, for example, reminds us of the patristic saying:

"Feed those dying of hunger, for not feeding them means killing them." But then we also find another curious situation. There is at least one case, the case of euthanasia, where most people pass extremely severe judgment on the act of killing a human being. At the same time these people also maintain that there are cases where it is ethically proper to let a person die when he is wasting away and suffering terribly. So on the one hand we are inclined to argue against a moral distinction between doing something and letting something happen, while on the other hand we turn this distinction into the boundary line between a good deed and a crime. Is there a lack of consistency in this?

Upon close inspection we may be able to see some regularity in this conflicting attitude after all. Despite the oft repeated assertion that a human life is beyond any attempt to set a price on it, we do in fact seem to assess the value of human lives. There are instances where we consider the lives of human beings and say: it would be a fearful misfortune if they were to die. One thinks of the case of a young child dying from hunger. There are other cases, however, when we judge that it would be better for some people if they were to die at last, that death would be a blessed release for them. Such is the case, for example, with a person who is slowly wasting away and suffering terrible pain.

Now whenever we say that it would be a misfortune for someone to die, we are tending to reject the validity of *any* moral distinction between killing someone and letting someone die. In such a case, letting that person die when we could save him is just the same as killing him. However, when we judge that it would be better for a person to die, then we are standing by the distinction between killing someone and letting him die. We are saying "no" to the idea of killing the person, but "yes" to the idea of letting that person die. In short, our ethical judgment here seems to run as follows: (a) death as a misfortune may not even be allowed by passive neglect or omission; (b) death as blessed release may not be brought about by active measures. It would seem that a *favor vitae* is being asserted here.

If this observation seems pertinent, then it might serve to give orientation to further and more complete analyses. In any case there is good reason for moral theologians to rethink the traditional teaching on human action. And even though this necessity first becomes clear from a teleological standpoint, this does not mean that proponents of deontology need not devote their attention to it.

Notes

1. C. D. Broad, *Five Types of Ethical Theory*, London, 1967, 9th edition, pp. 206f.

2. Wittgenstein, *Philosophische Untersuchungen*, 129.

3. Frankena, *Analytische Ethik*, Munich, 1972, p. 74.

4. Gundlach, "Die Lehre Pius XII. vom modernen Krieg," StdZ, 164, 1959, p. 13.

5. This problem-complex is examined in R. Ginters, *Die Ausdruckshandlung*, Düsseldorf, 1976.

Processive Relationism and Ethical Absolutes

Walter G. Jeffko

It is a widely held view in contemporary metaphysics that reality is fundamentally "processive" and "relational" rather than static and thing-like. From Hegel onward, this has been the prevailing metaphysical view of reality, not to mention the profound influence of both physical and biological science. The first term means, quite literally, that the universe is process, not that it merely involves process. In a processive universe, the elements of process—change, growth and development—are appropriately expressed by terms such as "novelty" and "the new." As one author puts it: "Man and his world are in process of becoming a new man, a new world."[1]

Correspondingly, the universe is not a system of substantial, independent entities which are then extrinsically related to each other.[2] It is fundamentally a field of ongoing interaction and interrelations. On the level of personal reality this implies, as Marcel has put it, that "the fundamental datum of human existence is *man with man*,"[3] or Buber's celebrated "I-Thou" concept,[4] or again, John Macmurray's concept of "the mutuality of the personal."[5] The central insight here is that interpersonal relatedness pertains to the essential core of man's being; persons are constituted as such by their relations with other persons; the unit of personal existence is not "I" in isolation but "I" and "you" in mutual relationship. Negatively stated, man is not first a fully-constituted person in his own right who then becomes related to others; sociality, culture and community are not merely peripheral and secondary to human existence.

It is then argued that this world of "processive relationism" excludes the possibility of absolute values. For, "if one sub-scribes, as I do, to a processive view of reality in which the 'total human situation' is itself in process, then it is not possible to sort out and safeguard any 'absolutes' which would exist and have their reality independent of the process."[6] The aim of this article, however, is to show that the concept of ethical absolute (in a sense to be explained) *is* valid in a processive and relational uni-verse. To make my point, I shall first specify the ethical context: the metaphysical realm out of which moral values, acts and prin-ciples arise. Then I shall indicate what bearing this metaphysics has on the question of ethical absolutes.

I

THE PRIMACY AND MUTUALITY OF THE PERSONAL

We must first distinguish "interpersonal relatedness" from "impersonal cosmic process," or more generally "personal" from "biological-material" reality (i.e., Nature). The personal is con-stituted by spiritual activities such as self-consciousness, reflec-tion, conceptualization, symbolization (language, etc.), loving, in-tending and culture-making in general (both on the theoretical and practical levels), which are missing from Nature, or from the cosmic. Hence, the personal is ontologically higher than or "more than" Nature. Indeed, contemporary currents of philosophy such as existentialism, phenomenology and personalism, not to men-tion much of traditional philosophy, have made it something of a commonplace that the person transcends the cosmos, that the subjectivity of the person cannot be adequately understood in terms of the impersonal structures of objective nature.[7] Or as one author, focussing specifically upon the question of "person and process," puts it:

What distinguishes the person from lower inorganic pro-cesses is a two-fold *ecstasis*. A person is more than a mere recapitulation of the past; there is a vectoral orientation away from the present, an element which gives the future a reality which it cannot have in lower beings. Every vow, promise, project, or plan mortgages the future and hurls the person toward a conscious rendezvous with that which is to come. This is the first ecstatic movement. . . . .

The second movement is expressed in the exodus of the self toward other selves. The human person can only expand in the existential order by seeking to lose himself in another and by coinciding with the other, by seeking to be not where one is, but where the other person is . . .[8]

The transcendence of the person to Nature, however, does not imply a dualism between them. For man is also immanent within Nature; he has his roots in it. Through his organic body he partially includes and indeed is partially constituted by Nature. His body is the medium between him and the rest of Nature, and without it his spiritual core or essence could not actualize and express itself. The human person, in other words, is embodied or incarnate spirit. Yet, the body is subordinate to the spirit; it is for the sake of the spirit and not the other way around. Moreover, man as spiritual and rational should control (or subordinate) Nature for the enhancement of the human condition. This does not imply, of course, that man abuses and pollutes Nature as he has done. Quite the contrary, man can only effectively control Nature for his own benefit if he respects it and adopts a properly aesthetic attitude toward it.[9]

All of this may be summarized in the following formula: the person partially includes, subordinates, and is partially constituted by Nature or the cosmos. I say "partially" to indicate two things: first, the person's transcendence to Nature; and secondly, Nature's objectivity in its own right. Or as Teilhard de Chardin has pointed out by his law of complexity-consciousness, the person possesses more being than the various levels of cosmic reality, while at the same time he possesses whatever being they have; the person is "more than" rather than "other than" Nature. In brief, the person is both transcendent to and immanent within Nature or the cosmos.

Consequently, although the person has his roots in Nature, he cannot be reduced to it. To attempt to do so is to commit the genetic fallacy. In view of man's transcendence, it is the personal, not Nature, which is the primary level of reality. This is *a fortiori* the case in a theistic universe—to which I subscribe—whose creator and sustainer is an infinite person. The structure of cosmic reality, then, is not definitive or determinative of the personal. Although the cosmic has a certain heuristic value for the personal, in the last analysis the latter must be examined and judged on its own terms. And since, as we shall see, it is precisely personal reality which is the moral context, what is determinative of the moral order is the structure of the personal—not the cosmos or Nature.

Mutuality

Now, a permanent and abiding characteristic of personal reality is, to use Macmurray's term, its mutuality; without mutuality there simply would not be any persons. Indeed, the mutuality of the personal is its *fundamental* feature. For the interrelation of persons covers, by definition, the whole field of persons-in-relation and is the inclusive context and matrix for all aspects of experience, culture, and those spiritual activities of man which were previously mentioned. There is nothing that is truly personal that is not related to and not dependent upon the mutuality of persons. Even an individual's biological make-up is transmitted in and through the interpersonal context; it depends upon the procreation of persons.

As including all persons, the mutuality of the personal refers to both the direct and indirect relations of persons. The first involves face-to-face contact, or personal acquaintance. The second lacks this quality, yet the persons involved are related to each other politically, economically or metaphysically. I am politically related to those Americans on the West Coast whom I do not know, since we all belong to the same nation. I am economically related to those Italians who built and exported my automobile. And I am metaphysically related to the people of India and China.

For we are all members of the human family; we are all brothers under the fatherhood of God. Since there are some four billion people on earth, it is clear that the vast majority of interpersonal relations are indirect rather than direct. Still, the direct relations are the basis for the indirect ones; without the direct relations of persons there would be no indirect relations.

Mutuality's emphasis on relatedness, however, does not deny the reality and importance of personal individuality. On the contrary, the mutuality of the personal is its necessary condition; it is only in and through the interpersonal context that the individual can exist and grow. Both relationality and individuality are essential dimensions of personhood; neither by itself constitutes a person's total reality. Still, relationality is primary, while individuality—both that which is given at birth and that acquired after birth—is secondary and derivative, yet necessary.

Historically, the mutuality of the personal may be contrasted with "individualism." For individualism, the realm of persons-in-relation is an "aggregate"; for the mutuality of the personal, it is a "field." An aggregate is a group whose members are extrinsically related to each other, e.g., a heap of stones. Take away the heap, take away the extrinsic relations among the stones, and each stone retains its full individuality. Similarly, for individualism, take away the relations of persons, and each person is left intact in his individuality. Each person is first fully constituted as an individual person in his own right and then, as a secondary and peripheral moment of his existence, becomes related to other persons. The aggregate view of persons-in-relation can be seen in the early Modern social-contract theory of society, in Descartes' conception of personhood as *cogito*, and in the Aristotelian-Scholastic definition of man as a rational substance in which relation is merely an "accident." On the other hand, the field theory holds that the relations among persons are *intrinsic* to their personhood; take away the relations among persons, and one *ipso facto* takes away the persons who hitherto were related. For the aggregate theory, there can be an "I" in isolation; for the field theory, there is no "I" apart from the "I-You" relationship.

Yet it would seem that in a hermitage there is an "I" in isolation. A moment's reflection, however, shows that this is not the case. Although the hermit does indeed *intend* his isolation from his fellow men, he cannot completely negate his *de facto* relatedness to them. To begin with, he was born and reared in an interpersonal context—first in a family and then in a larger society. Secondly, he carries a consciousness of others into his hermitage. Thirdly, although he might be able to abolish direct relations (and even this is doubtful), he certainly cannot eliminate indirect ones. Not only is he metaphysically related to all people; he is also dependent upon the larger society economically and politically. Finally, the mental well-being of most people—including the hermit—would undoubtedly suffer in lengthy isolation. Indeed, his hermitage may be the result of some kind of mental disorder. In this connection, solitary confinement has always been considered one of the worst punishments ever devised by man.

II
ETHICAL IMPLICATIONS

Mutuality, then, is fundamental to personal reality. This suggests that the moral order or context is the field of the interrelation of persons, "I" and "You" in mutual relation, not "I" in isolation. The moral problematic is the interpersonal situation. The possibility of an action having moral quality—the possibility of it being morally right or wrong—requires at least two persons in relation. In such a relational situation there arises the essentially ethical question as to how I should act toward you and how you should act toward me. If, *ex hypothesi*, only one person existed, there would be no morality; no action could have a moral character; the distinction between moral and immoral would be meaningless.[10]

Since the mutuality of the personal includes all persons, the interpersonal context of morality implicitly involves the whole of humanity; it includes the indirect as well as the direct relations of persons. This provides us with an ontological ground for what is often called the universality of the moral claim, i.e., the claim that when one acts, he does not merely choose what is good for him in that particular situation, but, more significantly, implicitly claims that his course of action is good for anyone acting in that type of situation. Moreover, that situation is implicitly and ultimately the whole of humanity. Whenever one acts, he must consider the bearing or consequences of his action on the entire human race—both in the future as well as in the present—and not merely on the immediate situation or direct relationships which involve him at the moment.[11]

The foregoing analysis has three implications. First, since moral quality or value arises from the mutuality of the personal, the primary purpose of ethical value is to promote and maintain the good (or well-being) of persons-in-relation.[12] This good, in its full and complete sense, I call "community," and it unites both of the persons' ecstatic movements: toward other persons and toward the future.[13] Secondly, since mutuality is a permanent and abiding feature of personal reality, community is likewise a permanent and abiding ethical value. Finally, since mutuality is the fundamental and all-inclusive given of personal reality, and since community is permanent and abiding, community is the supreme—i.e., absolute—ethical value. Let us now indicate its essential characteristics.

Community is an enduring type of human association or relatedness whose originating and sustaining motive is love,[14] whose constituent values are freedom,[15] equality,[16] and justice,[17] and whose fruition is the joy and communion[18] existing among its members. It is a relationship of persons *qua* persons rather than persons *qua* functions or objects; a relationship of persons in the wholeness of their personhood; an "I-Thou" rather than "I-It" relationship; a mutual being-of-oneself with and for the Other. In brief, it is the self-realization of persons-in-relation. It is defined in terms of quality rather than quantity. Its size can range from two persons in genuine friendship or marriage to a universal community involving all persons, i.e., the brotherhood or fellowship of all men. Community is the type of interpersonal relatedness embedded in the Christian Gospel. Thus, the establishment of a universal community could be characterized as the kingdom of heaven on earth.

To be sure, the community so far achieved by man is woefully inadequate. The family and friendship are probably its most prevalent examples,[19] although many families, of course, could not be considered communities in my sense. Certainly, there is nothing approaching universal community. Still, any instance of genuine community should also contain an implicit intention to create and maintain universal community. This means that in actually loving the personal Other in those communities of which I am a member, I also maintain the determination to love and help any human being with whom I am brought into contact, whatever the circumstances. The universalization and institutionalization of such a determination would *ipso facto* constitute an actual universal community.

Community, then, is the supreme ethical value; it provides an ultimate or absolute standard by which we can judge the morality of any action. An act is morally good if it promotes or maintains community and morally bad if it diminishes or destroys community. This does not mean, however, that community denies the good of individual persons. For it is precisely individual persons who make up community, and it is *their* self-realization which is intended in and through community. Consequently, apart from the good and self-realization of individual persons, community would be impossible. Conversely, apart from community, the good and self-realization of individual persons would be impossible. Community is neither an organic-type reality which suppresses individuality nor an atomistic-type reality in which the individuals can achieve their self-realization separately. Rather, in view of the mutuality of the personal, community is a personal-type reality which fulfills individuality by intending its condition—the good or well-being of interpersonal relatedness.[20]

Since community involves the whole self or person, it does not involve a purely "spiritual" relatedness. Implicit within community is an institutional and organizational arrangement to meet man's economic and material needs, as well as his spiritual and psychological ones. For example, any marriage or family involves some kind of division of labor and coordination of functions between husband and wife to meet each family member's economic needs. Yet, this arrangement is not an end in itself; it is in and for the family's total community, i.e., their mutual self-realization. Each member's economic relatedness and well-being must be subordinated to his spiritual or personal relatedness and well-being. This example may be generalized by saying that community includes, subordinates, and is partially constituted by a type of human association or relatedness which is essentially economic, and which we call "society."[21]

Since community is an absolute value, it is always better to intend it than not to intend it, or to intend its opposite. Moreover, as the supreme ethical value or ultimate ethical norm, it is the *one* ethical absolute; there cannot be a plurality of ethical absolutes. This does not mean, however, that all other ethical values, principles and acts are relative or provisional. In this connection, let us distinguish between the concepts of "intrinsic" and *prima facie* good and evil.

Good and Evil

Intrinsic evil denotes a specific act or principle which is universally and necessarily evil, or evil in all actual and possible situations as far as one can conceive.[22] In Kant's terminology, such acts can be formalized in synthetic *a priori* judgments,[23] in which case the act becomes a principle, e.g., "slavery is immoral (or evil)." Although "absolute" and "intrinsic" are the same in terms of universality and necessity, there are two important differences between them. First, absolute is a primary or fundamental concept: it is the basis for all acts and principles which are either intrinsic or *prima facie*. On the other hand, intrinsic is a derivative or secondary concept; it derives its moral character precisely from community, the ethical absolute. Secondly, since the ethical absolute—*qua* absolute—implicitly covers, or is coextensive with, the whole moral order, it is somewhat indeterminate. On the other hand, intrinsic refers to a specific or determinate act or principle.

Prima facie evil denotes a specific act or principle which is significantly evil and therefore evil in general, or evil in the ordinary run of situations, but not universally and necessarily evil, not evil in so-called extraordinary or exceptional situations. In Kant's terminology, *prima facie* evil acts or principles can be formulated in synthetic *a posteriori* judgments.[24]

Of central importance to *prima facie* evil is a distinction between the "common" and "particular" features of an act. The former denotes those features shared by all instances of a class of acts in virtue of which they are members of that class. For example, any individual war is included within the class "war" because of certain common features which apply to all wars without which they could not be so classified. The common features of an act constitute the definition of that act, or its "essential core."

On the other hand, the particular features of an act denote the individuating circumstances of a singular concrete act within a given class of acts, which circumstances make it *that* act and none other. For example, the Vietnam War has certain unique and individuating circumstances—i.e., particular features—which make it different from all other wars. The particular features of a singular act are excluded from the definition or essential core of the class of acts of which it is a member.

From a moral standpoint, then, any individual act is a combination of two kinds of features: its common features which constitute and define a given class of acts; and its particular features, which distinguish an individual act from every other one within that class. Now, the notion of *prima facie* evil applies to the common features, the essential core, of an act. It is the evilness of this essential core which makes a given class of acts evil in general, or evil in the ordinary run of situations. However, since *prima facie* evil as such does not apply to the particular features of an act, we cannot say that the evilness of the common features makes every instance of that act evil. For it is quite possible for the particular features of some of these instances to possess more good than the evil contained in its common features. Such instances, however, constitute so-called extraordinary situations; they are the exception rather than the rule. For the essential core, precisely as essential core, *tends* to override or outweigh the particular features. Therefore, a general bias or attitude ought to be established against the performance of *prima facie* evil acts.

On the other hand, the concept of intrinsic evil applies to the act as a whole—to both its particular and common features. And since such an act is evil as a whole, it is universally and necessarily evil, or evil in all actual and possible instances. Yet, this does not imply that *every* particular feature of all instances of such an act is evil. Rather, an act is intrinsically evil when its essential core is so gravely evil that no actual or possible set of circumstances, whatever goodness they may contain, could render an instance of that act good in the concrete; that it is impossible for any individual act's particular features to possess sufficient goodness to outweigh or even equal the evil of its common features; and that, therefore, the act as a concrete whole always possesses more evil than good. In other words, the essential core is so evil that its evilness diffuses and corrodes the act as a whole, and overrides whatever goodness the particular features may have, notwithstanding that a particular feature considered in isolation from the whole act may have more good than evil.

Let us exemplify these abstract notions. In my judgment, "slavery"—either on an individual or institutional level—is intrinsically evil. Slavery here is defined as an established or settled type of interpersonal relatedness—a *modus vivendi*, if you will—in which the self treats the other solely as a means and not as an end, or treats him merely as an object, thing or function and not as a person. As so defined, slavery so gravely violates the constituent values of community—equality, freedom and justice—that I cannot conceive of a situation in which it would be morally justifiable.

"War," on the other hand, is an example of *prima facie* evil. For all individual wars, whatever their particular features, possess certain common features such as armed conflict between two or more nations, and the large-scale destruction of life, property and economic resources, which are clearly evil and destructive of community. Hence, a general moral bias ought to be established against the performance of war.

Yet, it is possible to have a just war, one in which the good of its particular features outweighs the evil of its common features. In general, the conditions for a just war have been set forth in the traditional just war theory, which I think is basically sound.[25] In the light of the ethical theory I have sketched, the ultimate justification of war and, indeed, of the just war theory itself, lies in community. Accordingly, a just war is one which intends the protection and preservation of a certain community—e.g., a nation and its constituent families, friendships and institutions—against an unjust agressor, e.g., Hitler invading Poland.

The ethical theory presented here clearly has a bearing upon the situation ethics debate.[26] Perhaps the fundamental doctrine of situation ethics—at least of Fletcher's situationism—is that moral quality or value is an "extrinsic predicate" rather than an "intrinsic property" of acts.[27] What this means, in effect, is that no act has an *essential core* (or common features) which is good or bad as such. Apart from the concrete situation in which a specific type of act becomes embodied, an act is simply ethically neutral or amoral. The agent predicates goodness or badness of an act precisely when he concretizes it in an individual situation. And what determines the concretized act as good or bad is whether or not it is informed and directed by "love"—Fletcher's absolute moral standard.[28] Accordingly, the agent predicates moral quality extrinsically of an act, i.e., extrinsically of the essential core of an act, or the act considered abstractly.

Such ethical neutrality, however, is simply false.[29] As I have tried to show, an act considered abstractly or in its essential core is as much the subject of moral quality as is the concrete act, i.e., the act possessing particular features as well as common ones. Not only does Fletcher deny the validity of intrinsic evil, but of *prima facie* evil as well. For him all morality is located within the particular features of an individual concrete act. In this respect, his ethical theory is extremely inadequate.

To be sure, Fletcher is justified in criticizing "legalism" for its inordinate list of intrinsically good and evil acts. In the total moral order, the number of intrinsic evils is relatively small in relation to *prima facie* evils. However, just as legalism and much of traditional ethics absolutizes the relative (to borrow Fletcher's phrase), neither should we go to the opposite extreme and relativize the absolute. One of the major tasks of an adequate ethical theory is to mediate between these two extremes, and to re-examine the concepts of ethical absolute and intrinsic good and evil.

Notes

1. Eugene Fontinell, "Towards an Ethics of Relationships," *Situationism and the New Morality*, ed. by Robert L. Cunningham (New York: Appleton-Century-Crofts, 1970) p. 207.

2. For an attempt to interpret the category of substance as fundamentally processive and relational without losing its subsistence, see James M. Somerville, "Toward a More Dynamic Understanding of Substance and Relation," *Wisdom in Depth*, ed. by Vincent F. Daues, Maurice R. Holloway, and Leo Sweeney (Milwaukee: Bruce Publishing Co., 1966) pp. 218-234.

3. "I and Thou," tr. Forrest Williams, *The Philosophy of Martin Buber*, ed. Paul Arthur Schilpp and Maurice Friedman (La Salle, Illinois: Open Court, 1967) p. 43. (Marcel's emphasis.)

4. *I and Thou*, tr. by Ronald Gregor Smith, 2nd ed. (New York: Charles Scribner's Sons, 1958.)

5. *Persons in Relation* (London: Faber and Faber, 1961). See also my study, John Macmurray's Logical Form of the Personal: A Critical Exposition. Diss. Fordham University 1970.

6. Fontinell, p. 201, n. 2.

7. See, for example, Joseph de Finance "Being and Subjectivity" *Cross Currents* 6 (1956) 163-178. Unless otherwise indicated, "person" refers strictly to "human persons."

8. Somerville, p. 232. (Author's emphasis.)

9. For a brief development of this point, see my "Ecology and Dualism" *Religion in Life* 42 (Spring, 1973) 117-127.

10. Although the interpersonal context of morality refers primarily to human persons, it also includes God. That is, apart from the human interpersonal context, most of our moral acts and values would be nonexistent. But not all of them. For example, if someone were the last person on earth because of a nuclear holocaust, he would still have a moral obligation not to blaspheme God and not to commit suicide. Needless to say, however, this example is highly improbable.

11. This has been a persistent criticism of situation ethics, i.e., that it interprets the ethical situation too narrowly. As one critic of Joseph Fletcher—perhaps the best-known situationist—remarks: "It is terribly important how one understands his situation. Is it boy plus girl between 1 A.M. and 3 A.M. after a number of drinks in a motel room who feel affection for each other stimulated by proper knowledge of erogenous zones? Or is it boy, responsible to others than the girl, and responsible to and for her over a long period of time under a covenant of some sort, plus girl concerned not only for the present moment but for the past and future relationships as well, in a human community for whose vitality and order they have responsibility and which in turn has to seek its common good?" James M. Gustafson, "How Does Love Reign?" *The Situation*

Ethics Debate, ed. Harvey Cox (Philadelphia: Westminster Press, 1968) p. 80.

12. I equate the terms "value" and "good" but not "value" and "ought." In my view, value or good is the ground of ought or obligation rather than the other way around. Thus, my ethical theory is "axiological" rather than "deontological."

13. Somerville, p. 232.

14. "Love" denotes an attitude or disposition of the self which has the following characteristics. First, it is both cognitive and affective, although primarily affective. Secondly, it is heterocentric rather than egocentric, i.e., it aims primarily at the Other's good, and aims at the self's good only insofar as it contributes to the good of the Other. Thirdly, it is universal, directed toward any person. Fourthly, it is manifested primarily on the level of action. Finally, the perfection of love requires its reciprocation.

15. "Freedom" in this context implies three qualities. First, it implies being-oneself, the ability to spontaneously express oneself, the absence in all one's activity of undue emotional and social inhibition. Secondly, it implies the possession of significant alternatives among which the self can choose. Finally, it implies self-mastery, the self's ability and power to consistently direct himself toward self-chosen, meaningful and ethically significant goals.

16. "Equality" denotes what I call "personal" rather than either "natural," "social" or "legal" equality. Natural equality denotes any specific, *de facto*, genetic similarity among persons, e.g., physical and temperamental qualities, intelligence, talents, abilities, etc. Social equality refers to similarities among persons acquired in society, e.g., occupations, wealth, status, power, etc. Legal equality refers to uniformity of rights among persons guaranteed by the laws and constitution of a government. Personal equality simply denotes the intention of the self to treat the personal Other as a person and with the respect which is commensurate with his dignity as a person, or, as Kant put it, to treat the other person as an end and never merely as a means. Since both self and Other are persons who thus have the same personal nature—constituted by mutuality, agency and reason—to treat the Other as a person is *ipso facto* to treat him as an equal. Personal equality, I should add, is the foundation of legal equality, whereas, needless to say, there is a vast amount of natural and social inequality. However, although natural inequality is pretty much a fixed biological given, the present-day *extremes* of social inequality are not, in my judgment, morally justifiable. In general, social inequality is justifiable insofar as it is based upon natural inequality. Still, natural and social inequality should be subordinated to personal equality and, indirectly, to legal equality.

17. By *"justice"* I mean giving the other person what is due him as a matter of right. Cf. my "The Morality of Amnesty" *American Bene-*

dictine Review 24 (1973) 100-104. See also Macmurray, pp. 186-205. As pertaining to community, justice refers basically to what Aquinas called "commutative" justice, justice among equals. Especially in terms of larger communities, however, justice also involves "distributive" and "contributive" justice.

18. Here the basic attitude is: "We belong together and are glad for it."

19. It is extremely doubtful whether the commune-type living of some of our youth is a genuine example of community.

20. In this connection, ethical value is naturally oriented toward religion. Religious value covers what the ethical does—the interrelation of persons and community. However, it goes beyond ethical value in three important respects. First, religion, unlike morality, is based explicitly upon man's relation to God. For religion, the concept of a universal, infinite personal Other is a desideratum in thinking the ground and unity of community. With God, we can think not only the brotherhood of man, but also the brotherhood of man under the fatherhood of God. Still, although an ethical theory can get by without God, its perfection requires the concept of a theistic God as the ultimate ground of reality and of value. Secondly, religion involves celebratory values (celebratory of the brotherhood or communion binding its participants) expressed in rituals and ceremonies, which are missing from morality. This is the aesthetic moment of religion, while theology is its intellectual moment. Finally, religion involves a reference to the after-life, whereas such a concept is not essential to morality.

21. In turn, society includes a legal aspect, which beyond a certain size becomes the state. Marriage itself normally has a legal aspect. Yet, the legal aspect of marriage is in and for the social and communal, just as the social is in and for the communal. Thus, the three basic types of human association—from highest to lowest in terms of ontological inclusiveness—are community, society and the state.

22. I add the qualification "as far as one can conceive" because it makes little sense to speak of possible situations beyond one's conception.

23. They could not be formalized in analytic judgments without becoming tautologous and trivial.

24. On *prima facie* evil, cf. W. D. Ross, *The Right and the Good* (Oxford: University Press, 1930) especially pp. 19-47.

25. See, for example, Austin Fagothey, *Right and Reason* 4th ed. (St. Louis: C. V. Mosby Co., 1967) pp. 244-252. I do not believe, however, that this theory is entirely applicable to nuclear warfare.

26. Cf. *The Situation Ethics Debate*.

27. Fletcher, *Situation Ethics* (Philadelphia: Westminster Press, 1966) pp. 57-68; *Moral Responsibility* (Westminster Press, 1967) pp. 29-57.

28. Nevertheless, for Fletcher love does not possess moral quality independently of the situation; it is completely a function of the particular features of a situation. As he puts it: "When we say that love is always good, what we mean is that whatever is loving in any *particular* situation is good!" *Situation Ethics*, p. 61. (Fletcher's emphasis)

29. To be fair, however, Fletcher does say that the situationist enters into every situation fully armed with the ethical principles of his community and its heritage and that he treats them as "illuminators" of the situation. But at the same time he denies that these principles have any *prescriptive* force. (*Situation Ethics*, pp. 26, 31.) And since they are not prescriptive, does that not imply that they are amoral, or ethically neutral? Or is Fletcher trying to introduce a *tertium quid* between the purely prescriptive and purely descriptive? Unfortunately, he does not tell us.

The Direct/Indirect
Distinction in Morals

Albert Di Ianni, S.M.

The principal tool within the Catholic moral tradition for dealing with conflict-situations has been the principle of double effect. Reflecting upon and expanding certain remarks of Aquinas on the indirect voluntary, moralists have refined the principle and applied it to an increasing number of moral issues since the second half of the 16th century up to the present day.[1] The central nerve of the principle is the notion that evil should never be the object of direct intention whether as an end (*per se et propter se*) or as a means to a good end (*per se sed non propter se*). Three of the four well-known conditions for legitimate application of the principle are aimed at insuring indirect voluntariety (a permitting rather than an intending will) relative to an act which one foresees will have both a good and an evil effect. First, the *finis operis*, the inner object or constitutive intentionality of the act itself, as distinguished from the effects of the act, must be morally good or at least indifferent. Just as in structuralist thought a literary piece has an intersubjective intentionality or life of its own independent of the intentions of the author, so in traditional moral theology an act is viewed in its immediate and constitutive result (*finis operis*) as having an intersubjective moral meaning independent of the concrete intention of the agent and the consequences of the act. This *finis operis*, moreover, is the principal moral index; if it is morally evil the act can never be deemed objectively good, but at best subjectively inculpable due to extrinsic guilt-reducing factors such as ignorance, fear, passion and the like. The second condition is that the agent's intention must encompass only the good effect of the act and not the evil effect. The third condition is that the evil effect of the act must not mediate the good effect; the evil effect must not be the means willed whereby the good effect is produced. There is a fourth condition, viz., that there must be a proportionate reason for positing such a polyvalent moral act. This last condition has little bearing upon ensuring the indirect voluntariety of the act and can be viewed as a teleological or quasi-utilitarian consideration about consequences. It concerns more directly the production of the good than the deontological rightness or fittingness of the act.

I

Until recently most twentieth-century Catholic authors have acknowledged the broad moral relevance of the principle of double effect and of the embodied distinction between an intending (direct) and permitting (indirect) will. During the last decade, however, several authors, led by P. Knauer,[2] have insisted that in analyzing the moral meaning of a human decision, we have considered the act posited too abstractly and absolutely, treating it too readily as a unit of meaning which is by itself susceptible of a moral index.[3] These authors prefer to treat the posited act or means as a constitutive part or stage of a larger whole, which whole is the primary object of one's intention and thus is the only true unit of moral significance. The traditional emphasis, on the *ex objecto* evil of an act prior to consideration of any circumstance or intention, it is claimed, has led to conclusions which are too literal, mechanical or artificial, conclusions which are in some cases morally erroneous.

An oft-cited example is that of ectopic pregnancy where the embryo is developing within the fallopian tube. When medical authority began describing the tube as pathological in itself prior to the lodging of the embryo therein, Catholic moralists applied the principle of double effect and allowed doctors to excise the tube with the intention of curing the pathology in the realization that while the act saved the life of the woman it would destroy the non-viable embryo which was present in the excised tube. The object of the act performed was characterized as the good act of "excising a malfunctioning organ" and the death of the embryo was viewed as an oblique side effect only indirectly willed. These same moralists forbade doctors to shell out the embryo from the tube thus correcting the problem while leaving the tube and the woman's fertility intact. This was considered a directly intended killing of the embryo and the direct intention of an intrinsically evil act even as a means to a proportionate good was not allowed.

Today several contemporary Catholic moralists believe that the shelling out of the embryo is morally preferable on the grounds that on balance it causes less evil than the excising of the tube; even though both methods kill the embryo and save the mother, the former method avoids the mutilation and reduction of fertility of the woman. The more conservative among this group like G. Grisez attempt to construe the shelling out of the embryo in such circumstances as still comprising an indirectly intended causation of evil by placing less stress upon the physical action done and more upon the intention in their description of the act.[4] Others, however, criticizing more radically, feel that the whole traditional emphasis upon the distinction between direct and indirect intentionality is misguided, and that it should be downplayed or even discarded in favor of the principle of the proportionate good or the lesser of two evils, a principle which, in their view, more closely expresses the true substance of the moral enterprise and harmonizes more closely with our moral experience.

Among this second group we find Van der Marck[5] and Van der Poel.[6] Influenced by P. Knauer they begin by insisting that the question: "What act is being done?" cannot be answered by pointing to the immediate causal result alone of the intervention. Rather, a proper description of a human act must encompass and emphasize the foreseen end motivating the act. (The intention, in fact, becomes the paramount feature in a proper description of a human act *qua* human.) A human act is not merely a physical or causal intervention in the world. An act as *human* act must be viewed as an organic whole whose two aspects are the constitutive causal intentionality of the act (*finis operis*) *and* the end-in-view. The aspects considered isolatedly and in themselves should not be given any moral weight or index for the good or the bad. Only the totality of the act is a proper candidate for moral adjudication.[7] Finally, the sole criterion of moral desirability is whether or not this entire whole is seen to be community-building in the long term. In the example cited, the shelling out of the embryo would be preferable to the excision of the tube on the ground that it constitutes an intermediate *pre-moral* stage in a larger totality of intersubjective moral meaning whose principal determinant is the end-in-view, viz., the saving of the life as well as the fertility of the mother. The moral desirability of this complex of factors is judged on the grounds that it is more community-building (utility-maximizing) than the more conservative alternative of excising the tube with the embryo. It gains the day because, although it causes the death of the embryo, it preserves full fertility while the other alternative diminishes the woman's physical integrity while also killing the embryo. The human act comprehensively viewed, then, is deemed morally correct. The immediate physical intervention performed (the shelling out of the embryo) is construed as partaking of the *positive* moral good of the whole human act. As such, morally speaking, it can be not only permitted but even directly intended as part of the totality of factors which is seen as producing more good in the situation than any other possible complex of factors. The moral act is here analyzed in terms of decision / consequences rather than in terms of act / consequences; the emphasis on means (or action) so paramount in traditional moral theology falls away and the *finis operis* of the act performed must take its place alongside the more mediate effects of the action.

Though his own position owes much to this type of analysis, R. McCormick correctly criticizes these authors for not carving out precise criteria for deciding when a piece of behavior may legitimately be construed as "an intermediate stage" in a larger complex of meaning. He asks whether "every pre-moral evil which occurs in any way in conjunction with my activity 'may' be reduced to an intermediate stage."[8] For example, "Is the killing of innocent children to get at the enemy's morale simply an 'intermediate stage' of an action describable as 'national self-defense?' "[9] Irrespective of what these authors might personally hold on these questions, there is nothing in these theories to preclude an affirmative answer. So, it is difficult to see how these theories would differ from a thoroughgoing act-utilitarianism. Act-utilitarianism is a completely future-oriented theory which strives to choose the act in a situation which it is foreseen will produce the best consequences for society as a whole. It de-emphasizes almost entirely considerations concerning the causal act itself. It views all acts as ultimately morally neutral when viewed apart from a situation and is open to the possibility of any act becoming a *positive right-making characteristic* in some situation. Talk of intrinsic moral evil of acts in any sense is avoided and rules forbidding actions if invoked at all are secondary rules of thumb or open-ended empirical generalizations necessary only because people often lack the time, perspicuity or emotional control to assess each new situation *ab ovo*. The constant criticism of act-utilitarianism over the years has emphasized especially its inability to coherently encompass what philosophers have called "duties of perfect obligation" like justice, fidelity, reparation and gratitude.[10]

The more conservative ethicist Germain Grisez agrees with other contemporary moralists that the traditional textbook handling of the principle of double effect overstressed the physical causality of the act.[11] He retains, however, the importance of the direct-indirect distinction in morals and does not so thoroughly demote the relevance of the causal means posited. Grisez is concerned to avoid utilitarianism by remaining within the framework of the principle of double effect. But he does attempt a refinement on the criteria for determining when an evil produced in or by an act might be construed as indirectly willed in an act which in its overall thrust is aimed at the production of a proportionate good. He invokes the practical indivisibility of the act by human choice as a sufficient condition for deciding which aspects of the act are to be construed as means and which as effect. He maintains that when an act is posited with two effects (one good and one evil), if no other act *does* intervene or *could in practice* intervene between the action posited and one or other of the effects then the effects should be said to be produced with equal immediacy. In such a case, moreover, the good effect may without arbitrariness be considered as the sole object of direct intention while the evil is considered as merely permitted. In other words, if the good effect emanates from the act posited with equal causal immediacy as the bad effect it is not then related to the bad effect as means to an end and thus if there is present a proportionate reason, then the act is morally permissible. If the good effect does or could conceivably arise from a causal act which is posterior to a more original act which causes the evil effect, then this more original act must be construed as aiming at evil alone and is morally forbidden.[12]

Pursuant to his principle, Grisez contends that one cannot justify the commission of adultery by a mother aiming to be released from a concentration camp in order to succor her children, because the saving effect would not be present in the one act which is also adulterous but in a subsequent human act—that of the person who orders their release. In such an instance adultery would be intended as an evil means to a good end. On the other hand, a mother who saves her child by purposely interposing her body as a shield against an attacking animal is justified since the very performance which is self-destructive is also with equal immediacy protective. Organ transplants which involve the deprivation of the life of the donor (e.g., a father giving his heart for his son) are immoral because the two aspects, excision and implantation are factually separable; this for Grisez translates into the killing of one as a means to the saving of the other. Capital punishment is not morally justifiable: the argument from deterrence, even if factually defensible, is "ethically invalid, because the good is achieved in other human acts, not in the execution itself."[13] Grisez does, however, allow an abortion to save the life of the mother, because here the removal of the fetus produces at once (with equal causal immediacy) the good effect and the bad effect. The shelling out of the ectopic embryo is also morally permissible because the one same act which produces the death of the embryo produces with equal immediacy the saving of the life of the mother.

II

McCormick welcomes Grisez's refinements upon the criteria for discriminating between direct and indirect voluntariety but criticizes him for not pressing far enough his critique of traditional Catholic moral theory, and specifically for not bringing under question the very moral relevance of the direct-indirect distinction in general.[14] Why must we say that a person turns against the good when an evil means toward a good end is the direct object of an intending will? Is a directly intended homicide always an evil *in se* and if so, why? Does not the end sometimes justify the direct intention of an evil means? McCormick's own view is closer to that of Bruno Schüller by whom he is heavily influenced but whom he also criticizes, as we shall see. Schüller retains the moral decisiveness of the direct-indirect distinction only in a drastically reduced number of cases. In line with the traditional doctrine he agrees that one can never posit an act which is morally, intrinsically evil. But he differs from the tradition in the identification of such acts which are intrinsically evil. He draws a clear-cut distinction between two types of evils which may constitute the *finis operis* of human acts, moral evil and non-moral evil.[15] An act is intrinsically evil with the effect that it is never to be directly intended only if it in its immediate causal nature (*finis operis*) constitutes in itself a *moral* evil and not if it constitutes only a non-moral evil. And the only act which seems to qualify for Schüller is an act of scandal.[16] To directly will and commit scandal is never justifiable by a good end, no matter how important, because scandal is *ex objecto* a moral evil in itself. The *finis operis* of any of the other acts traditionally labelled intrinsically evil is for Schüller only a non-moral evil. As examples he cites, e.g., homicide, lying, sterilization, which effect the non-moral evils of death, error, infertility, and so on. For Schüller such acts may, morally speaking, be directly intended and performed if there is a proportionate reason, if, in other words, the positing of such non-morally evil acts constitutes the lesser of two non-moral evils in a situation. Concurring with Schüller thus far McCormick remarks relative to the axiom that the end does not justify the means, "If it means that a non-moral good (end) does not justify a morally bad means, it is correct. If, however, it is understood to mean that no good end (whether the good be moral or non-moral) can justify a *non-moral* evil means, it is false; for it is precisely the good end envisaged that justifies causing or permitting a non-moral evil."[17]

As I mentioned, McCormick will have difficulty with other aspects of Schüller's position, but before I enter into this allow me to set forth a confusion of which I believe this whole new school (Schüller, Fuchs, Janssens, McCormick *et alii*) is guilty. It is the confusion between 1) the *finis operis* of a human act and 2) the effect brought about in the act. The first refers to the tendency or intentionality of the act, which *includes* the note of the *causality* of the act as well as the effect; whereas the second is simply the immediate effect of the act. The first concept refers to the fact that the act is *aimed causally* at "X" while the second refers to the "X" in and of itself. Applied to the case of direct homicide, for instance, one must not conflate but distinguish between the non-moral evil immediately effected (death) and the free causation of that same non-moral evil (homicide).[18] What must be remembered is that what precisely demands justification here is homicide and not the immediate effect which is death; the question, in other words, is whether homicide can be the object of direct intention for a good end. We must agree that "death" is not, in itself, a moral concept—it refers to a non-moral, ontic or pre-moral evil—but the concept of the free causation of death has at least minimal *moral* meaning in itself prior to consideration of intention and circumstances; such an act might well be construed as intrinsically evil in a weaker sense than that of the manual tradition.[19] This would allow us to speak of the principle of the lesser moral evil as one of the basic principles guiding actions in morals.

Why does an act have always to be morally overriding in itself in a situation to be construed as a bearer of moral meaning in itself? (Let us grant for the sake of argument that "scandal" does constitute such an overridingly evil act.) It seems to me that "direct killing of an innocent," for example, might well be construed as a bearer of negative moral meaning, onstage as it were, even if one goes on to say that theoretically it might be morally tolerated in some drastic situation. It could be characterized as "intrinsically evil," though in a weaker sense than that of the tradition. This would mean that it would not always be forbidden whatever the circumstances. And if it is performed when it is morally tolerable it would *not* produce moral guilt but it would still be a bearer of certain moral claims and generate what I will call *creative regret*. This will demand further explanation below.

But the argument may be pressed in still another way—in terms of moral rules.[20] From this point of view the question which is being asked is whether the fact that we sometimes are allowed *not* to follow a particular rule in action entails that the rule does not apply in any way in that case, or that, in other words, it is not really a *moral* rule. Can two rules be said to apply to a situation in a moral sense even when they apparently give contradictory advice and we clearly cannot follow both in practice? Now if two such rules were constantly to clash, it would certainly be a sign of basic and systematic incoherence. Moral dilemmas do occur, however, where two rules which we usually follow happen in this particular case to point in divergent directions. In such cases what is the status of the rule we do not follow? I may, for instance, experience at one and the same time the moral obligation to return a gun by Saturday morning because of a promise to do so and the moral obligation not to return it because of my knowledge that the owner has decided to commit homicide with it on that day. It is clear that my overall moral duty is not to return it, but do I explain my decision by saying that no promise is broken, because a promise by definition does not hold in such cases? that the fact of the promise exercises no moral claim in such situations? The fact that we feel the need to apologize and make amends for a broken promise even in such a situation indicates an awareness of a continuing moral demand. It is clear that one should not feel remorse or guilt in such situations but he is certainly morally more sensitive if he feels regret. And part of the meaning of regret is that what I have freely caused is in some way evil and I wish I had not been pressured by the situation to do it. It is to the credit of such thinkers as Schüller, Fuchs, McCormick and Janssens that they at least speak of such acts in terms of non-moral, pre-moral or ontic *evil*. Their position is clearly removed from that of situationists like Fletcher (and possibly of Van der Marck and Van der Poel) who construe an act like homicide when it is called for as a positive moral good or a positive right-making characteristic within the situation and see no need at all of speaking of regret or mere toleration.

It is clear that where I would differ from the Schüller school is in the fact that I would construe concepts such as homicide as bearers of a negative *moral* meaning (as intrinsically evil in a weak sense) and not merely as bearers of negative ontic or premoral meaning. Death is clearly a non-moral evil, but a moral nuance must be maintained between death and homicide. In a moral system the willful causation of death (the human act of homicide) should retain a minimal negative *moral* index. To treat it as a mere non-moral evil leans too far in the direction of act-utilitarianism or situationism which demands the voiding of the intrinsic moral meaning of all action concepts. My view maintains that the *prima-facie* moral meaning of certain negative acts continues to make a moral claim even though such acts may be tolerated because of other features of the situation. The fact that homicide is not a complete or closed moral concept need not take it out of the arena of moral meaning even when it is viewed in isolation.

I would thus construe acts such as homicide, lying, stealing, etc., as morally intrinsically evil, but in a *weak* sense. By this I mean that they are not for this reason disallowed whatever the consequences, and here I abandon the strong sense of "intrinsically evil" found in the textbook tradition. Such acts are to be construed as the object of a negative moral "ought" but of moral "ought" which is not always decisive or overriding but is *always relevant* in every situation. Objects of such negative moral "oughts" or claims would never be viewed as positive right-making or love-making characteristics of a situation; they may at best become morally tolerable in some situations. The presumption is against them and they are in need of justification. A moral imperative (and meaning) is generated by them in the sense that if the good end sought could be achieved in some other way which avoids them and procures at least an equal amount of good this other must be done. Moreover, even when in some situation an action which is viewed as intrinsically evil in this weak sense can be legitimately posited it is viewed as a source of *creative* regret. In other words, in such cases one's moral obligation would not cease but one would be obliged to actively attempt to make up for the evil wrought. The perpetration of such acts is to be strongly avoided even if it is not necessarily always forbidden, but can never be considered a positive moral feature in any situation. Even though the telling of a falsehood, for example, may be allowed in a particular situation, it can never become a plus-moral feature—a positive right-making characteristic in any situation. As Arnold Isenberg has noted, one can never say of a situation that everything about it is bad except that a falsehood was told.[21]

III

Let us now turn to McCormick's disagreements with Schüller on the question of direct-indirect intention. As we said, he agrees with Schüller that the direct-indirect distinction is absolute and decisive only in the cases where full *moral* evil is what is directly willed (e.g., scandal). He disagrees with Schüller's further claim, not as yet mentioned in this essay, that the direct-indirect distinction has *no moral relevance whatsoever* in the other cases where what is being willed and caused is pre-moral evil like death, sterility, and the like. He claims that it does have some significance even here albeit not ultimate significance. With this I agree, but I must part company when he develops the justification for the significance. We must avoid direct killing more than we avoid indirect killing, he says, but not on the traditional deontological grounds, but solely on teleological ones.[22] He cites the oft-discussed case of judicial murder wherein a person is faced with the dilemma of allowing hundreds to die in a potential riot which might be prevented if he framed and had sentenced to death an innocent man. He claims that we feel it would be morally wrong to directly will the killing of this innocent man, not because the act is in itself unjust (deontological grounds) but because we feel that the long-range evil consequences which would accrue to direct killing are so much greater than those which accrue to indirect or accidental killing (teleological grounds). Direct killing is wrong in a case where indirect killing may be right because of the effects of the precedent set by justifying such killing. The logical implication is that, if in fact it could be shown that the effects were not more devastating, then the direct killing would be equally as acceptable as indirect killing. It is the high improbability that this would ever be true which for McCormick lends absoluteness to the rule against direct killing. Why is judicial murder wrong? "Is it not precisely because we sense that taking the life of this innocent man in these circumstances would represent a capitulation to and encouragement of a type of injustice which in the long run would render many more lives vulnerable? Yet our judgment would be different if the death of the one innocent man were incidental (indirect)."[23] It is clear that McCormick has espoused a type of rule-utilitarianism to cover the vast majority of moral issues. Rule-utilitarians while denying that there are any theoretical behavioral absolutes (rules of action never to be broken whatever the consequences) do espouse certain *practical* absolutes (rules which in the ordinary circumstances of life are never to be broken). The rules comprising these practical absolutes are virtually airtight. Individual acts are justified only by a direct reference to these rules. The utilitarian quality of the theory remains in the fact that the rules themselves (and changes of rules) are justified solely by the principle of utility, or community-building, that is, by showing that the universal conformity to such fundamental rules will produce a greater degree of happiness or wish-fulfillment in society at large, or in McCormick's case that the lesser evil will be produced. It is in principle possible, though in fact improbable, that society will change enough so that the most fundamental of these rules should cede to others which would now be seen to be utility-maximizing. Individual actions in situations are justified by their conformity to these rules while the rules themselves are justified by utility and utility alone; this last is the sole ultimate ground of morality. But the grounds adduced by McCormick and other rule-utilitarians in the judicial murder case are only partially correct. I agree with McCormick in his utilitarian-type assessment that more than likely the precedent set by the direct killing of the innocent man will brutalize sensitivities and thus lead to greater long-term evil than allowing the incidental death of even fifty men by riot. In a similar way the use of psychological bombing raids directly destroying whole cities in order to induce surrender of the enemy is a type of practice which if adopted would gradually debase the moral currency and produce more evil in the long-term. As Bernard Williams has pointed out such act-utilitarianism fosters the pre-emptive strike.[24] In a society of utilitarians known to be utilitarian a person knows that you feel obliged to do anything (even something very evil) if you can foresee that it will prevent something more evil. Knowing your readiness for this, he, as a proper utilitarian, will be ready to do something very evil to prevent your evil, and so on. The realization that there is a downspiraling, pre-emptive logic built into utilitarianism is sufficient to support the proposition that direct killing ought to be avoided with greater rigidity than indirect killing, or even that stringent rules should be set up in this regard. In the riot case the killing of the one man to save fifty could be forbidden even on long-term utilitarian grounds as McCormick holds.

But a closer reflection upon our moral experience reveals that the possible consequences are not the only reason *nor* the *principal* reason why we are appalled at the suggestion that the innocent man be directly framed and killed or that we exploit the psychological effects of bombing the innocent. The reason we are appalled, I submit and hope to show, is because of the crass indignity visited upon an innocent man, because we feel that an *innocent* bystander is being *used* as a means to avoid certain merely tragic deaths which it is foreseen will occur. We experience the same horror at a doctor who would deem to kill a perfectly healthy man in order to obtain transplants to save the lives of five other people. Our horror does not arise primarily out of the thought of what might happen to society if such a practice became the rule. The immediate and principal horror is directed toward the present injustice irrespective of precedents and long-term consequences. The feeling is that it is unfair—and the attempted reduction of fairness or justice to considerations of utility has been the stumbling block of utilitarians from Mill to the present-day.

A proof of our position can be constructed by slightly

modifying the last case. What if the killing of the one person in the case of the doctor in search of transplants to save five people could be kept completely *secret* and there were no question of bad precedent being set? Would not McCormick, making sole use of teleological criteria as he does, have to condone the doctor because the good consequences of what he does (saving five lives) is better than the evil consequences (the death of the one)? And yet our feeling still remains that injustice would have been done.

Defenders of rule-utilitarianism, using arguments developed by Rawls, attempt to wriggle out of this conclusion by stressing the publicity requirements of the rules of which they speak. Their rules, they claim, are not summary-rules or empirical generalizations, but rules of practice and "it is essential to the notion of a practice that the rules be publicly known as definitive."[25] Rule-utilitarian rules are rules which we are willing to universalize publicly, that is, rules which we prescribe publicly not only to ourselves but to all other men in relevantly similar circumstances. What I would be urging the rule-utilitarian to do, then, in the modified case I present, is to take a step backward and ask whether the rule "Never kill one to save five except when you can keep the affair a secret" would be a rule which he is willing to make part of the public moral code and to urge on *utilitarian grounds* alone as a part of moral education for our children. The rule-utilitarian might feel that when publicity requirements are highlighted then clearly consequential considerations alone will be sufficient to explain the moral outrage we experience at such a prospect. But what is clear is that even allowing for publicity and precedent-setting the proper evaluation of the consequences of such a rule is *prima-facie* still problematical. Asking ourselves whether or not greater welfare will accrue when secrecy is possible, the answer is that it may be the greater welfare would accrue if such a public rule were introduced or again it might not. A certain hesitancy remains. What is clear, however, is that there is *no* hesitancy in our immediate moral condemnation of this act. Prior to any consideration about potential repercussions upon society we feel that an injustice is being done which is at least *prima-facie* morally reprehensible whether it is kept a secret or not. And it is this aspect of immediate apodicity which is difficult to explain on utilitarian grounds.[26] It seems to us that even if in fact greater welfare could be produced by having such a rule of practice it would still be *prima-facie* condemnable on other grounds, e.g., on grounds that it is unfair, that it violates equal rights, the dignity of the individual or the like. And whatever the final moral resolution it is at least clear within our moral experience that independently grounded moral claims are clashing—I would dub them claims of dignity versus claims of welfare.

A closer analysis of McCormick's position shows that he really conflates two different and distinct claims. He cites teleological considerations as the sole ground for both 1) the central substance of our conviction that evil directly willed is worse than evil indirectly willed, and 2) our conviction that the rule against some directly willed evils (e.g., direct-killing of the innocent) should be airtight or virtually exceptional, a *practical* absolute. I can agree with the second point but not with the first. The practical airtightness of the rule may be dictated by extrinsic teleological considerations, that is, the play of human rationalization, the setting of precedents, the weakening of human determination not to be a cause of evil, and the like. However, in most cases, the primary intrinsic ground for our conviction that the direct willing of evil (as end or means) is worse than indirect willing arises from the fact that direct willing of evil often constitutes a violation of what I will call "dignity-values" as opposed to "welfare-values." I will attempt to clarify what I mean by this distinction.

IV

Historians of ethics classify the various theories for justifying moral obligations under one of two basic headings, teleology or deontology. Teleologists (utilitarians for one) derive moral obligations like justice from the sole moral imperative that welfare must be maximized. For teleologists the only reason why it is imperative that justice be done is because in fact it will produce a greater degree of some non-moral value, e.g., desire-fulfillment, in, say, society at large. At the heart of deontological theory, however, is the idea that certain obligations like justice are independently grounded and must be met even if a lower degree of desire-fulfillment might in fact ensue.

On my view, the intuitions which generate the distinction between teleology and deontology in obligation-theory relative to human actions give rise to an analogous distinction when one construes his moral theory in the form of an axiology or value-theory. And it is this felt-distinction which gives rise on the level of action to the felt-difference between direct and indirect causation of evil, as we shall see. It is my view that within an axiological framework there are at base two radically different kinds of reason why actions are wrong. They may be wrong because they violate one or other of two basic but variously important value types. They are wrong because they 1) affront dignity or 2) reduce welfare (desire-fulfillment). Values of welfare and values of dignity are two irreducible value-types and though they are ultimately commensurable in terms of degrees of value-in-general[27] values of dignity are to be considered as of far greater importance and must be given far greater weight in a conflict-situation than values of welfare.

Values of welfare center about the fulfillment of whatever potentials for action and enjoyment an entity might have, life, health, pleasure, power, etc. Thus the welfare-values of birds will be different from those of apes and the welfare-values of men will differ from those of both in that besides exercise and food they will include such things as aesthetic enjoyment, scientific knowledge and religious feelings.

Values of dignity, however, have little or nothing to do with the desirability of fulfilling potencies or exercising faculties, with what Rawls has summarized under the title of "the Aristotelian principle."[28] The values of dignity are such things as self-respect, autonomy, fidelity, justice, trust, integrity and the like. Though there will necessarily be some connection between these values and the values of welfare, values of dignity are in large measure independent of the latter. Values of welfare might be lost to a great degree or even entirely (when life is lost) without a person necessarily losing his dignity. Whether a man dies with dignity or without dignity, whether he dies the death of a free man or the death of a slave depends in large measure upon *how* he dies, upon the position of the will of free agents in regard to his death. The values of dignity introduce a quasi-aesthetic dimension into morality. It is these values which cause us to speak of certain actions as fitting or unfitting, as decent or indecent.

Because man's consciousness is self-consciousness his existence is characterized by freedom and precisely because of this freedom (but not solely) does he dwell in the dimension of dignity and indignity and does he experience the emotions of self-respect and indignation. Dogs can be afraid, or even jealous, but hardly indignant. Morality is only secondarily a system for maximizing welfare-values. It is more fundamentally a system regulating the interaction between free self-conscious agents who, because they are free and self-conscious, experience certain very special kinds of desires or needs which if trampled upon produce the special moral emotion of indignation.

Dignity values are of different types. In cases of social morality, e.g., abortion, killing one to procure organ transplants for five others, framing a black man to quell a riot, and the like, the dignity-values involved are primarily those of justice or fairness. A man may legitimately sacrifice his life to save that of others but this is an act of supererogation or what Russell Grice has called an ultra obligation, a weak type of obligation which does not imply that other people have a corresponding right to expect it from him[29] and *a fortiori* no right to directly extract it from him. In cases of *individual* morality like voluntary euthanasia and suicide, direct willing of death is worse than the oblique or incidental willing allowed under the double effect rule because another class of dignity-value is violated, what I shall call for want of a better name, "nobility-values." Under this category I include such values as courage, self-respect and religious gratitude. Durkheim in his classical work on suicide neglected the importance of these values. As a result he considered irrelevant the position of a person's will relative to the renunciation of his own existence. He lumped together under the title of "suicide" a martyr's dying for the faith, a mother sacrificing herself for her child and the merchant who kills himself to avoid bankruptcy. Schopenhauer was more sensitive to dignity-concerns when he remarked that the real reason why suicide must be condemned had to do with self-conquest. The Christian abhors suicide because he views his life as a gift from a "graceful reality" and suicide as the supreme act of ingratitude and lack of trust. He views suffering not as the ultimate evil but as redemptive and creative of depth of existence and dignity.[30] It is clear that different authors have located and grounded dignity in different ways but many have distinguished it against mere welfare.[31] The task of the Christian ethicist is to discover the religious (and distinctively Christian) dimensions of dignity.[32]

But what has all this to do with the direct-indirect distinction in morals? The direct-indirect distinction is, to my mind, an important second-level moral distinction. It is rooted in and is expressive of a more basic first-level moral distinction, the distinction between the more important dignity values and less important welfare values. It is valid because it generally generates conclusions which coincide with the conclusions generated by the more basic dignity / welfare value distinction. It is moreover practically valuable as a tool because of its greater tangibility. Because value-considerations are often murky, it is important to have a distinction and principle which nuances the more basic distinction but which trades directly on the level of actions. Actions are more tangible, clear and verifiable than are values, and for this reason rules-of action are important in moral education. We must not underestimate the human willingness to take the easier path when moral duties seem the least bit clouded. Without explicitly realizing it, many authors have emphasized the importance of the direct-indirect distinction in morals without understanding that its importance arises out of the fact that it parallels, at the level of action, the lived experience of the deeper distinction between dignity and welfare and out of the correlative fact that dignity is experienced as far more important than welfare in human interactions. I believe, for instance, that Paul Ramsey's reasons for opposing direct euthanasia even in sad or hopeless cases are dignity considerations.[33] He does not consider direct euthanasia to be an act of injustice but rather a copping-out on the obligation we have of caring for and companying with the dying. The primary operative imperative in these cases, he insists, is

"Never abandon care!" It is clear that this imperative centers about dignity-values because compliance with it may well actually lessen welfare and result in more suffering for the patient. For Ramsey this imperative is complied with by one who by using drugs to ease a patient's pain indirectly hastens the dying man's death. It is not complied with if one in his action aims at directly bringing about the patient's death. In direct euthanasia continued "companying" with the dying person in his dying is not possible; we, in a sense, walk off the scene and take the easy way out under the banner of "death with dignity."

Ramsey makes an exception of two cases where the distinction between direct and indirect euthanasia is no longer relevant. The cases he has in mind involve a person who is in a deep irreversible coma or one who is in ultra-severe intractable pain. The point is that since there is no apt recipient of care in these cases you fulfill the imperative "Never abandon care" equally as well by direct killing as by indirect or simply "letting die." McCormick disagrees with Ramsey's exceptions here on the ground that it is in principle impossible until death to know if some form of personality or consciousness remains and because on Ramsey's grounds it would be difficult to argue in favor of the personhood and protection of the unborn fetus.[34] But McCormick concurs that here the direct-indirect principle is parasitic upon the more substantive principle "Never abandon care!" What he does not realize is that Ramsey's operative principle is valid because it embodies concern for an important dignity-value and is not valid simply on utilitarian grounds, that is, simply because in the last analysis a greater welfare might be produced by erecting such a principle into a practice.

V

The Oxford moralist, Philippa Foot, feels that the distinction between doing and allowing (commission-omission) is really the fundamental operative moral distinction in most conflict cases where the principle of double effect was traditionally applied and that the distinction between direct and indirect intentionality is secondary and valid only because it happens to often coincide with the doing / allowing distinction.[35] Failure to bring aid to the starving blacks of the Sahel region of Africa, thus allowing them to die, may be evil but not as evil as would be sending them poison, which violates the negative duty not to kill. Doing something to procure someone's death is worse than doing nothing to prevent someone's death from occurring. Doing evil violates the stronger negative duty of non-interference with another's good while allowing evil violates the less stringent positive duty to bring aid to others.

Michael Tooley disagrees wholeheartedly with Mrs. Foot. He claims that the doing-allowing distinction (and the correlative distinction between negative and positive duties) seem basic only because of other distinctions present in the situations considered. He feels that the more basic distinction upon which the doing-allowing distinction is parasitic is a distinction within intention. "If a person performs an action he knows will kill someone else, this will usually be grounds for concluding that he wanted to kill the person in question. In contrast, failing to help someone may indicate only apathy, laziness or selfishness . . . the fact that a person knowingly allows another to die will not normally be sufficient ground for concluding he desired that person's death. Someone who knowingly kills another is more likely to be seriously defective from a moral point of view than someone who fails to save another's life."[36]

Tooley continues that if we assume identical intentions in the case of doing or allowing evil the distinction between doing and allowing left thus by itself seems morally irrelevant. By way of example he asks us to compare the following: 1) Jones sees Smith will be killed by a bomb unless Jones warns him. Jones's reaction is: "How lucky, it will save me the trouble of killing Smith myself." So Jones allows Smith to be killed by the bomb although he easily could have warned him. 2) Jones wants Smith dead and therefore shoots him. Tooley concludes, correctly I believe, that there is no significant difference between the wrongness of Jones's behavior in these two cases.[37] It is thus erroneous to draw a distinction between doing and allowing evil and hold that we have a stricter obligation to avoid the first more than the second. Performing an action in order to cause another's death is in itself no worse than omitting a performance with the intention of procuring his death. "The difference in our intuitions about situations that involve giving aid (positive duty) to others and corresponding situations that involve not interfering with others (negative duties) is to be explained by reference to probable differences in the intentions operating in the two situations and not by reference to a distinction between positive and negative duties. For once it is predicated that the motivation is the same in the two situations we realize that inaction is as wrong in the one case as action is in the other."[38]

I believe that Tooley's analysis goes far in dispelling the moral importance of the commission-omission distinction. This distinction is at best a practical rule of thumb, a third-level distinction which functions fruitfully only because of other truly operative distinctions with which it happens to coincide. What Tooley's analysis reemphasizes, however, is the importance of the position of the will, of intention, in our moral intuitions. If intention is so important, so also is the distinction between direct and indirect voluntariety which bears upon intention. What we must be careful to avoid is the growing utilitarian tendency of de-emphasizing means by construing them simply as somehow inter-ingredient with ends. The distinction between means and end must be maintained as well as the distinction between an evil directly aimed at as a means and an evil foreseen but not directly aimed at in the perpetration of an action (means). As I have noted, the position of the will, of freedom, relative to the evil performed is at the root of considerations of what I have called considerations of dignity and which I have strongly distinguished from values of welfare.

It is because of the lived-experience of a tension between two distinct types of value (dignity and welfare) that the distinction between deontology and teleology has constantly cropped up in the history of moral theory from Plato to the present day. It is the same lived-experience, I believe, which unconsciously motivated traditional moralists to introduce the distinction between the direct and indirect causation of evil as a practical rule mediating the more fundamental value distinction. The direct killing of the innocent, for example, is worse than the indirect killing thereof in most cases, primarily because it carries with it both types of disvalue, indignity and ill-fare, whereas indirect killing when there is a proportionate reason causes ill-fare alone. To aim at an innocent man's death as an end or even as a means to a good end is usually to treat him as an object, as a non-person (a non-freedom), as a mere means, whereas to aim at a proportionate good knowing that evil to another person will also arise as a not-aimed-at side-effect is to produce some ill-fare but is not a violation of dignity. Even this much should be avoided as much as possible but the latter may be tolerable whereas the former could hardly ever be.

And what must be re-emphasized against McCormick and others is that the central substantive reason why direct killing of an innocent (e.g., in the case of judicial murder cited above) is wrong is not because of extrinsic utilitarian considerations about the great good for society at large, but because the dignity of a person, an equal, a freedom, is being violated. Dignity values are most clearly in evidence in cases of justice and social morality, but they are also present in cases of individual morality, e.g., suicide or mutilation. Besides the general hierarchy of dignity values over welfare values a hierarchy within the realm of dignity-values itself would have to be established as well as within the realm of welfare values. This will prove to be a massive but richly rewarding task as the history of recent axiology has shown.[39]

VI

My insistence upon the immorality of the direct causation of evil as end or means need not be interpreted as a repetition of the strong traditional thesis of the manuals. There is, for example, the thorny problem as to whether the direct killing of the innocent is intrinsically evil in the very strong sense that it can never be done whatever the consequences. This would constitute a *theoretical behavioral absolute*, and it may not prove possible to ground such absolutes on the level of action in morals. It seems that theoretically some feature could always be conjured up to relativize any behavioral principle. But this possibility need not prevent me from maintaining that direct causation of evil is *always* morally intrinsically evil in the weaker sense which I have described above. The direct causation of evil falls, in other words, among those acts which have in themselves a negative moral index on which count they are generally to be avoided, and even in those situations where they may be allowed or tolerated because of the other features of the situation they retain their negative moral index and beget those moral claims of creative regret mentioned above. But over and above this, certain of these acts which are intrinsically evil in this weaker sense are so devastating for human dignity as well as human welfare that a *practical behavioral absolute* must be set up in their regard. The prohibition of the direct killing of the innocent is one of these as well as the prohibition of rape or of medical experimentation without informed consent. The absolute prohibition of even such an act may not be justifiable on intrinsic or theoretical grounds, but intrinsic factors coupled with extrinsic factors may warrant the absolute proscription of its perpetration in practice by means of setting up a quite airtight taboo. In fact this may be pedagogically necessary for the purposes of adequate moral education, given the "empirical" fact of human rationalization and egoism. Part of our moral duty may be to keep a distinction alive (here the direct-indirect distinction) by drawing a clear fixed line on the tangible level of action even though a theoretical clear fixed line does not exist at the level of values. As James Gustafson has noted in a rather recent article, the fact that a softening precedent is set may be sufficient reason for setting up a boundary of duty.[40]

For these extrinsic reasons, especially, then, I believe that Christians should be taught *never* to entertain the possibility of directly killing one innocent even for the purpose of saving the lives of many innocents. Theoretically, the absoluteness of the behavioral imperative not to kill an innocent may not be clearly sustainable (in a fantastic case where someone threatens to kill 100,000 if you do not kill one) because it is possible that an overwhelming quantity of welfare may override a small consideration of dignity. On the other hand, moral education should teach that in practice we should not even entertain the possibility in our imagination of ever perpetrating the direct killing of the innocent. It should not be a live option. "Act *as if* you should never directly kill the innocent" is our practical absolute. What I am maintaining is that we should retain certain "virtually exceptionless norms"[41] in ethics, or in other words that the "unthinkable"[42] should be retained as a category of moral thought. With Bernard Williams, I believe that the subversion of morality at the hands of utilitarianism must be resisted. Reflecting upon the pre-emptive logic within utilitarianism and the potential debasement of moral integrity of which it is capable, he advocates resistance in the form of adherence to practical absolutes. "Enough people, enough of the time, it seems, have to be prepared to stick at doing various things, whatever the consequences may be. That means that enough people, enough of the time do not have to think as utilitarians; they have quite definitely to think as non-utilitarians. Nor will it do for them to preserve at the back of their mind the utilitarian rationale in coexistence with the required moral bloody-mindedness. For they have to be able to resist utilitarian temptation in the most difficult circumstances, when much obvious harm will follow from resisting it, and for that their non-utilitarianism has to be very deeply engrained."[43]

It is clear that underlying Williams' emphatic plea is a concern for values other than utilitarian welfare, for values of dignity. It is also clear that he sees the need for absolutes on the level of action to which one is willing to commit oneself. The direct-indirect distinction and the correlative principle of double effect, both carefully nuanced, remain, to my mind, valuable principles in our effort to carve out this non-utilitarian road between right and wrong on the level of action.

Notes

1. For Aquinas, the indirect voluntary refers to the foreseen but unwilled effect of an *omission*, (cf. I-II, q. 6, a. 3). It was Medina, Vasquez and their followers of the latter half of the 16th century who extended the concept to apply rather to the foreseen but unintended effect of a *commission*. Cf. J. Ghoos, "L'acte à double effet,"

Ephemerides Theologicae Lovaniensis, 1951, v. 27, pp. 30-52. J. Ghoos, whom I here follow, disagrees with J. Mangan who believes that Aquinas actually developed the notion of the indirect voluntary to apply to commissions in his article on self-defense (II-II q. 64, a. 7) and that subsequent authors perfected the principle of double effect in meditation upon this article; cf. "An Historical Analysis of the Principle of Double Effect," *Theological Studies*, 1949, v. 10, pp. 41-61. P. Knauer disagrees with Ghoos's criticisms of Mangan; cf. "The Hermeneutical Function of the Principle of Double Effect," *Natural Law Forum*, 1967, v. 12, p. 133. An earlier study which Mangan attacks and Ghoos defends is that of V. Alonso, *El principio del doble efecto en los comentadores de Santo Tomas de Aquino*, Rome, 1937.

2. *Op cit.*, pp. 132-162.

3. The problem of describing human action is thorny, as Bentham knew and a number of modern philosophers have discovered. There seems to be room for many plausible descriptions of an action depending upon the *context*. Within a purely aesthetic context understood as such the action of killing a man with a gun might be legitimately described as a beautiful flourish of the arm and hand. In most ordinary contexts, however, and certainly in the context of morality, part of whose very definition includes the note of concern about the import of our interventions on sentient beings or persons as such, (Cf. Frankena, *Ethics, 2nd* ed., N. Y., Prentice Hall, Chap. 6) the immediate result of this kind of action is so important that it must be brought out explicitly in the description of the act. To answer the question: What did he do? in our moral context it does not suffice to stop at the physical movements of the agent and say merely "He fired a gun" or to elide the means into a good purpose and say simply "He saved the life of his friend." If so extreme a means is used to attain even so noble a goal it is necessary that the means be explicitated in our description of what is done. We must say: He killed a man in order to save the life of his friend. To maintain that moral experience demands this explicitation of "important" acts is not yet to commit oneself to a particular moral theory. Such a position on action-description is compatible with act-utilitarianism as well as with strict deontologism. Cf. Eric D'Arcy, *Human Acts* (Oxford, Clarendon Press, 1963), pp. 18ff. and Paul Ramsey, *Deeds and Rules in Christian Ethics* (N. Y.: Scribner's 1967), pp. 192 ff.

4. Grisez, as we will see below, attempts a more nuanced analysis of the causal relationship between the act and its effects.

5. Cf. *Toward A Christian Ethic*, N. Y., Newman Press, 1967, Chap. 2.

6. Cf. "The Principle of Double Effect," in *Absolutes in Moral Theology?*, ed. Chas. Curran, Washington, Corpus Books, 1968, pp. 186-210, and *The Search for Human Values*, N.Y., Paulist Press, 1971, Chap. III.

7. Cf. Bruno Schüller's criticism of Van der Marck for construing "homicide" as a mere physical aspect of an act, an aspect which in itself

does not yet constitute a unit of intersubjective meaning. "Neuere Beiträge zum Thema 'Begründung sittlicher Normen,' " *Theologische Berichte* 4, Einsiedeln: Benziger, 1974, pp. 137-138.

8. *Ambiguity in Moral Choice*, Pere Marquette Lecture, 1973, p. 30. See also Paul Ramsey's critique of these views as applied to the morality of organ transplants by Van der Poel, *The Patient as Person*, Yale Univ. Press, pp. 182-185. For a response to Ramsey by R. McCormick see "Transplantation of Organs: A Comment on Paul Ramsey," *Theological Studies* 1975, V. 36, No. 3, pp. 503-509.

9. *Ibid.*

10. Because of these criticisms many utilitarians have moved to a rule-utilitarianism (of which there are many variations) wherein greatest happiness considerations (utility) are seen as giving rise to certain very stringent rules of practice which must be adhered to strongly or for some even absolutely and universally if the greatest happiness for society at large is to be procured. These rules are justified by their utility and acts only by their conformity to the rules in question. Some have argued that the distinction between rule- and act-utilitarianism cannot be consistently maintained. (Cf. Lyons, *Forms and Limits of Utilitarianism* (N. Y. Oxford University Press, 1965) and Jan Narveson, *Morality and Utility* (Baltimore, Johns Hopkins Press, 1967), pp. 123-140.) John Rawls, himself not a utilitarian, presents the best defense of the coherence of a distinction between act- and rule-utilitarianism and the superiority of the latter in "Two Concepts of Rules," *The Philosophical Review*, Vol. LXIV (1955). pp. 3-32. Cf. also J. Margolis's criticism of Rawls in *Values and Conduct* (N. Y., Oxford University Press, 1971), pp. 160-171. Cf. also H. J. McCloskey's criticism of Rawls in "An Examination of Restricted Utilitarianism," in *Philosophical Review*, 1957, V. LXVI, pp. 466-485. For a nuanced version of rule-utilitarianism see Richard H. Brandt, "Toward a Credible Form of Utilitarianism," in *Morality and the Language of Conduct*, ed. Castaneda and Kakhnikian (Detroit, Wayne State Univ. Press. 1963). The similarities between philosophical discussions in utilitarian theory and contemporary discussion in Catholic moral theology are concisely presented by John R. Connery, S.J. in "Morality of Consequences: A Critical Appraisal," *Theological Studies*, 1973, V. 34, pp. 396-414. Cf. also McCormick's "Notes on Moral Theology," *Theological Studies*, 1975, V. 36, pp. 93-99 and Bruno Schüller, *op. cit.*. pp. 109-81.

11. Cf. Grisez, *Abortion: the Myths, the Realities and the Arguments* (N. Y., Corpus Books, 1970), pp. 321-346. The same doctrine is presented in less technical terms in Grisez and R. Shaw, *Beyond the New Morality* (University of Notre Dame Press, 1974), pp. 138-149.

12. "Regardless of intention, the structure of the act is what it is. It does not change simply because one's intention is directed toward one aspect rather than the other. Even though, in emotional terms, a person may not feel that he intends the destructive aspect of the action, nevertheless it is inescapable that he intend it inasmuch as it is required

as the means to reaching the end toward which his feelings are directed." Grisez and Shaw, *Beyond the New Morality*, p. 141.

13. *Abortion, the Myths, the Realities and the Arguments*, p. 336.

14. *Ambiguity in Moral Choice*, p. 49ff.

15. Other authors influenced by Knauer and Schüller speak of "pre-moral evil" (Fuchs) and of "ontic evil" (Janssens). All of these terms are synonymous and seem to be identical in meaning with the concept of *malum physicum* of the tradition. Cf. J. Fuchs, "The Absoluteness of Moral Terms," *Gregorianum*, 1971, V. 52, pp. 415-457 and L. Janssens, "Ontic Evil and Moral Evil," *Louvain Studies*, 1972, V. 4, pp. 115-56.

16. Cf. "Direkte Tötung—Indirekte Tötung," *Theologie und Philosophie*, 1972, V. 47, pp. 341-357.

17. "Notes on Moral Theology," *Theological Studies*, March 1976, V. 37, n. 1, pp. 76-77.

18. Cf. similar criticisms by G. Ermecke levelled especially against J. Fuchs in "Das Problem der Universalität oder Allgemeingültigkeit sittlicher Normen innerweltlicher Lebensgestaltung," *Münchener Theologische Zeitschrift*, 1973, V. 24, pp. 1-24 Cf. also J. Fuchs response, "Sittliche Normen-Universalien und Generalisierungen," *op. cit.*, V. 25, 1974, pp. 18-33. See also Paul Quay's searching critique of the trend to de-emphasize acts and means, "Morality by Calculation of Values," *Theology Digest*, 1975, V. 23, pp. 347-364.

19. This resembles closely the very strong tradition in Anglo-American ethics of *prima-facie* moral duties fathered by W. D. Ross in his works *The Right and the Good* (Oxford, Clarendon, 1930), and *Foundation of Ethics* (Oxford, Clarendon, 1939). For the most systematic critical evaluation of this whole tradition see O. Johnson, *Rightness and Goodness* (The Hague, Martinus Nijhoff, 1959).

20. I am indebted to Bernard Williams and Roger Trigg for the substance of this discussion. Cf. Williams, "Ethical Consistency," *Proceedings of the Aristotelian Society*, 1965, p. 124, and Trigg, "Moral Conflict," *Mind*, 1971 V. 80 pp. 41-55 (*passim*).

21. Cf. "Deontology and the Ethics of Lying," in *Ethics*, ed. Thomson & Dworkin, (N. Y.: Harper & Row, 1968), p. 178.

22. *Ambiguity in Moral Choice*, pp. 56-65, and 82-93.

23. Cf. *Ambiguity in Moral Choice*, 1973, Pere Marquette Theology Lecture, p. 64. (Parenthesis mine.)

24. Cf. *Morality: An Introduction to Ethics* (N. Y.: Harper & Row, 1972, p. 104).

25. Rawls, "Two Concepts of Rules," *Philosophical Review*, 1955, V. LXIV, p. 24.

26. Most Anglo-American moralists, both utilitarians and deontologists, agree that it is quite evident what the correct act is in hard cases like that of judical murder and the case we here present and that an ethical theory which leads to an opposite conclusion must be either modified or dropped. Schüller denies that the actual duty of the pro-

tagonist in such cases is so immediately evident. For the sake of argument one can agree with him. He fails to see, however, that there is a *prima facie* duty which is very evident and which seems to rest on non-utilitarian grounds. Cf. Schüller, *Theologische Berichte*, V. 4, pp. 172-173.

27. By value-in-general I mean the "good" which is the most fundamental concept in morals. It is equated neither with values of welfare nor with values of dignity, which are subsets of the good. My theory then is not ultimately deontological completely dissociating the right from the good. It conceives of both dignity-values and welfare-values as components of the good of man. It denies, however, that dignity values can be translated in terms of welfare values and vice-versa. The ultimate concept in my moral theory can then be termed love if love is understood as the will to do always in every situation what produces the greatest overall good for man with sensitivity for the differences between the different orders of values.

28. Cf. *A Theory of Justice* (Cambridge: Harvard University Press, 1971), Chap. VII, No. 65, pp. 424-439.

29. Cf. Russell Grice, *The Grounds of Moral Obligation* (Cambridge, University Press), Chap. 4.

30. For an interesting investigation into an adequate delimitation of the concept of suicide read R. F. Holland, "Suicide," in *Moral Problems*, ed. J. Rachels, (2nd ed., N. Y., Harper and Row, 1975), pp. 388-401.

31. In the words of Robert Brumbaugh, "Ever since there has been a discussion of choice, there has been an intuitive conviction that while some values are additively related, others cannot be. There is no cash price, no degree of comfort, that can persuade a Socrates to give up his pursuit of wisdom or a Beowulf his quest for glory and honor." "Changes of Value Order and Choices in Time," *Values and Valuation*. (ed. John W. Davis, Knoxville, Univ. of Tennessee Press, 1972), p. 51.

32. A fuller discussion would have to introduce a phenomenology of the religious dimensions of reality as "graceful," which would provide the deeper ground for the salience of dignity-values over welfare-values, a ground which undergirds the considerations of freedom to which we have pointed. For an interesting discussion in this direction see Frederick Carney, "On Frankena and Religious Ethics," *The Journal of Religious Ethics*, 1975, V. III, pp. 7-26.

33. *The Patient as Person*, (New Haven, Yale Univ. Press, 1970), p. 153. Cf. also "The Indignity of Death with Dignity," *Hastings Center Studies*, V. 2, No. 2, May, 1974, pp. 47-62.

34. Cf. "The New Medicine and Morality," *Theology Digest*, Vol. 21, No. 4, Winter, 1973, pp. 312-314.

35. "The Problem of Abortion and the Doctrine of the Double Effect," *The Oxford Review* 5, (1967), pp. 5-15, Cf. esp. p. 11 ff. Reprinted in *Moral Problems*, (ed. James Rachels, N. Y., Harper and Row, 2nd ed.), 1975.

36. "Abortion and Infanticide," *Philosophy and Public Affairs*, 2 (1972), p. 59.

37. James Rachels provides a similar example in an article which defends a position almost identical with Tooley's. Cf. "Active and Passive Euthanasia," *New England Journal of Medicine*. Vol. 292, No. 2, Jan. 9, 1975, p. 79.

38. Tooley, *op. cit.*, pp. 59-60 (Parentheses mine.) For an attempted refutation of Tooley's argument see Richard Louis Trammell, "Tooley's Moral Symmetry Principle," *Philosophy and Public Affairs*, 1976, V. 5, No. 3, pp. 305-313. See also Trammell, "Saving Life and Taking Life," *The Journal of Philosophy*, 1975, V. 72, No. 5, pp. 131-137.

39. For a review of the work which has already been done since the late 19th century see J. N. Findlay, *Axiological Ethics* (London, Macmillan, 1970). For a more elaborate treatment of Findlay's own theory of values see Findlay, *Values and Intentions* (London: Allen and Unwin, 1961), esp. 227-394. See also Nicholas Rescher's analysis of welfare-values in "Welfare: Some Philosophical Issues," *Values and Valuation* (ed. John William Davis, Knoxville, Univ. of Tennessee Press, 1972), pp. 221-232.

40. "Mongoloidism, Parental Desires and the Right to Life," *Perspectives in Biology and Medicine*, XVI, pp. 529-559.

41. Cf. Donald Evans, "Paul Ramsey on Exceptionless Moral Norms," *The American Journal of Jurisprudence*, 1971, V. 16, p. 209.

42. Cf. Bernard Williams, "A Critique of Utilitarianism," in *Utilitarianism For and Against* (Cambridge, University Press, 1973), p. 92.

43. *Morality: An Introduction to Ethics* (N. Y. Harper and Row, 1972), pp. 105-6.

Morality of Consequences:
A Critical Appraisal

John R. Connery, S.J.

The war in Vietnam has perhaps stimulated more interest in the moral issues connected with warfare than any recent conflict in history. Never before, at least in recent times, has the theory of the just war received so much attention; never before has there been so much concern over reports of atrocities, e.g., direct attacks on noncombatants, especially women and children, although these were not unheard of in recent wars in which we have been engaged. Even if this unprecedented interest and concern is traceable more to the unpopularity of the war than any growing moral sensitivity on the part of the people, it has to be regarded as a benefit. What is clear is that people, if they permit war at all, do make moral distinctions; they allow attacks on combatants and condemn attacks on noncombatants. What is not clear is the reason behind this distinction, and the underlying question here is one that runs through the whole of morality. Why do people judge certain acts morally right and others morally wrong? Is it because some have bad consequences, others good consequences? Or are there other features of these acts that must be considered morally relevant, at least in some moral judgments? One can presume, of course, that wrongful acts will generally be followed by bad consequences, and in many instances one may be able to conclude that an act is wrongful only after becoming aware of its consequences. But the basic question goes deeper: Is an act wrong precisely and solely because it has bad consequences, or are some acts wrong independently of their consequences?

Anyone acquainted with the recent writings of Catholic authors in the field of general ethics and morality will be aware of a movement toward a consequentialist response to this question. Such writers as Knauer, Schüller, Fuchs, and Crotty are among those who can be identified with this movement.[1] From their writings one can detect a certain dissatisfaction with the "deontological" response of traditional Catholic morality and an interest in a more "teleological" approach.[2] According to this latter view, what one ought or ought not to do depends entirely on the consequences of the act. If the consequences on the whole are undesirable, the act ought not to be done; if they are desirable, it ought to, or at least may, be done. Different ethicians use different terminology in enunciating this principle, and they even vary it considerably, but all are alike in putting the whole moral burden on the consequences of an act. Those who are knowledgeable in the history of ethical thought will know that the Catholic authors mentioned above are plugging into a school of thought which has a long history behind it. It will be the purpose of this article to relate these authors to this thinking and try to bring out some of the problems it presents.

The school of thought being referred to is commonly known as utilitarianism. It has its origins in ancient Greek philosophy (Aristippus and Epicurus), but more recently (from the end of the eighteenth century) it has gained great popularity through the writings of such philosophers as Hume, Bentham, J. S. Mill, Sidgwick, and G.E. Moore. Currently, at least in English-speaking countries, it has been the subject of much discussion and controversy.[3] Perhaps the best-known appeal to the utilitarian principle in this country, though on a more popular level, has been that of Joseph Fletcher, whose ethic is allegedly an ethic of love, but who uses the utilitarian principle of the greatest good of the greatest number as the criterion of the loving act.[4]

The utilitarian movement itself has undergone considerable evolution over the past two hundred years. It was originally presented as a theory of ethical hedonism. Pleasure and pain were considered the only intrinsic good and evil, and the judgment of the individual act was tied solely to this consequential calculus. If an act gave pleasure, or better, perhaps, a greater balance of pleasure than any alternative act, it was at least morally permissible. Initially, personal pleasure was the norm but this was later extended to include the pleasure of others. Some went on to identify pleasure with happiness and made the criterion "the greatest happiness of the greatest number." Others did not go this far, being satisfied with producing the "good" rather than the greatest good or the greatest happiness. Still others were satisfied with a negative utilitarianism, content with a norm that would tell them what one ought not to do. Finally, there have been utilitarians who admit other intrinsic goods besides pleasure or happiness, e.g., knowledge, virtue, power, etc.[5]

It should be clear from the way it has been described that utilitarianism, at least if considered as a method of determining the morality of the human act (the consequential method), is compatible with different theories of value, i.e., theories about what is intrinsically good or evil. It is true that most utilitarians have been hedonists but, as we have seen, there are utilitarians who accept other intrinsic goods besides pleasure or happiness. Catholic authors moving toward consequentialism have not gone into this question to any great extent, but they would undoubtedly not limit intrinsic good to pleasure or happiness. We are not, however, concerned with deciding what are good or bad consequences. What we are concerned with is the validity of a moral system that makes the judgment of an act depend solely on its consequences.

Traditional morality has not ignored the role effects or consequences play in determining the morality of the individual act. It is difficult to see how any moral system could ignore them, since there is probably no human act that will not sooner or later have some bad effects. Traditional moralists have solved this problem by the well-known principle of the double effect. If the evil effects are not intended and are balanced by good effects, an act which is otherwise good is still permissible according to this principle. But it is perfectly clear that in traditional morality effects or consequences have not played a solitary role in determining the morality of an act. They have shared this role with those other elements of the human act commonly known as object, end, and circumstances. Or perhaps it might be better to say that they have shared this role with the object of the act, since it is possible to include effects or consequences under the end (intended effect) and circumstances (other effects).[6]

Knauer actually attempts to explain his whole position in terms of the principle of the double effect and makes this his sole principle in determining the morality of the individual act. To do this, he must extend this principle far beyond its traditional usage; he must apply it even to those acts in which the good is mediated by evil. The only requirement for Knauer is that the good produced be commensurate with the evil involved.[7] As long as this commensurate good is present, it makes no difference that it is the product of evil. The mediating evil will be only *indirectly* intended, and the act will be morally good. The evil will be *directly* intended (and the act morally bad) only if the good effect is not commensurate with the evil involved. Knauer thinks that he finds support for this position in St. Thomas' treatment of self-defense.[8]

Whether Knauer can fit his approach into traditional scholastic patterns is highly questionable, but there is no doubt that he is presenting a morality of consequences. He puts the whole moral burden on the commensurate reason. It is the commensurate value of the goal that justifies the evil caused. His main concern is with an evil means, but he would certainly include any evil associated with the act, whether means or independent effect, in his moral assessment. What is clear is that a commensurate good will justify any evil connected with the act. If this good is lacking, the act will be morally bad, since the evil will be directly intended.

In presenting their own respective positions, Fuchs demands a *proportionate* reason and Schüller a *greater good* to justify any evil involved in a human act. Crotty simply states that the evil connected with human acts can be justified if these acts are *promotive of human welfare*.[9] It would be interesting to compare these norms with Knauer's as well as with the great variety of norms used by different utilitarians, but it would distract us too much from the purposes of this article, which is to consider these positions primarily insofar as they put the moral emphasis totally on consequences.[10] Although Knauer, and to a lesser extent Fuchs, have gone to some pains to fit their approach into traditional scholastic categories, there can hardly be any question that all these authors are tending toward consequentialism. [11]

Once a moralist or ethician has worked out a basic moral principle or norm, the next question that arises concerns the application of this norm. Thus, let us suppose that one proposes or accepts the principle of commensurate reason, or proportionate reason, or one of the other consequentialist norms. How does one use this norm in practice? Does it become an immediate measure of individual acts, or is it used rather in the formulation of rules?

In raising this question, we are moving into an area of great controversy among contemporary utilitarians and their adversaries. There is some reason to believe that J. S. Mill himself believed the rules themselves to be the expression of the greatest good of the greatest number. Observing the rules, then, would produce the best consequences. As he says, men by this time "have acquired positive beliefs as to the effects of some actions on their happiness: and these beliefs which have come down are the rules of morality for the multitude, and for the philosopher until he succeeds in finding better."[12] It appears from this that Mill would expect the individual to rely on the rules rather than on a personal application of the utilitarian norm to the individual act. In fact, Mill questions the "strange notion that the acknowledgement of a first principle is inconsistent with secondary ones."[13] There is some justification, then, for thinking that according to Mill the basic utilitarian calculus is reflected in our moral rules and there is no need for the individual to apply it directly to individual acts.

Whatever may have been Mill's understanding of utilitarianism, in the hands of some of his followers it became act-oriented.[14] According to act-utilitarianism (also called extreme utilitarianism), the utilitarian principle is applied immediately to the individual act. If the good effects of the act are greater on the whole than the bad effects (or however the principle be stated by the individual ethician), the act may be performed, even if it goes contrary to a rule. Rules are no more than summaries of past experiences; they tell us nothing about the present act. Judgment of the present act calls for an immediate application of the principle of consequences.

It should be said immediately in defense of act-or extreme

utilitarians that in spite of their theoretical position on rules they admit their practical need and usefulness. They admit that most people have not the time, the ability, the training, or the objectivity to work out a teleological calculus of their own acts. These people will achieve a utilitarian goal more often by following the rule than by going against it on the basis of their own calculus. Some utilitarians will go so far as to say that rarely, if ever, will the conditions that would warrant going against a rule be verified in practice.

Even though it may be toned down in practice, the theory of act-utilitarianism runs into serious difficulty in dealing with some actions that have been traditionally recognized as morally wrong. One author presents the case of a sheriff in a southern town faced with the alternatives in a rape case of framing a Negro suspect (whom he knows to be innocent) or carrying on a prolonged search for the real culprit.[15] The immediate indictment and conviction of the suspect would save many lives, as well as prevent other bad consequences, so that it would clearly be the best thing to do from the viewpoint of consequences. The act-utilitarian would seem committed in theory to this alternative, in spite of the fact that it goes against traditional norms of justice.

Another author, referring to the problems raised by act-utilitarianism, made the following observation:

> It implies that if you have employed a boy to mow your lawn and he has finished the job, you should pay him what you promised only if you cannot find a better use for your money . . . that when you bring home your check you should use it to support your family and yourself only if it cannot be used more efficiently to supply the needs of others . . . that if your father is ill and has no prospect of good in his life, and maintaining him is a drain on the energy and enjoyment of others, then, if you can end his life without provoking any public scandal or bad example . . . it is your positive duty to take matters into your own hand. . . .[16]

It is because of such problems that many have abandoned act- or extreme utilitarianism for what is called rule-utilitarianism or restricted utilitarianism. In rule-or restricted utilitarianism the teleological or consequential norm is the basis for the rule itself. The assumption is that the rule is calculated to produce the best consequences. Given this assumption, the norm for the individual act becomes the rule rather than a consequential calculus of the act itself. So, even if the consequences of following the rule in a particular act may be bad, one is still obliged to do so because observing the rule leads to the best consequences on the whole.

Rule-utilitarianism obviously attaches an importance to rules and tries to give them a theoretical role they do not have in extreme utilitarianism. The rule is not just a summary of the past but an expression of the utilitarian principle.[17] Observance of the rule is called for even where nonobservance might lead to better consequences. By calling for observance in these circumstances, rule-utilitarianism seems to evade the charge made above against act-utilitarianism. It would not permit the punishment of an innocent man, the violation of a promise or other covenant even in a case where this might lead to good results. In this respect rule-utilitarianism seems more in accord with ordinary moral convictions.

But many doubt that there is any real difference between act- and rule-utilitarianism and consequently do not feel that the latter escapes the charges made against the former. They argue that if there really is a situation in which the consequences of violating a rule would be better than those of observing it, one would have to ask whether the rule itself is the best utilitarian rule. The best utilitarian rule, which would maximize good consequences, would be one which allowed for this exception. So the rule-utilitarian, unless he accepts his rules uncritically, cannot avoid applying his consequential calculus to the individual act, and if he does apply it, it is difficult to see how he can avoid making the same exceptions the act-utilitarian makes.

There is undoubtedly good logic in this position and it certainly calls for a response, but not all rule-utilitarians would respond to it in the same way. Some would want to cling to a pure rule-utilitarianism and allow for no exceptions.[18] Others would allow for exceptions, but not based on the appraisal of a single act; they would demand that the appraisal be made of the practice. Their concern is centered around the question: What would happen if everybody did that? Behind this concern is the assumption that a single act may not have bad consequences, whereas a practice might. They would allow an exception only when the practice would not have bad consequences. They frequently illustrate their position with a rather trivial example. If one person walks on the grass, no harm is done; but if everyone walks on the grass, the lawn will be ruined. The same would be true of voting or paying taxes, or even promising or lying. This concern for the consequences of a practice, which is certainly a healthy one, would seem, at least superficially, to distinguish the rule-utilitarian from the act-utilitarian. The latter often claims that the conduct of others is irrelevant to the moral judgment of example. In this case it would have to be considered one of the consequences of his act and included in the moral assessment. But if others were not influenced by his conduct (because the act was done secretly), he would not have to be concerned, and if what he wanted to do would not have bad consequences otherwise, he could go ahead and do it.

Although one can hardly criticize the rule-utilitarian for his concern over the consequences of a practice, the logic that would rule out every individual exception on this basis has to be questioned. If bad consequences will not follow when one or a few persons perform a certain act, but only when everyone does, the only logical conclusion one can come to (according to a morality of consequences) is that not everyone should do it. One can hardly conclude that no one should do it and set up an exceptionless moral rule.[19] But there is undoubtedly some ambiguity here. One or two acts may not have bad consequences outside of a practice, but if they are part of a practice they may contribute to the damage resulting from the practice. As part of the practice, then, they will have bad consequences. It is possible, of course, that individual acts, e.g., walking on a path after the grass has already been beaten down, even if they are part of a practice, may not contribute to the damage. When relating individual acts to a damaging practice, the rule-utilitarian must limit himself to those acts which are part of the practice and contribute to the damage. A rule that will bear utilitarian investigation can cover only those acts which are univocal in regard to bad consequences. Thus, it can forbid walking on a lawn (still damageable) in a place where others either have walked or are likely to do so with a certain frequency. It could not forbid walking on the grass in an isolated spot where others would not likely follow or walking on a path where the lawn is already ruined. But if the rule-utilitarian limits himself, as he should, to acts which are univocal in regard to bad consequences, he will not, as David Lyons points out, condemn any act which should not be condemned by the act-utilitarian as well.[20]

Lyons also points out that the act-utilitarian cannot consider the conduct of others irrelevant to the moral judgment of his own act apart from scandal on his part. He shows clearly that the act-utilitarian cannot, at least in many cases, define his own act in terms of consequences unless he knows how others are going to act. For instance, the man who fails to vote cannot know whether his act will have bad consequences unless he knows what others are doing about voting. If he fails to vote in a situation in which his vote is necessary for victory, his failure will have bad consequences; otherwise it will not, or at least not such bad consequences. A knowledge of the conduct of others is obviously necessary for a consequential judgment of his own act. This may not always, or even often, be easy to come by, but it is still necessary. So an act-utilitarian may be just as dependent on a consideration of the conduct of others as a rule-utilitarian.

There is another factor that tends to bring act-utilitarianism closer to rule-utilitarianism. We have seen that the conduct of others is morally relevant to a consequential description of one's act. It is also true that the judgment which one makes of his act is morally relevant to the conduct of others. We are dealing here with what is called the principle of generalization.[21] One who judges that an act is right for him, whether on consequential or other grounds, implicitly judges that it is right for anyone in the same situation. The same act cannot be right for him and wrong for everybody else, or even anybody else. Thus, for instance, if one judges that it is all right for him to have sexual relations with his fiancée with whom he is deeply in love and planning marriage, he must allow this for everyone in the same situation if he is to be consistent.[22] So, when a person makes a moral judgment in a particular situation, he is making a judgment that must be valid not only for his own conduct but also for everyone else in that situation. What he is really doing is making a rule, or if a rule is already in existence (as in the present case) he is qualifying it. He is not making an isolated judgment of his own act; indeed he cannot.

It may be, of course, that the situation one is judging is unique in the sense that it is not likely to be repeated in all its details. It would be meaningless in such a case to speak in terms of an explicit rule or, if it were an exception, an explicit modification of a rule to include it. James Gustafson in an article on abortion presents a case that would fall into this category.[23] After enumerating several tragic circumstances connected with the case, he concludes that an abortion would be justifiable because of the accumulation of really serious problems connected with the continuation of the pregnancy.[24] The likelihood that such a case would be repeated in all its relevant details is perhaps very slight. But the judgment is still generalizable. Also, even though not repeatable in *specie infima*, the case may fall under a more general category that could be verified in practice more frequently. In other words, if all the circumstances in the case add up to very serious harm or need, there may be other cases in which the circumstances, though quite different, would add up to the same degree of harm or need. To be consistent, one who would allow an abortion in the present case would have to allow it in all other cases that fall into the same general category. Thus, even though a case might not be repeatable in *specie infima*, it might well be repeatable on a more generic level. It would involve, then, or at least presume, a modification of the rule on this level. So it can be said that anyone making an exception for himself is either qualifying the rule or at least presuming a qualification of the rule at some level. This is obviously true of the rule-utilitarian. It must also be true of the act-utilitarian, or anyone else for that matter, however unique his exception may be.

The only difference between the act-utilitarian and the rule-utilitarian in this respect is that the latter would be more inclined to make specific qualifications wherever possible (e.g., taking what belongs to another is wrong except when one is starving), since this would have a less weakening effect on the rule. Act-utilitarians, who are not as interested in secondary rules, would tend to settle for a more generic qualification, e.g., the principle of consequences itself.[25] But this difference is on the practical level and would not in any way put a theoretical gap between them.

To sum it all up, then, rule-utilitarianism is not as independent of a consideration of the individual act as it wants to claim, nor is act-utilitarianism as independent of the conduct of others or of rules. Whether he admits it or not, the act-utilitarian is involved in and involves the conduct of others in his moral judgments of individual acts. His judgments also imply the generalizations from which rules are made. So one is hard put to find any discernible theoretical difference between act-utilitarianism and rule-utilitarianism. It can hardly be alleged, then, that rule-utilitarianism can effectively evade the charges made against act-utilitarianism. If the act-utilitarian must allow (on the basis of good consequences) acts which go against common convictions, so must the rule-utilitarian. Nor can the rule-utilitarian condemn any act that would not also be condemned by the act-utilitarian.

The Catholic authors who have been moving toward consequentialism have not discussed the role of norms as thoroughly as recent utilitarians; therefore it is not easy to identify them as act-utilitarians or rule-utilitarians. Crotty seems to come closer to act-utilitarianism than the others, since he maintains that norms are just rules of thumb which tell us more about the past than about the present; they are no more than summaries of the past. The morality of the individual act must be worked out on the basis of its consequences. The other authors seem more rule-oriented, though by no means toward a pure rule-utilitarianism; rules are open to exception on the basis of the principle of consequences.

Although Knauer does not treat other norms very explicitly, it is quite clear that his principle of commensurate or proportionate reason is central to his moral system and that other norms are subject to it. Schüller, while insisting that the admission of a first principle (the greater good must be preferred) does not automatically do away with secondary or middle-ground rules, insists as well that these rules are subordinate to this principle. The only unconditional or exceptionless norm will concern a good which is superior to any conceivable good. The implication seems to be that few, if any, secondary rules would involve such a good. They should give way, then, when a higher good is the alternative. He does not come to any definite conclusions regarding such exceptions, but suggests that our rules pertaining to taking one's own life or the life of an innocent person may not be completely closed to exceptions for this reason. He intimates the same possibility regarding the rule of indissolubility where a sacramental or consummated marriage is concerned.

In his analysis Fuchs, like Schüller, though rule-oriented, takes the position that there are probably no exceptionless norms of human behavior. This stand derives from his view, in which he follows Knauer very closely, that an act cannot be judged morally apart from the circumstances in which it is performed and the intention of the agent. Since it would be impossible to foresee all possible combinations of acts (objects), circumstances, and intentions, it would be equally impossible to set down an absolute or exceptionless norm. Fuchs would therefore have to attach a rider to every rule, e.g., killing is wrong except when there is a proportionate reason.

In attaching to rules an escape clause of this kind, Fuchs does not want to weaken them or detract from their real worth. They do point to values or nonvalues in the premoral sense. If they are nonvalues, e.g., taking human life, they may never be the object of a human intention and may be actuated only for a proportionate reason, i.e., some higher value. Also, rules can be considered universal in the sense that we cannot think of any exception to them. Whatever one may say on the level of theory, e.g., that theoretically such a norm is open to exceptions, on the practical level one cannot conceive of any proportionate reason that would justify violating them. Finally, some norms may be stated as universals in the sense that they are valid for ordinary cases (*ut in pluribus*). They are meant to be valid for the cases that ordinarily occur, and hence for ordinary living.

The notion of exception is in no sense foreign to traditional morality. In some instances moral rules themselves have been qualified to exclude certain cases. The prohibition of killing, for instance, has been qualified to the point where it is limited to the direct killing of an innocent person. Specifically excluded is killing in legitimate self-defense, killing of combatants in a just war, and capital punishment. Excluded also is indirect killing of an innocent person where there is a proportionate reason. Similarly, in regard to taking what belongs to another, the act of stealing is defined in such a way that it excludes certain acts of taking something from another, e.g., taking what is necessary to relieve extreme need. Finally, it is generally recognized that the law of charity does not bind where it would cause serious harm to observe it. And these are just a few of the exceptions allowed in traditional morality.

The present issue is whether these rules must remain open to further exceptions, and on a consequential basis. Also, what of those norms which have not been qualified in any way up to the present, e.g., the prohibition of adultery, fornication, etc.? The Catholic moralists we have been dealing with have all committed themselves at least to the theory that all rules are subject in one way or other to the principle of consequences. In other words, whatever their status, rules will yield to consequences. As mentioned, Fuchs takes a somewhat guarded position on the practical level. He admits that some norms may be closed to exception on the practical level, in the sense that we cannot conceive of any good that would justify the violation of these norms. So, although his theoretical position is more liberal than that of traditional morality, it is not clear how far away from it he would be in practice.

I suppose it would be very difficult to prove that all our current norms are closed to all future refinement, even if one does not take the stance that morality depends solely on consequences. But whatever the future may hold, many would agree that some of our norms are presently closed to exceptions.[26] Fuchs takes this position, or at least a similar position, even in respect to a morality based solely on consequences, when he says that some norms, though theoretically open, are practically closed to exceptions. But it is just as possible that rules will be tightened up as it is that some relaxation might be introduced.

This has happened in the past in regard to slavery. It may also be happening in the present in respect to capital punishment, which is being questioned in many places today. In the future, killing as punishment may be considered immoral. Even today capital punishment is the last example of physical punishment remaining in our penal codes. This gives reason to expect that, along with flogging and other forms of physical punishment, it will give way in a society moving progressively away from this type of punishment. The future may also find it more and more difficult to justify killing in war, since it may become more and more difficult to fulfill the conditions of the just war.

The basic problem with a morality based solely on consequences is not precisely that it remains open to exceptions but rather that it seems to call for, or at least allow, exceptions which go against commonly held convictions. When faced with acts which people generally consider wrong, but which according to all available evidence have overriding good effects, utilitarians will frequently appeal to hidden effects to condemn them. We have seen that the rule-utilitarians attempted to do this by concentrating on the effects of a practice rather than the effects of the individual act. Other utilitarians tend to appeal to long-range effects, "secondary effects" (bad example, weakening of character, etc.), and insist that the consequential calculus be thorough and include all such effects.

There is no doubt that these are important cautions, but, as Marcus Singer points out, this line of reasoning begs the question.[27] It is not as it ought to be: "This act is not useful, therefore it is wrong." It is rather: "This act is wrong, therefore it cannot be useful." In other words, the principle of consequences is not being used as a criterion. The conviction that the act is wrong derives from some other criterion and the judgment is made independently of consequences. Moreover, it would be very difficult to prove that every act which went against common convictions would have decisive hidden effects, or that it would be impossible for an act which was commonly considered wrong to be without overriding bad effects.

One of the criteria on which these common convictions are based is that of justice, and it is in this area particularly (but not solely) that many ethicians find a morality of consequences inadequate. David Lyons argues very convincingly that the principle of consequences simply cannot handle problems of justice and fairness, and if it is followed, it will often conflict with justice. To illustrate his position, he uses the example of a car that has stalled on a hill.[28] The car has six occupants, but five can push it up the hill without any great strain. Since this is the case, maximal utility (the best consequences) will be achieved if only five push and one rests.[29] Let us suppose that X wants to rest. It may well be that the others would like to rest too. Why X? If he just opts out, his action would undoubtedly affect others and lead to bad consequences, e.g., hard feelings, quarreling, etc. But if he just feigns pushing, he can exploit the maximizing condition and avoid these bad consequences. Thus the best consequences will be produced.

There is an obvious conflict here between justice or fairness and utility. X is being clearly unfair, even though the best consequences are being produced. The only reason his action does not have bad consequences is that the others are pushing their weight. The benefit he receives is parasitic on the efforts of others. But if he pushes to satisfy the demands of justice and a just distribution, less value will be produced than if such a distribution were not called for. The principle of consequences here would clearly call for unfair conduct and thus conflict with justice.

An ideal utilitarian might argue that unfair conduct leads to a loss of intrinsic good because a just or fair distribution is itself an intrinsic good. According to an ideal utilitarian, an act would have to be considered from this angle before an assessment of consequences could be made. Thus, in the case above, if X does his share of pushing, he loses the good of rest but contributes to the good of a just distribution. But if he does not push, he gains the good of rest and does not contribute to a just distribution. Which alternative would maximize the good produced? David Lyons points out that in the ideal utilitarian approach fairness would not always win out, since the contribution to fairness may not always be that important. Yet the traditional argument for fairness would call for it universally, since no one can be justified in exploiting or trying to exploit others.[30]

Lyons points out another problem with the ideal utilitarian

position. Suppose that one of those who helped push the car up the hill decided not to ride any farther with the group. On the ideal utilitarian view, he would be producing intrinsic evil (unfair distribution), since he participated in the effort without sharing in the benefits. This is indeed a trivial example, but the problem becomes more real in the case of the soldier on the winning side who is killed or maimed in the war as well as the soldier on the losing side who survives intact. We do not ordinarily accuse such people of causing intrinsic evil.

In his book on ethics, William Frankena also argues against the adequacy of utilitarianism as a moral system.[31] After admitting that his arguments against act-utilitarianism would seem to point in the direction of rule-utilitarianism, he goes on to say that there is a decisive argument even against rule-utilitarianism that would require one to adopt some kind of mixed deontological theory. He presents the argument this way. Suppose there are two rules, only one of which can be adopted. They produce the same amount of good but distribute it in different ways. The rule-utilitarian could not choose between them; each one would serve equally well. But one rule gives the benefits to a relatively small group without any merit on their part; the other distributes the benefits over a larger part of the population. On the basis of justice, the second rule would be morally preferable. The point he is making is that a rule may maximize the amount of good that can be achieved and yet be unjust in the way it distributes it. He admits that Mill's norm, the greatest good of the greatest number, avoids this charge, but only because it includes the principle of justice as well as the principle of utility. The principle of utility itself would not provide for justice.

Frankena argues that even the position of the ideal utilitarian, who recognizes a fair distribution of goods as an intrinsic good, is not adequate. First, Frankena is not convinced that a pattern of distribution is a good thing in itself. But even if one does accept it as an intrinsic good, he thus "admits that the criterion for determining whether a distribution is just is not the principle of utility, but something else, for example, equality. He may still hold that utility is the criterion of rightness, but he cannot hold that it is the criterion of justice."[32]

These two ethicians show that the demands of justice differ

from the demands of utility and can even come into conflict at times. A utilitarian might want to continue a defense of his system by maintaining that these differences, and subsequent conflicts, are only apparent, and that the principle of justice is merely a refinement of the principle of consequences. He might argue that the principle of justice was arrived at through an empirical study of the consequences of just, and unjust, acts. When one appeals to the principle of justice, therefore, he is really and ultimately appealing to the principle of consequences, since the former is merely a derivative of the latter. But this forces the utilitarian into the position in a conflict situation where he either has to deny that there is injustice or else appeal to hidden bad effects. He will more often attempt the latter (since he is facing common convictions), although this is often not very convincing. But in choosing this course, he is admitting that the principle of justice is a more reliable guide than the principle of consequences. He is also admitting that somewhere along the line other considerations, e.g., equality, have replaced consequences in practical importance in some areas of morality. If he still wants to maintain that consequences are the only consideration, he can do this only on a highly theoretical plane and against very persuasive indications.

It may be best to organize the conclusion of this discussion around the question originally presented. Is an act wrong because it has bad consequences, or does it have bad consequences because it is wrong (for other reasons)? That teleological or consequential considerations are decisive in some moral judgments has never been in question. In traditional moral theology the principle of the double effect has been the guideline for this type of moral judgment. The current question is rather whether consequential considerations are always decisive in moral judgments. Our discussion leads us to conclude that on the practical level the principle of consequences is not a very reliable guideline, at least in comparison with so-called secondary rules. The act-utilitarians themselves admit this. The rule-utilitarians even attempted to interdict the application of the principle of consequences to the individual act, but only at the cost of inconsistency. A consistent adherence to the principle of consequences would reduce rule-utilitarianism to act-utilitarianism. On the theoretical level, the possibility of conflict, even frequent, between secondary rules and the principle of consequences leads one to suspect that these rules cannot be explained entirely in terms of consequences. It is much easier to explain these conflicts if one postulates factors other than consequences behind these rules, with which consequences can come into conflict. The only alternative to this is to deny the conflicts by appealing to hidden consequences, but this seems a much less credible approach. Consequentialism, then, is difficult to establish on the theoretical level and dangerous to apply on the practical level. Those Catholic authors who are moving in this direction must turn their attention to both of these problems in future discussions. If pressed, they might be forced to acknowledge in the end that it would be better to rely, for instance, on considerations of justice rather than consequences in assessing certain classes of conduct. Such a standard may illuminate far more adequately and make much more secure such cases as that against the direct killing of the innocent.

Notes

1. We are referring particularly to the following articles: P. Knauer, S. J., "The Hermeneutic Function of the Principle of the Double Effect," *Natural Law Forum 12* (1967) 132-62; B. Schüller, S. J., "Zur Problematik allgemein verbindlicher ethischer Grundsätze," *Theologie und Philosophie* 45 (1970) 1-23; Joseph Fuchs, S. J., "The Absoluteness of Moral Terms," *Gregorianum 52* (1971) 415-58; Nicholas Crotty, C. P., "Conscience and Conflict," Theological Studies 32 (1971) 203-32. This list obviously represents no more than a sampling of the articles written on this subject. A complete list would have to include the articles written by John Giles Milhaven, *Theological Studies* 27 (1966) 218-41; 31 (1970) 106-24; 32 (1971) 407-30, as well as many others. The present articles were selected because their content was more relevant to the discussion pursued in this article, a discussion which is limited to certain features of the problem.

2. C. D. Broad distinguishes a deontological, teleological, and logical approach to moral obligation. There are some people who judge that all or at least certain types of action ought to be done or avoided regardless of the goodness or badness of the consequences. This is the deontological approach to obligation. Others hold that everyone in his actions ought to aim at certain ends, e.g., his own happiness or the greatest

happiness of the greatest number, etc. This is the teleological application of ought. Still others do not accept any end that everyone ought to desire, but maintain that if a man chooses an ultimate end for his acts, he ought to be consistent in choosing acts which lead to it. This is the logical ought. Cf. *Five Types of Ethical Theory* (London, 1930) p. 162. Today any morality based solely on consequences is called teleological. Deontological morality maintains that there are at least some actions which are right or wrong despite consequences.

3. Several of the significant articles that have appeared on this subject have been collected in a volume edited by Michael D. Bayles, *Contemporary Utilitarianism* (Garden City, 1968).

4. Joseph Fletcher, *Situation Ethics* (Philadelphia, 1966) p. 95.

5. These are called ideal utilitarians. Hedonists also admit other goods besides pleasure. Differences of opinion pertain to whether these goods are intrinsically or extrinsically good. The ideal utilitarians hold that they are intrinsically good. Concern with the theory of value connected with utilitarianism has declined considerably in recent times, probably because all utilitarians tend to agree in practice about what is good. The dispute about intrinsic and extrinsic is perhaps more philosophical than practical.

6. While unintended effects may be classified as circumstances, it should be noted that there are other morally relevant circumstances besides effects in traditional morality.

7. The commensurate good or reason (good consequences or effects) of which Knauer speaks does not fall into the category of "end" in the traditional sense of this term, i.e., *finis operantis extrinsecus*. It is Knauer's position that the commensurate reason is included in the *finis operis (finis operantis intrinsecus)*, i.e., the moral object of the act. Apart from this reason the act has only a physical object, or what St. Thomas calls a *species naturae (Summa theologiae* 1-2, q. 1, a. 3, ad 3). So, e.g., the act of killing in itself has only a *species naturae*; it takes on a *species moris* when one considers the reason behind it. Killing in self-defense is a morally good act; killing out of anger or hatred is a bad act. According to Knauer, one cannot speak of a moral object *(finis operis)* apart from the reason behind the act. One can speak only of a physical object, and if evil, physical evil. This presents no problem in regard to killing, which can be morally good or morally bad. But it does raise questions in regard to actions which have been traditionally regarded as wrong, e.g., adultery, direct killing of an innocent person, etc., independently of whatever reasons the agent might have had. By including the commensurate reason in the *finis operis* or moral object of the act, Knauer attempts to avoid the charge that he is violating the axiom that the end does not justify the means. This has usually been interpreted to mean that a good end or intention *(finis operantis extrinsecus)* will not justify an act which is morally bad *ex objecto*. But if the end is really part of the object and gives it a moral species, there is no question of a morally bad object, i.e.,

morally bad means. So there is no violation of the axiom.

8. *Summa theologiae* 2-2, q. 64, a. 7. The meaning of this article has been the source of much controversy over the centuries. For a brief history of the controversy, cf. Joseph T. Mangan, S. J., "An Historical Analysis of the Principle of Double Effect," *Theological Studies* 10 (1949) 41-61. Knauer argues that St. Thomas' total concern in this treatment is that there should be proportion in the defense. Since self-defense is a proportionate reason, taking the life of another is morally permissible. I am not sure this accurately represents the position St. Thomas takes in this article. Before taking up the problem of proportion at all, he makes a much more basic moral statement, namely, that it is natural to defend one's life. This provides for Thomas the basic justification for the use of violence. The question of proportion seems secondary; even if one is justified in using violence, one may do wrong by using more than is necessary. Also, when he takes up the question of proportion, Thomas is not speaking of a proportionate end justifying a violent means, but rather of a proportionate means, i.e., a means that does not go beyond the requirements of the goal. It is quite possible to speak of self-defense as a proportionate reason for violence against an aggressor, and interpret Thomas' basic statement on the morality of self-defense in this way. But even if justifiable, it would not do full justice to his position. A faithful rendering of this position would state that, according to Thomas, self-defense is a proportionate reason for *proportionate* violence against the aggressor. Where Knauer clearly goes beyond Thomas is in generalizing this rule.

9. When Crotty says that these acts can be justified, he does not mean that they are good. He follows the distinction some Protestant ethicians use between right and good. An action which involves evil, but which is promotive of human welfare, may be right but it is not good. Knauer, Schüller, and Fuchs rely more on the distinction between moral evil and premoral (ontic, physical) evil. An act may be morally good according to this distinction even though it involves premoral evil.

10. Our failure to deal with other problems connected with a consequential morality should not be interpreted as a lack of appreciation of these problems. It would be interesting, e.g., to discuss whether the principle of consequences is really a principle of morality or simply a principle of responsibility. If one is thinking in terms of actual, or perhaps even probable, consequences, how can he expect to make an objective moral assessment of an act unless he limits himself to more or less immediate consequences? To illustrate this difficulty, one author presents the fictitious case of the doctor who was called in to save the life of the infant *Adolf Hitler*. Is an objective estimate of his obligation possible on the basis of consequences? He can certainly make a judgment on the basis of foreseen consequences, and this will solve the problem of responsibility, but it may be far from reflecting the objective morality of the act.

11. Fuchs does not seem as much concerned with making the proportionate reason part of the *finis operis* or the moral object of the act. He takes the stand that the moral judgment must be made of the whole act: object, end, and circumstances. It cannot be made of the object independently of the other elements. All these elements are premoral in themselves, i.e., considered apart from the other elements of the act, so that any evil in the object will be premoral. There is no question, therefore, of the object being a *morally* bad means, and hence no violation of the axiom that the end does not justify the means. This principle would be violated only if a morally bad act (the judgment being made on the basis of all three elements) was justified by appealing to another intended act (judged morally good on the same basis). It is a little difficult to see how this would work out in practice.

12. J. S. Mill, *Utilitarianism* (New York, 1910) p. 22.

13. *Ibid.*

14. Responsibility for this orientation is frequently attributed to G. E. Moore, *Ethics* (London, 1912) pp. 7-45.

15. This case was first introduced by H. J. McCloskey in an article in the *Philosophical Review* 66 (1957) 466-85. The whole problem of the utilitarian approach to punishment was treated subsequently by the same author and responded to by T. L. S. Sprigge in two articles published in *Inquiry* 8 (1965) 249-63, 264-91. Alan Donegan discusses the same problem briefly under the formality of what he calls "Caiaphas's Rule" (Jn. 18:14) in a paper read at the University of Pittsburgh. All these articles have been reprinted in *Contemporary Utilitarianism*.

16. Richard Brandt, "Toward a Credible Form of Utilitarianism," *Contemporary Utilitarianism* (Garden City, 1968) pp. 146-48.

17. No rule-utilitarian has ever worked out a set of rules on a utilitarian calculus. Like everyone else, the rule-utilitarian starts with the *de facto* rules. The immediate issue is whether these are the best rules from a utilitarian viewpoint . . . and therefore closed to exceptions. I think the answer to this would have to be in the negative.

18. McCloskey distinguishes four different kinds of restricted utilitarianism. According to the *pure* theory, the principle of utility is appealed to only when considering the rules in practice, and never when considering the rightness or wrongness of actions. McCloskey says that restricted utilitarians write as though they wish to defend this view, but none of them hold to it in an undeviating way. According to the mixed variety of rule-utilitarianism, the principle of utility justifies the rules in practice, but is also used as a secondary rule which competes with other rules on the level of the individual case. *Unconditional* rule-utilitarianism allows for exceptional cases, e.g., stealing by a starving man from a wealthy person. The mixed and conditional varieties are obviously meant to meet difficulties which the pure and unconditional variety cannot handle.

19. Marcus Singer concludes that *no one* should violate the rule in

this case by introducing the principle of generalization (cf. below). Whether he does this validly may be questioned, but he admits that he cannot come to this conclusion on the basis of consequences alone. Cf. *Generalization in Ethics* (New York, 1961) pp. 90 ff.

20. *Forms and Limits of Utilitarianism* (Oxford, 1965) chaps. 2-4. Lyons admits a type of rule-utilitarianism, which he calls ideal rule-utilitarianism, which cannot be reduced to act-utilitarianism, but he does not find this very satisfactory (*ibid.*, pp. 136 ff.).

21. Singer, *op cit.*, pp. 13-33.

22. The rules of sexual morality have been traditionally considered closed. Unfortunately, utilitarians and those promoting a morality of consequences have been preoccupied with the problems of lying, promising, and punishment of the innocent, so that little thought has been given to these rules. But one author, Knauer, when asked explicitly about the application of his principle of commensurate reason to the sexual area, did respond in a final note to his article. He was questioned about the case of the woman who commits adultery to rescue her children from a concentration camp, or the woman for whom prostitution is the only way to keep from starving. Knauer could not see his way clear to allowing either of these two cases, since he looked upon both as yielding to a kind of extortion: Making a living or saving one's children from a concentration camp would not be a commensurate reason to justify such yielding. Life or freedom have no value if they result from yielding to extortion. Cf. *art. cit.*, p. 162, note. This response might surprise those who would expect a morality of consequences to open up many doors. But it must be admitted that other consequentialists might make a different assessment.

23. "A Protestant Ethical Approach," in *The Morality of Abortion*, ed. John T. Noonan (Cambridge, 1970) pp. 107 ff.

24. The moral judgment must rest on morally relevant details. Many of the details that would make an act unique may not be morally relevant. Jonathan Harrison gives the example of a "red-haired man with one eye, a wart on his right cheek, and a mermaid tattooed on his left forearm (telling) a lie on a Tuesday" (*Contemporary Utilitarianism*, p. 36). Obviously these details, although they make for the uniqueness of the act, are not morally relevant. So the moral act may not be as unique as a full description of the act might lead one to believe. But it may not always be easy to determine what details are morally relevant.

25. Exception-making criteria make for what Lyons calls concise rules. Rules listing specific exceptions (excepting conditions) he calls expanded rules (*op. cit.*, pp. 125 ff.). It would be clearly impossible to include a taxative list of exceptions in some rules, e.g., the rule of secrecy. The best one could do would be to include the exception-making criteria.

26. Ramsey suggests that the rule against rape, e.g., might be one in which no morally significant change might be expected; cf. "The Case of the Curious Exception," in *Norm and Context in Christian Ethics*, ed.

Gene H. Outka and Paul Ramsey (New York, 1968) pp. 127 ff. For a lengthy but interesting critique of Ramsey's position on exceptionless norms, cf. Donald Evans, "Paul Ramsey on Exceptionless Moral Norms," *American Journal of Jurisprudence* 16 (1971) 184-214.

27. *Op. cit.*, pp. 209 ff.

28. *Op. cit.*, chap. 5.

29. We are dealing here with what David Lyons calls "maximizing conditions." He also speaks of "minimizing conditions." These will prevail in a situation in which less than the required number are observing a rule which has certain threshold effects, so that the good will not be produced anyhow. In the example given above, if three of the occupants refuse to push the car, the good consequences will not be achieved, since it will take five to get the car up the hill. There is no obligation on X to push in this situation. Similarly with lying, killing, etc.: if everyone is lying, killing, etc., the good consequences resulting from the practice of telling the truth, respecting the lives of others, etc., will not be achieved. Some refer to these as "state of nature" situations. cf. *op. cit.*, pp. 128 ff.

30. The exaggerated notion of justice, epitomized in the saying *fiat justitia, ruat caelum*, is not being recommended here. There may be times when justice should give way to consequences or other considerations (*Summa theologiae*, 1-2, q. 94, a. 4).

31. *Ethics* (Englewood Cliffs, 1963) pp. 32 ff.

32. *Ibid.*, p. 35.

Morality by Calculation of Values

Paul M. Quay, S.J.

Many widely known moralists of recent times have been seeking to eliminate "absolutely binding" moral norms. They deny, that is, that any norm known antecedently to the ultimate assessment of the agent's existential situation and of what appears to him his full set of alternative lines of action can specify either the moral goodness or moral badness of the line of action actually chosen. In other words, they assert that no antecedently binding moral norms can be universally applicable; none are unconditional and independent of the situation and the subjective dispositions of the agent.

Presumably because this tendency first gained notoriety through the "situation ethics" of Sartrian existentialism and certain forms of Protestant sentimentalism, attacks upon it have focussed largely upon its demand for a moral judgment based on the entirety of a concrete situation, including all subjective elements. But, in fact, the flaws lie elsewhere. For, St. Thomas and, I think, the whole Catholic tradition have maintained that every component of reality concretely contained in or related to a given moral choice and its alternatives needs in principle to be considered in one fashion or another in the formation of the moral judgment.

The question then is this: are there any concrete (not purely formal, not tautological) prohibitions and/or precepts of Christian morality which bind a duly informed conscience antecedently and universally? Of the many arguments for the negative, only one is considered here, that based on the philosophy of values as more or less recently elevated into a theology of values. Whatever may be said from a purely speculative point of view as to the possibility or usefulness of such a theological approach, this article will center exclusively on the principal use to which a number of current moralists are putting it,[1] i.e., to "relativize" so-called "absolute prohibitions" against defrauding laborers, adultery, abortion, and the like.[2]

I

A THEOLOGY OF VALUES

The main elements in their argument from values can be summarized as follows:

1. Every element of the concrete moral situation facing a particular human agent (most particularly, possible courses of action, both in themselves as modes of activity and in their previsioned consequences, what he sees of circumstances and relationships, his interior dispositions and purposes, his ends and goals, his moral and religious convictions, the social, political, and cultural contexts operative) is (or has) a value, positive if helpful to man, negative (and then often called "disvalue" or "physical evil") if hurtful or injurious. Most elements will contain more than one value and often may have aspects of both value and disvalue.

Moral norms embody and protect the particular values which a society has learned to esteem and has made its own through past observation of their helpfulness; thus these norms protect and foster the society itself. They enter into the moral evaluation precisely as value-affirmations deeply rooted in historical experience.

While not absolute or determinative, they represent values which experience has shown to be so great within this cultural context that it is highly unlikely (in that same context) that any congeries of oppositely directed values which might arise because of circumstances, intentions, and the rest will ever countervail their worth. Nonetheless, on principle, the possibility of such countervailing value must always be left open until the concrete moral situation has been evaluated.

2. The over-all value, then, of each alternative course of

action is grasped through a moral calculus in which the human agent, after assessing the values of each of the elements belonging to that alternative, sums these values, and, in a moral judgment, perceives and asserts the aggregate worth of each course of action physically open at the moment. That is judged to be bad which has a negative total value; and that to be good which has a positive total value.

All the values thus far discussed are considered to lie at the pre-moral level, i.e., to be physical goods or evils for man, society, family, etc. They are values which, even when summed by the moral judgment are, as yet, antecedent to moral good or moral evil, which enters only with the engagement of one's liberty in an act of free choice.

Positive Total Value Intended

3. Having judged as best one can the total value of each alternative, one is then obliged to intend and choose that particular action which has the greatest total value or, at least, some action whose net value is positive. The intention is to be directed to the positive total value, considered as a whole, which is attainable through the particular action. To intend a negative total value is always morally wrong.

Because of the mixed nature of most situations, the intention will usually bear on a line of action that contains a certain number of disvalues as well as of positive values. In such a case, if indeed the aggregate value of the whole is positive, still, for the action to be morally good, the intention must bear on the totality only, without intending directly, or as such, any negative elements. Thus, such heavily negative premoral elements as killing the innocent, sex with another's husband or wife, and the like, form part of a morally good action whenever, rare as the case may be in practice, they are incorporated into and coalesce in a single act of choosing a net positive value.

One may rightly will an abortion, for example, but only when the death of the child is seen as but one of many premoral elements whose values when summed result in an overriding positive value for the action as a whole. Since all the values present, positive and negative alike, are premoral values, there is no question of first making an evil moral choice, directly intending to kill the infant and then using that evil choice or its results as means to one's good end. There is only one human action, one which has—in this presumably rare situation—a net positive premoral value; hence, the action is good. There is no morally bad action anywhere in the process which one might order to some good end.

4. It is then pointed out that no human or created value can be absolute; none is such as to weigh infinitely in the balance regardless of what is placed in the other pan. This follows not merely from reason but also from the fact that no human value has ever been recognized as absolute by the Scriptures or by the Church. God alone is absolute. Nothing and no one else can have absolute weight. Hence, no one may ever choose anyone or anything in direct preference to God. Since most moral choices, however, are not between God and a creature but between one line of creaturely conduct and another, one must say that, apart from direct blasphemy, no value-judgment can be antecedently determined by appeal to some absolute value supposedly present.

5. Often an ultimate relativization is obtained by restricting the values to be considered to intra-worldly ones, those which bind individuals or societies to their world-of-experience. It is then argued that Christianity does not appreciably change even the weights to be ascribed to the various values entering into the moral assessment. Apart from the moral "forms" of faith, hope, and charity, revelation has directed its concrete imperatives only to the culturally conditioned and highly mutable value-systems of its day, instructing us that, as Christians of that day were to avoid the things then quasi-universally regarded as immoral, so the Christians of our day are to adapt their conduct to the moral judgments of their cultural milieu.

In Section II we shall indicate some of the key elements in any moral situation or in the alternative responses open to free choice which cannot be reduced to any complex of values whatever: physical good, physical (or ontic) evil, qualitative differences between values, relations of cause and effect, persons, and personal relations. Then, in Section III, we shall consider some of the unfortunate consequences of confounding such irreducible elements with values.

II
ELEMENTS NOT REDUCIBLE TO VALUES

Now, is it possible to reduce to values all the elements needed for the making of a moral judgment, as these positions assume, and thus reduce the moral judgment itself simply to evaluation? Alternatively, is a correct moral judgment possible if and only if it is based on consideration of all the premoral *values* concretely present, and only these?

Some aspect of value can doubtless be distilled from most elements in the moral situation. But the full reality of that situation and, consequently, its significance for moral choice cannot be adequately described by any listing of its values. This is obvious *a priori*: for, unlike the good, value is not transcendental; hence, it is not convertible with being; hence, there are aspects or modes of being which must perforce escape any discussion in terms of values. But the matter is too important to leave at this level of generality.

Value vs. Good

1. How, in detail, does a value differ from a good? Obvious as the answer may be, we must discuss it, since perhaps the commonest error is to think that a physical or indeed any premoral good can be treated simply as a positive value.

Now, the good is whatever is (i.e., any being or mode of being whatever) considered under those aspects in which it is all that it ought to be, i.e., perfect and, therefore, evoking in any intellectual being who knows it in its existential totality a willed response of love, complacency, or desire.

A value, on the other hand, is that which can be, is, or ought to be prized, esteemed, or thought to have worth by some human agent (whether an individual, a group, or a collectivity such as state, society, or culture); more abstractly, a value is that formal aspect of a being which is the ground of its being thus prized. Thus, value-theologians call human life a value in the former sense and, in the latter sense, speak of the capacity for loving, interpersonal relationships as the value of human life. A value, then, may rightly be subjected to a weighing of its worth by men. In the sense of that which ought to be prized, a value is something of intrinsic worth to man, which of its nature is related to human advantage or the furtherance of human ends. For example, an activity which leads to or constitutes a given mode of self-realization is such a value.

A value, then, is not simply convertible with what is good for man but with that which is good for him in terms of his needs, desires, or purposes. To be free is a metaphysical good for man, whether he knows or admits the fact or not; food is good for him physically, again independently of his awareness of the fact; but values require his consciousness, his own perception, estimation, and choice of what he will consider good for man. It is, I believe, the recognized need for just such personal assimilation of the morally good that has been chiefly responsible for the current exaggeration of the role of values in moral choice.

Thus, a value is not merely valuable to some prospective agent but is of value to him *for* some purpose or goal. A value stands in relation, therefore, not only to man in his physical and metaphysical constitution, like the good, and to his conscious and subconscious views of reality, but to his already accepted goals. The more a being contributes to a desired goal, the greater value it has. But the goal itself must already be given. *Qua* goal, it is good, but not of value; obviously, though, most goals receive a value when considered in relation to yet further and more nearly ultimate ends.

Worth for Exchange

If a value differs from a good by its web of qualifying relations, it is also these relations which define the value concretely, which give an object its value. Hence, anything else so related is equally valuable—*value implies the possibility of exchange*. So long as one object has as great effectiveness for the attainment of given ends as some other, it is of equal value with it or with anything else which is no more, no less effective in the same respect. Thus the commercial origins of the word in English are still evident; and "values" never wholly sheds its denotation of a worth-for-exchange. Thus the valuable as such is the interchangeable, not in the sense of identity and, so, of anonymity, as of one penny for another, but in the sense in which a nickel has the same value as five pennies, i.e., in all that matters for the given context, there exists complete interchangeability or convertibility.

Further, it is a common experience to find good and value in conflict. Who has not had to part with things because they are of no value to him whatever and yet which he recognizes as truly good, e.g., a fine old mansion, now far too expensive to maintain? Conversely, who has not felt disgust or sadness on seeing some trifling good become the center of men's attention and interest, taking on enormous value, or even some evil thing becoming a major value?

The good can be of value under many different aspects; but since it grounds and, in some sense, contains not only all these values but an infinity of other, merely possible ones, the good cannot be reduced to any finite set of values. More simply, the good, since it is not defined by any relationship to human advantage, cannot be adequately replaced by any set of elements, such as values, which are in this way relative. On the other hand, values can be exhaustively described in terms of complex goods and so be reduced to them, hence, the traditional concern of moral theology with the good, physical as well as moral, rather than with value.

Disvalue vs. Evil

2. If, then, positive value and good are not equivalent, we may expect to find that negative values (disvalues) are not the same as premoral (ontic) evils. Thus, it might be for me a negative

value in the defense of a client in court that I cannot simultaneously attend a performance of an opera that I should very much like to hear. But that is not an evil, not even a physical one. It may be retorted that "negative value" is the wrong way to put the matter; rather, defense of my client at this time is merely of slightly less, aggregate, positive value than were it compatible with my also hearing the opera. Yet the very notion of aggregation and balance of values renders this an evasion. That which, when added to anything, makes this latter less than it would otherwise be is just what is meant by a negative quantity.

Nor can one avoid the point by arguing that I might in time do both. Perhaps; but the quintessential drama of all moral existence is precisely that of those great choices (and their lesser analogs) where the taking of any option destroys in the choosing the very possibility of all others, e.g., marriage now to this woman.

How Premoral Evil Differs

A physical (or premoral) evil is quite different. It represents not merely a contingent aspect of a good as a result of which its advantage to me is or seems diminished, i.e., a negative value, but contains a true privation of a good called for. The good that naturally belongs to or is intrinsically part of some being is, in fact, destroyed or prevented. Operas are no essential part of pleading a case or of human life; I am deprived of nothing, therefore, in the example above, no matter how great the negative value. Removing, on the other hand, a human fetus, "animated" or not, from the nourishing shelter of its mother's womb is to deprive it of its natural conditions for and possibility of life and growth—a negative value indeed, but worse than that, a grave evil. The difference between physical evil and disvalue can be made still more evident by obvious modifications of the arguments given above concerning good and value.

3. A third element, also recalcitrant to value reductionism is that of qualitative difference. To attempt to judge an action solely by the aggregate of value it contains leads logically to seeing the determination of moral good as a merely quantitative process—a "moral calculus" as these moralists say—a quasi-algebraic addi-

tion of pluses and minuses. For, things cannot be added save insofar as they are of one kind. Two apples and three oranges can be added only if one ignores their diversity and regards them as "pieces of fruit." Hence, the addition of values must lead ultimately to the discarding of all elements of uniqueness and nonconvertibility even among diverse kinds of values.

Thus reduction to values is a reduction to the quantitative but without the carefully wrought methods of quantifying the qualitative which have been the hallmark of science. It is less a calculus than a mercantilism of values, an exchange and weighing for trade. Everything can in principle be evaluated and scaled in accord with utility, worth, and price; as values are balanced, exchanged, and traded off for one another, the moral judgment becomes a commerce and merchandizing in human conduct and Christian behavior.

It is the mercantilist spirit applied once again to human behavior, defending its present relativism with essentially the same arguments as those with which it once defended trading glass beads and brass buttons for the wealth of furs in the Pacific Northwest: Indians valued the beads more than the furs; the white man, the reverse; each got the things he valued. So what is this talk of injustice?

Intention and Causal Relations

4. Though the matter is not entirely clear, apparently a majority of value-moralists, rightly, do not regard the moral intention as one among the premoral values entering into the determination of the moral judgment. Yet often they seem overly insistent that all intentions concretely present at the time of a choice be considered in order adequately to grasp the human meaning of the act ("opposed usually to grasping merely its physical nature"). Such language is at least open to misunderstanding in its context. This position is called "new" or "newly recovered." Yet, who of moral theologians of past or present has held that the intention of the agent is less important concretely than the physical structure of his action? Who has regarded an unintended killing, say, as murder? In any event, it will be helpful to make the point entirely

clear, since the untangling of some serious confusions will depend upon it.

The intention is the intellectually grasped end or *finis* to which an action, if chosen, will be directed (or, about as commonly, the intellectual act which grasps this end). It serves primarily to map out and delimit the precise elements which will constitute the moral activity I choose. I can choose freely and so am responsible solely for that which I in some way intend (both positively and negatively—that is, I am responsible for intending A; I am responsible as well for not intending B along with A).

So, then, the intention is not one factor among others in the concrete situation or concrete alternative actions but is that by means of which I delimit and bind together all the elements needed to form the pattern of possible action which constitutes such an alternative. It determines net values (and all else) from the outside, not as an element or component of the alternative but as that which defines the alternative to have such and such components.

The crucial tie-in between intention and value-morality lies in the fact that the reduction of all internal aspects of the moral judgment to values or relations among values renders impossible or irrelevant consideration of other intrinsic connections between the different elements, connections which, however, have an essential role in the specification of one's intention.

In particular, the relation of cause to effect cannot be expressed solely in terms of values, though it is essential for the moral judgment. The values, individual and aggregate, of someone's dying and my escaping with my life would seem to be the same, all else being equal, whether there is a causal link between them or not. But the moral importance of his death's being the cause of my survival is not negligible. As we shall see in Sect. III, a radically false view of moral intention is generated by ignoring causal relations.

Person Neglected

5. Finally, let us look at what are for the Christian the most basic and important elements omitted in the attempt to carry all

by the way of values: human persons and their relations, especially with God. Now, the value-moralists do often assert that the human person is the most basic or fundamental of values. Yet, while it is evident that a person may well be designated a "fundamental good," these moralists never tell us by what right he may be regarded as a "fundamental value." That he is not an "instrumental value" is also clear—but why "value" at all?

At the level of fact, it need not be true. Many a person— tragedy though it is—has lived for months or years without being a concrete value for anyone; he is unknown or despised by all. Yet this person need not be less good because he is valued less by anyone or by all others, save God.

At the level of possibility, can a person as such be evaluated? There is already a theoretical problem in evaluating a person merely as an athlete or as a scientist, still more as a lawyer or a mother. For a person's "performance" as any of these never depends merely upon his observable abilities and skills but also upon his basic character, virtues, and personal relationships. These latter suffuse all he does in a manner which does not permit sharp separation of his worth as "man," as "physician," as "otolaryngologist." Yet here one only has to answer such questions as: how well does he do this work or relate to particular people in certain specified manners? But how judge his value as person? Indeed, it is not easy even to say what we might mean by "the value of a person." His value to whom? For what ends?

It would seem precisely this attempt to assay our fellows as persons which the Gospel excludes when it forbids us to "judge" them, i.e., to make a judgment about their goodness in God's eyes, on the basis of their conformity with our values, even when these seem to be based on revelation. No one can be weighed or evaluated as a person, nor can the attempt legitimately be made to do so, by anyone but God himself.

The Person Is Unique

Even were it possible truly to evaluate a person as such and licit to do so, would seeing him as of value to man, as one who ought to be esteemed, be a morally sound way to see him?

First of all, equivalence for exchange and convertibility are simply incompatible with a Christian understanding of the person. For the person, in what makes him truly such, is unique and irreplaceable and unexchangeable. He is literally invaluable; for whatever is the only one of its kind cannot be evaluated from that aspect in which it is unique. Quantitative measure, even of the fairly indefinite sort involved in premoral values, requires at least two of a kind, one of which can be used to furnish a measure for the other. Hence, no person can be adequately regarded for any human purposes simply as a value, as "for others."[3] Indeed, the central problem of a Christian morality is just the opposite: namely, how is it possible to have objectives and universal norms for beings who are precisely non-universal and unique? Since Christ died for each man, not just for a global "all," a satisfactory response can be given; but it cannot lie in the direction of denying the uniqueness and the irreplaceability of the person, as value-moralists seem to allow.

Yet do we not sense that a truly good person is of great value to society? We see him as a good example, know him to be reliable in danger or difficulty. He is of service to all, for all good ends. Yet he is not a means to anyone's ends. One cannot use him in order to have good example, though each can profit by the example he offers. His "value" is gratuitous; there is no predetermined way in which he will be of value to anyone or to society. And he is unique; even his work in this world is not replaceable by others'. Is it not clear, then, that the greater the good, the greater the variety and magnitude of the values it can ground and sustain—but that it is the good at which we are looking, and that our proper response to it is not evaluation or esteem but love? And is not the evil that afflicts family life so widely today just this, that parents *value* their children and that husbands *value* their wives, with reasonable accuracy, indeed, and "love" them accordingly?

Valuing and esteeming are, at best, ancillary virtues in the moral life of the Christian, where charity has primacy. It is the unique quality of charity to love a person—because God loves him and in Christ—who is not (yet? ever?) worthy of love at his deepest level. It is the love with which God loved us when we were still in our sins and worthy only of damnation, valuable only as a vine-branch for burning. Charity is a love which seeks indeed to give value and worth (in relation to God, however, and not in relation to man directly) to a person who lacks all worth, or to increase it beyond its present measure where it already exists; further, charity seeks to help him become good, to call forth from chaos, as God did at the first Creation, the unique goodness of this person whom we must love before he has in himself any ground for our love.

Induced Desirability

6. We may note here in passing a further difficulty which this example of charity raises for a value-theology: not only is it true that all morally relevant elements of a situation cannot be expressed as values in a self-consistent manner, but a highly pertinent class of values is not to be found at all in the antecedent situation and possible courses of action, so that it is impossible to make the moral judgment on the basis of *all* the values which are chosen in the free act.

This is the phenomenon of "induced" desirability, whereby my free choice itself becomes the source of at least part of the value of the object chosen—the simplest case being found in the choice of one among several identical chocolates, stamps, or the like (Buridan's ass died for failing to realize this). But in fact, this investing of something with value by the very act of liberty which chooses it enters into all free choice. It is this which explains some of the destructive power of sin to blind the sinner, in the act itself, to his own sinfulness, preventing repentance through disguising the need for it: for the mind seeks justification for the sinful action by objectifying this increment of value as if there were true grounds for it in the antecedent reality. In a good action, the person tries rather to bring into being (or at least into consciousness) the element of goodness which could ground such an increment of value within the real situations where this value was not grounded (or perceived). And, as mentioned, this sort of induction of value reaches its transcendent and higher-than-human perfection in charity.

In brief, then, neither the persons involved in the moral situation nor their relationship with one another nor, least of all, those relations to the Persons of the Trinity which are charity, hope, and faith, can be dealt with adequately in a moral framework concerned primarily with human values.

III
NEW PROBLEMS ARISE

Though any moral system must devote an appreciable place to problems concerned with values, there arise novel and serious problems wherever the assignment of values to the elements of the action-in-context is made to carry the entire burden of the moral judgment.

Whose Values Count?

1. Assuming, then, for the sake of discussion, that a morally good action is one which is of net positive value to man as man, we must still ask: how can the values belonging to the elements of this concrete action be *uniquely* prescribed?

For, any element of premoral good may have, and properly so, very different values for every different person—even for the same person at different times. For example, the good that my continuation in life represents at a given time could be more or less objectively discovered by each person who wished to do so regardless of his own situation, so long as the same definition of good was used. The same is not true of value. My life may be much more valuable to one person than to another, though both understand "value" indentically; it may be a disvalue to yet others.[4] Are their moral obligations not to shoot me down equally diverse?

Whose values then are to count? Since we are speaking of the moral quality of some individual's free choice, presumably these values must be those of this moral agent, though evidently they will be so shaped as to include some sort of reference to those of other people. But do his actual values count? Or the values he ought to have?

If the former, we should have to approve Hitler as morally good since he clearly chose fairly effective means for developing the "pure Aryan" stock which he valued; and in general he seemed to act consistently with his value-system. That this value-system itself was monstrous and that he was acting immorally when acting in accord with it can be shown only if one admits that his value-system was, ultimately at least, a matter of free choice. And since no values can be assigned to all till some value-system has already been chosen, one cannot determine the moral quality of any choice of a fundamental value-system by summing the values which would be realized through the choice of this system rather than of some other. Further, if it is the agent's actual values which determine the morality of his action, by what right may the state pass laws to force him to act otherwise? Law becomes nothing more than a device for behavioral conditioning, and fundamentally unjust.

If, on the other hand, we insist that a man act in accord with values one does not hold but ought to hold, at least in these circumstances, this sounds suspiciously like an antecedent moral norm of universal applicability. Whence else comes the "ought"? It clearly is meant to represent a moral obligation, binding in conscience. Nor is it a grudge against Hitler personally, for *no* one at all can rightly hold such values. If someone knowingly refuses the values he should have, we consider him to be acting immorally. But on the basis of what values would *he* make the moral judgment that he ought to reject the fundamental values he holds and embrace others which he sees only as disvalues at present?

Other Men's Values

Further, does the reference one man's values *should* show towards those of others relate to others' actual values or to the ones they ought to have? Or to both? Again, if something is of great value to the agent but a disvalue for the great majority of his fellow men, how should the agent take these values of others into account?

Suppose I am a sodden and single derelict, but innocent of misdeed against others. Have I the right to defend myself against an attacker who is a pillar of society, one who is, apart at least from his hostility to me and the dispositions from which it springs, of great value to millions of people? It has been urged by value-moralists that killing in self-defense is still permitted because, in the long run, such killing best protects the value it seems to harm: human life for as many as possible. But whose value is this? Not mine; I may defend my life against the two other survivors of a nuclear holocaust. Not, clearly, my attacker's. Then society's?

But how can other persons, even a whole society, demand, in any way obliging on my conscience, that I shift my value-system to conform to theirs, unless there is within my value-system (therefore, in principle, universally) one value greater than all other possible values together, namely, to follow the basic values of the society in question—something for which there seems little enough evidence. Why should I feel obligated to conform, especially if in my actual value-system the key values of society count for little—as true of St. Paul vis-a-vis both his native Judaism and the Graeco-Roman world as, in a less worthy manner, of some individualistic struggler for wealth and power?

The One Against the Many

Moreover, the quantitative summing of values has this inconvenience, that whoever is acting for the state, that is, in the name of or for the benefit of the people as a whole, has automatically a factor of millions with which to multiply one or other relatively minor value. If the value of my life, drunken bum that I am, is to be laid in a scale against the far smaller values of, say, good business and avoiding offense to the sensibilities of many millions of citizens, then, innocent though I be of crime, how could the value of my life ever prevail? The objection that to give such power to the state in one case would, by implication, give it such power in all others and that this would be a negative value large enough to block an assault on me, presumes a state acting irresponsibly. But suppose a responsible statesman who would, every time, assiduously weigh the appropriate values in accord with suitably accurate laws before snuffing out some fellow citizen, so that indeed the values of all others were truly served. How could he be faulted?

An obvious response would be to deny that the values of different agents are additive, to insist rather that every agent must make the common good of all a major value of his own. "Must . . . "? Do his antecedent values necessarily and in all cases determine this to be the choice of greatest net value for him? Is this knowable antecedently to any knowledge of his case? In any event, is it not cheating a little to invoke the common *good* here rather than some common value—else, why should good not replace value everywhere? The problem recurs: how *ought* I take into account the values of others if the grounding of all my moral activity lies not in the good but in my values?

One final and more fundamental difficulty may be noted in this context. If other people's good, as well as their values, are to have weight in the formulation of my moral judgment only insofar as they can be transformed into values of my own, then I would seem to be inescapably locked into a wholly self-centered moral attitude. For, again, unlike the good, even if it is only good-for-me, a value-for-me has no necessary implication of value for anyone else. Nothing, then, would be admitted into my moral judgment except in terms of my own advantage and perspectives—an approach to morality incompatible not only with the God-centered orientation of Christianity but even with a psychologically sound attitude towards reality.

Ignoring Causal Relations

2. As mentioned in Section II, n. 4, the tendency to see all in terms of value leads to nearly complete neglect of the implications for morality of the metaphysical structures of causation, most particularly, that of efficient cause and effect. It is in connection

with the intention of the agent that this neglect becomes crucial.

In the real order, an intention cannot, save by ignorance or mistake, bear on only one or other link in a single causal chain. If I know that this (valuable) effect comes about only through the placing of this (premorally evil) cause, then it is simply hypocrisy to pretend that I can will *only* the net value, the cause somehow vanishing in the addition. Rather, the exact opposite obtains. My moral intention bears upon and makes me responsible for *all* the individual elements that are, to my knowledge, interrelated by causal necessity. Whoever wills the effect wills the cause, or else his willing the effect sinks to the level of velleity. After all weighing of values, for example, suppose that I decide that the greatest net value is obtainable by a line of action taking me on a pleasure-cruise by means of money obtained by the mercy-killing of my slowly dying and cancerous father. All the "willing" in the world of this net value is of relatively little moral consequence unless I decide finally to kill him. And if I so decide, the basic moral quality of the act is fixed, whatever modifications are introduced by other elements.

On the other hand, what is not connected causally with the desired end need not enter my choice, though its value be the same as if it were so connected. Recall the permission classically accorded me to run down a child playing in the middle of a narrow road between cliff and chasm as I flee from those intent on killing me. The running down is physically necessary (so the case assumes) if I am not to lose my own life; but it is not the cause of my staying alive and I, therefore, am able and, indeed obligated, while confronting the whole reality of what will keep me alive, to avoid intending that child's death. If (as in the old Saturday-afternoon "serials" at the movies) it happens that there is a hidden escape-mechanism available for the youngster at the last moment, I am delighted, once I learn of it, and nothing has happened to prevent my escape.

But change the case a bit. Let the road be wide enough at this point for me to get by without either hitting the child or slowing down; let me recognize him as my pursuer's only son, innocent entirely of his father's misdeeds; and let me know for certain that running him down would cause my enemy to call off his pursuit, indeed, that at this juncture there is no other means to escape death. In no way could I be justified in killing this boy. His death would now be the means of my escape and there is no way I could intend the global "escape-from-my-enemy-by-killing-his-son" without bearing the full guilt of intending to kill an innocent man.

It is this clear regard for reality in all its relationships that lies at the heart of the principle of double effect—rejected by a majority of value-theologians or restated in terms of that same dreamy unreality, the undiscriminating global intention. This principle does not merely state, as some seem to think, that if there exist two effects, one good, one bad, of a single action, I can will the good and permit the bad. Rather, I may will or choose *only* the good and *must*, by my willing, *reject* the bad, even if I see no way of avoiding it concretely (and, of course, have sufficient reason for acting anyway). The question is not whether I cause the bad effect or not (I do, by supposition) but whether the bad effect is causally related to the good intended.

The Global Intention

Consider the matter from a slightly different point of view. It is always the agent's option to intend as large or small a domain of choice as he wishes, provided that, in drawing his boundaries, he always respects the real relationships, especially those of causality, linking what he is doing with all else; for, freedom involves among its functions the specification, in and by the free act itself, of this domain. But if, as the value-moralists would have it, the intention need not attend to causal linkages, provided only that the net value of whatever domain is chosen is concretely positive, then we may well inquire into the criteria for drawing the boundaries of one's intention. Might I pull the trigger on a loaded gun which happened to be pointing at someone's head, intending only the exercise of my trigger-finger and practice in the steadying of my hand? If one looks only this far, till the bullet is in the air and no further, then is not the value-summation positive and the act good? The case is not absurd. One may severely restrict one's intention, coming to intense, often deadly concentration on the very present act, assiduously not looking so far as its first consequences lest the horror there surmised freeze the heart and weaken the determination, as Althaea did when she burned the log on which her son's life depended—and how many murderers since! Only knowledge of cause and effect justifies us in calling such ostensible limitation of intention insincere and morally ineffective.

Or, what of those Marxist enthusiasts who do not hesitate to loose destruction for millions in the hope of a better humanity in the future, rising rejuvenated from the ashes of its former self? "We must break eggs if we wish an omelette." So long as the intention need bear only on the total value of all that it embraces, without being constrained by the relational configuration of reality, then whenever a given span of intention is insufficient to provide a positive counterbalance to one's presently envisaged premorally evil act, one can shorten or extend the intention, shrink the range of elements included or broaden it even to all things known and foreseeable.

Intrinsic Consequences

It is strange, with their strong emphasis on the moral significance of foreseen extrinsic consequences of an action, that these moralists do not grasp more clearly the still greater importance of intrinsic consequences—those which, by the nature of the action, are produced, for good or ill, in the one acting, independently of whether he knows of them or not (premoral good or evil), though having a far stronger impact and making a far deeper modification of his being when lifted to the moral level. Thus, as I have shown elsewhere, (*Theological Studies* 22 [1971] 18-40), an act of sexual perversion, even if we suppose it to be carried out in good conscience, still damages the properly human personality of the agent, conforming it to the falsity such an act symbolizes. Now, if one knows the evil of such an act, there is still no way his intention can truthfully separate the act from its inner and immediate effects—if he intends the act, he intends these. To call these negative values and to perform the action for some extrinsic good is simply to do evil that good may come.

A Shabby Empiricism?

3. If the metaphysical grounding of the value-theologies is this weak, one may expect their epistemology to be little better. Indeed, the same false notion of intention will be operative here also to prevent them from extricating themselves from situations to which they are not necessarily bound by other demands of consistency.

Central to their argumentation is the assertion that no single element can antecedently determine the moral quality of a proposed course of action independently of all other factors; for, if the element has a non-infinite value, then sets of circumstances must be conceivable with aggregate value sufficient to outweigh it. It is conceded, indeed, that this would not have to be the case were we able to know every possible set of circumstances, consequences, and the rest; but this is patently impossible in principle, still more so in practice.

Now, such a position seems no different from the crudest sort of empiricism, according to which we can know only what has been directly given us in our experience. Even in the physical sciences, till recently so dominated by both British empiricisms and Continental positivisms as to seem their source, it has always been admitted that proper deductions can be made, *via* abstract thought and logic, to conclusions of strict impossibility. Given some set of empirically valid principles, e.g., Newton's laws or the principles of quantum mechanics, one can immediately deduce all sorts of "absolute" statements (i.e., which do not depend on further circumstances at all) about objects of specified properties. No circumstances could combine to make certain prescribed behaviors possible for these objects.

True enough, some sort of "background knowledge," "theoretical framework," or "contextual presupposition" is always necessary for such deduction. But it was just the empiricists' difficulties-in-principle with this background for deduction that have contributed in large measure to the recent total collapse of positivist philosophies of science.[5] It would be a shabby empiricism that could not sustain deductions of this sort in moral questions as well. And, of course, once made and checked and tested for validity, such deductive conclusions can be taught to others as sure guides, enabling the concrete morality to be determined as soon as this or that feature is discerned, regardless of the range of other elements and values involved.

Vitiating Defects

Yet one might expect even an empiricist ethics to advert to the asymmetry between the good, with its requirement of integrity, and the evil, which can result from a multiplicity of possible defects, even if not every defect is such as to convert the good to evil. Even values, especially intrinsic ones, can reflect such asymmetry with regard to disvalues. Almost daily we experience how single defects can reduce dramatically or even destroy both great goods and great values. Some defects may only render an object less good and less valuable, but others spoil it altogether, making it to be of no value or positively to be rejected or even bad. Nor is this a matter of the size of the defect to the eye of the non-expert, but only of the real effectiveness in damaging the object in question. A nut only an imperceptible fraction of a millimeter too large is useless for its bolt. An icepick can make as deadly a hole in someone as a meat-cleaver; an invisible crystal of botulinus toxin is deadlier than either.

So, then, in morality: one element of evil, not necessarily obvious or easily discernible, can vitiate a whole act. If I cannot choose to do something without willing directly, even if implicitly, what is evil, then the concrete act is evil. If, further, the evil is an intrinsic consequence of the action, then the action is intrinsically evil. It must surely be obvious that a bad intention can by itself vitiate any action, even what would otherwise be the holiest, e.g., saying Mass, with the intention of profanation. It is possible, likewise, to think up circumstances or extrinsic consequences that would render any normally good act evil. Why, then, cannot the act itself be intrinsically vicious, as, e.g., sexually perverse acts, or conditionally vicious, e.g., if the person I am about to kill has not forfeited his right to life? Recognition of intrinsic evil in actions in no way restricts one to discussing only the "objective act" or confines morality to an essentialist level. To say that would be merely a dodge to avoid seeing or admitting that if the act is bad, then no extrinsic consequences, circumstances, or intentions can remedy the situation any more than any amount of good in the act itself can remedy a malicious intention or vitiating consequences or circumstances.

If all this is unclear to the theologians in question, the root reason seems to be, again, their insistence on regarding all in terms of *additive* positive and negative values, so that the components melt together as indistinguishably as abstract numbers do. Just as no mathematician can tell whether a net sum of +10 was reached from summing +6 and +4 or from −100,000 and the product +10,001 times +10, so for the value-moralist. Having abstracted from physical evil merely the one aspect of negative value and having similarly denatured the good, he is left with abstractions which are, indeed, wholly symmetric with one another but therefore, utterly inadequate to deal with the moral drama of human good and evil.

Why Positive Values?

4. A further element missing from the value-approach is some indication of why it is morally necessary for man to choose a net positive value or to avoid direct choice of a negative one. Whence comes the moral link? What is there in what is for me the *most valuable* (in any of its senses) which forces me to consider its choice to be *morally* good? The omission is the more serious in that most of the moralists in question argue that no created value can be absolute; that consequently, no concrete moral norm can bind without exception (cf. Sect. I.4). Problems of internal consistency arise at once.

Is not the requirement that one choose directly only positive values itself a moral norm? A norm, moreover, according to these theologians, antecedent to every concrete choice and universally applicable? It will be objected that this norm is not concrete. True, perhaps, in an "ordinary language" sense. But it is certainly not a merely formal or tautological norm,[6] the only alternative to "concrete norms" which these moralists offer. For, "most valuable" and "morally good" are not even roughly equivalent in their vocabulary—it is the *pre*moral good and evil which they claim to be the elements of the final, summed, and still premoral value.

Further, and even more strikingly, this norm is considered absolute in the sense of admitting no exceptions, whatever the circumstances or extrinsic consequences. A free and direct choice of a net, premoral, negative value (which is not absolute in any sense) is said to be always morally evil; and, so far as I can tell, even according to these moralists, I am never free to do a morally evil thing for the sake of any consequent and separately conceived good or value. Thus a moral evil *is* absolutely forbidden; and my free assent has somehow mysteriously removed the relativity of the negative value.

On the other hand, the argument drawn from the non-absoluteness of created values seems to leave out of account the fact that God is personal and has a mind and will. Not merely is God the Absolute; his will is absolute also, though he need not will absolutely all that he wills. Hence, any truly moral act involves, at least implicitly, a judgment that something is good or bad or, in a value-context, positively or negatively valuable, and that God forbids or permits or desires or commands it accordingly.

But God does not forbid whatever it is that might be meant by the term "absolute evil" nor protect a putative "absolute value." But he forbids absolutely that we choose evil, albeit relative; he may command absolutely that we do some relatively minor good. And any refusal to act in accord with his will thus signified, even though we seek only created and limited values, is a rejection of the Absolute. Some at least of the value-moralists are in explicit agreement with this position. For them, the question is rather how to discover what *is* God's will in matters of moral values.

Values under Judgment

While it seems clear enough that God wills things that are for our good and forbids things that would harm us, what he wills as to our human values is not so clear. Our human values are rarely in full consonance with what he desires our values to be; hence, the need of continuous conversion of mind and heart, of continually submitting to his judgment. And, as the value-moralists rarely fail to remark, our human values are always highly relative to our particular cultural context and are highly mutable. Obviously then, these men are right in thinking that no assessment of values alone is sufficient unconditionally to determine moral good or evil. But that shows only the inadequacy of their value-approach.

The Christian moral theologian has as a major charge, perhaps his chief one, to assess all human values in the light of the Gospel, to judge them by his own norms of faith (with all it gives us of concrete moral norms), hope, and charity, accepting what is compatible with these, rejecting the rest. To subject the moral conduct of the Christian as prescribed in the New Testament (with all that this implicitly takes over from the Old) to a weighing against human values would be to undo the Gospel.

Only Intra-Worldly Values?

5. The restriction to intra-worldly values would seem to nullify the morality built thereon. It is possible, indeed, to draw out of our experience and from Christian teaching that law of nature which shows what is good or bad for man in virtue of his nature and to know that this is not overturned by grace though the latter's demands may be more exigent. Yet it is not possible—as the very argument about the cultural, social and individual relativity of values presumes—to do a "natural-law analysis" of values, which, at least so far as our weak human knowledge goes, are always contingently modifiable and inextricably linked with our entire, sinful history.

Thus, one cannot deal usefully with such an abstraction as "intra-worldly values" (taking it to mean true values but belonging to the order of nature alone) nor licitly take the concrete and actual "intra-worldly values" of our morally purblind society as normative for men as such. Nor, since actual human values are largely suffused by sin and the refusal of grace, is it possible to consider them as values formed by faith, hope, and charity in interaction with the "purely human" or the "concretely human."

The scriptural argument will not concern us here, since it

needs special treatment. But the questions the value-theologians must answer in that regard are now clear: where in Scripture do they find support for the value-imperative at the base of their whole system? How can they show that the concrete moral norms of the New Testament are intended not to identify what is morally good or bad for the children of God but only to reinforce particular and contingent values or value-systems? Since, however, the rest of the framework of value-morality seems untenable, it is not clear that Scripture scholars need undertake the task.

Notes

1. The moralists whose writings are directly of interest here are: Joseph Fuchs, Richard McCormick, Giles Milhaven, John Dedek, Charles Curran, and Bruno Schüller.

2. Something should be said about the purpose and method of this paper. Its purpose is to disengage one single thread which runs through the writings of many, not always concurring, moral theologians, to show its influence upon the moral theories into which it has been woven, and to indicate the errors to which such theories are exposed if wholly self-consistent. I am primarily concerned, therefore, with certain generic modes of argumentation and only secondarily with details, though to the best of my ability I seek to preserve the integrity of the arguments given by these authors. My effort is to highlight a flaw which, to different degrees and in different manners, is found in the works of each of these men, some of whom perhaps attribute to it no other importance than that of a shift of language. I seek here to show that, whatever their intentions, the shift is important, inept, and often deleterious.

This is, then, a summary paper, a digest of many articles, on the one side, and an outline of generic response on the other. Direct refutation of an individual's arguments would clearly call for a different method; my concern here is rather to give warning with regard to a global tendency.

3. Sensitivity to this uniqueness of the person has always been the distinguishing characteristic of the professions, which are concerned with services to persons in the invaluable, inestimable aspects of their existence. And to the extent that money or personal advantage becomes a goal of the professional man, to that extent he begins to treat his clients as interchangeable sources of income or prestige and to that extent he falls away from his profession.

4. I am speaking here solely of "objective values." Thus, anyone who objectively considers me and my life-situation adequately would see that my life has a greater value for my parents than for some total stranger. A "subjective value," on the other hand, is imposed or ascertained only

by the valuing subject. I am not concerned with subjective values save where explicitly indicated.

5. For a detailed analysis of the structure of empirical thought, cf. my "Estimative Functions of Physical Theory," *Stud. Hist. Phil. Sci.* 6 (1975), 125-157. Much of what is developed there finds easy application to questions of the epistemological structure of morality.

6. "Good is to be done; evil, to be shunned" is commonly supposed to be tautologous or true by definition.

Reflections on the Literature

Richard A. McCormick, S.J.

I

Joseph Fuchs, S.J., has written a lengthy study which appears to contain a significant shift in his methodology toward a morality of consequences.[1] As one would expect from Fuchs, the essay is a careful, subtle, ranging, and balanced piece of writing. There are times, however, when it is less than absolutely pellucid. Fuchs is primarily concerned to discover whether there are any concrete norms which are absolute, i.e., without exception. His key ideas can be distilled as follows.

First, he distinguishes premoral evil from moral evil and insists on the crucial nature of the distinction.[2] Killing, wounding, deceiving, sterilizing, etc. are premoral evils, not necessarily moral evils. "Whoever sets up negative norms, but regards exceptions as justified, by reason of overriding right, or warranted compromise, or for the sake of the lesser evil (or the greater good), shows by this that the *malum* repudiated by the norm is *not* (yet) to be understood as *moral* evil."[3]

Secondly, Fuchs asks: when do these premoral evils become moral evils? Or—which is the same—when is human action or the man in his action morally evil? His answer: when he *"has in view and effects* a human non-good, an evil (non-value)—in the premoral sense, for example, death, wounding, wrong etc."[4] The next question clearly is this: when must one be said to "have in

view and effect" premoral evil? The answer: when he causes it
without proportionate reason. Thus Fuchs says:

> A surgical operation is a health measure, its purpose is to
> cure, but it is at the same time the cause of an evil, namely
> wounding. This, however, appears to be justified in view of
> the desired cure and is capable of being incorporated in the
> *one human* act—a curative measure. The surgical operation
> is *morally* right, because the person acting desires and effects
> only a good—in the *pre*moral sense—namely, restoration of
> health. If the surgeon were to do more than was required in
> performing this operation, that "more" would not be justified
> by the treatment indicated; that is, it would be taken up *as an*
> *evil*—in the *pre*moral sense—into the surgeon's intention; it
> would be morally bad.[5]

Therefore for Fuchs premoral evil caused becomes moral evil
when it is "taken up as an evil into one's intention." This happens
when there is no proportionate reason for causing the premoral
evil.

Obviously, then, intention has a great deal to say about the
moral quality of an act. Indeed, Fuchs says that the moral quality
of an act cannot be determined without reference to the intention.
And in this sense he qualifies the traditional understanding of
object, end, circumstances. Traditional moralists said that certain
actions were morally evil *ex objecto* in the sense that no good
intention could purify them. The basic morality of such acts was
determined by the object. Fuchs says, in contrast, that "a moral
judgment of an action may not be made in anticipation of the
agent's intention, since it would not be the judgment of a 'human'
act."[6] In other words, the object must be taken with the intention
before the meaning of the action, its true moral character, can be
stated. In light of this Fuchs asks:

> What value do our norms have with respect to the morality of
> the action as such, prior, that is, to the consideration of the
> circumstances and intention? We answer: they cannot be
> moral norms unless circumstances and intention are taken
> into account. They can be considered as moral norms only

because we tacitly assume to judge the action in the light of possible circumstances and intention.[7]

However, since this tacit advance judgment is theoretically impossible, we cannot rule out the possibility that in practice there will be an exceptional instance. Therefore, when treating of the traditional notion of intrinsic evil, Fuchs notes: "Viewed theoretically, there seems to be no possibility of norms of this kind for human action in the inner-worldly realm." For a behavioral norm universally valid would presuppose that those who arrive at it "could know or foresee adequately *all the possible combinations* of the action concerned with circumstances and intentions, with (premoral) values and non-values."

Even though there can be no theoretically exceptionless norms of behavior, Fuchs sees a genuine practical worth in norms properly formulated as universals. First, they do point out values and disvalues. Secondly, certain norms can be stated as universals "to which we cannot conceive of any kind of exception; e.g., cruel treatment of a child which is of no benefit to the child." Thirdly, in a specific culture or society universal norms can develop which "suffice for ordinary use in practical living." However, the existence and validity of such norms does not mean that we are exempt from rethinking them. Such rethinking is warranted where faulty evaluations in the past generated faulty norms or where a norm grew out of a culturally conditioned situation which no longer obtains. In this latter case moral reformulation is not only conceivable but demanded.

Fuch's debt to Knauer and Schüller is obvious and acknowledged. Because I agree with so much of what he says, it might be helpful to indicate some remaining areas of unclarity.

First, because Fuchs has followed Knauer so closely, the question of what he means by "intending" premoral evil arises, much as it did with Knauer. Knauer, it will be recalled, proposed that when there is a commensurate reason for causing premoral disvalue, the evil is *indirectly* willed. When there is no commensurate reason, the evil caused is *directly* willed. As noted above, Schüller has rightly challenged the usefulness of this terminology. Fuchs states that when there is no proportionate reason, the premoral evil caused "would be taken up *as an evil.*" He also says that premoral evil must not be "intended as such." Is "intending evil as such" equivalent to direct intent? Fuchs nowhere says this, but his heavy reliance on Knauer leads me to raise the question. Would it not be clearer and more precise to say that it is legitimate to intend premoral evil *in ordine ad finem proportionatum?* I may choose and intend the pain of a child or a patient if it is the only way or the most reasonable way to secure his greater good. This "greater good" (proportionate reason) does not mean that the premoral disvalue is not intended; it means that it is not intended *propter se.* Therefore would it not be better to say that it is legitimate to intend a disvalue *in se sed non propter se?* When there is no proportionate reason, the disvalue caused is chosen and intended *in se et propter se*, and it is this *propter se* which makes the act immoral. I believe this is what Fuchs means by "intending evil *as such,*" but his occasional use of the simple and unqualified word "intend" leaves the matter a bit murky.

The second question raised by Fuchs's analysis is closely connected with the first. It is also a question Knauer did not face satisfactorily. In treating premoral evil (wounding, deceiving, killing), Fuchs insists in the examples he gives that the evil or disvalue is not an isolated action "but only an element of the one act." Thus he notes: "In the *one* human action (health care, transplant) the performing of the evil is not an isolated (human) action, but only an element of the one action. Therefore, a morally bad (human) action is not being used as a means to a good end."[8] The evil is justified because it "is capable of being incorporated in the *one human* act—a curative measure." The example of surgery serves Fuchs well, for obviously the harm (or "wound") is part and parcel of the one healing act or process.

Yet, if I understand Fuchs correctly, there is some unclarity here. There are two elements Fuchs appeals to in justifying the doing of premoral evil: proportionate reason and the fact that the evil is simply an element of one human action. What does it mean to say that the evil must be "incorporated in the *one* human act"? Does he mean to say that every time there is a proportionate reason, the act is really one by reason of the intent of this good, and therefore the evil caused is really only an element of one human action? Or does he mean that first we must discover whether there is in human terms one single action (as, e.g., in surgery) into which the premoral evil is "capable of being incorporated"? If Fuchs means the first alternative, it would seem that he is pushing language too far; for if an action is truly one human action, it is realistically describable as such. Thus we can say realistically that a leg amputation is a "healing action." If, however, the intended effect does not allow one to redescribe the action in terms of this effect, then are we still dealing with a single human action? If so, in what sense? Not all actions with good consequences are describable in terms of intended results—a point Paul Ramsey has made very sharply.[9] And when they cannot be so redescribed, can we really speak of the premoral evil caused and chosen as only an element in *one human action*? Or if we do, what does this mean? The earlier analysis of Knauer never got off this reef.

Take the now classic case of Mrs. Bergmeier. Can her extramarital intercourse and subsequent pregnancy (whereby she was able to achieve her release from a Soviet concentration camp) be said to be simply an element of one human action describable as "bringing her family happiness"? Can it be called this simply because this is her ultimate intent? Hardly, I should think. Not only does this stretch human language beyond its limits, but it ignores all the other possible or probable consequences and describes this act in terms of just one. Rather it seems we should say that she performed one human action (extramarital intercourse) which had, among other effects, the intended good consequence of bringing her to her family. If this is a correct rendering of the example, what does it mean to say that premoral evil must be only an element of "one human action"? The example of surgery is a bit too simple; for in surgery the very same physical act which amputates also removes a threat to life. Obviously the healing intent is present, but it is not precisely this intent which makes the amputation one human action.

Therefore how far is Fuchs willing to stretch this example? I am not sure what he would say to the case of Mrs. Bergmeier; but if the ultimate justification is that the premoral disvalues must be an element of "one human action," then this one human action should be describable in terms of the intended value—much as amputation can legitimately be called a "curative procedure." Perhaps Fuchs's insistence that the premoral evil be incorporated into the one act overstates the requirement a bit. However this may be, such insistence either (1) very sharply limits the premoral evils one may cause in the pursuit of good or (2) expands the notion of "one human action" to the point where human language will no longer sustain the unity.

The third reflection constitutes a matter of emphasis. In treating the notion of intrinsic evil, Fuchs rightly claims that theoretically "there seems no possibility of norms of this kind for human action in the innerworldly realm." He refers to *behavioral norms*—i.e., norms which take a materially described action (killing) and say of it that it is always unjust. The reason for this: an action cannot be judged apart from circumstances and intention. This seems certainly correct, but three reflections are called for.

First, it must be said that the theological problem only begins here. For instance, a prohibitive behavioral norm (e.g., against killing) is based on the perception of the value of human life and the disvalue of taking human life. Where exceptions are concerned, the real problem is to show that there are higher values involved, and what they might be. Fuchs admits this clearly when he says: "Hence the attempt on the part of moral theology to discover which values realizable in this world can justify 'killing' and which cannot."[10] Circumstances and intention justify exceptions only when they are concerned with higher, nonpostponable values. If we moralists seriously propose exceptions as possible (and they are), our most basic task is to discover those values which do and do not justify causing the disvalue. Unless we do so, are we not inviting people to except themselves without providing any hierarchy which would make such a decision rational, and therefore promotive of greater humanization? The point is emphasized here because recent literature has understandably been concerned with the fact of exceptions, while it has almost never treated the extremely difficult and unfinished task of describing the kinds of values which alone make the causing of disvalues reasonable.

A second point. While it is impossible to foresee all the possible combinations of concurring values and disvalues (circumstances and intention), still through experience and reflection it is possible to foresee at least very many of them. Therefore Fuchs is certainly correct when he says of concrete behavioral norms that "they suffice for ordinary use in practical living." They "suffice" because they include the ordinary circumstances in practical living. This is the same as saying that the significance of the action (drawn from object and ordinary circumstances) is ordinarily clear. And this in its turn is the same as saying that *ordinarily* a person will achieve the greater good by following the norm, because it incarnates the greater good. Negatively stated, this means that one who makes an exception of himself has the burden of proof that his case is truly exceptional.

Thirdly, Fuchs does admit "norms stated as universals . . . to which we cannot conceive of any kind of exception." In this sense I suppose he is admitting a kind of "relative absolute."[11] But his example is "cruel treatment of a child which is of no benefit to the child." One could and should argue that cruel treatment of a child (or anyone) is never permissible, although a treatment which visits hurt, harm, or deprivation on someone need not be cruel. Here Fuchs has introduced a formal element (cruel) into the description; this makes his example a very poor one.

A final observation. Fuchs has obviously taken a rather giant step in the direction of a consequentialist methodology. But how far this stride takes him is not altogether clear. In discussing the formation of concrete moral norms, he mentions that the significance of an action is a prime criterion. He then continues: "It is not only the 'meaning' itself of experienced realities that constitutes a criterion for the evaluating *ratio*, but also practical knowledge of the outcomes and consequences which determined modes of conduct can have . . . "

Here Fuchs seems to contrast meaning and practical knowledge of consequences. Actually these should not be contrasted in this way; for the very "meaning" of an action can only be gathered when all aspects of the action, especially its consequences, have been weighed as far as possible. The fact that Fuchs contrasts meaning and consequences implies that he is willing to speak of the meaning of an action apart from its consequences. This raises the question of just what importance he does want to attribute to consequences. The matter remains obscure.

II

John R. Connery, S.J., has reviewed the work of Fuchs. Schüller, Knauer, and others and related it to the whole utilitarian school of thought.[12] Basically Connery sees these authors as representing a form of consequentialism, "a moral system that makes the judgment of an act depend solely on its consequences." After exposing and criticizing in highly knowledgeable fashion the two prevailing forms of consequentialism (act-utilitarianism, rule-utilitarianism), Connery judges both as vulnerable to allowing acts that go against common convictions, especially convictions about justice. He then associates Knauer, Fuchs, and Schüller with rule-utilitarianism in the sense that "all rules are subject in one way or another to the principle of consequences." The basic problem he finds in this is that "it seems to call for, or at least allow, exceptions which go against commonly held convictions."

When faced with this problem, rule-utilitarianism appealed either to hidden effects or to long-range effects. Connery's explicit conclusion is: practically, so-called secondary rules are more reliable guidelines than "the principle of consequences." Theoretically, such rules "cannot be explained entirely in terms of consequences." His implicit conclusion is that the arguments of Fuchs, Schüller, and Knauer are vulnerable to these same challenges, i.e., those urged against utilitarianism.

Bruno Schüller presents a long and careful reaction to Connery's study.[13] He agrees with Connery that utilitarianism as a theory of moral norms is untenable, but he insists that no one should conclude from the contemporary critics of utilitarianism that traditional moral theology has found new allies in its defense of its deontological norms; for the very critics of utilitarianism reject (as "naturalistic fallacy") the way traditional theology defends as exceptionless the prohibitions against, for example, contraception and homologous artificial insemination. Rather, a philosopher such as H. J. McCloskey suggests that such norms are prima-facie duties (or conditioned norms) much as Peter Chirico and Denis Hurley had done earlier but in different language.[14] So one need not move to utilitarian theory to hold different conclusions than traditional theology held on these points. Indeed, one need not enter the larger theoretical discussion of moral norms at all to contest such conclusions.

However, Connery has made his argument against Schüller, Fuchs, and Knauer by appeal to the critics of utilitarianism and by use of the arguments they make. The argument in substance is this: teleological grounding of norms = reductively utilitarian theory = untenable, as the long discussion in Anglo-Saxon philosophical circles has shown.

Schüller brings several objections against this. First, he objects to forcing the discussion into the logically elegant division deontological-teleological as defined by C. D. Broad. Broad has defined teleological theories as those that determine the moral character of an action exclusively by its consequences. Deontological theories, by contrast, are those that claim there are actions that are morally wrong whatever the consequences. Schüller protests the apparent neatness of Broad's division. It simply overlooks the vast differences between those who regard themselves as deontologists. For instance, Kant and W. D. Ross are regarded as being in this category; but there is a chasm between them. Kant held that the duty not to speak falsehood is absolute; Ross holds it to be a prima-facie duty (*bedingtes Erfüllungsgebot*). What is it, then, that divides Kant, Fichte, and the Catholic tradition from Ross, McCloskey, and other critics of utilitarianism? Schüller's answer:

> Only Kant, Fichte, and the Catholic tradition assert that there are actions that are morally wrong without any regard for their consequences. W. D. Ross and the modern critics of utilitarianism, on the contrary, assert that for the moral rightness of an action consequences always play a determining role, but not alone. . . . In this light, only Kant and the

Catholic tradition, but not the modern critics of utilitarianism, know deontological norms as defined by C. D. Broad.[15]

So, by accepting Broad's definition of deontologist and teleologist, Connery has made it appear that all teleological tendencies conform to Broad's model, and therefore can be faced with the standard arguments brought against utilitarian theory. Schüller rejects this.

Second, with many critics of utilitarianism, Connery asserts that an action's moral rightness or wrongness cannot be determined by the amount of good it does. He uses the example of a person who promises money to a young man to cut his lawn. Should he give the young man the money? If *that* action is morally right which does more good, then he should give it only if he finds no better use for the money. This type of argument has led critics of utilitarianism to deny that only one principle determines the morality of any act. Thus Frankena calls for two principles; love (benevolence) and justice; David Lyons calls for three; love, justice, fairness. And so on.

Here Schüller says that the Christian theologian is perplexed by the notion of love implied in such fragmentation. "The Christian theologian who, under the influence of Romans 13:8–10, declares that love as benevolence and beneficence must be seen as the final criterion for the moral rightness of an action, does not understand under 'love' something next to justice and fairness. Rather he understands by this term the general root of all other particular principles."[16] It is a strange concept of love that has nothing to do with justice and fairness, as if these were separate and independent sources of moral rightness. Schüller accepts the identity of the principle of utility—when adequately understood—with love-as-beneficence.

Several examples are used by Connery and the critics of utilitarianism to show the impossibility of a teleological theory of norms. One concerns justice, the other fairness. Schüller speaks to both. The justice example is that of a sheriff in a Southern town faced with the alternatives in a rape case of framing a Negro suspect (whom he knows to be innocent) or carrying on a prolonged search for the real culprit. The immediate indictment and conviction of the suspect would save many lives and prevent other harmful consequences. If an action's moral rightness is determined solely by consequences, it is argued, the sheriff ought to frame the one innocent man—a conclusion that shocks our moral sensitivities, but one that a teleologist would be forced to draw.

Schüller argues that a teleologist would not be forced to draw any such conclusion. Overlooked completely is the fact that in the example not only is there question of the life of one versus the lives of many others; the entire institution of criminal law is at stake. The conclusion that the sheriff should frame the one to save others is only justified if this conclusion, raised to a universally acknowledged and practiced rule, would actually promote the common good. Since that is at least highly doubtful, such an exception must be judged contrary to the common good and unjust.

This is clearly a form of teleological argument and it is, Schüller contends, familiar to Catholic tradition. To illustrate this, he cites de Lugo's defense of the absoluteness of the confessional secret.

If it [revelation of sins] were allowed in some circumstances because of some extremely important need, this alone would be sufficient to make sacramental confession always difficult. Penitents would always fear that the confessor would reveal their sins because he would think this is an example of the exceptional instance. To avoid this evil, it was necessary to exclude any exception. That rare evil which would be obviated by revelation of sins is in no proportionate relationship to the perpetual evil and continuing harm which would be associated with the difficulty of confession if an exception were allowed.[17]

The example of fairness is that of a person who wants a certain candidate elected. He knows that the vast majority of his fellow citizens feel the same way and will vote for this candidate; so he himself stays home. Viewed in terms of consequences, his vote would be useless. Therefore, as useless, it is not morally right if it is viewed within a teleological framework. Yet it is unfair, for the stay-at-home enjoys the good of getting his candidate elected even though he spares himself the trouble of a trip to the polls. Therefore, it is asserted, beyond love (as usefulness, *beneficentia*) there is required a principle of fairness.

Schüller does not deny that fairness demands the person's vote. Rather he is amazed that one thinks such fairness has nothing to do with what we Christians call love of neighbor. Furthermore, he is perplexed at how narrowly the critics of utilitarianism interpret the term "useless." Of course, the vote is in one sense useless (it will not change results). But precisely because the vote is useless, it has the peculiar aptitude to be an expression of solidarity, much as the gesture of the woman who poured perfume over the head of Jesus (Mk 13:3–19) was seen as useless by some but was actually an act of love. One should not confuse the principle of utility (*beneficentia*) to one's neighbor and neighbors with mere efficiency.

In summary, then, Schüller leans heavily toward a teleological theory of moral norms if the term "teleology" is not too narrowly understood. Connery, he urges, can find justification for a deontological theory neither in traditional morality nor in the critics of utilitarianism; for the grounds on which these critics demand, in additon to love (*benevolentia* and *beneficentia*), principles of justice, fairness, etc. are mistaken. He summarizes as follows:

> Traditional moral theology factually represents a deontological theory. Frankena does the same thing. But they do this from reasons that have nothing in common. Frankena believes he must hold a deontological theory because the necessary principle of justice is logically independent of the principle of love. Traditional moral theology states, on the contrary—so it seems to me—that the principle of justice is contained already in the principle of love. Therefore traditional moral theology must deny that Frankena has a legitimate ground for counting himself a deontologist. This theology itself represents a deontological theory, because it believes that there is, first, a class of actions that are morally

wrong because of their unnaturalness (contraception). Second, there is a class of actions that must be seen as wrong because of a lack of divine permission (e.g., killing of the innocent). As far as I can see, Frankena, on the basis of the rest of his ethics, must contest that these two classes are justified. Therefore he could not admit that Catholic tradition has a legitimate ground for holding to a deontological theory. If one admits that Frankena is correct, yet if he holds with Catholic tradition that the principle of justice (and fairness) is contained in the principle of love, *then the result is a teleological theory of moral norms.*[18]

Because Connery's work is so economical, precise, and disciplined, and because the points he raises are so important to this entire discussion. I should like to attempt my own formulation of a few problems that seem to remain.

First, after noting that the Catholic authors discussed are all "tending toward consequentialism," Connery repeatedly describes this approach as "a morality based *solely* on consequences."[19] If we understand by consequences "intended consequences," we have here the same objection raised by Ermecke against Fuchs on the place of intention ("eine letzlich *allein* . . . entscheidende Bedeutung . . . "). This is not what these authors are saying nor, in my judgment, what they can be forced to say. All would admit, for example, an inherent value in keeping secrets and an inherent disvalue in breaking them. The question is not that it is morally wrong to break secrets simply because of bad consequences. It is rather: when is it legitimate to bring about the admitted disvalue of breaking secrecy, and why? Schüller, Fuchs, Knauer, and Janssens insist that we are talking about an *evil* (nonmoral, premoral, ontic) where revelation of a secret is concerned. Therefore, as soon as the action involved is seen as containing such evil, it is no longer a matter of "consequences alone," but of the proportion between the evil involved and the good sought. If they regarded the action as "based on consequences alone," revelation of secrets would have to be seen as neutral in itself, not as an ontic evil.

Second, Connery notes that it is the position of Knauer—

and actually of Fuchs also—that the intent (Fuchs) or commensurate reason (Knauer) is included in the moral object of the act. Apart from such a reason the act has only a physical object.[20] Thus, killing can be morally justified or not depending on the reason or intent behind the act. Of this Connery notes: "This presents no problem in regard to killing, which can be morally good or morally bad. But it does raise questions in regard to actions which have been traditionally regarded as wrong, e.g., adultery, direct killing of an innocent person, etc., independently of whatever reasons the agent might have had.[21]

It is to be noted that Connery refers here to "direct killing of an innocent person." But it must be asked: where did such a qualified and circumscribed description come from? Why is only "direct killing of an innocent person" regarded as wrong at all times? Why is this not true of any killing? The only answer seems to be that in some instances of conflict[22] (self-defense, warfare) killing can represent the better protection of life itself, can represent the lesser evil when compared to the only other available alternative. Obviously such a conclusion roots in the weighing of the effects of two alternatives. It traces to a judgment about what would happen if some killing were not allowed. Now if such a calculus is necessarily implied in the sharpening of forbidden killing down to "direct killing of an innocent person," then it seems that this sharpened category itself must be similarly tested; otherwise we are inconsistent. So when one says that "direct killing of the innocent" is forbidden, he need not and should not imply that such killing is morally wrong "independently of whatever reasons the agent may have had. He may and ought to imply that the conceivable reasons for killing in such circumstances are, under careful analysis, not proportionate to the harm done; for if it was a weighing of alternatives that honed the rule to its present precision, it is a weighing of alternatives that must test its continuing viability.

In this regard Connery notes that "Fuchs would therefore have to attach a rider to every rule, e.g., killing is wrong except when there is a proportionate reason." Exactly so. But has traditional theology not done exactly this—and then gone about deciding which reasons are proportionate and which not? I believe so.

Otherwise we would not have a theory of just warfare, a theory of self-defense, a theory of tolerable indirect killing.

Third, in supporting certain claims of justice (e.g., against direct killing of an innocent person in a situation where great good might seem to accrue as a result), Connery notes that one who develops and restricts his rules by considering the only alternatives (teleologist) and in this case prohibits the killing must appeal to hidden bad effects, "although this is often not very convincing." I agree that it is not always very convincing. But then the issue is one of clarity and certainty. How much clarity and certainty do we need? The underlying supposition seems to be that we must have rather exhaustive clarity to support a justice norm. Scholastic analysis supports this tendency of thought. However, even a strong suspicion that taking life in these circumstances may undermine rather than support (may be disproportionate to) the value of life seems sufficient to uphold the prohibition. The norms of justice and their limits, no more nor less than other norms, are the conclusions of a type of prudence that involves or can involve feared or suspected implications in alternative courses of action.

Finally, Connery concludes that Fuchs, Schüller, *et al.* "might be forced to acknowledge in the end that it would be better to rely, for instance, on considerations of justice than consequences in assessing certain classes of conduct." I do not see that the two are that distinct. It must be noted that "considerations of justice" involve an appeal to a certainty that is achieved only after another alternative has been, to the best of our ability, weighed. For example, why is not indirect killing a violation of the right (justice) of the one "only indirectly killed"—e.g., the innocents indirectly killed as I blast at the enemy's war machine? What do fish, so to speak, think of the morality of fishing?

Traditional moral formulations say that indirect killing need not be a violation of right, that it is morally legitimate when proportionately grounded. It can say this, I believe, only after having considered the alternative, scil., what would happen in conflict cases if we did not allow such killing? Because the answer to that alternative possibility is more disvalue to life itself, more ontic evil, it was concluded that such killing may be tolerated, and is not therefore a violation of the right of the one indirectly killed.

Therefore behind and before the ascription of what is just and unjust is a prudential judgment—in a world of conflict and tragedy—of where the lesser evil lies.

I address these questions to Connery because we have already learned so much from his work that his continuing attention to these problems promises only gain.

III

Some basic aspects of normative ethics have also occupied Catholic moral theologians in the past decade. During this period, at the invitation of Vatican II, Catholic moral theologians have been re-examining certain aspects of their discipline. It is no secret that some of the results have not been to the liking or comfort of all in and out of the Church.

Paul Quay, S.J., has made this re-examination the object of a long study.[23] He focuses on six moral theologians[24] and sees their writings—what he calls a "theology of values"—as attempts to " 'relativize' so-called 'absolute prohibitions' against defrauding laborers, adultery, abortion, and the like." He states explicitly that his purpose is "to show that, whatever their intentions, the shift is important, inept, and often deleterious."

Quay first summarizes "the elements in their argument." Moral norms embody and protect values. While these norms are not absolute, it is highly unlikely that "any congeries of oppositely directed values" will arise that will countervail them. In principle, however, the idea is that a moral agent looks at all the values of two alternative courses of action and "sums these values." Quay continues: "That is judged to be bad which has a negative total value; and that to be good which has a positive total value." Having decided what course of action embodies the "greatest total value," the agent directs his intention to the positive total value. Quay gives abortion as an example. "One may rightly will an abortion, for example, but only when the death of the child is seen as but one of many premoral elements whose values when summed result in an overriding positive value for the action as a whole."[25]

Quay's response to this "thread" or direction is twofold.

First, it overlooks the fact that there are elements in human situations not reducible to values. He mentions several: qualitative difference between values, relations of cause and effect, persons and their uniqueness. Quay then specifies these. For instance, he notes that premoral good cannot be treated simply as a positive value. A value is not just what is good for men, but *what is good for him in terms of his needs, desires, purposes.* Thus, standing as it does in relation to one's already accepted goals, it implies the possibility of weighing and exchange. This is not true of the good. The same analysis, Quay argues, is true of the terms "premoral evil" and "disvalue." They are not the same. By treating them as such, the "value theologians" get involved in seeing "the determination of moral good as a merely quantitative process." As Quay words it: "Everything can in principle be evaluated and scaled in accord with utility, worth and price; as values are balanced, exchanged, and traded off for one another, the moral judgment becomes a commerce and merchandizing in human conduct and Christian behavior."[26]

This mercantilist spirit and calculus, Quay argues, cannot deal adequately with the relation of cause and effect and the realities of human intentionality. For instance, "The values, individual and aggregate, of someone's dying and my escaping with my life would seem to be the same, all else being equal, whether there is a causal link between them or not." Furthermore, this approach, in putting a value on persons, does not deal adequately with the uniqueness of persons. Indeed, in regarding a person as a "value for others," it is contrary to the gospel.

Secondly, Quay attempts to show the unfortunate consequences of confounding irreducible values. For instance, whose values are to count, the individual's or someone else's? On what grounds? Again, systems built on a "quantitiative summing of values" can submerge the individual in favor of relatively minor values touching millions of others. The many objections Quay levels cannot be detailed here, but he concludes that the approach of these theologians is no different from "the crudest sort of empiricism." I think it fair to say that Quay sees the basic error of these theologians in the reduction of premoral goods and evils to values and disvalues. Once this move has been made, everything follows: the weighing of values (including persons) against other values, the quantitative summing up of net values, the neglect of causal relations, intentionality, and intrinsic consequences,

Any serious study that concludes that the recent direction taken by some theologians is "inept, even deleterious," "no different from the crudest sort of empiricism," "to undo the gospel," must be taken with utmost seriousness. I intend to do that; for there are probably many who share the fears that lie behind this study and therefore there is real danger that it will be taken seriously. First, an introductory remark. Quay has adopted a device unfamiliar to the academic community: an indictment of individual theologians, without citation or footnote references, in terms of global or overall tendencies. Though Quay may repeatedly disown the fact, and insist that he is concerned only with a "global tendency" or a "flaw which, to different degrees and in different manners, is found in the works of each of these men," the impression is unavoidable that each is vulnerable to the alleged implications Quay adduces. The serious theologian is justifiably uncomfortable with such lumping; for if one denies the allegation, Quay can always say: "Yes, but Milhaven (or Fuchs, or Curran) words it that way." If one is going to level such utterly serious moral indictments against *individuals*, careful documentation is called for. Having noted that, I turn to a few specifics in as fair a way as possible, though it would be impossible in so short a space to attend to all the deficiencies I believe are present in Quay's study.

Relativizing so-called absolute norms. Quay asserts that several moralists "have been seeking to eliminate 'absolutely binding' moral norms." His examples: defrauding laborers, adultery, abortion, "and the like." Here several remarks. First, there is a confusion here between fact-description (*Tatsachenbegriff*) and value-description (*Wertbegriff*). "Defrauding laborers," like adultery, murder, theft, is a value-description; indeed, a morally pejorative one. To state the contemporary discussion as if it were an attempt to justify what has already been labeled as morally wrongful is to indulge in circular discourse closely resembling homiletics. The issue is: What concrete conduct is to count for murder, for "defrauding laborers," etc.? And on what criteria, with what implications? Quay's study repeatedly confuses such questions.[27]

Secondly, what recent Catholic theologians are attempting is to approach their own tradition from within the tradition itself, not with some outside system. Acknowledging the undeniable achievements of that tradition and the over-all validity of its value judgments, they are testing its formulations at key points to see whether the formulation accurately conveyed the substantive value judgment. These theologians could be wrong in their analysis, but to neglect the task is to freeze moral theology in a way repudiated by Vatican II. This effort does not deserve to be labeled "seeking to eliminate 'absolutely binding' moral norms," even if elimination is the outcome of the rethinking; for such language seems to impute motives.

2. *Good and value (evil and disvalue)*. Quay faults recent theologians for not distinguishing these notions carefully. Failure to do so leads to assessing certain goods as values for man in terms of his needs and goals. In other words, it makes what is good for man a measurable and hence negotiable thing. This is at the heart of Quay's objection, for from it follows everything else he says.

I cannot answer for all the indicted theologians individually; but I can say that the contemporary discussion uses "premoral good" and "value" *synonymously* (as also "premoral evil" and "disvalue"). There may be a dictionary difference in the notions and words, and indeed the difference Quay describes: value implies value to man in terms of his needs and desires. But that is not the way these terms are used by Schüller, Fuchs, myself *et al*. We understand by "value" an intrinsic good to man, not something that is good simply because it is evaluated as such by human beings.[28] And it is only if premoral good and evil are understood as value and disvalue *in Quay's sense* that the multiple aberrations he details would follow. If one is going to enter and understand contemporary moral discourse, the terms used must be accepted as the authors use them, not as one thinks they ought to be used.

There is a long and honored tradition identifying "premoral good" and "value" in the philosophical community. It can be found in contemporary philosophers such as William Frankena. It is used repeatedly in Vatican II. Take the Decree on the Apostolate of the Laity: "All of these [elements of the temporal order] not only aid in the attainment of man's ultimate goal but also possess their own intrinsic value. This value has been implanted in them by God, whether they are considered in themselves or as parts of the whole temporal order. 'God saw all that he had made, and it was very good.' "[29] Here "value" = "own intrinsic value" = "implanted by God" = "good." In a similar vein Paul VI spoke recently of the "value of every human life."[30] The recent pastoral letter of the American bishops (*To Live in Christ Jesus*) repeatedly uses value and good synonymously. With such impeccable precedents, I will continue with peaceful grammatical and philosophical conscience to use these terms synonymously, and hence to deny that usage of value (as identical with premoral good) collapses the "what is good for man" into a negotiable thing in the way Quay adduces. Once that has been said, most of Quay's subsequent objections fade into the genre of *non sequitur*.

3. *Quantification of values*. Quay repeatedly asserts that the determination of moral goodness (the more accurate term is "rightness") for value theologians is a "merely quantitative process." Thus, over and over again we read of "greatest total value," "net positive values," "quantitative calculus," and so on. First, I know of no one who does this, who understands the resolution of conflict of values in such a quantitative sense. There are times, of course, when there is commensurability along quantitative lines. For instance—to use Philippa Foot's example—if one is steering a runaway tram and there are two directions in which it can be turned (both involving killing people), one ought to steer the tram in the direction where the smaller number will be killed, other things being equal. I believe there is a similar commensurability in some rare abortion decisions where the alternatives are to save one or lose two.

Secondly, the authors in question cannot be *made to say* that moral judgments are a "merely quantitative calculus." They do not understand the terms "value" and "disvalue" as Quay does, as goods (or evils) to persons only in terms of their needs, desires, purposes, and therefore as goods that can be balanced, exchanged, and traded off. That there are serious and unresolved theoretical problems involved in the use of terms such as "the lesser evil," "proportionate reason," and so on, I do not doubt. But these problems are common to all philosophers and theologians who would, e.g., make *any* exception to the proscription "Thou shalt not kill." They are not restricted to the so-called "value theologians."

4. *Intentionality*. Quay believes that "they" seem overly insistent that all intentions be considered before a meaning is assigned to an action, rather than considering merely the "physical nature" of the action. To this he says: "Yet, who of moral theologians of past or present has held that the intention of the agent is less important than the physical structure of his action?" I shall not cite the many examples from manualist literature; let one suffice: self-stimulation for sperm-testing. This was explicitly condemned as *contra naturam* and illicit masturbation by many theologians, the Holy Office, and implicitly by Pius XII in my judgment. Very many contemporary theologians—I would say most of my acquaintance—believe that such a procedure for testing and treating infertility is a different human and moral act than masturbation as generally understood, and it is different precisely because of its purpose or intention. To Quay's question ("Who of moral theologians past or present. . . ?") I answer: very many, or, as we used to say, *consulas auctores probatos*.

5. *Moral evil and nonmoral evil*. Quay repeatedly overlooks this distinction. E.g., he writes: "One element of evil, not necessarily obvious or easily discernible, can vitiate a whole act. If I cannot choose to do something without willing directly, even if implicitly, what is evil, then the concrete act is evil. If, further, the evil is an intrinsic consequence of the action, then the action is intrinsically evil."[31]

These statements hold ("the concrete act is evil") only if "what is evil" is understood as *morally* wrongful. There is, e.g., a long tradition that allows us to *intend* the deception of another (*falsiloquium*) if this is a necessary means for the protection, e.g., of the confessional secret. Similarly, we may *intend* the amputation of a leg when this is necessary to prevent spread of cancer.

We may *intend* the death of the criminal as a necessary means in capital punishment (or so tradition argued) and in self-defense (as very many theologians argued against what is taken to be the Thomistic understandings of things). We may *intend* the pain of the child as we spank him/her pedagogically. Now these are all evils, but nonmoral in character. By stating, as he does, that the concrete act is evil "if I cannot choose to do something without willing directly . . . what is evil," Quay must *suppose* that the evil in question is *morally* evil. But that is to overlook the distinction between nonmoral (ontic, premoral) and moral wrongfulness. Doing that, one begs the entire question of intentionality.

There is, then, a long tradition that nonmoral (tradition called them "physical") evil may be intended *in se sed non propter se*.[32] Two categories of actions were excluded from this: (1) actions *against nature* (certain sexual actions, e.g., contraception, masturbation); (2) actions wrong because of a *lack of right* (direct killing of the innocent, dissolution of a sacramental and consummated marriage). As Schüller has shown,[33] these actions were regarded as intrinsically evil because of the unnaturalness or lack of right. And it was for this reason that indirectness was required in the tradition when an action involved the death of an innocent person or sterilization of the sexual power. It is these qualities (unnaturalness, lack of right) that we ought to be discussing. One does not help the discussion by first describing the act as a "perversion" and *then* saying it ought never be directly willed.

Much else in Quay's presentation calls for comment,[34] but the above must suffice. I have spent a good deal of space on this article because it is important that recent probes and revisions by Catholic theologians be not misunderstood and distorted. Theologians such as Janssens, Fuchs, Schüller, Curran, Dedek, *et al.* may be wrong—that is a risk we all run; but first they must be properly understood.

For that reason it may help to cite two examples of what two of the indicted theologians think they are about. The first is drawn from a conference of European moral theologians held at Strasbourg.[35] There Franz Böckle stated several theses on moral norms. One was drawn from Schüller's writings and was stated as follows:

All ethical norms that concern interpersonal behavior rest on a judgment of preference. They are so many reflex and formulated applications of the following preference rule: "Put in the presence of two concurring but mutually exclusive values, a person ought to examine which of the two merits the preference." Concretely, therefore, what is involved is hypothetical imperatives, even if this does not always get expressed verbally.[36]

Schüller wrote a brief reply indicating that he himself was not fully satisfied with this formulation, it being a first attempt.[37] He restated the problem. Where concrete norms for conduct are concerned, some norms were interpreted as moral absolutes or in a deontological manner. He gives the two examples noted above (intrinsically evil because unnatural, e.g., contraception; intrinsically evil because of lack of right: direct killing of an innocent person). The reasons given by tradition for the exceptionless character of such norms involve, he believes, fallacies. In the case of contraception, the fallacy consists in the assertion that preestablished (natural) finalities of certain organs or functions are untouchable. In the case of killing, the fallacy consists in an undue restriction of human powers.

However, he continues, tradition has known other norms as well, teleological ones. These are understood as those which judge an act *also* by its consequences. The crucial problem is to discover the criteria that allow proper assessment of consequences. The great danger is naivete; where this exists, the preference rule (above) is rendered unintelligible. One needs other rules as mediations of the preference rule. The moral theological problem of today, as Schüller sees it, is to discover plausible teleological justification for norms in control of actions that were interpreted deontologically in the past. This is the case precisely because the traditional reasons adduced for deontological understanding of these norms will not bear scrutiny. Schüller does not regard this as discontinuous with traditional value judgments, if one is careful not to confuse a value judgment with a historical formulation of it.

My second example is Charles Curran. In the final essay of this volume, "Utilitarianism and Contemporary Moral Theology," Curran relates recent writings by contemporary Catholic moralists to a similar discussion in the field of moral philosophy.[38] He first points out that the objections of philosophers such as Rawls, Frankena, and Williams to "utilitarianism, teleology, or consequentialism" are threefold: (1) aspects other than consequences must be taken into account; (2) the good cannot be determined independently of the morally right; (3) not only the consequences of the action but also the way in which the actor brings about the consequences have moral significance. Thus to oppose utilitarianism, teleology, consequentialism (Curran uses the terms as synonymous), these philosophers need not maintain that certain actions are right whatever the consequences.

Secondly, Curran points out that the antiutilitarian argues that, in addition to consequences, other aspects of the action must be considered, e.g., the obligation of fidelity in promise-keeping. Something other than consequences counts as important in assessing right and wrong, even if these other considerations do not yield an absolute behavioral norm. It is these other considerations that separate Frankena, Rawls, etc. from the utilitarian.

Thirdly, there is a third current in philosophical literature represented by G. E. M. Anscombe, who indicts all of contemporary philosophy because it is even willing to consider the possibility of exceptions based on consequences. Concretely, Anscombe condemns modern moral philosophy "for proposing a philosophy according to which the consequences of such an action could be morally taken into account to determine if one should do such an action." In other words, there are actions that are right or wrong whatever the consequences. Thus, in her terminology, W. D. Ross is a consequentialist.

In summary, then, Curran believes there are three positions. The first is properly described as utilitarian, strict teleology. The position of Anscombe *et al.* may be described as nonconsequentialism or even deontology. The second and middle position, Curran states, differs from strict teleology because it maintains the following points: (1) moral obligation arises from elements other than consequences; (2) the good is not separate from the right; (3) the way in which the good or evil is achieved by the agent is a moral consideration. Since such an opinion does not necessarily hold that certain actions are always wrong no matter what the consequences, it has been called consequentialism by Anscombe.

When I first encountered Curran's threefold division of positions within modern philosophy, I was pleasantly astounded. I had arrived independently at a similar division. Specifically, I had concluded to the usefulness of the following divisions: (1) absolute deontologists: Kant, Catholic tradition on certain points (e.g., contraception), Grisez, Anscombe; (2) absolute consequentialists: J. Fletcher, some utilitarians; (3) moderate teleologists: Ross, McCloskey, Frankena, Fuchs, Knauer, Schüller, Böckle, Curran, and a host of others.

Curran next asks where "reforming Catholic moral theologians" fit into this division. Exactly as I had, he concludes that "as the debate progressed it became quite evident that the reforming Catholic theologians, generally speaking, do not embrace utilitarianism or what Rawls, Frankena, Williams and others have called teleology or consequentialism." They are Curran's "mixed consequentialists" or my "moderate teleologists." Why? Because these theologians, in their explantions of *materia apta* (Janssens), commensurate reason (Knauer), proportionate reason (Schüller), insist that elements other than consequences function in moral rightness and wrongness. I include myself among those who so insist.

Somewhat similarly, Schüller lists three general approaches.[39] (1) The moral rightness of all actions is exclusively determined by their consequences. (2) The moral rightness of all actions is always also but not only determined by consequences. (3) There are some actions whose moral rightness is determined in total independence of consequences. The first position, he notes, is called "teleological" or "utilitarian" (though Schüller argues that the latter term needs rehabilitation), the second and third "deontological." He regrets that there is no terminology distinguishing the second and third positions—a fact that does not disturb Anglo-American philosophers, since practically no one (except, e.g., Anscombe) holds the third position.

William May has, I believe, accurately identified the second approach listed by Schüller as a "mixed deontological" approach (Frankena's phrase).[40] It might just as well be called "moderate teleology," as I suggested above. Whatever the term used, the type of moral reasoning involved is shared by many moral philosophers and theologians, and is the type present in Catholic tradition except in the two general areas mentioned. May contrasts this with the approach of Ramsey, Grisez, and himself.

I think he is right in this contrast, but his development calls for comment at several points. First, May uses the preservation of life to illustrate his problems with the type of "mixed deontologism" he associates with Schüller, Janssens, Curran, and others. After noting my statement that life "is a value to be preserved only insofar as it contains some potentiality for human relationships,"[41] he writes: "In other words . . . life itself, in the sense of physical or biological life, is what an older terminology would have called a *bonum utile*, not a *bonum honestum*, whereas such relational goods as justice and friendship and compassion are 'higher' goods, *bona honesta*."[42]

May is troubled by this usage. Among other reasons he adduces is that we are images of God, "and God is absolutely innocent of evil. He *permits* evil but does not directly intend it . . . " Furthermore, he sees a dualism in the position; for it considers life as a *conditional* good, whereas it is a *personal* good, "not something subhuman or subpersonal."

This is not the place for a prolonged discussion of the intricate matter of the direct and indirect voluntary, but several remarks are in order. First, to say that life is a good to be preserved insofar as it contains some potentiality for human experience is not to make life a *bonum utile*, a kind of negotiable thing, as Quay suggests. It is merely to talk about our duties—and especially the why of those duties—toward the preservation of a *bonum honestum*, the dying human person.[43] Secondly, I believe it is inaccurate to say what May says of God and evil ("God *permits* evil but does not directly intend it") unless one distinguishes between physical (nonmoral) and moral evil. Finally, it seems inaccurate to contrast life as a conditional good with life as a personal good. The proper pairs are conditioned-unconditioned, personal-nonpersonal. Life is a personal good, yet it need not be, even as personal, unconditioned.

In conclusion, I would suggest that Paul McKeever has the matter very well in hand when he refers to contemporary Catholic discussions as an "evolution," with an organic relation to the past, rather than a "revolution."[44]

IV

I would like to advert to two key notions in the discussion in an attempt to clarify continuing exchanges. They are "consequentialism" and "intrinsic evil."

As for so-called consequentialism, let the statement of William May introduce the matter. In speaking of what he calls "consequentialism," May writes that it is "at root a form of extrinsicism in ethics. It derives the meaning or intelligibility of human acts from their consequences or results, and these are not inherent or intrinsic to the acts but are extrinsic to them, added on to them. For the consequentialist, in other words, human acts are *of themselves* meaningless, neither good nor bad, neither right nor wrong."[45]

In my judgment, several things are seriously wrong with that account, and I believe that it no longer serves the purposes of constructive moral discourse to argue as May does here. First, the statement trades on the generic and misleading term "consequentialist." There are many forms of teleology, just as there are many forms of deontology. I do not see the service to moral science to volunteer, for example, that all deontologists are at root physicalists or are guilty of a kind of naturalistic fallacy. Some may be. The same is true of teleology. Some teleologists may be extrinsicists. But there is nothing in the notion that demands it, otherwise Catholic tradition for centuries must be accused of extrinsicism; for this tradition was teleological in its understanding of norms in nearly all areas.

Secondly, it is simply erroneous to assert that writers like Böckle, Janssens, Schüller, Weber, Fuchs, *et al.* (all of whom are "proportionalists" in their understanding of moral norms) derive the meaning of actions from something "extrinsic to them, added to them," and that for such writers "human acts are *of themselves* meaningless." What these writers are asserting—and I include myself amongst them—is that the inherent goodness (and therefore meaning) of a promise is a *limited* goodness and may concur with a more urgent value demanding value preference. Catholic tradition has held this for centuries. In other words, if a promise need not always be kept, that conclusion does not deny, nor can it be logically forced to deny, the inherent meaning and value of promise-making. It denies only that this inherent good and meaning is an *absolute* value. That is what these authors mean when they refer to "breaking a promise," "deceiving another by falsehood," "killing a person," as premoral (or ontic) *evils*.

Finally, May asserts that for these writers "human acts are *of themselves* meaningless." Here he must inform us what he has in mind when he refers to a "human act." Breaking a promise perhaps? Directly killing a person? Using a contraceptive device? Obviously, no one of these is a human act. They become human acts, and patient of a judgment of rightness and wrongness, only when sufficient circumstances have been added to complete the picture. Thus, one breaks a promise (e.g., to attend a wedding) in order to give a dying accident victim life-saving first aid. *That* is patient of a moral assessment and we would all agree that the action is morally right. Now, why cannot something similar be said of, e.g., sterilization? As yet, that is not patient of a final judgment of rightness or wrongness. Or if it is, it is so only on the ground that integral intercourse is an *absolute* good, one that, regardless of conflicting goods and circumstances, always deserves the preference. One can, of course, maintain that. But in doing so, he is saying something about the integrity of intercourse that Catholic tradition has been unwilling to say about life itself. In my judgment, that is exactly what W.D. Ross has in mind when he speaks of breaking a promise or uttering a falsehood as prima facie (and that only) morally wrong.[46] In summary, proportionalists cannot be accused of holding, or being forced to hold, that actions have no meaning in themselves. They maintain only that no final assessment of rightness or wrongness can be made until more has been said of the action than that it is "breaking a promise." And if that is the case, they wonder, correctly, why this must not apply to all acts so described.

The second very misleading usage in this discussion is the

central importance attributed to the notion of "intrinsic evils." Thus May, Stoeckle, Ermecke, *et al.* have accused Schüller, Fuchs, Janssens, *et al.* of espousing a methodology which does not allow for this concept, and hence one that allows for exceptions to norms proscribing, e.g., adultery.

Several things need to be said here. First, the notion of intrinsic evil has such a variety of understandings[47] that it is all but useless in contemporary discourse. Secondly, many contemporary theologians are primarily concerned with departing from the term *as it has been used in recent theological and magisterial literature*, a point that will become even clearer in the next section of these "Notes." In that literature, certain kinds of actions (directly killing an innocent person, direct sterilization) have been proscribed as always wrong regardless of circumstances or consequences. These theologians argue that these contentions have not been satisfactorily established. In other words, they are primarily discoursing with their own tradition, and arguing that one cannot isolate the object of an act and say of it that it is *always* wrong in *any* conceivable circumstances. One can, of course, begin to add a variety of circumstances to the description of an object so that such an action is always wrong. For instance: abortion of a fetus in order to avoid a medical (delivery) bill. That is always wrong—and, if one wishes, intrinsically wrong (scil., *praeceptum quia malum*, not *malum quia praeceptum*). There are a whole host of actions that fit this category; but when one says that, he must realize that he is no longer speaking of the object of the action *as used in recent theological and magisterial literature*.

Thirdly, and therefore, these theologians are arguing that when an action is always morally wrong, it is so not because of unnaturalness or defect of right (as recent tradition contends), but because when *taken as a whole*, the nonmoral evil outweighs the nonmoral good, and therefore the action is disproportionate. One can legitimately continue to call such an action intrinsically evil,[48] but I see no great gain in doing so. Indeed, it is confusing; for the term is associated unavoidably with its usage in recent tradition. This association suggests the validity of the analysis of actions (described without circumstances) as morally wrong *because unnatural* (contraception) or *because of lack of right* (direct killing of an innocent person) Thus the term is tied to a kind of deontological understanding of moral norms that (a) has been persuasively argued to be invalid, and (b) has been shown to be inconsistent with the teleological grounding of norms in every other area of Catholic tradition.

These analytic differences between theologians should not blind us to the vast area of agreement we share and ought to be reflecting to the world. We are at one in treasuring basic human values such as life, the family, and childbearing, and it would be a pastoral disservice to allow our differences to usurp center stage; for more than ever in our time we need to support people in their desires and efforts to avoid failure "against the very meaning of conjugal life" (Pius XII).

For many decades, even centuries, some crucial moral conflicts have been approached and solved through use of the principle of the double effect. This is intimately associated with the discussion of moral norms, but it deserves separate treatment.

Franz Scholz approaches the moral relevance of the direct-indirect distinction through the study of two sets of notions: object-circumstances, essential effect and side effect.[49] In the narrow sense of the word, found in the manual tradition, "circumstance" referred to an aspect of human action which was "extra substantiam existens" (Thomas). Thus there grew a gradual association of the notion of circumstances with that of accident. But, as Scholz points out, some circumstances effect the very essence or substance of human action. This variability of circumstance is too easily overlooked when the idea is associated with "accident."

Scholz next turns to the notions of accidental and essential effects. Essential effects are those that proceed from the substance or essence of the action. Accidental effects are not produced by the substance but indicate that more than one cause is at work. Now when circumstances pertain to the very essence or object of the act, they cannot be said to produce side effects that are merely accidental. Thus the key question is: Which circumstances must in a given case be counted in the object itself, which remain accidental? This cannot be determined a priori; rather, reality itself is the test. Once we have determined this, we will know which actions are necessarily direct and which indirect.

To illustrate these rather fine speculative points (which he gives in considerable detail), Scholz cites three examples from the manual tradition. (1) An unarmed person meets a deadly enemy intent on killing him. The only escape is by horse and on a road occupied by a group of blind and crippled persons. He rides down the road, killing and maiming many people as he escapes. Traditional manuals argued that the presence of the cripples was accidental; thus there is question of a circumstance that remains external to the object: hence the deaths were side effects. (2) Innocent persons are present in a fortress attacked by the enemy. The attacker says he does not will their deaths, but only the cause (the explosion) and not the effect. (3) A person performs an act *minus rectum* (scandal) and foresees that another will thereby be given an occasion of sin.

Scholz asks: Are we concerned with side effects in these examples, which are patient of indirectness? To the first two he says no; to the third, yes. In the first case, e.g., some authors describe the act as "fleeing down the road on a horse." By what principle do they set the boundaries between object and circumstances? Excluding the blind and the crippled from the object contradicts reality. Scholz sees this as "preprogrammed object." One degrades what is essential to the action to a side effect, but at the cost of a mistaken reading of reality. The presence of the blind and crippled on the road is of such significance that it pertains to the very *object*. And if it dies, it is a part of essential effects, not side effects. The escaper cannot say he only "permitted" the deaths. The deaths and injuries are *means*. "But the means, just as the ends, can only be directly intended."[50] We would have a true side effect if, in the case described, the victims threw themselves at the last moment unavoidably into the path of the horse. In that case the rider could say: "I must permit what I cannot prevent."

As for the second case, the attacking general might say that he wishes only to kill combatants. But actually the one natural effect of the bombing is destruction—of soldiers, civilians, beasts. His regret at the death of innocents means only that their deaths are not *propter se sed propter aliud*. Their deaths are a *conditio sine qua non*. But "he who is ready—under the call of the end—to realize the condition *sine qua non*, acts exactly as the one who chooses the appropriate means, scil, directly."[51] Therefore, in these first two cases Scholz does not believe the deaths are indirect. Rather, they are a modified form of direct willing (scil., *secundum quid*, with regrets).

In the third case (scandal) we have a true side effect. He who seeks his goal by an *actio minus recta* does not cause the neighbor's sin. The operation of another cause is necessary for a true side effect. Therefore, the psychology of the will does not demand that the evil effect be willed either as a means or a *conditio sine qua non*.

Since so many of the conflicts that were previously solved by the direct-indirect distinction really represent qualified forms of direct willing, Scholz moves to another model and espouses it: "direct, yes, but only for a proportionate reason." He sees this as not only more honest to reality but as advantageous. First, the direct confrontation of the will with the evil caused by it "ought to be to the benefit of a weighing of values" (*Güterabwägung*). Secondly, looking in the eye is healthy. It avoids development of an "exoneration mentality" associated with phrases such as "not directly willed," "only permitted." Finally, "the broken human condition with its tragic character appears more starkly. Unavoidably we become conscious of the fact that man not only cannot have, hold, and protect all goods simultaneously, but that he can be called, in the service of higher goods, to injure lesser premoral values, and that without any *animus nocendi*."[52]

Here, then, is yet another theologian who argues that every human choice is the resolution of a conflict, that the direct-indirect distinction is only descriptive, and that when actions were legitimated as *indirect* permitting of evil, actually they were morally direct in most cases, even if in qualified form (*secundum quid*, with regrets: "I would not be prepared to do this unless I had to"). Hence Scholz is arguing that there is no morally significant difference between direct and indirect actions where nonmoral evils are concerned.

Albert R. Di Ianni, S. M., accurately reviews the work of Grisez, Schüller, Fuchs, Janssens, Van der Marck, Van der Poel, and myself in this area.[53] He makes two moves. One is a kind of terminological adjustment. The other, the second half of his long essay, exposes his own understanding of the importance of the direct-indirect distinction.

He first insists on the distinction between a nonmoral evil (death) and the free causation of that evil (homicide). Then of homicide he states that "the concept of the free causation of death has at least minimal *moral* meaning in itself prior to consideration of intention and circumstances." This minimal moral meaning makes the act "'intrinsically evil' though in a weaker sense than that of the tradition." That is, it would not always be forbidden regardless of the circumstances. And when it is tolerable, it will generate what Di Ianni calls "creative regret." Why does he insist on this "minimal *moral* meaning"? In his own words: "To treat it as a mere nonmoral evil leans too far in the direction of act-utilitarianism or situationism which demands the voiding of the intrinsic moral meaning of all action concepts."[54]

His second step is to explain positively why he believes the direct-indirect distinction (as in killing) is morally relevant. Some years ago I had argued that direct killing of the innocent, as in indiscriminate bombing, is wrong because of the long-term effects such killing would have, scil., life itself would be worse off by the brutalizing of sensitivities, the release of violence associated with it, and the ultimate unavoidable debasing of the moral currency.[55] Di Ianni agrees with this assessment of consequences but does not believe it is the reason the direct killing is wrong in the first place. It is wrong because it is violative of what he calls "dignity-values" (vs. "welfare-values"). What do these terms mean? "Values of welfare center about the fulfillment of whatever potentials for action and enjoyment an entity might have; life, health, pleasure, power, etc." Values of dignity have little to do with these things. "The values of dignity are such things as self-respect, autonomy, fidelity, justice, trust, integrity and the like."[56] These dignity values are of far greater importance and must be given greater weight in conflict situations.

What has this distinction to do with the direct-indirect distinction? Di Ianni sees the latter distinction as both valid and practically valuable. "It is valid because it generally generates conclusions which coincide with the conclusions generated by the more basic dignity/welfare value distinction. It is moreover practically valuable as a tool because of its greater tangibility."[57] By this he means that while value considerations are often murky, the direct-indirect distinction trades directly on the level of action. Concretely, Di Ianni asserts that to aim at an innocent person's death as an end or even as a means to a good end "is usually to treat him as an object, as a non-person (a non-freedom), as a mere means, whereas to aim at a proportionate good knowing that evil to another person will also arise as a not-aimed-at-side-effect is to produce some illfare but is not a violation of dignity."[58]

How far would Di Ianni carry this? Not, he says, to the extent of a theoretical behavioral absolute, so that direct killing of an innocent could never be done whatever the consequences. Rather, it is a practical behavioral absolute. He cites a "fantastic case where someone threatens to kill 100,000 if you do not kill one." Of this he says that an "overwhelming quantity of welfare may override a small consideration of dignity."

This interesting study deserves several comments. First, I want to put a question to Di Ianni about the moral relevance of the direct-indirect distinction. He argues that direct killing of an innocent person, in addition to visiting illfare upon him, also visits indignity on the victim, "whereas indirect killing when there is a proportionate reason causes illfare alone." Why? Because, he says, direct killing is to treat him as an object, a mere means. Here it must be asked why this is not true also of foreseen indirect killing. Unless Di Ianni says more about the meaning of direct and indirect intent, that difference seems stipulative. That is, it supposes the very thing that is to be established, scil., that there is a *morally* significant difference in the two types of action. As stipulative, therefore, it seems to beg the question.

An indication of this is Di Ianni's statement that the distinction between direct and indirect "is valid because it *generally* generates conclusions which coincide with the conclusions generated by the more basic dignity-welfare distinction." Furthermore, he says that to kill another as a means is *usually* to treat that person as an object. If the distinction is valid as such, why is it not *always* applicable? The fact that it is not indicates that it is not the morally decisive element.

Secondly, Di Ianni has engaged the author of these "Notes" and disagreed with my explanation of the wrongfulness of, e.g., indiscriminate bombing. In this I believe he is correct. Through the kind criticisms of thoughtful colleagues, I have modified this teleological understanding of the wrongfulness of many direct killings, without, however, abandoning the teleology itself, as I shall attempt to indicate below. In other words, there is another understanding of proportionate reason than the one I gave.

Third, Di Ianni insists that actions such as homicide, prior to the addition of circumstances, have "minimal moral meaning." He contrasts this with the position on evil of Fuchs (premoral), Schüller (nonmoral), and Janssens (ontic). These latter terms, he says, refer to "mere nonmoral evil" and thus "lean too far in the direction of . . . situationism" because they void actions of intrinsic moral meaning. Actually, we have here a *lis de verbo*; for these authors all have obligational statements to offer about our attitudes and actions with regard to nonmoral evils—scil., that they are to be avoided insofar as compatibly (with other conflicting values) possible. And all would agree with Di Ianni that there is a place for "creative regret." Several (e.g., Janssens) explicitly mention this.

Fourth, one might argue that Di Ianni has but an artificial distinction when he contrasts dignity values with welfare values. I mean that actions which assault or promote dignity pertain to one's welfare, are for or against a person's welfare. Certainly, the authors who appeal to proportionate reason as that which in principle justifies disvalues in our actions include in the notion of proportionate reason what Di Ianni calls dignity values. This is clear, e.g., in the insistence we find in Janssens and Schüller on the notion of expressive actions (*Ausdruckshandlungen*) in measuring proportion. Therefore, dignity values do not eliminate teleology in the understanding of norms; rather, they form a part of it.

Fifth, it is necessary to ask Di Ianni how big a disaster would have to be before he is willing to call a direct killing of an innocent person "a small consideration of dignity." If he proposes, as he does, that a hundred thousand lives saved would be an "overwhelming quantity of welfare," why not one hundred, or even ten?

Sixth, it is clear that Di Ianni shares in the teleological tendencies of the theologians he cites, insofar as he rejects "intrinsic evil in the very strong sense." How far he departs and in what areas would be much clearer had he said more about falsehood, sterilization, and other (than killing) problems. This strong sense of the term is the sense in the writings of authors like Paul Ramsey, Germain Grisez, and William May. This rejection of "intrinsic evil in the strong sense" is what is common to theologians like Fuchs, Böckle, Weber, Janssens, Schüller, and Scholz, and is where the discussion really originates. Furthermore, I believe it is the heart of the matter. But such a rejection necessarily implies *some form* of teleology. Whether it is useful to retain the term "intrinsic evil" at all once this move has been made is highly questionable, as was noted above.

This brings us to the notion of proportionate reason. Above I suggested that it is the crucial notion in this discussion. Di Ianni would agree in principle to that statement. There are many ways in which that term can be explained, just as there are many considerations that go into its proper understanding. That is why reference was made to *some form* of teleology. For instance, Schüller and Janssens have emphasized the importance of expressive actions and institutional obligations in reading proportion. The former are very close to so-called "dignity values." The latter (institutional obligations) refer to duties that stem from the existence and necessity of institutions (like contracts) for stable social life. Thus, in the case of judicial murder (the judge who frames one innocent person to prevent a rioting mob from killing more in reprisal), Schüller argues that the action is morally wrong because the entire institution of criminal law is at stake.

Where proportionality is concerned, a further word about the term "consequences" is called for. Böckle noted above that an ever-increasing number of theologians trace rightness and wrongness to consequences. Many react immediately against such a notion, because it suggests to them all kinds of unacceptable things. It suggests, e.g., that torture or extortion or adultery may be morally right if they produce sufficiently good results or net good. In other words, it suggests in undifferentiated form that "a good end justifies an evil means." Thus the reaction.

Actually, that is not what is meant by the term in recent Catholic writing nor what the term can be forced to mean. By referring to consequences, recent writing means two things. First, and negatively, it means a rejection of the notion of intrinsic evil *in the strong sense* (Di Ianni's phrase). This strong sense states moral wrongness of an action (e.g., direct sterilization) independently of consequences and circumstances. Secondly, and positively, the term "consequences" means that all things must be considered before a final moral judgment of rightness or wrongness can be made. By saying "all things must be considered," these authors do not mean *total net good* as this term is often understood (scil., mere welfare values). The usage "total net good" (or evil) too easily excludes from consideration factors that go into determining proportion (expressive actions [dignity values], institutional obligations, etc.).

Another study suggests possible ways of reading proportion.[59] The oft-repeated argument of some authors (e.g., Ramsey, Grisez, May) for resisting analyses such as those of Knauer, Janssens, and Schüller is that the basic goods are incommensurable. Those who shift the major emphasis in cases of conflict to proportionate reason are (so the argument goes) measuring the incommensurable. If one attempts to do that, he is unavoidably involved in a form of consequentialism that determines the moral wrongness and rightness of an action according to "greatest net good"—not only an incoherent notion, as the long philosophical discussions of utilitarianism have revealed, but also one that is at odds with some basic Christian convictions. In other words, one does not suppress one basic good for the sake of another one *equally* basic. The only way to cut the Gordian knot when basic values are conflicted is to only indirectly allow the defeat of one as the other is pursued. As Paul Ramsey words it in a forthcoming study:

My own view is that the distinction between direct and indirect voluntariety is pertinent and alerts our attention as moral agents to those moral choices where incommensurable conflicting values are at stake, where there is no measurable resolution of value conflicts on a single scale, where there are gaps in any supposed hierarchy of values, and therefore no way to determine exactly the greater or lesser good or evil. . . . Where there is no single scale or common denominator, or where there is discontinuity in the hierarchy of goods or evils, one ought not turn against any human good.[60]

Those who put the major emphasis on proportionality in situations of conflicted goods might respond in any number of ways. For instance, negatively they might urge that if proportionate reason involves measuring the unmeasurable, then what is the meaning and function of proportionate reason in the standard understandings of the double effect? They might ask why an "indirect killing" does not involve one in turning against a basic good? In other words, they would press the matter of the *moral* (not merely descriptive) relevance of directness as this was understood traditionally.

A concrete vehicle for bringing these questions into clearer focus is the classic, even if rare, obstetrical case where the physician faces two options: either he aborts the fetus and thus saves the mother, or he does not abort and both mother and child die. Both those who defend the moral relevance of the direct-indirect distinction in such instances (e.g., Ramsey, Grisez) and those who question it agree on the conclusion; that is not at issue. What is at issue is the reason for the conclusion. The defenders of the traditional distinction would argue that the conclusion is correct insofar as, and only insofar as, the death of the fetus can be said to be indirect. The revisionists, so to speak, would argue that the real reason for the conclusion is that *in such circumstances* the abortion is proportionately grounded, is the lesser evil. When one is faced with two options both of which involve unavoidable (nonmoral) evil, one ought to choose the lesser evil. To argue that the intervention is morally right because it is "indirect" is, on this view, to use a notion that is adventitious, unnecessary, and ultimately indecisive.

The common response to such an argument is that if this is true, then what is known in philosophical circles as "the Caiphas

principle" is valid. That is, one is justified in sacrificing one innocent person to save five. The example often used is that of a
sheriff or judge in a Southern town faced with the alternatives in a
rape case of framing a black suspect (whom he knows to be innocent) or carrying on a prolonged search for the real culprit. The
immediate indictment and conviction of the suspect would save
many lives and prevent other harmful consequences. If an action's moral rightness is determined solely by the consequences
(one innocent killed vs. many innocent killed), then it seems that
the sheriff ought to frame the one innocent person—a conclusion
that shocks our moral sensitivities, but one that a revisionist on
the double effect would seem forced to draw.

At this point the revisionist would return to the insistence on
the words "in these circumstances" in the abortion dilemma
given above. In the abortion dilemma the situation is not simply a
save-one vs. lose-two dilemma. It is not simply quantitative. It
must be added that the deadly deed is intrinsically and inescapably connected with the saving of the mother's life, whether that
deadly deed be a craniotomy or the removal of the fetus to get at a
life threatening aneurysm. That is to say, there is in the very nature
of the case no way of saving the mother. There is an essential link
between the means and the end. By contrast, however, I argue
that such a link does not exist in the sheriff instance. There is no
inherent connection between the killing of an innocent person and
the change of mind of a lynch mob. For those who hold to the
notion of free will in the doing of evil (and good), there is never an
inherent connection between killing an innocent person and
changing the murderous mind of a lynch mob. In other words, in
the abortion case one chooses to save the life that can be saved
because in such circumstances that is the lesser evil, is proportionately grounded. In other circumstances it would not be the
lesser evil, would not be proportionate.

The article further argues that seeing proportionate reason as
the crucial element in situations of conflict need not at all involve
one in measuring the immeasurable. There are times, of course,
when genuine measuring in the strict sense is appropriate: e.g.,
when merely instrumental goods and basic goods conflict. One
sacrifices the instrumental for the basic, because instrumental

goods are lesser in the order of goods. Thus, one prefers life to property. This is a strict weighing of values.

But such is clearly not possible where basic goods are concerned. But neither is it necessary. While the basic goods are not commensurable (one *against* the other), they are clearly associated goods. Thus, one who unjustifiably takes human life also undermines other human goods, and these human goods, once weakened or undermined, will affect the very good of life itself.

Let marriage and birth control be another example. Two distinct but closely associated goods are involved: the procreative good, the communicative (unitive) good. With this in mind, Paul Ramsey justifies contraception as follows: "In these matters . . . there are no moral judgments for which proportionate reason is not the guiding preference-principle." He immediately explains this as follows: "Will not the manner of protecting the good (procreative) undermine it in the long run by serious injury to an associated good (the communicative good)."[61] The "manner of protecting it" means here periodic continence or the so-called rhythm method. Practically, this means that the possible ineffectiveness[62] and forced and perhaps prolonged periods of abstention can easily harm the communicative good and *thereby* the procreative good itself. The Second Vatican Council said something very similar when it stated that "where the intimacy of married life is broken off, it is not rare for its faithfulness to be imperiled and its quality of fruitfulness ruined."[63] That seems to me to be a reasonable account of things. It is precisely concern for the procreative good, but as related to and supported by the communicative good, that leads Ramsey to conclude to the moral rectitude of contraception and, if necessary, sterilization.

Clearly *some kind of measuring* is going on there. The incommensurability of goods (procreative, communicative) is reduced by seeing them in interrelationship. And it is this interrelationship that provides the context—a kind of single scale—in which decisions are possible and reasonable, and adoption of personal and community policies (hierarchy) is not completely arbitrary.

Could not something very similar be said of the case of the Southern sheriff above (and, by extension, of the immorality of obliteration bombing)? The manner of protecting the good (human life—by framing one innocent person) will undermine it in the long run by serious injury to an associated good (human liberty); for by killing an innocent person to prevent others from unjustly killing five innocent persons, one equivalently denies the freedom of these others. That is the very moral meaning of extortion. One supposes by his action that the cessation of others from wrongdoing is necessarily dependent on my doing harm. Such a supposition denies, and thereby undermines, human freedom. And because such freedom is an associated good upon which the very good of life itself depends, undermining it in the manner of my defense of life is undermining life itself—is disproportionate.

Here, again, one does not exactly weigh life *against* freedom; one merely associates the associable and reads proportion within such an interrelationship. That is why Schüller seems absolutely correct in insisting that in this and similar cases it is not simply a matter of the life of one versus the life of many others; the entire institution of criminal law is at stake. And that is how proportion must be read.

Let obliteration bombing be another test case. Those who would defend such counterpeople (vs. counterforce) attacks argue that they will save more lives. This was Truman's argument. The choice is seen as between taking a hundred thousand Nagasakian lives or losing double or triple that number from both sides in a prolonged conventional war.

If the article under review is correct (that proportionate reason reigns even where the taking of human life is concerned), then there must be a way of showing that Truman's understanding of proportion was wrong—if we hold it to be such, as I do. I believe there is.

Let us again use Ramsey's formulation. "Will not the manner of protecting the good (human life—by ending the war) undermine it in the long run by serious injury to an associated good (human liberty)?" Making innocent (noncombatant) persons the object of our targeting is a form of extortion in international affairs that contains an implicit denial of human freedom. Human freedom is undermined when extortionary actions are accepted and elevated and universalized. Because such freedom is an "associated good" upon which the very good of life heavily depends, undermining it in the manner of my defense of life is undermining life itself—is disproportionate. John Locke understood this association of goods very well:

> For I have reason to conclude that he who gets me into his power without my consent, would use me as he pleased when he got me there, and destroy me too, when he had a fancy to it. . . . He that in the state of nature would take away the freedom that belongs to any one in that state must be supposed to have a design to take away everything else, that freedom being the foundation of all the rest. . . .[64]

Perhaps it would be helpful to put this in another way and in explicitly Christian terms. It is the Christian's faith that another's ceasing from his wrongdoing is *never* dependent on my doing nonmoral evil; for the Christian believes that we are truly what we are, redeemed in Christ. We are still threatened by the *reliquiae peccati*, but are free and powerful in Christ's grace. We rejoice in our infirmities, that the grace of Christ may abound in us. And we know the powers of that grace—in Magdalen (and many Magdalens), in the martyrs, in the likes of Thomas More, Matthew Talbot, and a host of others. Others can cease their evil-doing without our connivance in it, without our doing harm to persuade and entice them. We are free. That is our Christian bet as persons who know our freedom in Christ.

That is why the *essential connection* between aborting and saving the one who can be saved is so important in the classical abortion case. No such connection exists in the instance of the rioting mob. They can erase their evil-doing without our doing harm to make them cease. To yield to their demands would be a denial to them of their own freedom. And that freedom is an associated good which must be asserted and protected if the good of life itself is to survive. We may lose some lives in sticking to this conviction, but that is where our trust in God's providence is on the line. Because people can, with God's gracious help, cease evil-doing, our doing harm to make them cease is unjustifiable, disproportionate. The judicious Christian reads his proportions not just by looking at numbers, but by looking at many other features of the situation within which the numerical must be interpreted.

Something very similar can be said, I believe, about the conduct of warfare. But before saying it, we must recall the teaching of Pius XII, the most extensive and detailed papal elaboration of the just-war-theory in all of history, Pius XII, contrary to some earlier theological formulations, restricted the *jus ad bellum* (the just cause for going to war) to national self-defense. War, he taught, can be justified as a response *ad repellendas injurias* (to repel injury or aggression), not for settlement of other disputes, even the most serious (*ad vindicandas offensiones*, *ad recuperandas res*). Now the implication of this limitation of just cause to self-defense means that the other nation is the aggressor—in short, is engaged in wrongful conduct. It may at times be difficult to say who was the original aggressor, but that does not eliminate the need of *an aggressor* as the sole justification for going to war.

If a nation is wrongfully aggressing, once again it is the Christian's faith, and a well-founded one, that that nation can and must cease and desist from wrongful aggression without our doing harm to noncombatants to make that nation do so. There is no *necessary connection* between our doing harm to noncombatants (e.g., killing innocent civilians to stop that nation) and that nation's ceasing unjust aggression. To say that there is would be to insult the humanity of the aggressor by denying his liberty; for unjust aggressors are free to cease unjust aggression. Christ did not invent that idea, of course, but by his graceful redemption he powerfully restated it to a world that too often came to terms with its inhumanities as "necessary," "culturally imposed,"etc. And by denying the aggressor's freedom, we deny our own by implication, thus removing the conditions for any rationality in war. That is why, I believe, the Christian judges attacks upon noncombatants as disproportionate.

Ultimately, then the article concludes, revisionists admit a descriptive difference between actions involving nonmoral evil directly and indirectly. That is, the directness or indirectness of an effect tells us what is being sought and by what means and in what circumstances. These in combination reveal the significance of the action. Whether the action is, as a whole, morally right or wrong depends on this significance; for significance reveals what other values are at stake, and therefore whether the manner of the pursuit of the good here and now is destructive of it or not. In other words, it reveals whether in the action as a whole the good outweighs the evil, whether there is a truly proportionate reason or not. And it is the presence or absence of such a reason that determines whether the attitude of the agent is adequate or not, whether he is choosing rightly or wrongly, whether he remains open to the basic goods or closes one of them off in pursuit of another, whether or not one chooses against a basic good, or, in Pius XII's words, whether one "sins against the very meaning of conjugal life."

This analysis is quite tentative. But it seems not without points to recommend it. Moral theologians will undoubtedly clarify their analyses as this exchange progresses. But one thing seems increasingly clear: there are fewer and fewer theologians ready to defend "intrinsic evil in the strong sense," as Di Ianni phrases it.

Notes

1. Joseph Fuchs, S.J., "The Absoluteness of Moral Terms," *Gregorianum* 52 (1971) 415-58.

2. Fuchs uses "premoral" where Schüller had used "nonmoral."

3. Fuchs, *art. cit.*, p. 443.

4. *Ibid.*, p. 444.

5. *Ibid.*

6. To what extent this departs from the traditional understanding is not altogether clear. That depends on how many circumstances traditional moralists allowed to enter the statement of the *objectum* and how many Fuchs excludes.

7. *Ibid.*, p.446.

8. *Ibid.*

9. Paul Ramsey, *Deeds and Rules in Christian Ethics* (New York: Scribner's, 1967) p. 196.

10. *Ibid.*, p. 450. Cf. also Franz Böckle, "La morale fondamentale," *Recherches de science religieuse* 59 (1971) 331-64, at 358.

11. On this point cf. David Blanchfield, "Balancing in Moral Theology,"*American Ecclesiastical Review* 164 (1971) 90-96.

12. John R. Connery, S.J., "Morality of Consequences: A Critical Appraisal," *Theological Studies* 34 (1973) 396-414.

13. Bruno Schüller, S.J., "Neuere Beiträge zum Thema 'Begründung sittlicher Normen,' " *Theologische Berichte* 4 (Einsiedein: Benziger, 1974) 109-81. Schüller's review includes much more than a response to Connery. It surveys and critiques much of the literature on this entire subject. e.g., Curran's principle of compromise and Hurley's principle of overriding right.

14. Cf. Denis E. Hurley, O.M.I., "In defense of the Principle of Overriding Right," *Theological Studies* 29 (1968) 301-9; Peter Chirico, S.S., "Morality in General and Birth Control in Particular," *Chicago Studies* 9 (1970) 19-33.

15. *Art. cit.*, p. 177.

16. *Ibid.*, p. 170.

17. Cited in Schüller, p. 174. from *Tractatus de fide*, disp. 4. sect. 4. n. 57.

18. *Art. cit.*, p. 176.

19. Connery, *art. cit.*, p. 398.

20. Schüller criticizes this language in his review of W. Van der Marck, *art. cit.*, p. 137-38. Killing, e.g., even when its moral evaluation is left totally open, is not merely a physical act; it is a kind of human action.

21. *Art. cit.*, p. 399, n. 7.

22. For a much broader study of the notion of conflict, cf. H. Thielicke, "Anthropologische Grundtatbestände in individuellen Konfliktsituationen." *Zeitschrift für evangelische Ethik* 18 (1974) 129-45.

23. Paul M. Quay, S.J., "Morality by Calculation of Values," *Theology Digest* 23 (1975) 347-64.

24. The six mentioned are Joseph Fuchs, Richard McCormick, Giles Milhaven, John Dedek, Charles Curran, Bruno Schüller.

25. Quay, *art. cit.*, p. 349.

26. *Ibid.*, p. 352.

27. The same confusion is notable in Quay's treatment of sexuality. He notes that "an act of sexual perversion . . . damages the properly human personality of the agent." If one knows this and still performs the act, then "he intends these [harms]." Quay then concludes: "To call these negative values and to perform the action for some extrinsic good is simply to do evil that good may come." So it is—at least it is to do premoral evil. But the entire issue is, what forms of sexual conduct are to count as "perversion"? One does not define the action as "perversion" and then set about seeing how we can justify it: for "perversion" = morally unjustifiable.

28. In this respect cf.Ph.Delhaye,"A propos de'*Persona humana*,' " *Esprit et vie* 86 (1976) 197. He writes: "Il existe une liste universelle des valeurs capables de susciter l'attention et l'amour de tous les êtres humains et dès lors objectivement fondées. Elles sont, *en même temps*, des

'bien-en-soi' et des 'valeurs-pour-nous.' Pourquoi? Parce qu'elles pren-nent naissance dans les exigences, les besoins, l'inspiration à la dignité de *tous les êtres humains"* (emphasis added). Cf. also a declaration of the German bishops, "Les valeurs fondamentales de la société et le bonheur humain," *Documentation catholique* 73 (1976) 868-71.

    29, Cf. *The Documents of Vatican II* (tr. Abbott) p.497.

    30. Address in St. Peter's Square, Sept. 26, 1976. Cf. *Catholic Chronicle* [Toledo] Oct. 1, 1976; cf. *L'Osservatore romano*, Oct. 7, 1976 (English edition).

    31. *Art, cit.*, p. 361.

    32. Cf., e.g., W. Brugger, *Theologia naturalis* (Pullach, 1959) p. 412.

    33. B. Schüller, S.J., "Direkte Tötung—Indirekte Tötung," *Theologie und Philosophie* 47 (1972) 341-57.

    34. E.g., his understanding of premoral evil. He insists that this refers to a "true privation of a *good called for.*" This is not the way the notion is understood in contemporary moral discourse. Louis Janssens puts it as follows: "We call ontic evil any lack of a perfection at which we aim, any lack of fulfillment which frustrates our natural urges and makes us suffer. It is essentially the natural consequence of our limitation" ("Ontic Evil and Moral Evil," *Louvain Studies* 4 [1972] 134).

    35. Cf. *L'homme manipulé*, ed. Charles Robert (Strasbourg: Cerdic, 1974).

    36. *Ibid.*, p.180.

    37. *Ibid.*, pp. 194-96.

    38. Charles E. Curran, "Utilitarianism and Contemporary Moral Theology: Situating the Debates," *Concilium*, Dec. 1976.

    39. Bruno Schüller, S.J., "Anmerkungen zu dem Bergriffspaar 'teleologisch-deontologisch,' " *Gregorianum* 57 (1976) 315-31.

    40. William May, "Ethics and Human Identity: The Challenge of the New Biology," *Horizons* 3 (1976) 17-37.

    41. Richard A. McCormick, S.J., "To Save or Let Die," *Journal of the American Medical Association* 229 (1974) 172-76.

    42. *Art. cit.*, p. 35.

    43. Here an interesting text of Thomas is in place. "Some change could happen that would entirely take away a man's happiness by hinder-ing virtuous action altogether. For example, some sickness could cause madness or insanity or any other mental breakdown. Since happiness may not be attained except by living humanly or in accord with reason, when the use of reason is gone, human living is not possible. Con-sequently, in what concerns living humanly, the condition of madness must be equated with the condition of death" (Commentary on the *Nicomachean Ethics* I [Chicago: Regnery, 1964] 85).

    44. "Moral Theology: Evolution or Revolution? *Priest* 32, nos. 7-8 (July-Aug. 1976) 12-13 (an unsigned editorial, but moral theologian Paul McKeever is editor).

45. William May, "Contraception, Abstinence and Responsible Parenthood," *Reason* 3 (1977) 34-52.

46. W.D. Ross, *The Right and the Good* (Oxford, 1965).

47. Cf. James Murtagh, *Intrinsic Evil* (Rome, 1973).

48. Walter Jeffko does; cf. his careful study "Processive Relationism and Ethical Absolutes," *American Benedictine Review* 26 (1975) 283-97.

49. Franz Scholz, "Objekt und Umstande, Wesenswirkungen und Nebeneffekte," in *Christlich glauben und handeln*, ed. Klaus Demmer and Bruno Schüller (Düsseldorf: Patmos, 1977) 243-60, This is the *Festschrift* honoring Joseph Fuchs, S.J.

50. *Ibid.,* 256.

51. *Ibid.,* 257.

52. *Ibid.,* 259.

53. Albert R. Di Ianni, S.M., "The Direct/Indirect Distinction in Morals." *Thomist* 41 (1977) 350-80.

54. *Ibid.,* 362.

55. *Ambiguity in Moral Choice* (Milwaukee: Marquette Univ., 1973).

56. Di Ianni, "The Direct/Indirect Distinction" 370.

57. *Ibid.,* 372.

58. *Ibid.,* 377.

59. Richard A. McCormick, S.J., "Le principe du double effect," in *Discerner les valeurs pour fonder la morale* (= *Concilium* 120) 105-20, This is not available in English but only in French, Spanish, Italian, Dutch, and German.

60. Paul Ramsey and Richard A. McCormick, S.J., *Doing Evil to Achieve Good: Moral Choice in Conflict Situations* (Chicago: Loyola University Press, 1978).

61. Cf. n. 60 above.

62. I say "possible" in deference to those who urge that when properly practiced (precise and recent knowledge, high motivation) periodic continence has a very high rate of success.

63. Cf. *Gaudium et spes*, no. 51.

64. John Locke, *An Essay concerning the True Original Extent and End of Civil Government,* in *Of Civil Government* (New York: Dutton, n.d.; no. 751 of Everyman's Library) 125.

Utilitarianism and Contemporary Moral Theology: Situating the Debates

Charles E. Curran

Within the last decade in Roman Catholicism there has been a growing theological literature questioning the existence of absolute behavioral norms in moral theology. More specifically, many theologians have objected to exceptionless moral norms in which the moral action is described in terms of the physical aspect of the act. At the same time there has been a growing debate in philosophical ethics about the adequacy of a utilitarian approach. Often these debates have been taking place in isolation. The purpose of this study is to compare the different debates that have taken place within utilitarian thought, to examine the arguments proposed against a utilitarian position in order to clarify the terms of the discussion, to situate the debate which has taken place in Roman Catholic ethics in the light of the discussion about utilitarianism, and to suggest approaches for Roman Catholic ethics.

I

Debates Within Utilitarianism

Utilitarianism is described as the ethical attitude which seeks to produce the greatest good for the greatest number. Since the morality of an action depends in some way on producing good and/or avoiding evil, utilitarianism is generally understood as a

341

form of teleological ethics or consequentialism. Teleological theories are generally contrasted with deontological theories which maintain that it is possible to have a moral obligation to do an act which does not produce the most good or avoid the most evil in the manner suggested by teleologists. Utilitarianism is a form of consequentialism because moral obligation is determined by the good or bad consequences produced. J.J.C. Smart, a contemporary defender of utilitarianism, describes it as the view that the rightness or wrongness of an act depends only on the total goodness or badness of the consequences.[1]

Calculating Consequences

Utilitarians themselves as well as their opponents have frequently recognized some difficulty in calculating consequences. Bentham attempted a calculus of pleasure and pain by indicating seven different dimensions which had to be taken into account. John Stuart Mill, reacting to Bentham's calculus based on quantity, introduced a qualitative distinction between higher and lower pleasures.[2] But the problem of calculating the consequences is even more complex. Whatever utility means, the theory of utilitarianism calls for it to be maximized. Since our actions very often affect more than one person and many societal institutions, it must be possible to calculate the total net utility to all affected by the various alternative actions which are open to the subject. Different theories of calculation are still being proposed by various contemporary thinkers (e.g., Braybooke, Rescher, and Brandt).[3] Most philosophers recognize the difficulty in constructing such a calculation of the consequences of acts.

Two points deserve mention in response to the problem of calculating consequences. Utilitarians do not believe that human beings should always attempt to make such exhaustive calculations before acting. They readily accept rules of thumb often called summary rules. Such summary rules are not absolute and should be violated if the violation brings about better consequences, but ordinarily one can follow such rules of thumb as the distillation of experience about what usually produces the most utility.

Secondly, one must admit there is no universal agreement even among utilitarians on how consequences of acts should be calculated. The difficulty or lack of agreement does not constitute a totally convincing argument against utilitarianism or any consequentialist theory. Calculating consequences is a problem for all other types of ethics as well. Roman Catholic manualistic moral theology has often appealed to consequences to justify the morality of particular actions. The principle of proportionality in war maintains that the good to be achieved by the war must outweigh the evils involved. Here one is asked to consider the consequences of alternative actions involving many different human values including the taking of human lives and the very existence of peoples and nations. Traditional Catholic moral theology thus had to face the same difficulty as utilitarians although not all the time.

Act-Utilitarianism and Rule-Utilitarianism

A very significant and important debate among utilitarians concerns the difference between act- and rule-utilitarianism. Until the last two or three decades utilitarianism was understood in terms of act-utilitarianism—the rightness or wrongness of the action is determined by the consequences of the act itself. Antiutilitarians brought up a number of objections to utilitarianism because by making the consequences of the individual act morally determinative one goes against many accepted moral teachings. e.g., punishment of the innocent, judicial murder, not voting in an election, not keeping secrets, not telling the truth, etc. Michael Bayles has collected an anthology of essays to show the development of rule-utilitarianism as a refinement of the basic utilitarian approach which was proposed in the intervening years to overcome some of the above objections.[4] According to rule-utilitarianism acts are to be regarded as right only if they conform to rules which can be supported on utilitarian grounds. Urmson maintains that John Stuart Mill himself was really a rule-utilitarian and not an act-utilitarian.[5]

In the 1960's David Lyons and others maintained that rule-utilitarianism and act-utilitarianism, if properly understood as including all the circumstances, especially threshold phenomena, are equivalent, so that there is no real difference between them.[6] Lyons' thesis of equivalence has been attacked,[7] but it is safe to describe the present state of the debate by indicating that there is a growing consensus among utilitarians themselves that rule-utilitarianism very frequently if not always collapses into act-utilitarianism.[8]

The debate within utilitarianism about act- and rule-utilitarianism does not have any immediate parallels in the current debates in Roman Catholic moral theology. However, it seems that Roman Catholic moral theology might profit from this discussion with its emphasis on the principle of universalizability. Richard A. McCormick has recently proposed that some norms (e.g., direct taking of innocent life, direct killing of non-combatants, difference between commission and omission as seen in so-called passive and active euthanasia) are "teleologically established and yet are virtually exceptionless." In weighing all the consequences of actions one comes to the conclusion that the actions are wrong and that the dangers and risks that might result from any exceptions are so great that the norm is virtually exceptionless. The establishment of such a norm is based on an analogy with the establishment of a positive law on the basis of a presumption of common and universal danger.[9]

McCormick's argument for exceptionless norms consists in a wedge argument that any possible exceptions would ultimately lead to greater evils than the good that might possibly be achieved in the one exception. The debate about act- and rule-utilitarianism has frequently made use of the principle of universalizability or generalizability which might be employed here to allow certain exceptions without necessarily involving all the evils that McCormick fears might come from any exceptions.

McCormick himself maintains that the existing laws or norms accepted in Catholic moral theology have ultimately come about by refining the principle that killing is wrong except where there is a proportionate reason. Exceptions have been made in this general norm for proportionate reasons (self-defense, killing in war, etc.) without endangering the value to be perserved by the norm itself.[10] Now one might attempt to push the question one step further—can exceptions be made in the now accepted norms of no direct killing of the innocent and no active euthanasia which could allow for some exceptions without entailing all the evil consequences that McCormick fears if one no longer accepts the existing distinctions?

In the case of directly killing noncombatants in war I am in basic agreement with McCormick's fears, but in the case of directly killing the innocent, it might be possible to make some very limited exceptions. Consider a case which was proposed by Williams. A foreigner comes across a scene where a tyrannical military captain is prepared to shoot a group of villagers taken at random to discourage other protesters in the village and bring about loyalty to the existing government. The captain offers the foreigner the privilege of killing one of the villagers with the promise that he himself will then let the others go free. The presuppositions are that the captain will do as he threatens and there is absolutely no other way to save the villagers or any number of them.[11] Is it not possible to acknowledge some exception clause for hard cases like this without necessarily involving the many long-range consequences feared by McCormick? Could one not accept the rule—directly killing the innocent is wrong except in those cases where one has certitude that this is the only way a far greater number of innocent persons can be saved? Such a restricted exception clause could allow such killing in a few cases and still maintain the general principle of not killing innocent people in almost all situations. Here it is necessary to insist on the certitude that one has that this is the only way in which a far greater number of innocent persons can be saved. Such a condition is rarely present and impossible in the complex situation of warfare and the direct killing of noncombatants.

In the case of the difference between killing and letting die as acts of commission and omission, is it not possible to make some nuanced distinction which acknowledges there is not always an absolute difference between the two but still avoids some of the bad consequences that McCormick fears? I have proposed that once the dying process begins the distinction between omission and commission ceases to be of decisive importance. More practically, the dying process can be identified as the time that extraordinary means could be discontinued as now being useless, since there is no hope of success in thus treating the patient. Is there that great a difference between turning off the respirator with the intention of allowing the person to die and positively interfering at the same time to bring about the same effect? The presumption is that in both cases the death of the person will follow certainly, inevitably and with about the same degree of immediacy from either the act of omission or commission. In the vast majority of cases the two acts of omission and commission would not be the same regarding certainty, inevitably and immediacy of the effect of death, and thus one avoids most of the dangers mentioned by McCormick. However, there is the difference that in the case of shutting off the respirator I am not the cause of the death in exactly the same way as in an act of commission, but the difference does not seem to constitute the basis for a different moral judgment where the conditions mentioned above are the same.

II
UTILTARIANISM, TELEOLOGY AND CONSEQUENTIALISM

Clarifications and Rejection of Utilitarianism

In the recent literature there has been a general tendency to point out the insufficiency of utilitarianism as a moral theory and to advocate other approaches as at least modifications of the utilitarian approach. The terms involved have been defined in different ways, but in the context of the utilitarian debate utilitarianism, teleology and consequentialism are generally understood as ethical theories which determine the moral rightness or wrongness of the act (or rule) solely on the basis of the consequences of the act (or rule). J.J.C. Smart maintains that the rightness or wrongness of an action depends only on the total goodness or badness of the consequences, i.e., on the effect of the action on the welfare of all human beings.[12]

In a critique of utilitarianism, especially with the theory of Smart in mind, Bernard Williams devotes a large section of his monograph to the structure of consequentialism and emphasizes that the alternative to consequentialism does not involve the acceptance of the position that there are certain actions which one should do or never do whatever the consequences. Williams himself admits some circumstances in which direct killing of the innocent would be morally good. The denial of consequentialism only involved the admission that there would be some situations in which acts would be good, even though the state of affairs produced by doing these acts would be worse than some other state of affairs accessible to the actor. In other words, to oppose consequentialism it is necessary to hold that consequences are not the only morally relevant considerations; one does not have to affirm that it is always wrong to do acts no matter what the consequences.[13]

In the more recent debate authors who modify or reject utilitarianism such as Rawls and Lyons employ the word teleological in this same sense. Lyons states in the very beginning of his book that teleologists claim that the rightness of acts depends solely on their utility, whereas deontologists claim that rightness is not simply a function of utility.[14] Rawls insists that in teleological theory the good is defined independently of the right. In accord with this description Rawls maintains that if the distribution of the good is also counted as a good and perhaps a higher order one, we no longer have a teleological view in the classical sense.[15] Such an understanding of teleological is in accord with the position of William Frankena who defines teleology as the system in which the moral quality or value depends on the comparative nonmoral value of what is produced or brought about. Deontological theories, as opposed to teleological theories, affirm that there are at least other considerations which make an action or rule right or obligatory besides the goodness or badness of consequences. Frankena recognizes that deontologists can be of two types, either those for whom the principle of maximizing the balance of good over evil is not a moral criterion, or those for whom such a principle is not the only basis or ultimate one.[16]

Objections to the theory of utilitarianism or teleology or consequentialism as proposed by Rawls, Frankena, Williams and others in the contemporary debate are not based on the fact that these authors necessarily maintain that some actions are always right or wrong whatever the consequences. Rather, their objections to utilitarianism, teleology or consequentialism may be summarized as follows: 1) Aspects other than consequences must be taken into account. 2) The good cannot be determined independently of the morally right. 3) Not only the consequences of the action but also the way in which the actor brings about the consequences has moral significance. To refute utilitarianism, teleology or consequentialism, these authors do not have to maintain that certain actions are right or wrong whatever the consequences, but they must accept that acts can be the right thing to do even though the state of affairs produced by those acts would be worse than other states of affairs accessible to the actor.

A consideration of promise keeping which is often mentioned in the literature about the adequacy of utilitarian ethics well illustrates the differences between utilitarians and their opponents. The case is often proposed about a promise to a dying person on a desert isle to give this person's money to a jockey club. When the survivor comes back to civilization, should he say the dying man wanted his money given to the jockey club or to a hospital which could do much more good for people. The utilitarian or consequentialist would judge only upon what would have the best consequences—giving the money to the jockey club or to a needy hospital. The consequentialist recognizes the importance of promise keeping in society and must consider this aspect, but in this case the presupposition is that no one knows about the promise. Since no one else knows about the promise, there would be no harm done to society if the maker of the promise did not keep it. Working on the supposition that the promisor is a good utilitarian such a person would never feel guilty about now giving the money to the hospital.

The antiutilitarian argues that in addition to consequences there is an obligation of fidelity on the part of the promisor, which must be taken into account. The antiutilitarian, together with the traditional textbooks of Catholic moral theology, acknowledges that promises are not always to be kept, for a change in the matter or the person might make the promise no longer obliging. The antiutilitarian argues here that the good consequences cannot be considered apart from the criterion of the right and something other than consequences (namely, the obligation of fidelity) must be taken into account. Likewise, the integrity of the person who made the promise is involved.

In the light of this understanding of utilitarianism, consequentialism and teleology, the antiutilitarians attempt to show the inadequacy of utilitarianism in the following areas: questions of fidelity, gratitude and punishment; questions of distribution involving justice and fairness; intentionality and integrity of the person. The antiutilitarian appeals to questions of fidelity, gratitude and punishment because here there are sources of moral obligation other than the future consequences. In fidelity, moral obligation arises from the promise made in the past. In gratitude, moral obligation arises from the past act of generosity or beneficence. In punishment, moral obligation arises from the wrong act which the person did in the past. It is not necessary to assert that an absolute moral norm can be derived from these other sources of obligation, but at least it must be asserted that these sources of moral obligation must be considered as well as the future consequences. However, very often the utilitarian and the antiutilitarian conclusions will coincide.

Questions of distribution, justice and fairness have frequently been proposed as problems for a utilitarian ethic. The only controlling moral criterion cannot be the net aggregate of good over evil achieved by the act, for one must also consider the distribution of the good. Rawls first proposed a form of rule utilitarianism in his famous essay on "Two Concepts of Rules" as a means of strengthening the utilitarian view especially in matters of justice and promises. On the basis of that article Rawls was often wrongly called a rule-utilitarian, but he himself expressly indicated he was not proposing the rule-utilitarian position as completely defensible.[17] Later in his *Theory of Justice*, Rawls indicates that utilitarianism needs to be modified by considerations of justice and fairness which call for a proper distribution of benefits and burdens, rights and duties. Rawls develops these principles of justice relating to the basic equality of all and to the way in which all inequalities in societies are to be arranged.

In this connection of justice, one can consider the frequently debated example of the sheriff who, to avoid a race riot in which many blacks would be killed in a southern town in the United States, frames and executes one innocent black person. Philosophers have been arguing about this case and now Catholic moral theologians, e.g., Connery and Schüller, have taken different sides of the argument. However, both in the philosophical literature and now in the theological literature it seems as if the exact force of the particular case is often overlooked by both sides. Some argue that if all the consequences are properly taken into account, then one could never accept judicial execution. However, a staunch act-utilitarian such as Smart recognizes the bite of this particular case. If no one knows an innocent person was framed, and the presupposition is that no one can find out about it, then there would be no harmful effects on the role of justice and criminal law in society if the innocent person were executed. Smart admits that it is logically possible for such a situation to exist and that the utilitarian must logically opt for the judicial murder in this case, but existentially he hopes the case would never happen.[18] Again the importance of the illustration shows what the differences are between the two approaches.

Another series of objections proposed against utilitarianism emphasizes the intentionality of the agent. The bottom-line consideration of the net good over the net evil is not the only factor to be considered—one must also consider how the good and evil were accomplished. There is a difference between effects or consequences that are merely foreseen by the agent and those that are intended by the agent. The way in which the agent brings about the effects is also important. The case of judicial murder also illustrates this problem as exemplified in the already mentioned case of a foreigner who in a South American country comes upon a military captain who is about to kill innocent villagers. The point is that the foreigner is not the cause of the death of the others in the same way he would be the cause of the death of the one. An individual's actions and decisions flow from one's projects, but in this case the foreigner's action is determined by the project of the captain. It is absurd to demand that the foreigner leave aside his own deepest projects and decisions and base his actions only on the utilitarian calculus of the number of lives ultimately lost when this has been greatly determined by the project of another. Williams who proposes such a case leans toward doing the deed, but considerations other than consequences enter into the moral decision.[19]

Another Antiutilitarian Position

Within the body of recent literature specifically discussing utilitarianism, the antiutilitarian approach generally agrees with the position just expounded and does not directly appeal to or accept the principle that certain actions are right or wrong no matter what the consequences.[20] However, within the philosophical literature in general, if not in the utilitarian literature specifically, there is another form of the antiutilitarian approach which is based primarily on accepting such a principle.

G.E.M. Anscombe includes all modern philosophy under indictment for leaving open to debate whether such a procedure as judicial murder might not be the right one to adopt. Although some of the present Oxford moral philosophers think it permissible to make a principle never to do such a thing as judicial murder, Anscombe condemns them for proposing a philosophy according to which the consequences of such an action could morally be taken into account to determine if one should do such an action. Anscombe opposes such a theory because it is willing even to consider the possibility of exceptions based on consequences. She thus places all modern moral philosophy under the indictment of what she calls consequentalism. (One can thus see the terminological problem which exists in the philosophical literature.) Anscombe and her followers accept the principle that there are actions which are right or wrong whatever the consequences.[21] In subsequent literature the position defended by Anscombe and others has been called absolutist,[22] conservative[23] and Catholic.[24] This position can properly be called Catholic (even though authors like Bennett reject the term) because it describes the position generally taken in the manuals of moral theology—certain actions are intrinsically wrong, e.g., contraception, sterilization, direct killing of the innocent, and can never be justified no matter how much good might result. Likewise, Catholic philosophers such as Anscombe and John Finnis defend this position.[25]

In conclusion, an overview of the philosophical literature indicates that there are three different positions, but terminology differs in describing these different opinions. The following descriptions will not agree with the terminology employed by many of the authors themselves, but it seems to be necessary to bring about needed clarifications. The first position is properly described as utilitarianism, strict teleology or strict consequentialism. The third position, Anscombe *et al.*, may be described as nonconsequentialism or even deontology—some actions are wrong no matter what the consequences. I will call the middle position a mixed consequentialism or mixed teleology. This middle position differs from strict teleology or strict consequentialism because it maintains the following three points: 1) Moral obligation arises from elements other than consequences. 2) The good is not separate from the right. 3) The way in which the good or evil is achieved by the agent is a moral consideration. Since such an opinion does not necessarily hold that certain actions are always wrong no matter what the consequences, it has been called consequentialist by Anscombe. The good consequences are able to be determinative of the right and wrong of actions. The terminological confusion increases when one realizes that some proponents of this middle position can also properly be identified as deontologists, e.g., W. D. Ross who speaks about *prima facie* obligations. Ross acknowledges morality consists in such *prima facie* obligations but also recognizes the existence of conflicts in which the consideration of good consequences can be equally determinative of which obligation one must follow.[26]

III
SITUATING CATHOLIC MORAL THEOLOGY

Where does Catholic moral theology fit into such a schema? The moral theology of the manuals definitely belongs under the third position—the nonconsequentialist position which maintains that some actions are intrinsically wrong no matter what the consequences (I realize that some contemporary theologians are trying to reinterpret what this meant, but at least there is no doubt that as generally understood the teaching of the manuals belongs under this category.)

In the 1960's some Roman Catholic moral theologians reacted in general, and especially in the context of the debate over artifical contraception, against what I have called physicalism—the tendency to identify the moral act with the physical structure of the act. The physical is only one aspect of the human and the totality of the human cannot be identical with just this one aspect. Many authors refer to physical or premoral or ontic evil as distinguished from moral evil. In this light these theologians (rightly in my judgment) rejected the traditional teaching that contraception, sterilization, masturbation for seminal analysis, artificial insemination even with the husband's seed and the killing of the fetus to save the mother were always wrong. Beginning with Knauer an appeal was made to commensurate reason to justify some of the actions which the manuals described as intrinsically wrong.[27] Schüller and others spoke of a teleological justification and a consequentialist calculus to determine if such actions were right or wrong.[28] Reforming Catholic theologians thus appealed to commensurate reason, proportionate reason or the calculation of consequences to indicate that premoral evil could on some occasions be justified. Knauer also argued that one should not speak of the evil as being an effect with the act as its cause but rather spoke of the effect as an aspect of the act so that one might see here some similarity with the position maintaining there is no difference between effects which are foreseen and effects which are intended. In the light of the terminology and of some of the reasoning, the question arises if these Catholic authors are utilitarians or consequentialists in the strict sense.

Notice that early in the discussion within Roman Catholicism the debate centered almost exclusively on problems present in the Catholic theological tradition such as contraception and sterilization. The questions that were being discussed in the debate about utilitarianism such as promise keeping, fidelity, gratitude, justice, punishment, and integrity were not even discussed by the Catholic moral theologians. Once some of these questions such as the prohibition of direct killing of noncombatants or questions of jud·

icial murder began to be discussed by the reforming Catholic ethicists, their understanding of consequentialism and teleology became clear. McCormick rightly insists on a difference between an intending and a permitting will.[29] Schüller recognizes that the consequences are always considered in the light of what is right.[30] Thus as the debate progressed it became quite evident that the reforming Catholic theologians generally speaking do not embrace utilitarianism or what Rawls, Frankena, Williams and others have called teleology or consequentialism. In the schema proposed above, they fit into the middle category which can be described as mixed consequentialism.

Even in the general statement of their theories, it is clear that the reforming Catholic theologians do not belong to the first position of strict consequentialism or utilitarianism. Knauer, himself insists on commensurate reason, and thus attributes some value to the physical act in relationship to the end which is sought. Fuchs gives attention to all three aspects of the human act—object, end and circumstances.[31] Janssens sees a reciprocal causality existing between the material and the formal element of the human act so that the consequences alone are not determinative.[32] Milhaven requires an objective evaluation of the consequences in light of moral criteria.[33] Yes, there is a problem in terminology, but as the debate continued it became more evident that these Catholic authors do not embrace utilitarianism, or strict consequentialism or strict teleology. Thus I disagree with the contention of John Connery that many of these Catholic authors are tending to consequentialism, which he understands in the strict sense.[34] In light of the three different positions explained above, most of the reforming authors in the Catholic tradition fit into the second position called mixed consequentialism, but perhaps this position should be described differently.

IV
CLARIFICATIONS AND RELATIONALITY

Problems exist both in the philosophical literature and in the literature of Catholic moral theology about the exact meaning of the terms teleology and consequentialism. Teleology is generally contrasted with deontology, yet the second position described above as mixed consequentialism also includes people like Ross who are often classified as deontologists.

In my judgment, at least part of the confusion arises from the fact that the difference between teleology and deontology can refer to two different realities in ethical discussion—the general model of the moral life and the more particular question of the establishment of normal norms or the criterion for decision making in concrete cases. When referring to the model of the ethical life, teleology refers to an approach which sees the moral life primarily in terms of goals and ends. In this view Aristotle and the manualists of moral theology are teleologists, as well as all utilitarians. Deontology understands the moral life primarily in terms of duties, obligations, and laws. Kant serves as an example of deontology, but Ross with his emphasis on *prima facie* obligations also fits under this category. From the viewpoint of theological ethics, Rudolf Bultmann's insistence on morality as radical obedience also makes him a deontologist.[35] However, in terms of the more limited aspect of determining moral norms or the criterion of concrete obligations one could characterize these ethicists differently. Certainly Aristotle and some manualists of theology would not be characterized as determining moral norms on the basis of consequences and strict teleology. Ross has been classified as a consequentialist (at least by Anscombe). Bultmann is often described as a situationist. There is a difference between the level of ethical model and the level of the formulation of the ethical norms.

One of the unfortunate aspects of the debate about situation ethics and norms in the last decade has been that moral theology is often reduced to the one question of whether or not there is a law. Questions of attitudes, dispositions, ideals, values, goals, perspectives and intentionalities have not received the attention they deserve in a complete consideration of moral theology. The ultimate model of the ethical life therefore should be broad enough to consider all the more specific questions and topics that form part of ethics and moral theology. Therefore both in practice and in theory one can legitimately distinguish between the level of the ethical model and the level of establishing norms or the criterion for decision making in specific cases.

On the level of ethical model I prefer to accept an ethical model of relationality and responsibility as a third model distinguished from both teleology and deontology. Such a model seems to be more in keeping with both theological and ethical data. Theology views the life of grace and the reality of sin primarily in terms of relationships, as is evident in the concepts of covenant and love. In the perspective of Christian eschatology the individual does not have that much power and control over one's end and destiny. The cross and the paschal mystery remind us that our end or goal is not completely in our hands. We as Christians live in the hope that the evils and problems of the present can be transformed somewhat even now by the power of God and ultimately transformed into the fullness of life.

A phenomenological reflection on all human existence also seems to indicate that our lives are more understandable in terms of responding to the many happenings of human existence rather than adhering to a prearranged plan in search of our goal. Teleological and consequential models emphasizing only the goal or consequences obviously laid the foundation for a technological model of human existence, but technological progress can never be identified with truly human progress. Likewise an emphasis on consequences, goals and ends very readily places all value in terms of what one does, makes or accomplishes. The Christian approach does not seem to react in the same way, for there will always be a Christian bias in favor of those who do not accomplish or are not successful—the poor, weak and the outcast. One might retort that the teleological model does not necessarily involve the kind of problems that I have described here, but even at its most refined understanding, the teleological model seems less apt than the relationality-responsibility model of the ethical life of the Christian.[36]

On the level of the formulation of moral norms and the criteria for concrete decision making I would opt for the second position described above as mixed consequentialism. The problem of terminology has already been pointed out since strict teleology is different from this position, and both teleologists and deontologists rightly fall into this category. Here again I am trying to develop.a relationality approach as a third type distinct both from teleology and deontology, but this needs much greater development in my thought at the present time. At the very least it solves the terminological problem which now exists. Such a relational type has the advantage of including all the elements that should be considered and not reducing reality only to consequences or to duties. One might also argue that the relationality approach is not merely a middle approach between the other two but in a sense also opts for a somewhat different understanding of the moral decision making process. Certainly it is not as rationalistic as the consequentialist approach. Likewise, it avoids the inflexibility that might often be associated with various aspects of the nonconsequentialist approach. By seeing all reality in terms of relationships one is less willing to absolutize any one aspect or one individual, since the individual by definition exists in multiple relationship with others; but the theory can still insist on the fundamental importance of the individual person. However, this approach obviously needs much further development.

V
CONFLICT SITUATIONS

In general one might say that the entire discussion deals with conflict situations—a point which is even more true when it is limited to the discussion of philosophical literature but which can also be verified in the literature of Catholic moral theology. In my judgment it is important to recognize that there are different sources of conflict situations. Specifically, I propose four sources of conflict situations which Christian ethics can and should distinguish— 1) conflicts arising from the difference between the subjective and the objective aspects of human acts; 2) conflicts arising from creaturely finitude and limitation; 3) conflicts arising from eschatological tension; 4) conflicts arising from the presence of sin. In concluding this essay it is not possible to develop these different sources of conflicts at length, but a brief description will suffice. However, since my theory about the source of conflicts resulting from sin has often been misunderstood, some further clarification is necessary.[37]

Catholic moral theology traditionally recognized the distinction between the objective and the subjective aspects of the human act. An act might be objectively wrong, but the individual is not subjectively guilty or responsible for it because of various impediments to a voluntary act. The manuals traditionally referred to the question of invincible ignorance of the obligation, but many contemporary authors rightly insist that the notion of invincible ignorance today must be seen in the perspective which emphasizes the existential totality of the human person, so that invincible ignorance is a matter of the inability of the person to realize a moral obligation because of the situation in which one finds oneself. Moral philosophers recognize the same reality in the distinction between reasons which justify an act and reasons which excuse an act. Here the objective evaluation of the act is not changed, whereas in the other three types of conflict situations the objective evaluation of the act is changed.

The second source of conflict situations is human finitude and limitation. Here one finds most of the problems in which the physical aspect of the act has become absolutized, for different premoral values will often exist in conflict with one another so that one cannot be absolutized. Here too the principle of double effect has been employed to solve some conflict situations such as the birth room dilemma of mother or child. The third source of conflict situation arises from the tension between the eschatological fullness and the present. Since Catholic moral theology in the past was so heavily based on natural law and did not appeal to grace and eschatological realities as being morally obligatory for all, this type of conflict seldom arose. However, it is quite present in the situation of divorce, which in my judgment cannot be an absolute prohibition. The fourth source of conflict situation is the presence of sinfulness. In response to the presence of sin I have developed a theory of compromise which in the light of subsequent debate needs to be properly understood.

The theory of compromise was never meant to apply to all conflict situations but only to those conflict situations in which sinfulness predominates. The problem of physicalism or what others call physical evil as distinguished from moral evil constitutes a distinct question. The conflict here most often arises from finitude and limitation either of time or space. I do not appeal to compromise to solve the questions of contraception, sterilization, artificial insemination, many cases solved by double effect, etc. However, it was a mistake to use the term the "theory" of compromise as if it were primarily an ethical term, for it refers primarily to a theological reality—the source and the cause of the ethical conflict. The ultimate ethical solution of the conflict requires an ethical approach such as those discussed earlier. I would apply in these situations the second or mixed approach which I prefer to call a relational approach which involves weighing all the values involved.

From a theological perspective it is more accurate to distinguish the various sources of conflict, even though in particular cases it might be difficult to discern if the conflict is due primarily to one or the other sources, e.g., finitude, sin or the eschaton. Even in the ethical order there are important ramifications in distinguishing the conflicts arising from sinfulness. Sinfulness as the origin of conflict situations might be understood in three different ways—the universal sinfulness existing in the world which was the basis for Thomas Aquinas' teaching on the ownership of private property; the sinfulness incarnate in the human situation which in my judgment affects the person who is an irreversible homosexual; and the sinful actions of another person affecting my action as illustrated in the case of the captain threatening to shoot a large number of innocent villagers unless I shoot one of them myself.

Some philosophers claim that many of the examples proposed in the debate about consequentialism are rather bizarre.[38] To a certain extent this is true, but the bizarre character of the examples often comes from the fact that personal human sinfulness is present as in the South American example. The exceptions will be less and severely limited when it is a case of the personal sinfulness of another. Likewise the sinfulness of the social situation affects a limited number of people. Finitude affects all in a more comprehensive way than sin when it is not the universal sin of the world. The Christian must try to limit all evil, but evil resulting from finitude and limitation will always exist together with the human. Evil resulting from sin is somewhat different. Its presence does not come from the human condition as such, and the Christian has an obligation to try to overcome the effects of sin. However, in the imperfect world in which we live it is never possible to overcome all the effects of sin this side of the eschaton—sometimes one must accept the limitations of the sinful situation. This explains the theological concept of compromise because of which an act which in ordinary circumstances would be wrong for this person in the sinful situation is not wrong. But the exact determination weighing all the values involved depends upon ethical criteria.

This article has not attempted a complete discussion of the philosophical debates about utilitarianism but has considered only those aspects most instructive for the current considerations of Roman Catholic moral theologians. In the process it has been possible to clarify and perhaps advance the discussions within Roman Catholic ethics.

Notes

1. J.J.C. Smart in J.J.C. Smart and Bernard Williams, *Utilitarianism: For and Against*. Cambridge, Cambridge University Press. 1973, p. 4.

2. J.B. Schneewind, "Introduction," in *Mill's Ethical Writings*, ed. J.B. Schneewind, New York, Collier Books, 1965, pp. 19, 20.

3. For an analysis of the present debate on the measurement of utility and for a comprehensive view of recent debates in utilitarianism, see Dan W. Brock, "Recent Work in Utilitarianism," *American Philosophical Quarterly* 10 (1973) 245-249.

4. *Contemporary Utilitarianism*, ed. Michael D. Bayles, Garden City, New York, Doubleday Anchor Books, 1968.

5. J.O. Urmson, "The Interpretation of the Moral Philosophy of J.S. Mill," *The Philosophical Quarterly* 3 (1953) 33-39.

6. David Lyons, *Forms and Limits of Utilitarianism*, Oxford, Clarendon Press, 1965.

7. J.H. Sobel, "Rule-Utilitarianism," *Australasian Journal of Philosophy 46 (1968) 146-165.*

8. *Brock, American Philosophical Quarterly* 10 (1973) 261.

9. Richard A. McCormick, *Ambiguity in Moral Choice*, 1973 Pere Marquette Theology Lecture, Marquette University, 91 ff.; McCormick, "The New Medicine and Morality," *Theology Digest* 21 (1973) 319 ff.

10. Richard A. McCormick, "Notes on Moral Theology," *Theological Studies* 36 (1975) 98.

11. Smart and Williams, *Utilitarianism: For and Against*, p. 98.

12. Smart and Williams, *Utilitarianism: For and Against*, p. 4.

13. Smart and Williams, *Utilitarianism: For and Against*, pp. 82-93.

14. Lyons, xii.

15. John Rawls, *A Theory of Justice*, Cambridge, Mass., Harvard University Press, 1971, p. 25.

16. William K. Frankena, *Ethics*, Englewood Cliffs, New Jersey, Prentice Hall, 1973, pp. 13, 14. In the light of these definitions, it seems that what is often called ideal utilitarianism would not fall under this description of utilitarianism.

17. John Rawls, "Two Concepts of Rules," *The Philosophical Review* 64 (1955) 4.

18. Smart and Williams, *Utilitarianism: For and Against*, p. 72.

19. Smart and Williams, *Utilitarianism: For and Against*, pp. 108-118.

20. Brock, *American Philosophical Quarterly* 10 (1973) 261-269.

21. G.E.M. Anscombe, "Modern Moral Philosophy," *Philosophy* 33 (1958) 1-19.

22. Thomas Nagel. "War and Massacre," *Philosophy and Public Affairs* 1 (1972) 123-144.

23. Jonathan Bennett, "Whatever the Consequences," *Analysis* 26 (1965-66), 83-102.

24. R.W. Beardsmore, "Consequences and Moral Worth," *Analysis* 29 (1968-69) 177-186; R. G. Frey, "Some Aspects to the Doctrine of Double Effect," *Canadian Journal of Philosophy* 5 (1975) 259-283.

25. John Finnis, "Natural Law and Unnatural Acts," *Heythrop Journal* 11 (1970) 365-387; Finnis, "The Rights and Wrongs of Abortion," *Philosophy and Public Affairs* 2 (1973) 117-145.

26. W.D. Ross, *The Right and the Good*, Oxford, Clarendon Press. 1930; and *The Foundations of Ethics*, Oxford, Clarendon Press, 1939.

27. P. Knauer, "La détermination du bien et du mal moral par le principe du double effet," *Nouvelle Revue Théologique* 87 (1965) 356-376; Knauer, "Das rechtsverstandene Prinzip von der Doppelwirkung als Grundnorm jeder Gewissensentscheidung," *Theologic und Glaube* 57 (1967) 107-133.

28. Bruno Schüller, "Zur Problematik allgemein verbindlicher ethischer Grundsätze," *Theologic und Philosophic* 45 (1970) 1-23; Schüller, "Typen ethischer Argumentation in der katholischen Moraltheologie," *Theologie und Philosophie* 45 (1970) 526-550.

29. McCormick, *Ambiguity in Moral Choice*, 72 ff.

30. Bruno Schüller, "Neuere Beiträge zum Thema 'Begründung sittlicher Normen'," *Theologische Berichte* 4, Einsiedeln, Benziger, 1974, 109-81.

31. Joseph Fuchs, "The Absoluteness of Moral Terms," *Gregorianum* 52 (1971) 445 ff.

32. Louis Janssens, "Ontic Evil and Moral Evil," *Louvain Studies* 4 (1972) 123 ff.

33. John Giles Milhaven, "Objective Moral Evaluation of Consequences," *Theological Studies* 32 (1971) 407-430.

34. John R. Connery, "Morality of Consequences: A Critical Appraisal," *Theological Studies* 34 (1973) 396-414. I do have one difficulty with many of these authors—the use of premoral evil to cover diverse realities which at best are only analogously related. For example, killing a person and contraception are not premoral evils in exactly the same way. Many people in society rightly see little or no premoral evil in contraception. Catholic authors tend to call contraception premoral evil because they want to maintain some continuity with the official teaching that contraception is morally evil. Why is contraception a premoral evil? The same is true of sterilization so that there in no practical moral difference in my judgment between direct or indirect sterilization. Also these authors must consider more questions of social ethics. Even here one might properly say, for example, that discrimination because of race, creed or color is only a premoral evil which in extreme situations of compensatory justice to others in society might be morally overridden. One could also argue that in social ethics we are often dealing with formal and not material norms as in Rawl's concept of justice. However, these questions deserve greater attention.

35. Thomas C. Oden, *Radical Obedience: The Ethics of Rudolf Bultmann*, Philadelphia, Westminster Press, 1964.

36. For a further development of this model, see my *Catholic Moral Teaching in Dialogue*, Notre Dame, Indiana, Fides Publishers, 1974, pp. 150-183.

37. These different conflict situations have been discussed in my other writings, especially *Ongoing Revision: Studies in Moral Theology*, Notre Dame, Indiana, Fides Publishers, 1976.

38. E.g., Anscombe, *Philosophy* 33 (1958) 13.

Biographical Notes

Peter Knauer, S.J. is Professor of Systematic Theology at Sankt Georgen, West Germany.

Louis Janssens is Professor of Moral Theology at the Catholic University of Louvain.

Joseph Fuchs, S.J. is Professor Moral Theology at the Gregorian University, Rome.

Bruno Schüller, S.J. is Professor of Moral Theology at the University of Münster, West Germany.

Franz Scholz is Professor of Moral Theology at the University of Augsburg.

Walter G. Jeffko is Professor of Theology at the University of Augsburg.

Albert Di Ianni, S.M. is Professor of Philosophy at Holy Cross College, Massachusetts.

John R. Connery, S.J. is Professor of Moral Theology at Loyola University, Chicago.

Paul M. Quay, S.J. is Professor of Physics at St. Louis University.

Richard A. McCormick, S.J. is Rose F. Kennedy Professor of Christian Ethics at the Kennedy Institute of Ethics, Georgetown University.

Charles E. Curran is Professor of Moral Theology at the Catholic University of America.